Canadian Macroeconomics

Problems and Policies

Second Edition

READER'S GUIDE

Canadian Macroeconomics

Problems and Policies

Second Edition   BRIAN LYONS *Sheridan College*

MAJOR FEATURES:

Secondary School Division
Prentice-Hall Canada Inc.

1870 Birchmount Rd., Scarborough, Ontario, M1P 2J7 (416) 293-3621

Canadian Macroeconomics

Problems and Policies

Second Edition

BRIAN LYONS
Sheridan College

PRENTICE-HALL CANADA INC.,
SCARBOROUGH, ONTARIO

Canadian Cataloguing in Publication Data
Lyons, Brian.
  Canadian macroeconomics: problems and policies

Includes index.
ISBN 0-13-113184-2

1. Macroeconomics.   2. Canada — Economic conditions.
I. Title.

HB172.5.L96   1987   339′.0971   C86-094202-3

Prentice-Hall, Inc., Englewood Cliffs, New Jersey
Prentice Hall International, Inc., London
Prentice-Hall of Australia, Pty., Ltd., Sydney
Prentice-Hall of India Pvt., Ltd., New Delhi
Prentice-Hall of Japan, Inc. Tokyo
Prentice-Hall of Southeast Asia (Pte.) Ltd., Singapore
Editora Prentice-Hall do Brasil Ltda., Rio de Janeiro
Prentice-Hall Hispanoamericana, S.A., Mexico

ISBN 0-13-113184-2

Production Editor: Chelsea Donaldson
Cover Design: Bruce Bond
Illustrations: Helmut Weyerstrahs
Manufacturing: Matt Lumsdon

1 2 3 4 D 90 89 88 87

Typesetting by DSR Typesetting Limited
Printed and Bound in Canada by John Deyell Company

All quotations from the Royal Commission on Economic
Union and Development Prospects are reprinted by
permission of the Privy Council, Minister of Supply and
Services Canada.

TABLE OF CONTENTS

11.   Stabilizing the economy: government policies to
      control the money supply   180

PREFACE

This book is an introductory macroeconomics text that addresses itself to the major economic problems facing Canada and Canadians today, and the policy choices confronting governments in dealing with these issues. It is not oriented toward rigorous, abstract or elegant economic theory, nor to a mathematical approach to economics—students of introductory economics neither want nor need these. Rather, its approach tends to be practical and pragmatic, introducing theory only insofar as it contributes to an understanding of the problems being discussed.

The organization of the book follows the evolution of economic problems and policies over the years, starting with the problems of *depression, recession* and *unemployment* that dominated much economic thinking and policy-making from the 1930's until the 1960's. The focus then shifts to the problem of *inflation* that dominated much of the 1970's and the *stagflation* that characterized the latter part of this period. Finally, consideration is given to the problem of *unemployment,* which became severe in the 1980's. The intention of this approach is to gain a better understanding of current economic problems by viewing them in the perspective of recent problems and policies.

Throughout the book certain *basic concepts* and themes appear and reappear for emphasis. Some of these are: the fundamental importance of *productivity* (output per worker) to prosperity, the contribution of *saving and investment* to prosperity, the *role of markets* in promoting prosperity through effective and efficient use of economic resources, and the real nature of *inflation* and its effects upon our prosperity. In analyzing macroeconomic problems throughout the book, the concept of the interaction between *aggregate demand* and *aggregate supply* is used. These frames of reference for analysis are more appropriate for the introductory student, as they are easier to grasp intuitively than some of the more commonly used approaches.

Many economists believe that, until recently, economic progress occurred so readily that some of these basics of economics were forgotten or ignored by Canadians and their governments. However, now that the economic situation has become much more challenging, it is more important than ever that the basics be remembered and emphasized: only by doing this can Canada achieve its tremendous economic potential. The relationship between government economic policy and the public's understanding of economic issues is fundamentally important here. If political necessity dictates that government policy must be framed to appeal to the public, the present economic situation makes it vital that the public understand economic realities, issues and policies. Only such knowledge can ensure that economic policy will be directed toward the long-term economic advantage of Canadians rather than being framed for short-term political expediency. If governments must be more responsive to the public than to their economic advisers, perhaps the time has come when economics is too important to be left to the economists.

Some people believe that this task is impossible, that economics (and especially macroeconomics) is too difficult a subject to be comprehended by most people, and must therefore be left to the experts. This view is not correct. Economics is not a particularly difficult subject at all. The real task in teaching introductory economics is to organize many things that people either already know or can grasp quite readily into a systematic framework that promotes greater understanding of important economic problems. Hopefully, this book can help people to do this in a readable, not unduly painful and maybe even enjoyable way.

A person undertaking a project such as this is indebted to a great number of people. In particular, I would like to express my gratitude to Bill Trimble, who said I should do it, Len Rosen, who didn't let me say I wouldn't, and all those instructors and students who used the first edition and offered helpful comments and suggestions. I would also like to thank the people whose reviews of both editions of the manuscript were so helpful: for the first edition, Ray Canon, Gord Cleveland, Ward Levine, Jim Thompson and Ian Wilson, and for the second, Alan Idiens, Kris Mundt and Greg Streich. In addition, I would like to express my appreciation to the many excellent Prentice-Hall editing and marketing people whose help and support have been indispensable, especially Chelsea Donaldson for her conscientious, patient and instructive editing. Finally, I want to acknowledge my indebtedness to my family—Barbie, Marnie and Amber—who have provided support and understanding over unduly long periods of time.

I have no doubts that there are many improvements that can be made to this book, and welcome any suggestions from teachers or students. Please write to me at Sheridan College, Box 4700, McLaughlin Road, Brampton, Ontario L6V 1G6.

for Barbie, Marnie and Amber

CHAPTER 1

What is economics?

What is "economics"? To the householder, economics is the difficult task of balancing the family budget in the face of rising prices, so that there is not too much month left over at the end of the money. To the business leader, economics is the problem of producing a product at sufficiently low cost that it can be marketed profitably in competition with the products of other producers. To a government leader, economics means difficult policy choices between goals that often conflict with each other, making it impossible to please everyone and thus ensure re-election. To the general public, economics is usually associated with vague, incomprehensible and often contradictory pronouncements of people called "economists," concerning matters of great national and international importance that seem, unfortunately, impossible to understand, much less resolve.

While each of these views may be accurate, each is only a part of the real meaning of economics, because each represents only the viewpoint of a particular group (householders, business leaders, government leaders, voters). From the viewpoint of the economist, however, economics covers a broader field, dealing in the widest sense with how well a society's economic system satisfies the economic needs and wants of its people. Since the basic task of an economic system is to produce goods and services and to distribute them among the people of the society, the most commonly used definition of *economics* is

> the study of the decisions a society makes concerning the production of goods and services and how the society distributes these goods and services among its members.

This somewhat dull and simple definition leads us into a variety of areas of much broader concern and greater interest, such as:

- What is the real significance of the federal government's large budget deficits?
- How likely is it that the severe inflation of the 1970's will return?
- Why did the international value of the Canadian dollar fall by approximately 30 percent from the mid-1970's to the early 1980's, and what does this mean for Canadians?
- Is foreign investment in Canada desirable or not?
- Are strikes really bringing the Canadian economy to the brink of ruin?
- Must a million Canadians be unemployed?
- Why are some people paid hundreds of thousands of dollars per year, while others receive less than one percent of that?
- Should the government place legal limits on the rents charged by landlords?

Some aspects of economic matters such as those above raise *philosophical* questions; for instance, is it proper for the government to control apartment rents, or people's wages, or workers' strikes? Other aspects of economics, however, involve more *technical economic analysis*. For example, if apartment rents are kept low by law, how will this affect the construction of new apartments? In many cases, also, economics becomes involved with questions of *value judgments*. For example, if the government acts to reduce unemployment, inflation may well become more severe: is this a worthwhile price to pay for reducing unemployment? This question is a value judgment, in that there are legitimate economic arguments in favor of either opinion.

Folklore versus economic analysis

Probably the greatest obstacle to the effective learning of economics is the fact that most people already think that they know a great deal about the subject. In fact, much of this knowledge consists of widely believed but not necessarily accurate ideas, such as:

- The way to eliminate poverty is to increase the minimum wage dramatically.
- Increases in the National Debt are always bad.
- Proper use of government policies can eliminate both unemployment and inflation.
- Reductions in interest rates will help to combat inflation.
- A decline in the international value of the Canadian dollar is economically harmful to all Canadians.
- The government should always balance its budget.

None of the above statements is true, but they are widely believed by the public. The objective of this book is to replace this type of folklore about economics with the tools for accurate analysis of economic issues of importance to Canadians.

The limitations of economic analysis

Because it deals with the behavior of people (consumers, business people, government policy-makers), economics cannot be a precise science such as physics or mathematics. Similarly, economic analysis does not provide clear and simple answers to important questions, such as whether the government should reduce taxes. However, economic analysis can do a great deal to illuminate the consequences of reducing (or not reducing) taxes, thus clarifying the choices to be made. Therefore, while economic analysis does not provide us with decisions, it provides us with a much better basis for making decisions.

Can economists agree on anything?

"Ask five economists what should be done about a problem and you'll get six different recommendations" is a jibe frequently directed at economists, whose credibility is often considered in the same category as that of weather forecasters. Given the disagreements among economists (and others who describe themselves as economists) on matters of importance, it is easy to get the impression that the field of economics is one of confusion and chaos. While economics, like all other fields of study, is continually evolving toward a fuller understanding of its subject matter, the present state of the subject is not as chaotic as it may seem. First, many of the disagreements among economists arise not from economic analysis but rather from differences concerning policy recommendations (value judgments) which arise from that analysis. Second, there are many generally accepted facts, concepts and theories that constitute a sort of mainstream of economic thought that is less publicized but more important than disputes between various economists. This book attempts to build around this mainstream of thought, while considering the major alternatives to it where these are important.

What is economics about, then?

Economics used to be known as the "dismal science," because of the economic theories of Thomas Malthus (1766-1834). Malthus, an English clergyman, theorized that because population could grow faster than the world's food supply, humanity was destined to live with a constant struggle with starvation. While no one can say what the future will bring, a combination of lower birthrates and modern production technology has brought living standards in many societies far beyond anything dreamed of in Malthusian theories, and has brought the study of economics to matters which, while serious, are much less depressing.

Economics, then, is about many matters both small and large. On a small scale, *microeconomics* (after the Greek word "micro," for small) focuses on particular aspects of economics, such as consumer demand, supply, demand and prices under various conditions, the role of big business, labor unions and government in the economy, and the economics of particular industries such as agriculture and oil.

On a large scale, macroeconomics (based on "macro," for big) deals with broader matters pertaining to the performance of the economy as a whole, such as recession, inflation and unemployment. The purpose of this book is to develop an understanding of these macroeconomic matters which are of importance to all Canadians. Before examining these issues, however, we will consider the basic problems of economics and the various types of economic systems which exist, in Chapters 2 and 3 respectively.

SOME SCIENCES ARE MORE EXACT THAN OTHERS

An alumnus, returning to his college for a reunion, found his old economics professor preparing the examination for her course. "But professor," said the former student, "don't you realize that these are exactly the same questions that were on my exam 20 years ago?" "Yes," answered the professor, "We always use the same ones." But don't you know," asked the graduate, "that students pass these around, and therefore will surely know by now what questions will be on their exam?" "It doesn't matter," said the professor. "In economics, we don't change the questions, we change the answers."

Isn't this all terribly difficult?

Not really. Probably the most insightful observation ever made about economics as a field of study is that it is a *complex* subject but not a *difficult* one. Unlike nuclear physics or differential calculus, there is little in economics that many people find conceptually difficult. Rather, economics deals with people and their behavior and decisions as consumers, business people and government policy-makers. Much of this behavior is already known to the student of introductory economics; what needs to be done is to organize these fragments of knowledge into a framework for analyzing and understanding economic events. This book attempts to do this in a way that eliminates the use of abstract theories and higher-level mathematics, instead focusing on developing an understanding of real and relevant Canadian economic problems in a readable and, hopefully, enjoyable way.

QUESTIONS

1. What has economics meant to you? From what viewpoints have you viewed the economic system?

2. How well does Canada's economic system fill the needs and wants of Canadians? What shortcomings do you perceive, and what do you think could be done about them?

3. "The inability of economists to make accurate economic forecasts shows that they know so little about the workings of the economy that their advice on economic matters should be disregarded." Do you agree with this statement? Why?

4. What are some of the specific developments that have enabled us to escape the dismal predictions of Malthus? Do you believe that Malthus's theories will eventually come true? Why?

CHAPTER 2

The economic problem

As we have said, economics is basically the study of the decisions a society makes regarding the production of goods and services and the division of these among its people. As we shall see, different societies make these decisions in very different ways, but all societies are faced with essentially the same problems—how to use their economic resources to the best possible advantage.

Using economic resources to satisfy human wants

A modern industrial economy is a very complex mechanism, involving a baffling number of factors, such as the level of output, employment, unemployment, prices, interest rates, money supply, exports, imports, the international value of the nation's currency, government tax revenues, government spending, consumer spending, banks, stock markets, big corporations, small businesses, labor unions and many others. Furthermore, each of these factors is related to the others in ways that are often subtle and complex. It is no wonder that many people find economics confusing and have difficulty "seeing the forest for the trees." Worst of all, such complexities often make it difficult to see the *basic economic principles* involved in an issue.

In examining basic economic principles, it can be very helpful to eliminate the many complexities associated with a modern economy which tend to obscure the principles involved. Suppose, then, that you are one of a group of people stranded on a desert island. With none of the complexities of a modern economy to distract you, your group must come to grips with the most basic economic problem: how to best satisfy your economic wants and needs using the three types of economic resources, or *inputs*, available to you — labor, capital equipment and the natural resources of the island.

(a) Labor

The largest single economic resource, or input, available to any society is the labor of its people, including all types of work, mental as well as physical, from manual labor to professional employment. In our desert-island mini-society, various people will have skills (hunting, fishing, building and so on) appropriate to the situation.

(b) Capital equipment

A vitally important economic resource is society's stock of capital equipment, which contributes greatly to the production of goods and services. While a modern industrial economy possesses a vast array of factories, machinery, equipment and tools, your desert-island mini-society has built only a few basic tools, such as spears, fish nets and hoes.

Capital equipment is of crucial importance because it increases *production per person (productivity)*, making possible a higher material standard of living (more goods per person) for the people of the society. Thus, while the mini-society's stock of capital equipment is presently low, its people may wish to increase it, and thus increase their standard of living.

(c) Land (natural resources)

The third economic resource available to the mini-society is the natural resources of the island, including land and plants, streams and fish, forests and animals, minerals, and so on. Economists lump these together under the name land. A difference between land and capital is that capital equipment is man-made and reproducible while not all natural resources are reproducible. On the other hand, there is a relationship between a society's technology and stock of capital equipment, and what it can use as natural resources. For example, until the development of nuclear reactors, uranium could not reasonably be considered an economic resource. Many people hope that technology can solve the energy crisis by similarly developing new energy resources. Thus, while some natural resources deplete, new technology is capable of creating new additional resources.

The task of any economic system is to organize and use these economic resources, or productive inputs, to produce goods and services (*output*) of the types and quantities that will best satisfy the needs and wants of the people of the society, as shown in Figure 2-1. This process can sometimes be quite complex. For instance, the production of an automobile involves people (labor) with a wide variety of skills and talents, very sophisticated capital equipment, and resources of various types. On the other hand, food production in some countries consists of peasant farmers tilling the soil with only the most primitive equipment. In organizing and using their economic resources, however, all societies face the same basic problem.

FIGURE 2–1   *The Basic Operation of an Economic System*

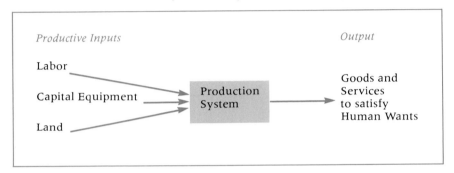

The "economic problem": scarcity

The basic problem of economics is simply that society's economic resources, or productive inputs, are scarce or in limited supply, while people's wants seem to be unlimited. Like all societies, our desert-island mini-society would like to have more goods and services than it is able to produce with its available inputs.

The production-possibilities curve

One way of illustrating the problem of scarcity is with a *production-possibilities curve*. Suppose our desert islanders can only produce two items—vegetables and fish. If all their economic inputs were devoted to producing vegetables, they could produce 15 kilograms of vegetables daily, but no fish. This option is shown as combination **A** in Figure 2-2, which indicates vegetable production of 15 kg and fish production of 0. If the desert islanders went to the opposite exteme and used all their productive inputs to produce fish, the result would be fish production of 5 kg and vegetable production of 0, as shown by combination **F** in Figure 2-2.

FIGURE 2-2 *Production-Possibilities Curve*

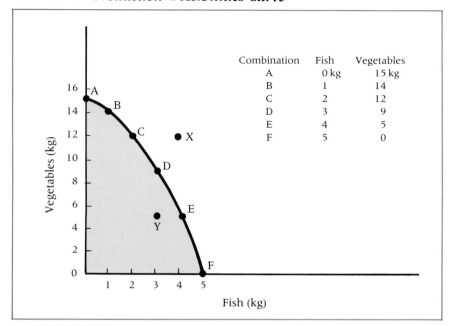

Combination	Fish	Vegetables
A	0 kg	15 kg
B	1	14
C	2	12
D	3	9
E	4	5
F	5	0

Of course, it is more likely that the islanders would choose to produce some combination of fish and vegetables, such as combinations **B** (14 kg vegetables and 1 kg fish), **C** (12 kg and 2 kg), **D** (9 kg and 3 kg) or **E** (5 kg and 4 kg). In making their choice, however, they will be restricted by the limitations of the production-possibilities curve: since their economic resources are limited, *producing more of one product necessarily means being able to produce less of the other*. The islanders may want to have 4 kg of fish and 12 kg of vegetables, (combination **X**), but they will not be able to. Resource scarcity dictates that if they want 4 kg of fish, they can only have 5 kg of vegetables, and if they are to have 12 kg of vegetables, fish production can only be 2 kg. Thus, while it is possible to produce 4 kg of fish or 12 kg of vegetables per day, it is not possible to produce this much of both on the same day. The islanders must make choices between various combinations of products, and the production-possibilities curve reflects the limitations that resource scarcity imposes upon their choices.

However, the combinations shown by the production-possibilities curve are based on two important assumptions—that the islanders use *all of their available productive inputs*, and that they utilize them as *efficiently* as possible. If some of their productive inputs were not used (if, for instance, some of the workers were sick, or one or their spears was broken) output would be below the potential level shown by the production-possibilities curve. Point **Y**, at which fish production is 3 kg and vegetable production is 5 kg, reflects such a situation. With fish production at 3 kg, vegetable production could be as high as 9 kg rather than 5 kg, and with vegetable production at 5 kg, fish production could be as high as 4 kg rather than 3 kg. However, if the islanders do not employ all of their productive inputs, their production will be below its potential. Even if all inputs are employed, production may fall short of its potential. If the islanders' inputs (labor and capital equipment) were not producing fish and vegetables as efficiently as possible, production could be below its potential level and the islanders could still wind up at point **Y**.

It is important to recognize that the production-possibilities curve indicates the economy's *potential* output, assuming that economic inputs are fully employed and efficiently utilized. Production can be at any point on the production-possibilities curve (if inputs are fully and efficiently utilized) or within the shaded area (if they are not), but cannot be outside the curve.

However, the islanders need not live forever within the limitations imposed by the curve shown in Figure 2-2. This curve represents the situation at a *particular point in time*, given the economic resources available to the islanders at that time. If, in the future, they were to add to their economic resources, say, by building *new capital equipment* or developing *new technologies*, their potential output of both fish and vegetables could increase. Figure 2-3 shows the new production-possibilities curve that could be created by additions to or improvements in the islanders' economic resources.

The inquisitive reader may wonder why the production-possibilities curve is bowed outward as it is, rather than following a straight line. The shape of the curve reflects the *changing efficiency* of resources as they are shifted from one use to another. For instance, in Figure 2-2, the table shows that to increase fish production from zero to 1 kg, we must sacrifice only 1 kg of vegetable production. But as we push fish production higher, we must forego ever-higher amounts of vegetable production to achieve the same increases in fish production. The second kilogram of fish costs 2 kg of vegetable; the third kilogram of fish requires the foregoing of 3 kg of vegetables, and so on.

To produce the first kilogram of fish, we would shift resources (labor and capital) out of their *least efficient use* in vegetable production (say, from the least productive land or using the least efficient capital equipment) into their *most efficient use* in fishing (say, using the best available equipment to fish the most productive waters). However, as we push fish production higher and higher, the trade-off between fish and vegetable production becomes less attractive. Increasingly, we have to shift labor and capital

FIGURE 2-3 *Economic Progress: Shifting the Production-Possibilities Curve Outwards*

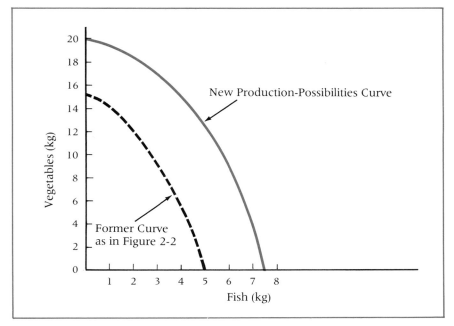

out of more efficient uses in vegetable production and into less efficient uses in fishing. The fifth kilogram of fish production is particularly costly in terms of vegetable production lost (5 kg of vegetables), as it requires that we shift labor and capital out of our last (and most efficient) use in vegetable production and into our least efficient use in fish production. As a result of these factors, the production-possibilities curve is not a straight line, which would reflect a constant trade-off between fish and vegetable production, but rather a curve which reflects *changing efficiencies* and trade-offs.

We have used a very simplified situation, involving a production-possibilities curve for only two products, in order to illustrate the basic nature of the problem of scarcity. While the real world is much more complex, involving many more inputs and outputs, the basic reality shown by our simple production-possibilities curve still exists. Because our economic resources are limited, our output of goods and services is also limited, and society must somehow make choices between various goods and services: we cannot have as much of everything as we would like.

THE CONCEPT OF OPPORTUNITY COST

The trade-offs between fish and vegetable production as shown
by the production-possibilities curve are referred to by economists as *opportunity costs*. The opportunity cost of using economic
resources to produce any item is the amount of any other item
that those same economic resources could have produced instead. The production-possibilities table in Figure 2-2 provides a
good illustration of this concept.

Combination	Fish Production	Vegetable Production	Opportunity Cost of:
A	0 kg	15 kg	
B	1	14	The 1st kg of fish = 1 kg vegetables
C	2	12	The 2nd kg of fish = 2 kg vegetables
D	3	9	The 3rd kg of fish = 3 kg vegetables
E	4	5	The 4th kg of fish = 4 kg vegetables
F	5	0	The 5th kg of fish = 5 kg vegetables

The opportunity cost of producing the first kilogram of fish is
the loss of 1 kg of vegetable production, which declines from 15
to 14 kg. The opportunity cost of the second kilogram of fish is
the 2 kg of vegetable production lost when their production
falls from 14 to 12 kg, and so on, as shown by the table above.

We can express opportunity cost in terms of vegetable
production foregone for *each additional kilogram* of fish, as shown
in the table. Alternatively, we can calculate the opportunity cost
of *any given amount* of fish production. For instance, the table
shows that the opportunity cost of the third kilogram of fish
production is 3 kg of vegetables, while the opportunity cost of 3
kg of fish production is 6 kg of vegetables, because if the entire
3 kg of fish had not been produced, vegetable production could
have been 15 kg rather than 9 kg.

To calculate the opportunity cost of anything, ask yourself,
"What could have been produced instead of it?" For instance,
the opportunity cost of building a $15-billion oil and gas pipe-
line is not the $15 billion, but rather the other products (hous-
ing, roads, machinery and so on) that could have been produced
by the inputs used to produce the pipeline. And, to a student,
the opportunity cost of riotous living on the weekend could be
viewed as the 16 extra marks that he or she could have obtained
on the economics test if the time had been spent studying.

The task of the economic system, then, is to use its scarce economic inputs in the way that best satisfies the needs and wants of the people of the society. This problem, however, is not nearly as simple as it may look. How do we determine what people's needs and wants really are? How should we go about producing those goods and services that we believe people need and want? And who should get how much of our total output of goods and services — how should we divide it up among the population?

These considerations can be summed up as the three basic questions that every society must answer, regardless of the particular type of economic system it has chosen.

The three basic questions of economics

(a) What to produce?

Because economic resources, or productive inputs, are scarce, no society can have all the goods and services it would like to have. Instead, it must *make choices*. For example, the people in our desert-island mini-society would have to decide whether they should use their inputs to produce fish, vegetables, shelter, nets, spears, traps, plows or other things. These choices will not be easy to make, because the more you produce of one thing you want (such as fish), the less you will be able to produce of other things you want (such as vegetables).

Even wealthy societies such as Canada cannot avoid the necessity of having to choose what to produce (and therefore what not to produce). Should Canada produce more housing? More schools? More hospitals? More gas and oil pipelines? More highways? More cars? More boats? More color televisions?

One of the most basic "what to produce" decisions that must be made is whether *consumer goods* or *capital goods* will be produced. Consumer goods (such as food, clothing, automobiles) can be enjoyed now, but do not contribute to longer-term economic prosperity. Capital goods (such as tools and equipment), on the other hand, provide less immediate enjoyment but will contribute to society's production and prosperity for many years. Obviously, the degree to which a society decides to produce capital goods (as opposed to consumer goods) will have a strong bearing on the direction and growth of its economy.

As noted, the decision to use scarce economic resources to produce more of one good involves a decision not to produce other goods. Who should make these choices: consumers? business people? the government? Different societies make these decisions in different ways, as we will see.

(b) How to produce it?

Once we have decided *what* we want to produce, we must decide *how* each product or service is to be produced. This is a question of production methods: how should we combine our scarce inputs of labor, capital equipment and land for use in production?

As a simple example, suppose our desert-island mini-society has decided to produce (catch) fish. The next question is, how should it do this? Should it catch them by hand? Or use spears? Or nets? Before the people can actually produce the fish they want, it is essential that they make a decision about how to produce them.

Production methods vary greatly from product to product; some are almost completely manual while others are almost totally automated. In general, we try to use the inputs in the most efficient way possible, so as to get the *maximum output per unit of input*. This avoids wasting our scarce inputs and thus increases our economic prosperity.

Different societies often produce the same products in quite different ways. For example, farming in North America uses a great deal of capital equipment and very little labor, while farming in Southeast Asia uses a great deal of manual labor and very little capital equipment. Yet both production methods make economic sense, because labor is relatively scarce and thus costly in North America while capital equipment is scarce and labor is plentiful in less advanced countries. So both production methods are efficient, in the sense that they economize on the use of those inputs which are most scarce relative to the others: capital equipment in Asia and labor in North America.

(c) Who gets what?

The final basic question is: *how will the society divide its output of goods and services among the members of that society?* Who will receive what shares of the output?

Suppose our desert-island mini-society consists of ten people whose daily total output of food is twenty fish. How should these be divided among the ten people? Should everyone receive the same share? Or should some have more than others? If so, who? And why? Should each person get only as many fish as he or she catches? What if someone can't catch any?

Somehow, our mini-society must answer this basic question, as must every society. This is certainly the most controversial of the three questions; indeed, revolutions have been fought over it.

Obviously, in an economy such as Canada's, which uses money, a person's share of the society's output depends on how much he or she can buy—it depends on his or her *income*. If an accountant's income is twice as large as a laborer's, the accountant's share of the economic pie will be twice that of the laborer's.

But how should society decide who gets what share? Should doctors have a larger share (income) than dentists? Should engineers have a larger share than accountants? Should teachers have a larger share than nurses? Should professional athletes have a larger share than doctors? Somehow, every society has to work this out and thus divide the economic pie among the people of that society.

Answering the three questions

In this chapter we have considered the three basic questions of economics, which every society must answer—what to produce, how to produce it and how to divide it up. As noted earlier, different societies answer these questions in very different ways. In the next chapter, we will examine the different approaches to the basic questions of economics as we consider the different types of economic systems that exist in the world today.

DEFINITIONS OF NEW TERMS

Economics The study of the decisions a society makes regarding the production of goods and services and the division of these among its people.

Inputs Economic resources such as labor, capital equipment and natural resources that are used to produce goods and services.

Labor The largest single productive input available to any economy, labor includes all of the productive talents of the people of a society, mental as well as physical.

Capital (Equipment) The tools, equipment, machinery and factories used by labor to increase production per person and thus living standards.

Land Short form for all the natural resources available to a society's economy as economic inputs.

Scarcity The problem that, while economic inputs (and thus potential output) are limited in availability, people's wants and needs are apparently unlimited.

Production possibilities curve A graph showing the maximum possible output of one product that can be combined with any given output of another product, assuming full and efficient utilization of all available productive inputs.

Opportunity Cost The concept that the real economic cost of producing something is the foregone opportunity to produce something else that could have been produced with the same inputs.

CHAPTER SUMMARY

1. The basic task of an economic system is to use its productive *inputs* (labor, capital equipment and land) to produce goods and services so as to satisfy the wants and needs of the people of the society.

2. This task encounters the problem of *scarcity*: whereas society's economic resources are limited in quantity, people's wants and needs are apparently unlimited; thus, not all wants and needs can be satisfied.

3. The task of an economic system, then, is to make the best possible use of its scarce economic resources by providing answers to the following three questions:
   (i) *what* to produce,
   (ii) *how* to produce it, and
   (iii) *how to divide it* among the people so as to best satisfy the needs and wants of the society.

QUESTIONS

1. In the affluent society of Canada today, have we overcome the problem of scarcity or do we still face it?

2. Of the three productive inputs (labor, capital and land), which is the most important today? Which is gaining in importance the most rapidly?

3. In some societies, old people who are unable to work any longer are left to die. What might explain such a custom?

4. How does the custom referred to above compare to Canada's attitudes toward those who are unable to support themselves? What might explain this difference?

5. Ed Schreyer, while Premier of Manitoba, suggested that the highest paid people in industry and government should receive no more than two-and-a-half times as much take-home pay as the lowest-paid workers. Do you agree with him? Why? What do you believe would happen if such a policy were implemented?

6. Following is a table showing the production possibilities for widgets and reemistrams.

Combination	Number of Widgets	Number of Reemistrams
A	0	20
B	1	18
C	2	14
D	3	8
E	4	0

What is the opportunity cost of producing:
- **(a)** the first widget?
- **(b)** the second widget?
- **(c)** two widgets?
- **(d)** the third widget?
- **(e)** three widgets?
- **(f)** the fourth widget?
- **(g)** four widgets?

7. While all economic resources are scarce in the sense of being in limited supply, the problem of scarcity is particularly dramatic when the physical amount of a resource is actually diminishing, as with some agricultural land.

According to a government inventory of Canada's land resources carried out in the 1960's and 1970's, only 11 percent of Canada's land is capable of sustaining agriculture of any kind, less than 5 percent is capable of sustaining crops and less than 0.5 percent is valuable, class-one land capable of sustaining the whole range of Canadian crops. 37 percent of Canada's class-one agricultural land and 25 percent of the nation's class-two land can be seen from the top of Toronto's CN Tower. Under pressure of "urban sprawl", this prime agricultural land continues to be converted to residential, commercial and industrial uses.

- **(a)** Why does this high-quality agricultural land continue to be converted to other uses?
- **(b)** Should the government permit this to happen?
- **(c)** What could be done to arrest this trend and protect our agricultural land?

8. The following table shows production possibilities for two commodities — fradistats and kadiddles.

Combination	Fradistats	Kadiddles
A	0	6
B	6	5
C	11	4
D	15	3
E	18	2
F	20	1
G	21	0

- **(a)** What is the opportunity cost of producing:

  the lst kadiddle: _____

  the 2nd kadiddle: _____

  the 3rd kadiddle: _____

the 4th kadiddle: _____

the 5th kadiddle: _____

the 6th kadiddle: _____

(b) Draw the production-possibilities curve for fradistats and kadiddles on a graph, placing kadiddles on the vertical axis and fradistats on the horizontal axis.

(c) If the economy achieved greater efficiency in the production of kadiddles, how would the production-possibilities curve change?

(d) If a more efficient method of producing fradistats were developed, how would the curve change?

(e) Suppose more economic resources (labor, materials and capital) became available. How would the curve change?

9. Fred's Fradistats Ltd. can produce fradistats using either of two production methods: manual or mechanized. Using the manual production method, 10 employees are required, working 8 hours per day at $10 per hour. Overhead costs (rent, office, etc.) are $200 per day and material costs are $5 per fradistat. The manual method produces 50 fradistats per day.

Using the mechanized production method, 5 employees are required, working 8 hours per day at $10 per hour. Overhead costs (rent, office, etc.) are $200 per day and material costs are $5 per fradistat. Depreciation expenses on the fradistat-forming machine are $300 per day and the machine uses $150 of energy per day. The mechanized production method also produces 50 fradistats per day.

(a) Use the table below to calculate the cost of producing each fradistat using each of these two production methods.

	Manual Method	*Mechanized Method*
Labor cost per fradistat	$	$
Material cost per fradistat		
Overhead cost per fradistat		
Depreciation cost per fradistat		
Energy cost per fradistat	_____	_____
Total cost per fradistat	$_____	$_____

According to the above figures, which production method would be chosen as the most efficient method?

(b) Suppose wage rates increased to $12 per hour. What effect would this have on:

(i) production cost per unit under the manual method.

(ii) production cost per unit under the mechanized method.

    (iii) the choice of production methods.

    (iv) the number of workers employed.

(c) Suppose wage rates were still $10 per hour and energy prices declined by 40 percent. What effect would this have on:

    (i) production cost per unit under the manual method.

    (ii) production cost per unit under the mechanized method.

    (iii) the choice of production methods.

    (iv) the number of workers employed.

(d) Suppose a new fradistat-forming machine is developed which still requires 5 workers, costs twice as much as the old machine (making depreciation expenses $600 per day), uses $320 of energy per day (compared with $150 for the old machine), and produces 80 fradistats per day. Would it be economical for the company to introduce the new machine?

(e) Sections (b), (c) and (d) show that the most efficient production method depends on _____, _____, and _____

CHAPTER 3

Types of economic systems

In Chapter 2, we identified the three basic economic questions faced by any society: what to produce, how to produce it, and how to divide it up. In order to focus on these basic problems and possible solutions to them, we placed ourselves in a desert island setting. Now that we have identified our basic economic problems, our island mini-society will have to devise an *economic system* to decide the answers to these questions. While there are in reality a great variety of economic systems, the two most basic *types* from which we may choose are the *command* system and the *market* system.

The command system

If the economy is organized along command lines, all basic economic decisions will be made by the *government*. In the case of a large-scale modern economy, these decisions would probably be made through a central economic planning committee or agency. On our desert island, however, the "government" might consist simply of one individual, or a small group, who would take over the task of directing, planning and overseeing production. This government would consider the economic resources (labor, capital equipment and natural resources) available to the islanders, and establish priorities for their use (for instance, whether to spend time producing capital goods or consumer goods, and what types of each). In establishing these priorities and translating them into specific requirements for particular products, an economic plan will be established. The person or group in charge would then make decisions regarding the three basic economic questions.

How the command system answers the three questions

The virtue of the command system, at least in the context of our theoretical mini-society, is its *simplicity*. All three questions would be decided by the same person, or group. The government decides what to produce, and directs individuals as to their *production quotas*, so that the types and volumes of goods produced conform to the overall plan that has been set. The government would also decide how to produce each good, by designating the *production methods* to be used by each worker, and allocating them the equipment necessary to reach their quotas. Finally the government would settle who receives what share of the economic pie, by determining what *economic reward* (how much fish, or vegetables, or meat) each individual deserves for his or her contribution to the society's welfare. The command system, then, can help to ensure an equal or fair distribution of goods among the islanders, in theory at least, by allocating more to people who are in need.

Practical experience with the command system

The command system has certain attractions in a situation such as our desert island mini-society. It offers a relatively simple way to organize people's economic activities according to a *plan*. The very concept of a plan is attractive, as it implies the provision of order to the complex tasks of deciding how best to utilize society's scarce economic resources and determining what to produce, how to produce it and how to share it among the people. In short, the government makes the basic economic decisions, and requires the people to follow these decisions, for their own economic benefit.

Actual experience with command systems has been considerably more complex — and less favorable — than this simple introduction suggests. In the Soviet Union, after the Bolshevik Revolution of 1917, the Communists established what has become the world's most famous command economic system. The state owned all production facilities (factories, farms, mines and so on), and each produced according to production quotas determined by the government's central economic planners, in conjunction with a grand economic plan covering the entire economic system. Since virtually everyone worked for the state, the central economic planners also decided the incomes that would be received by various types of workers, and thus decided the division of the economic pie among these groups.

The single greatest achievement of the Soviet Union's command system was the transformation of an economically backward nation into an industrial power in a remarkably short period of time. The command system can achieve such *rapid industrialization* because the economic planners can dictate that great emphasis be placed on producing the capital goods (basic industrial facilities, factories, machinery, and so on) that are required for industrial development. Because economic resources are scarce, such a strong emphasis on the production of capital goods necessarily means that the population must accept low levels of consumer-goods production, and therefore a *low material standard of living*. The magnitude of the Soviet Union's capital-building task has been such that the Russian people have been required to make great sacrifices during most of the twentieth century, for the longer-term benefit of future generations. The Soviet government planned its economic growth through its famous *Five-Year Plans*, the essence of which was emphasis on capital-goods production at the expense (opportunity cost) of low production of consumer goods.

The Soviet Union's experience reveals some real weaknesses of the command system. Probably the major problem of command systems is their *lack of incentives*: state-owned enterprises lack the profit motive to be efficient, and Soviet workers, who are in effect government employees, lack motivation to work efficiently. As a result, productive efficiency tends to be weak, which in turn impairs economic progress; at present, the Soviet authorities' major economic concern is to improve productivity, or output per worker. Productivity has been a particularly severe problem in the agricultural sector of the economy, in which the most capitalistic group in the society—the farmers—have been transformed from self-employed entrepreneurs into less-than-enthusiastic government employees on state-owned farms.

Another increasingly severe problem has been the inability of the *central economic planning system* to cope with the task of planning, directing and coordinating the production and distribution of the vast number of products of a modern industrial economy. While central planning was able to direct the development of the basic industrial facilities of the Soviet Union in the 1920's and 1930's, the planning and coordination of the millions of products associated with today's modern economy is an infinitely more complex task. The task is made more difficult by the fact that today's output includes many more consumer goods, which by their nature are less suited to planning by a central authority than are basic industrial projects.

> The latest index of products has twenty million articles. The plan can't detail that amount.
>
> Official of Gosplan, the Soviet State Planning Committee

KARL MARX (1818-1883)

Karl Marx was a German philosopher who began studying economics seriously after moving to London in 1849, when he became a prominent member of the British classical school of economics. His theories have always been highly controversial.

Marx's views were undoubtedly influenced by the era in which he lived and wrote — the period of the Industrial Revolution, with its extreme exploitation of labor. In the *labor theory of value*, Marx turned the predominant economic theory of the day — that the value of goods is mainly determined by the amount of labor required to produce them — against capitalism itself, attacking it at its very base.

Marx argued that because labor was the source of economic value, workers should receive the entire value of the products they produced. So, where capitalists view profits as a necessary and justifiable incentive, a reward to producers for supplying desired commodities, Marx viewed them as a *surplus value* gleaned from the unfair exploitation of other people's labor.

Marx developed an extensive definition of *social class*, and claimed that, since the capitalist system relied on the exploitation of a particular group (workers), class differences and inequalities could never be abolished under capitalism. In the increasing alienation of workers from owners, Marx foresaw the seeds of a possible socialist revolution, in which the working class would take over the means of production and the economic planning for the whole state, to the equal benefit of all members of the society.

Unfortunately, Marx never set down his ideas on exactly how a post-revolutionary socialist economy would operate. Nevertheless, his ideas have inspired many to attempt to work out a systematic approach to a state-run economy, with varying degrees of success. While he did not foresee that the Industrial Revolution would create such a broadly-based middle class in the West, it is important to remember that today, more people world-wide live under some form of socialism than under capitalism. Where communist revolutions have occurred, the societies have been agrarian, rather than industrial, in nature, and have used communism and economic planning to build an industrial state.

As a result, the Soviet Union's economic planning system has had increasing difficulty coping with the tremendously complex task of coordinating all aspects of a large modern industrial economy, and has increasingly tended to make errors. Some of these errors (such as the production of large numbers of eyeglass lenses but not the frames to hold them), seem somewhat amusing, but others are more serious. For instance, long delays in the opening of a major electrical generating plant were caused by the omission of a few vital components. Planning problems have been particularly persistent in the consumer-goods sector of the economy because the planners have been unable or unwilling to anticipate or cater to consumer preferences. As a result, despite the general shortage of all consumer goods, and severe shortages of some, the system produces many consumer goods that are so inappropriate or of such poor quality that consumers will not buy them. Such problems constitute a serious misuse of scarce economic resources.

Not only are such planning problems quite common; they can also be difficult to correct. A master economic plan for a nation is an incredibly complex document that must be drawn up for a considerable period of time (at least one year), making it very rigid. The complexity of the plan causes errors to be quite frequent, while its rigidity makes it difficult if not impossible to correct the errors promptly. This situation represents a fundamental problem of the command system with which Soviet authorities have wrestled, with little success, for many years.

In summary, the command type of economic system is capable of generating quite rapid industrialization, but tends to be relatively ineffective and inefficient in its use of economic resources. This holds true especially with respect to consumer-goods production, which lends itself less to the central planning approach than do the production of capital goods and military goods.

The "market" system

Under the command system, all economic decisions are made centrally by the government. The market system provides a completely different way of organizing society's economic resources, with no central planning or control. The process of economic decision-making is completely decentralized, with individuals, rather than the government, making the decisions.

To introduce a market system into our island mini-society, suppose that some form of money is introduced and each person is encouraged to produce, sell and buy whatever he or she wishes. Obviously, this would lead to the production, buying and selling of a great variety of goods and services. To simplify our examination of this system, we will consider the production of two items—vegetables and meat. From this simplified analysis we can gain insight into the overall workings of a market system.

Suppose that vegetables are quite plentiful and are relatively easy to pick, while meat is much more difficult to obtain. Let's say that the animals are not plentiful, must be hunted in comparatively inaccessible and inhospitable parts of the island and have been known to fight back, a fact that introduces some risk into hunting. As a result of these considerations, on the first day of economic activity, eight people decide to pick vegetables because it is the easier activity, while only two people are prepared to undertake the harder work and risk of hunting animals. At the end of the first day, when the people come to sell their products, there will be many more vegetables than people want, and much less meat than people want. Clearly, our mini-society did not use its economic resources very wisely on the first day—it produced too much of one product and too little of the other. Equally clearly, the mini-society would be better off if it were to shift some economic resources (mostly labor) out of vegetable production and into meat production, or hunting.

In a market type of economy, this will tend to happen *automatically*. Because there is an oversupply of vegetables on the market, the price of vegetables—and therefore the incomes of vegetable pickers—will be *low*. Conversely, the shortage of meat on the market will cause the price of meat—and the incomes of hunters—to be *high*. Thus, there will be an economic incentive for people to shift out of vegetable production and into hunting, or meat production. That is, there is an economic incentive for producers to produce what consumers will buy. There is also, of course, an economic incentive for producers to produce their products as efficiently as possible, because higher efficiency means lower costs and greater profits.

Market equilibrium

When the adjustments referred to above have worked themselves out, the market is said to have reached a state of equilibrium, or a more or less stable condition. Perhaps six people will be picking vegetables, compared to eight before. Vegetable pickers' incomes, while higher than they were originally, will still be low compared to the hunters' incomes. However, the difference between their incomes is less than it was originally, so that the remaining vegetable pickers do not view the incomes of hunters as being sufficiently high to attract them into that more difficult task. As for hunters, there will now be four of them, compared to the original two. As a result, the supply of meat will be greater than it was originally, and the price of meat (and the incomes of hunters) lower. While hunters' incomes are not as high, compared to those of vegetable pickers, as they were originally, they are still sufficiently high that the four hunters are content to remain as hunters rather than switch to the easier (but less well-paying) task of picking vegetables.

Changes in equilibrium

To gain some insight into just how a market system works, we will examine how it would respond to certain changes which would require adjustments within the economy.

(a) *A change in the demand for a product*

If the demand for vegetables increased relative to the demand for meat, the *price* of vegetables would rise.

Thus, vegetable pickers' incomes would rise, attracting more people into that field and increasing the supply of vegetables, *automatically*, in response to consumer demand.

(b) *A change in the supply of a product*

Suppose that the existing vegetable plots became less productive, causing a decline in the supply of vegetables. The *price* of vegetables would then rise, making it feasible for producers to buy and use better fertilizers and equipment, or to extend cultivation to new areas, thus increasing the supply of vegetables. If more labor were required for vegetable production, the higher incomes of vegetable pickers would attract people into that field. Thus, a shortage of a product *automatically* causes, through *price changes*, developments that tend to offset the shortage.

(c) *Changes affecting production methods*

Suppose that a particular productive input, such as the fertilizer used in farming, were to become less plentiful. Obviously, it would be economically desirable to use less of this scarce resource. In a market system, the price of this fertilizer would rise, increasing farmers' costs and reducing their profits, creating an economic incentive for them to use less of this fertilizer or to turn to an alternative. Furthermore, the higher price of this fertilizer would provide an incentive for fertilizer producers to increase their production of it or of alternatives to it. As before, the necessary economic adjustments take place *automatically*, in response to *price changes*.

The foregoing examples show how a market type of economic system adapts to changing circumstances: the system adjusts its production or production methods automatically as people respond to the *economic incentives* created by price changes. Because of the key role played by prices and price changes in such a system, the market system is sometimes referred to as the "price system."

How the market system answers the three questions

The operation of the market system provides a strong contrast with the command type of economic system. In a very decentralized way, without any direction or control from the government, the people of the island community have themselves provided answers to the three basic questions.

What to produce is decided by the demand of consumers, as the profit motive and price changes give producers an economic incentive to produce what consumers want.

How to produce each product is decided by the producers. The profit motive provides an incentive for each producer to use the most efficient production methods available, thus contributing to the economic efficiency and prosperity of the society.

The question of *for whom to produce it,* or how to divide the economy's output among various individuals and groups, is a more complex matter. The answer is determined by the incomes of individuals and groups, which are in turn determined in the marketplace by the supply of and demand for each type of productive skill. The *demand* for a particular productive skill depends ultimately on the demand for the product produced by it. The *supply* of that type of labor depends on the number of people who are willing and able to do that type of work. Thus, in a very real sense, no one decides incomes and the division of the economic pie — this is determined quite impersonally in the marketplace, by supply and demand.

The market system in a modern economy

In the simple desert island economy, individual people were both producers and consumers of products. In a modern economic system, the *production* of goods and service is done by privately owned business — mostly by corporations (owned by many shareholders and managed by hired professional managers) and also by smaller enterprises owned by one or more individuals (sole proprietorships and partnerships, respectively). *Consumption,* on the other hand, is done by households, which buy and use consumer goods and services. Members of households contribute to the production of goods and services by providing businesses with productive inputs, the most important of which is labor. Also, by purchasing stocks and bonds[1] issued by businesses, households provide businesses with funds (capital) for the purchase of capital equipment. In exchange for productive

---

[1] *Stocks,* or corporate *shares,* represent part ownership of a corporation. *Bonds* are the equivalent of IOU's issued by businesses to people who lend money, or "capital," to the business. Both stocks and bonds are sold by businesses to the public to raise capital to finance the expansion of the businesses' productive facilities.

inputs such as these, businesses pay households incomes in the form of wages, salaries, interest and dividends.[2]

As Figure 3-1 shows, this process involves two pairs of flows within the economy. The black lines represent the flows of money between the business and household sectors, while the blue lines depict the "real flows" of real goods and services and real productive inputs. The real flows depict the most basic and essential economic activities — the production and distribution of goods and services.

A modern market-system economy (also known as a "free enterprise" or "capitalist" system) answers the three basic questions of economics in essentially the same way as our simplified desert island market system did. Since the fundamental goal of business is to earn a profit, businesses

FIGURE 3–1 *The Operation of a Market Economy*

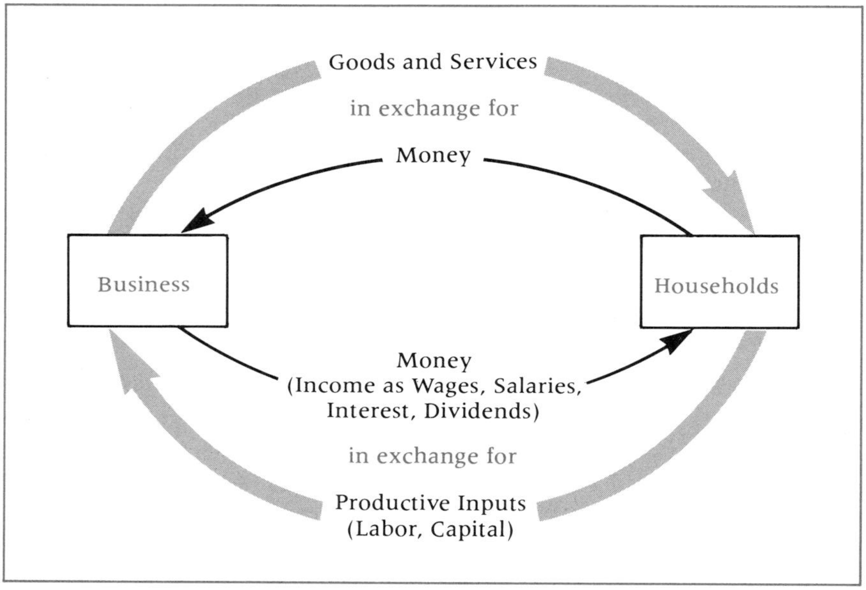

will produce those goods and services that are in demand. Therefore, ultimately, the question of *what to produce* can be said to be decided by the consumer. This process is described by the phrases "consumer sovereignty" (meaning that the consumer is viewed as "king of the marketplace") and "dollar votes" (meaning that the consumer's purchase of a product is, in effect, casting a vote for the production of that product).

[2]*Interest* is money paid by a borrower (here, a business) to lenders, (here, bondholders) for the use of the lenders' money; it can be likened to rent paid for the use of bondholders' funds. *Dividends* are the share of the corporation's profits received by shareholders as owners of the corporation. While interest payments to bondholders must be made regularly by a business, dividends may or may not be paid to the shareholders, depending on the level of profits.

The question of *how to produce it* is decided by producers, or businesses, who will strive for the most efficient possible method of producing the product. Lower costs mean higher profits, and, in a highly competitive industry, may mean survival. The most efficient method may change as the relative cost and productivity of various inputs changes. For example, rising wages may cause businesses to substitute capital equipment for labor (to automate). On the other hand, if labor is inexpensive relative to capital equipment, a business would use less capital equipment and more labor in its production processes. Whatever the decision, in a market type of economy it is privately owned producers — businesses — that make the decision.

PRODUCTION METHODS IN THE CANADIAN ECONOMY

The production methods used in the Canadian economy vary widely, with the greatest degree of mechanization in "capital-intensive" primary industries such as prairie grain, forest products and mining. In the manufacturing sector of the economy, production methods range from technologically sophisticated automobile plants and steel mills to "labor-intensive" industries such as clothing and footwear, which use considerable amounts of labor. Generally, those Canadian industries that are "capital-intensive" are best able to compete internationally, while "labor-intensive" industries such as clothing and footwear suffer from heavy foreign competition. We will consider the problems and choices facing Canadians with respect to such matters in more depth later in this book.

The *division of the economic pie* among various individuals and groups is influenced by many factors, the most important one being the interplay between the supply of and the demand for various productive skills. For example, highly skilled people are in short supply *as compared with the demand for them*, so their incomes (and share of the economic pie) tend to be quite high. There may be an even larger demand for semi-skilled labor (as measured by the numbers employed), but their incomes are quite low because of the large supply of them *as compared to the demand for them*. As the contrasts between the incomes of professional athletes, nurses and farm laborers show, market forces (supply and demand) can generate some incomes that are extremely high and others that are extremely low, in a way that is quite unrelated to how hard people work or to most people's view of the social value of the work done. On the other hand, such a system provides strong incentives for people to move

ADAM SMITH (1723-1790)

Adam Smith was a Scottish professor of moral philosophy who in 1776 wrote *The Wealth of Nations*, which was to become the most famous and enduring book in the (as yet not founded) field of economics. The essense of *The Wealth of Nations* was that economic liberty, in the form of sellers and buyers competing freely in the marketplace, was the best way to promote the general economic welfare of society. In perhaps the most famous quotation from the book, Smith said, "Every individual endeavours to employ his capital so that its produce may be of greatest value. He generally neither intends to promote the public interest, nor knows how much he is promoting it. He intends only his own security, only his own gain. And he is in this led by an invisible hand to promote an end which was no part of his intention. By pursuing his own interest he frequently promotes that of society more effectually than when he really intends to promote it."

Smith was very critical of monopolies, which restricted the competition that he saw as vital for economic prosperity. He also disliked government policies that protected the monopoly positions of some groups, such as apprenticeship laws restricting the entry of people into certain occupations. By showing how economic freedom could promote the interests of the general public, *The Wealth of Nations* became the rallying point for those who believed in economic liberty and free markets, unhampered by government regulation — that is, "laissez-faire" capitalism.

It is interesting that, more than 200 years after *The Wealth of Nations* was written, similar sentiments again became fashionable. After a long period of growing government regulation of business and the economy in North America, the trend by the mid-1980's was toward "deregulation," on the grounds that competition would promote efficiency and prosperity more effectively than an extensive system of government regulations.

into occupations that are in demand and to work harder. Both of these factors contribute to society's economic prosperity.

Thus, people's incomes (and the division of the economic pie) are basically determined in markets, by the forces of supply and demand. There are, of course, other factors, including labor unions and government regulations such as minimum wage and taxation policies, that influence the distribution of society's output among various groups and individuals. These matters, however, are microeconomic in nature and are therefore considered in a separate text.

The role of profits in the market system

Of all the aspects of a free enterprise economy, the most misunderstood is *profits*. The very word "profit" evokes for many people images of exploitation of workers and consumers. As Figure 3-2 illustrates, the *level* of manufacturers' profits is greatly exaggerated by the general public. While surveys indicate that the public believes profits to amount to 30 or 40 cents per dollar of sales, they actually amount to about 7 to 10 cents per dollar. (Ironically, the public believes 20 cents per dollar of sales to be a fair profit.) After taxes, most manufacturers' profits amount to 4 or 5 cents per dollar of sales.

FIGURE 3-2 *The Public's Attitude to Manufacturers' Profits*

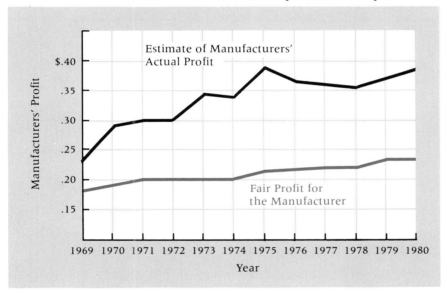

The public also has many misconceptions concerning the *uses* of profits, which are widely regarded as being hoarded away in corporate coffers or being paid out lavishly as dividends to wealthy shareholders. In fact, roughly 30 percent of corporate profits go to taxes and most of the remainder is reinvested by businesses in capital equipment. Dividends to shareholders generally amount to about a 5.5 percent return on their investment, and these "capitalists" include not only the wealthy but also all Canadians who have money in pension funds, bank or trust company deposits, life insurance policies, mutual funds and so on. Because of the public's misconceptions about profits and the negative emotional overtones to the word, many companies prefer to call their profits "earnings."

From the viewpoint of the economist, profits play two vital roles in the operation of a market system economy. First, profits provide *incentives for businesses* to produce those goods and services that consumers want, and to produce them as efficiently as possible so as to maximize economic benefits and minimize waste of scarce economic resources. It must be emphasized that using economic resources *effectively* (producing goods that are valued, or wanted) and *efficiently* (so as to maximize production and minimize waste of scarce inputs) are two fundamentally important economic objectives, and that no better way has ever been devised to attain them. Even some communist "command" systems have moved in recent years to introduce the profit motive into their systems, to give plant managers incentives to be both more efficient and more responsive to consumers' wants.[3]

PROFITS: IT'S ALL IN HOW YOU LOOK AT IT

Suppose a corporation has annual sales of $600 million, profits after taxes of $24 million, 4000 employees and $300 million of shareholders' capital invested in the company.

From the viewpoint of *the employees*, it might seem that they are being underpaid. If the $24 million of profits were divided among them, each would receive $6000 more ($24 million ÷ 4000).

From the viewpoint of *consumers*, $24 million in profits might seem to indicate that they are being overcharged for this company's product. Realistically though, the total elimination of the manufacturer's profits would only reduce prices by 4 percent ($24 million ÷ $600 million).

From the viewpoint of *the shareholders* of the company, their capital invested in the company is earning a rate of return (after tax) of only 8 percent ($24 million ÷ $300 million). Compared to other investments, this is not an attractive rate of return.

Thus, while employees and consumers may complain about this company's high profits, investors could very well be deciding to sell their shares in the company.

---

[3]It should be noted that profits also provide incentives for business to behave in socially harmful ways, such as dumping pollutants (cheaply) into the air and water and monopolizing markets so as to be able to charge excessively high prices. Thus, it is the task of government to ensure that these harmful side effects of the profit motive are controlled.

The second important role of profits is the provision of funds for the *financing of purchases of capital equipment.* While businesses do this to improve their own efficiency and profitability, the result, on a wider scale, is improved productivity. This is the basic source of higher living standards for society generally. Thus, reinvestment of profits by business contributes to a society's economic prosperity.

A baffling and contentious concept, profit has been the subject of debate, discussion and misunderstanding for centuries. Eminent men have variously extolled or denied its value to the community. Those who today consider profit as a "corporate rip-off" are, probably unknowingly, echoing the assertion of Michel de Montaigne, the 16th century philosopher, who said: "No man can profit except by the loss of others, and by this reasoning all manner of profit must be condemned." To this way of thinking, it follows, profit is by definition a "rip-off," and the profit motive nothing more than institutionalized greed and covetousness.

On the other side of the question, 19th century economist David Ricardo declared: "Nothing contributes so much to the prosperity and happiness of a country as high profits."

Reprinted from the Annual Report of the Royal Bank of Canada, 1974.

Thus, profits not only serve essential economic purposes, but also are not nearly as high as is generally believed. Many economists are concerned, in fact, that the level of profits may be too low to provide the heavy investment in capital goods needed in the near future to ensure energy supplies, keep Canadian industry internationally competitive and provide Canadians with the rising standard of living to which they have become accustomed.

PROFITS ARE EVERYBODY'S BUSINESS

About one dollar of every four in *pension funds* in Canada is invested in corporate shares. Thus, millions of Canadians have billions of dollars invested in shares. Not only do these Canadians receive part of corporate profits; they are in part dependent upon the prosperity of those corporations for their future financial security.

The market system in perspective

There is no economic system that is more responsive to consumer demand than the market system, which will adjust its production automatically to reflect changes in consumer preferences. Also, no system provides greater incentives for efficient use of economic inputs than the profit motive; as we have seen, it can contribute greatly to productivity and prosperity. The ability of this economic system to automatically coordinate the decisions of millions of businesses and individuals in response to changes in consumer demand has been referred to as "the miracle of the market." Adam Smith, the earliest advocate of this system, described businesspeople as being led by an "invisible hand" (the profit motive) "to promote (the interest of) the society more effectually than when they really intend to promote it."[4]

On the other hand, the market system is not without its weaknesses and problems, some of which we will examine in subsequent chapters. One problem is its tendency to slump into periodic recessions during which economic progress slows and unemployment rises. Also, the modern large corporation is not as powerless as the producers portrayed in our desert island illustration. In some cases, industries or markets can to a degree become monopolized either by one monopolist or by a few large producers acting together to increase prices and profits by reducing competition among themselves. A similar situation can develop in labor markets when strong labor unions can sometimes secure for their members a disproportionate share of the economic pie, leaving less for less powerful groups. Another problem is the tendency in market economies for great inequalities to develop in the distribution of income, with a few people enjoying very high incomes while others live in poverty. Macroeconomics is particularly concerned with problems, such as recessions, unemployment and inflation, that affect the entire economy. These problems, and the efforts of governments to remedy them, will be the main subject of this book.

The mixed economic system of Canada

The command and market systems described in the foregoing were quite pure in form, with the government making all economic decisions in the one case and playing virtually no role in the economy in the other. In actual practice, neither extreme has proven workable and neither exists — virtually every major economic system involves some combination of command and market forces.

Canada's economic system is best described as a "mixed free enterprise" system, in which both markets (or free enterprise) and government play

[4]Adam Smith, *The Wealth of Nations* (1776).

important roles. Basically, the Canadian economy is a market system, in which most Canadians work for privately owned businesses operating in a market environment, producing goods and services for sale for a profit. However, there are also extensive elements of government involvement (command) in the Canadian economy.

Governments *buy* about one-quarter of all the goods and services produced in Canada. Governments are also a major *producer* of goods and services, mostly through government-owned *crown corporations* such as Petrocan and Atomic Energy Canada Limited in the energy field, Air Canada and Canadian National in the transportation field, and the Post Office. By 1983, there were 60 such crown corporations owned by the federal government alone, with assets of over $75 billion and more than 200 000 employees.

Governments also sometimes *provide capital* for certain business undertakings, one of the most notable of which has been the Syncrude Athabasca Tar Sands oil project, in which the federal and Alberta governments invested $500 million of share capital.

Furthermore, governments *regulate* in many ways the operations and practices of businesses; for example, the prohibition of monopolistic practices, the regulation of the conduct of labor relations, laws regulating advertising practices, and the regulation of the production of some farm products by government-sponsored marketing boards. Also, many prices are regulated by governments, including electrical rates, many rents and transportation rates, some energy prices and tobacco and alcohol prices. It is estimated that about 25 percent of all the prices included in the Consumer Price Index are government-regulated prices.

Another major activity of government is the *redistribution of income* through transfer payments such as unemployment insurance, welfare, old age security allowances, family allowances and so on. Finally, as we shall see in more detail in subsequent chapters, governments undertake to use certain large-scale economic policy *tools* to steer the entire economy away from the extremes of inflation and depression.

Taken together, these involve a great deal of government participation in and regulation of the economy, making the term *mixed free enterprise* an appropriate description of the Canadian economy.

The traditional system

To complete our discussion of economic systems, we should consider the *traditional* system. Under this system, all economic decisions are made according to historic tradition. Today, this type of system is quite rare, existing mostly in tribal societies in remote regions such as the Amazon region of Brazil. In such societies, a person's economic activities and status are dictated by tradition. People perform the same economic activities (hunting, fishing, cultivating) as their parents did, using the same production methods and dividing up the economic pie into the traditional shares for various groups. This is a very static economic and social system that is of little interest to economists.

DEFINITIONS OF NEW TERMS

Corporation   A business firm owned by shareholders who, in many cases, are numerous and do not take part in the management of the corporation; most large business firms are corporations.

Stocks (Shares)   Financial securities representing part ownership of a corporation.

Dividends   That proportion of a corporation's profit paid to shareholders as owners of the corporation.

Profit(s)   Those funds left from a business' sales revenues after all expenses have been paid; such funds are therefore available (after taxes have been paid) for dividends to shareholders and reinvestment in the business.

Bonds   Financial securities issued by businesses to people who have loaned funds (capital) to the business.

Interest   Money paid by a borrower to a lender for the use of the lender's money.

Rate of Return   The annual income received from an investment, expressed as a percentage of the capital invested. For example, $5 annual dividend income received on $100 invested in stocks represents a rate of return of 5 percent.

Standard of Living   A measure of the economic prosperity of the people of a society, usually expressed in terms of the volume of consumer goods and services consumed per household (per year). Also referred to as *material* standard of living, because it ignores other factors that influence human welfare.

CHAPTER SUMMARY

1. There are two basic types of economic system — the command system and the market system.

2. In a command system, the government's central economic planners decide what to produce, how it will be produced and the division of the economic pie.

3. The main strength of the command system is its ability to generate rapid economic growth, while its main weaknesses are a lack of incentives and the errors and inflexibilities associated with the complex task of planning in detail the operations of an entire economic system.

4. The market system (also called the price system and the free enterprise system) operates in a decentralized manner, through markets. In these markets, what to produce is decided by consumer demand, how to produce it is decided by producers, and the division of the economic pie is decided by people's incomes.

5. Profits play a vital role in the operation of a market system. Profits provide incentives for the efficient use of economic resources and are a major source of funds for capital investment, which contributes to economic prosperity by increasing output per worker.

6. The main strength of the market system is its high living standards, which are the result of the strong incentives this system provides for efficient use of resources. The main weaknesses of the market system are its tendency toward periodic recessions, the domination of some markets by monopolistic corporations and strong labor unions, and a tendency for incomes to be distributed very unevenly.

7. Canada's economic system is a mixed free enterprise system: while it is basically a market or free enterprise system, it includes significant elements of government involvement in the economy, or "command."

QUESTIONS

1. Three of the following are essential to the operation of a free-enterprise market economy. Which one might such an economy operate without?
   (a) the profit motive
   (b) markets
   (c) corporations
   (d) prices

2. Not all economists agree that we in North America have "consumer sovereignty." Some economists argue that big business is able to control the consumer to the point where the situation would be better called "producer sovereignty." Do you agree or disagree? Why?

3. Our economic system is not purely a free-enterprise market system because the government (command) is involved in the economic process to a significant degree.
   (a) What are some of the "rules of the game" that the government sets and enforces?

(b) To what extent does the government (that is, command) play a role in deciding what to produce, how to produce it, and the division of the economic pie?

4. Do you agree with de Montaigne's statement that "No man can profit except by the loss of others, and by this reasoning all manner of profit must be condemned"? Does every economic transaction necessarily involve a "winner" and a "loser"?

5. If you were a Soviet economic planner
   (a) how would you make decisions about what to produce (and not produce)?
   (b) how would you decide which consumer goods to produce (and not produce)?
   (c) how would you decide to divide the economic pie (that is, the wages and salaries to be received by each type of occupation)?
   (d) how would you encourage your workers and managers to work efficiently?

CHAPTER 4

Measuring the performance of the economy

In Chapter 3, we examined the macroeconomic flows of money, goods and services between the business sector and the household sector of the economy, as illustrated in Figure 4-1. Obviously, the more economic activity that is occurring within the economy, the larger these flows will be, and the greater the economic prosperity of the society will be.

In order to monitor the performance of the economy, and to provide businesses and government policy-makers with information upon which to base their decisions, it is very useful to have economic statistics. While there are many such statistics relating to particular sectors of the economy (such as housing, agriculture, exports), the most all-embracing economic statistic is a measure of the total output of the entire economy of the nation.

Gross National Product

This statistic, called the Gross National Product (GNP), measures the ebb and flow of economic activity across Canada by adding up the output of all the sectors of the nation's economy. The only way to add together the many products of the nation's economy is to add up their values, or prices, expressed in dollars. The total figure which results is the Gross National Product. It is defined as *the market value of the total annual output of final goods and services produced in the nation.*[1]

---

[1]Another way of saying the same thing, which many students find helpful, is "the sum of the price tags of all final goods and services produced in the country in that year."

FIGURE 4–1 *Macroeconomic Flows in a Market Economy*

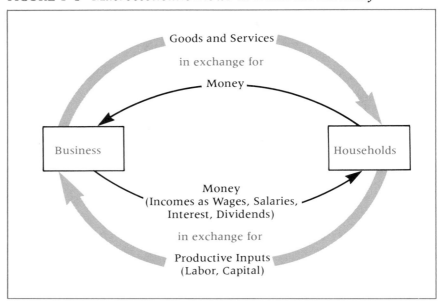

Note that the Gross National Product includes *final goods* only: it does not include goods that are used only in the production of other goods. An example of this is the production of bread, as shown in Figure 4-2. The final good here is obviously the bread; the wheat and flour are only intermediate products which go into the production of the bread. The contribution to GNP made by this process is obviously the value of the final product: $.60. If we had counted the flour and wheat into the GNP, we would have concluded that the contribution to GNP was

FIGURE 4–2 *Intermediate and Final Goods*

$1.16—almost twice the actual figure. The GNP would have been badly overstated because we would have been guilty of "double-counting." To avoid double-counting, the GNP is calculated in such a way as to include only the final goods and services produced: only the value of the bread is included.

Subdivisions of Gross National Product

The Gross National Product consists of a vast number of diverse goods and services . . . all of the automobiles, televisions, haircuts, entertainment, houses, factories, machinery, roads, military equipment, police services, education, wheat, minerals, lumber and so on that are produced in one year. This variety of goods and services can be organized into four major categories according to their destination, or purchaser.

(a) Consumption (C)

This category includes all *consumer goods and services* purchased by households, such as cars, appliances, food, clothing, entertainment and travel. This sector of the economy is sometimes referred to as the "private individual sector."

(b) Investment (I)

This category of production includes all additions to society's stock of *capital equipment, buildings* and *inventories* of products. The major part of the investment category is business spending on plant and equipment. Additions to business inventories of products and new housing construction are also included in the investment statistics.[2] Business investment spending is sometimes described as the *private business sector* of the economy.

(c) Government (G)

Governments (federal, provincial and local) constitute another major purchaser of goods and services. Some of these purchases, such as police services, are of a consumption nature because they are used up quickly. Others, such as schools and roads, are of an investment nature in that

[2]If a manufacturer's inventory of finished products increases by $2 million over last year's inventory, this represents $2 million of production during the year that must be included in the GNP statistics. However, it cannot be counted as consumption, since it has not yet been purchased by consumers, so we add it into the investment statistics instead. While construction of new housing is purchased by households, rather than being counted as a consumer item, it is included in the investment statistics because of its nature as a long-term asset.

they provide social benefits over long periods of time. However, *all purchases of governments* are lumped together under the category of government. This sector of the economy is known as the "public sector" or the "government sector."

(d) Net Exports (X-M)

So far we have accounted for all purchases by Canadian households (consumption, or **C**), business firms (investment, or **I**) and governments (government spending or **G**). Now we must account for two facts arising from Canada's trade with foreign nations.

(i) Products and services produced in Canada and sold to foreign buyers (Canada's **exports**) must be added to our figures.

(ii) Some of the Canadian purchases (C+I+G) that we have recorded include purchases of foreign-made goods **imported** into Canada. These should not be included in Canada's production (GNP) figures.

To correct our GNP figures to allow for these effects of foreign trade, we must *add* to our C+I+G total the value of all Canadian exports (X) and *deduct* from our C+I+G total the value of all imports (M) purchased by Canada. By making this adjustment, we ensure that we are measuring what was produced in Canada, as opposed to what was sold in Canada. The net effect of these adjustments **(X-M)** is called **net exports**. It may be a positive or negative factor, depending on the relative size of imports and exports in any particular year. This sector of the economy is also referred to as the *"foreign sector."*

In summary, the Gross National Product, which measures the total output of goods and services of the economy, is the sum of four components: consumption (C), investment (I), government spending (G) and net exports (X-M). This relationship is summarized in the equation

$$GNP=C+I+G+(X-M)$$

The limitations of GNP statistics

Gross National Product and other economic statistics that measure the performance of the economy are followed closely by governments, business and the media. While these statistics are important, we should always remember that they do not represent a simple and perfect measurement of the nation's economic prosperity. Like any statistics, GNP figures have certain limitations, some of which are examined in the following sections.

(a) The problem of price changes

The main problem in using GNP at market prices as a measure of total output is that price changes tend to distort the figures. Since GNP is the sum of the price tags of all final goods and services produced, GNP statistics can rise for two quite different reasons.

The following table shows some actual GNP statistics for Canada in selected years, all in billions of dollars.

	1980	1982	1984	1985
Consumption				
Consumer expenditure on goods and services	$170	$210	$247	$271
Investment				
Business investment in plant and equipment	$47	$55	$51	$55
Residential construction	14	13	16	19
Addition to inventories	0	–9	+2	+3
Total investment	61	59	69	77
Government				
Government expenditure on goods and services	68	88	103	109
Exports and Imports				
Exports of goods and services	$91	$102	$131	$141
Imports of goods and services	93	100	130	145
Balance	–2	+2	+1	–4
Gross National Product	$298	$358	$421	$454

(Totals do not always add to GNP because of statistical discrepancies.)

SOURCE *Bank of Canada Review.*

(i) *Increased production of goods and services*

If society's *output* of goods and services rises, GNP will tend to rise. This is called "real economic growth," because the society has more real output (of goods and services) at its disposal.

(ii) *Higher price levels*

If the *prices* of goods and services rise, GNP will tend to rise too, because it is stated in terms of current market prices. If real output were exactly the same as last year's level but prices were eight percent higher, the GNP would register an eight-percent increase over last year. This is obviously not "real economic growth," but because the GNP is higher it looks like growth has occurred. General price increases such as this are called inflation, and cause the GNP to rise faster than the real output of goods and services is rising.

We call these inflated GNP statistics "GNP at market prices," or "money GNP." The problem with such statistics, as we have seen, is that a ten-percent increase in money GNP could mean that real output has risen ten percent or that prices have risen ten percent, or that both real output and prices have risen, with the combined effect of a ten-percent increase. To make money GNP statistics more meaningful, we must adjust them to eliminate the effects of price increases. The result will be a statistic that measures only the real output of the economy and changes in it. This adjusted statistic is known by several names, including "real GNP," "GNP in constant dollars," and "GNP in 1971 dollars."[3]

Because prices have risen considerably in recent years, the statistics in Figure 4-3 show a considerable difference between the inflated **money GNP** figures and the adjusted real GNP figures in 1971 dollars.

In reading and interpreting economic statistics, it is important to be sure whether you are using statistics that have been adjusted for the effects of inflation or not. Generally, the adjusted (real) statistics are more useful because they reflect the level of and changes in real production

FIGURE 4-3 *Money GNP and Real GNP 1971–84*

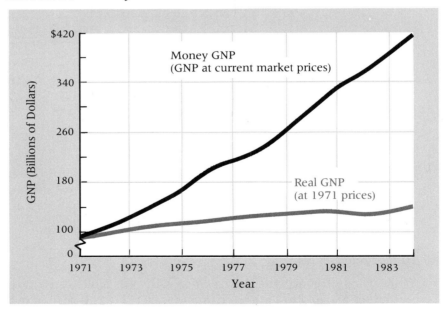

[3]This reflects the fact that the adjustment has the effect of calculating, for example, 1986's GNP *as if* prices had not changed from their 1971 levels.

rather than price changes. For example, from 1981 to 1982, Canada's **money GNP** increased by 5.3 percent—an apparently reasonable gain. However, **real GNP** actually *fell* by 4.4 percent during the same period, indicating a serious economic recession. Because prices continued to rise rapidly in 1982, the money GNP statistics made it look like economic gains had been made when in fact real output had fallen, as shown by the real GNP figures.

(b) GNP statistics omit many items

Gross National Product statistics omit a considerable amount of economic activity either because it is not reported or not marketed. For example, it is estimated that there is a significant "underground economy" in operation in which ordinary people buy and sell goods and services for cash (or even barter) in order to avoid paying income tax. Thus, while a plumber's or accountant's evening work for a neighbor may constitute a valuable service, it may not be included in the GNP if the earnings from it are not reported. Another major source of economic activity that goes unreported is income from illegal activities such as gambling, prostitution and the production and distribution of illicit drugs.

Another major omission from GNP statistics arises from the fact that not all goods and services that are produced are marketed and, lacking price tags, such items cannot be added into the GNP. Probably the largest of such items is the work done at home for free. Others include volunteer work, do-it-yourself projects and food grown for personal consumption.

(c) Total GNP does not measure living standards

While the Gross National Product does measure the total output of the economy, it does not necessarily measure the standard of living. A nation like India or China may have a large GNP, but its population is also large, making the GNP per person relatively low. Thus, *GNP per capita* is a more meaningful measure of economic performance for some purposes. Even this statistic may not measure the society's living standards very accurately, though. The Soviet Union's GNP per capita has risen significantly, but consumers have benefited relatively little from this because the economic planners have concentrated on increased production in the capital goods and military sectors of the economy rather than in the consumer goods sector.

For measuring living standards, *real disposable income per capita* (that is, after-tax income per person, adjusted for inflation) is generally considered to be the best statistic. By this measure, the purchasing power (and living standards) of the average Canadian doubled in the 1947-77 period, an average rate of increase of 2.4 percent per year.

(d) GNP does not measure the "quality of life"

GNP statistics, however adjusted to reflect real income, consumption or production per person, are not the only things that determine human welfare. For instance, increased leisure reduces the GNP but may add to our happiness. Canadians could have even more than twice their 1947 living standard if they were prepared to work more hours per week, something which most people probably would not do. Also, the GNP includes many goods that make a dubious (or negative) contribution to our welfare, such as cigarettes. GNP statistics do not distinguish between medical facilities, cigarettes, military equipment and beef. All are treated as additions to the nation's production and thus receive an implicit stamp of approval, regardless of their contribution to human welfare. A final irony is that the products of pollution-control equipment—cleaner air and water— are not even counted in the GNP statistics because they are not marketed. Thus, Gross National Product statistics are probably overrated by most people as a measure of how well our economy contributes to human happiness. On the other hand, to adjust the GNP figures to allow for all the problems we have discussed would be an impossible task. As a result, we have to use the GNP statistics for what they are—a far from perfect reflection of the welfare of society but a useful approximation of an important part of that welfare.

Measuring prices: the Consumer Price Index

Earlier in this chapter, we referred to the effect of price changes on GNP statistics and the fact that such price changes could be estimated and adjustments could be made to the GNP statistics to eliminate their effects. Obviously, then, it is just as important to measure *prices* and price changes as it is to measure the economy's output. Since there are millions of prices to be measured, they have to be combined into some kind of average, called an *index*. There are various price indexes. Some cover broad areas of the economy while others are quite specific, such as an index for housing prices. However, the price index with which most people are familiar is the **Consumer Price Index (CPI)**, which measures only the prices of consumer goods and services.

The Consumer Price Index is an average of the prices of the goods and services bought by representative or typical urban households. A common way of expressing this is to say that the CPI is the cost of a "basket" of goods and services bought by a typical household. As the prices of these goods and services rise, so does the CPI. To determine what types of goods or services should be included in this "basket" and in what quantities, Statistics Canada undertakes a nationwide survey of spending habits concerning 375 goods and services. The most recent such survey was completed in 1982. To determine the CPI for each month, survey takers in 51 cities record the prices of goods and services in the "basket." By feeding these prices into a computer, Statistics Canada is able to calculate the monthly CPI.

In calculating the CPI, it is essential to take into account that some items in the "basket" are more important than others: a 10 percent increase in the price of oil would have a far greater impact on the consumer than a 10 percent increase in the price of salt. To recognize this, each item in the "basket" is given a *weight* in the CPI, based upon the proportion of the typical household's income that is spent on it. For example, if the typical household spent 10 percent of its income on oil and one-tenth of one percent on salt, oil and salt would be given weights of .10 and .001 respectively in the CPI to reflect their relative importance. Figure 4-4 shows the weights assigned to each broad category of items in the CPI; within each category there are many individual goods and services, each with its own weight.

Rather than express the CPI in terms of the actual cost of the "basket" of goods and services, the CPI is expressed in terms of how much it has changed from a *base year* (presently 1981) in which the CPI was 100. This is illustrated in Figure 4-5, which shows not only the CPI in general ("all items"), but also the various major components of the CPI since 1961. In the base year of 1981, the CPI (and all its components) are

FIGURE 4-4 *Weights of the Major Components of the CPI 1982*

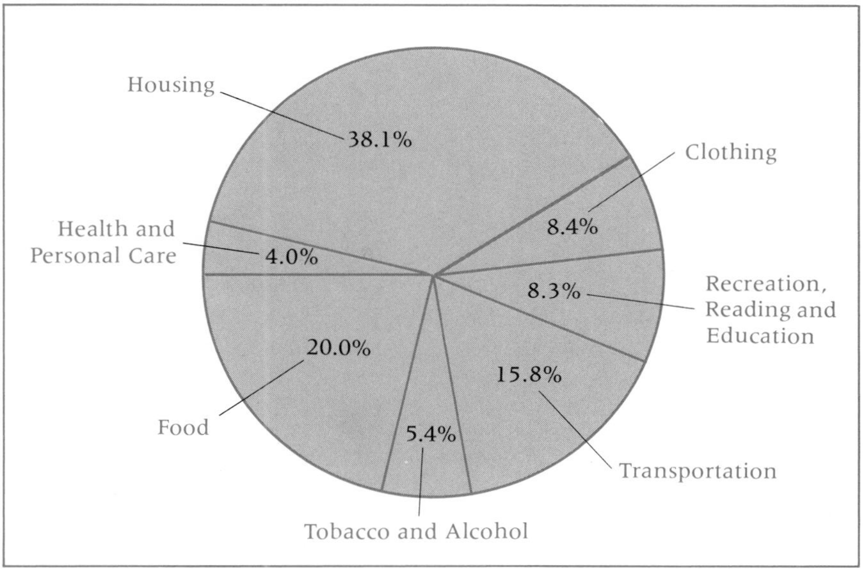

100.0. A CPI of 122.3 in 1984 means that the index (the cost of the "basket") was 22.3 percent higher in 1984 than it was in 1981. Similar calculations can be made for the various components of the CPI. For instance, in 1984, the cost of the clothing items in the "basket" was 12.5 percent higher than in 1981. It is not necessary to use 1981 as the base year for such calculations. For example, from 1983 to 1984 the CPI rose from 117.2 to 122.3, an increase of 4.3 percent (122.3-117.2÷117.2).

FIGURE 4-5 *Consumer Price Index by Categories 1961–85*

Year	All Items	Food	Housing	Clothing	Trans-portation	Health and Personal Care	Recreation and Reading	Tobacco and Alcohol
1961	31.6	26.2	32.3	40.6	32.4	31.8	38.6	37.2
1962	32.0	26.7	32.6	41.0	32.4	32.4	39.0	37.6
1963	32.6	27.5	33.0	42.0	32.4	33.2	39.5	37.7
1964	33.2	28.0	33.6	43.1	32.7	34.3	40.1	38.4
1965	34.0	28.7	34.1	43.8	34.0	35.9	40.8	39.1
1966	35.2	30.5	35.1	45.5	34.8	37.0	41.9	40.0
1967	36.5	31.0	36.6	47.7	36.2	38.9	44.1	41.0
1968	38.0	32.0	38.3	49.2	37.2	40.5	46.2	44.7
1969	39.7	33.3	40.3	50.5	38.9	42.4	49.0	46.5
1970	41.0	34.1	42.3	51.5	40.4	44.3	50.7	47.0
1971	42.2	34.4	44.2	52.2	42.1	45.2	52.4	47.8
1972	44.2	37.1	46.2	53.6	43.2	47.4	53.8	49.1
1973	47.6	42.5	49.2	56.3	44.3	49.7	56.1	50.7
1974	52.8	49.4	53.5	61.7	48.7	54.0	61.0	53.4
1975	58.5	55.8	58.8	65.4	54.5	60.2	67.3	59.9
1976	62.9	57.2	65.4	69.0	60.3	65.3	71.3	64.2
1977	67.9	62.0	71.5	73.7	64.5	70.1	74.7	68.7
1978	73.9	71.6	76.9	76.5	68.3	75.2	77.6	74.3
1979	80.7	81.0	82.2	83.5	74.9	82.0	82.9	79.7
1980	88.9	89.7	89.0	93.4	84.5	90.2	90.8	88.6
1981	100.0	100.0	100.0	100.0	100.0	100.0	100.0	100.0
1982	110.8	107.2	112.5	105.6	114.1	110.6	108.7	115.5
1983	117.2	111.2	120.2	109.8	119.8	118.2	115.8	130.0
1984	122.3	117.4	124.7	112.5	124.8	122.8	119.7	140.6
1985	127.2	120.8	129.0	115.6	130.8	127.2	124.5	154.0

SOURCE Department of Finance Canada, *Economic Review: A Perspective on the Decade*, April 1980 (page 215).
Statistics Canada, *Canadian Statistical Review* (Section 5, Table 2).

The upper part of Figure 4-6 shows how the *level* of the CPI has increased since 1961. However, it is more important to know *how rapidly* the CPI is rising in any given year. The lower part of Figure 4-6 shows us how fast (in percent terms) the CPI has risen since the previous year, or the **rate of inflation**. This graph shows that the CPI rose quite slowly in the 1960's, that the rate of inflation increased sharply during much of the 1970's, then declined back to the 4-5 percent per year range after 1982.

FIGURE 4-6   *The Level and the Rate of Increase of the Consumer Price Index 1961–84*

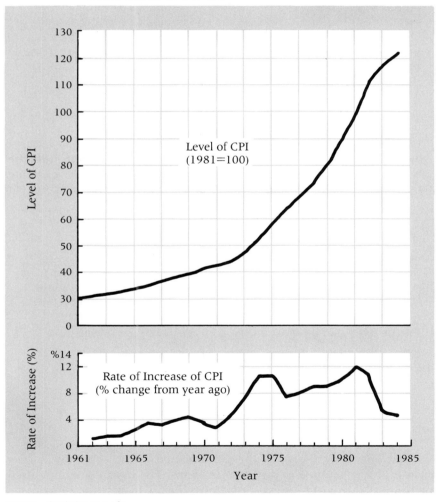

SOURCE   Statistics Canada.

THE CONSUMER PRICE INDEX IS *NOT* A "COST OF LIVING" INDEX

While people commonly refer to the CPI as the "cost of living" index, this is not correct. One reason for this is that the CPI does not include income taxes, which represent a major part of most people's cost of living. Another reason is that the CPI only measures the cost of a *constant* "basket" of goods and services; it does not allow for the fact that consumers tend to adjust to rising prices by buying less of those products whose prices are rising most rapidly. For instance, the rapid increases in the price of oil have caused the CPI to rise more rapidly. These increases in the CPI tell us what it would cost consumers to buy the same "basket" of goods and services, including the same proportion of oil as before. However, to the extent that consumers buy less oil than before, their actual "cost of living" will rise less rapidly than the CPI.

The rate at which the CPI is increasing is referred to as the **rate of inflation**. In this chapter, we have been concerned only with how the rate of inflation is measured. In Chapters 12 and 13, we will examine the causes of inflation, the effects of it and what can be done to combat it.

THE CPI AND YOU

A ten-percent increase in the CPI does not affect all Canadians equally, because individual householders' patterns of consumption may differ substantially from the weights used in the CPI. For instance, an increase in the CPI caused by increases in tobacco and alcohol prices will have no effect on people who neither smoke nor drink.

The unemployment rate

Another important aspect of the performance of the economy is how successful it is in *providing jobs* for Canadians. The most commonly used measure of this is the **unemployment rate**, which is the percentage of the labor force that is unemployed. The **labor force** refers to those

Canadians who are either employed or unemployed and available for work; thus, it is an approximation of the pool of labor available for work in Canada.

The statistics on employment, unemployment and the unemployment rate are obtained monthly by Statistics Canada through a sample survey of about 56 000 representative households across Canada. The results of this survey for the period 1966-84 are shown in Figure 4-7.

FIGURE 4-7 *Labor Force Statistics 1966–85*

Year	Labor force	Employed	Unemployed	Unemployment rate
	(	000's of persons	)	%
1966	7 493	7 242	251	3.4
1967	7 747	7 451	296	3.8
1968	7 951	7 593	358	4.5
1969	8 194	7 832	362	4.4
1970	8 395	7 919	476	5.7
1971	8 639	8 104	535	6.2
1972	8 897	8 344	553	6.2
1973	9 276	8 761	515	5.5
1974	9 639	9 125	514	5.3
1975	9 974	9 284	690	6.9
1976	10 203	9 477	726	7.1
1977	10 500	9 651	849	8.1
1978	10 895	9 987	908	8.3
1979	11 231	10 395	836	7.4
1980	11 573	10 708	865	7.5
1981	11 904	11 006	898	7.5
1982	11 958	10 644	1 314	11.0
1983	12 183	10 734	1 448	11.9
1984	12 399	11 000	1 399	11.3
1985	12 639	11 311	1 328	10.5

SOURCE Statistics Canada

The survey uses the following definitions:

Labor Force: that portion of the civilian non-institutional population 15 years of age and over who are employed or unemployed.

Employed: all persons who, during the survey week, did any work at

all or had a job but were not at work due to their own illness or disability, personal or family responsibilities, bad weather, a labor dispute or vacation.
Unemployed: those persons who, during the survey week, were

(a) without work, had actively looked for work during the past four weeks and were available for work,

(b) had not actively looked for work in the past four weeks but had been on layoff for 26 weeks or less and were available for work,

(c) had not actively looked for work in the past four weeks but had a new job to start in four weeks and were available for work.

The unemployment rate is the number of unemployed expressed as a percentage of the labor force. For example, if there were 9.1 million Canadians employed and 900 000 unemployed, the labor force would be 10 million and the unemployment rate would be nine percent (900 000÷10 million).

One problem with unemployment-rate statistics is that some jobs (such as farming or fishing) are seasonal in nature. As a result, the unemployment rate tends to rise every winter, due to purely seasonal factors. This can make unemployment statistics more difficult to interpret: is the unemployment rate rising because the economy is slipping into a recession or just because of seasonal factors? To make the statistics easier to interpret, Statistics Canada makes a "seasonal adjustment" to them, by eliminating

FIGURE 4-8 *Unemployment Rates in Canada 1966–84*

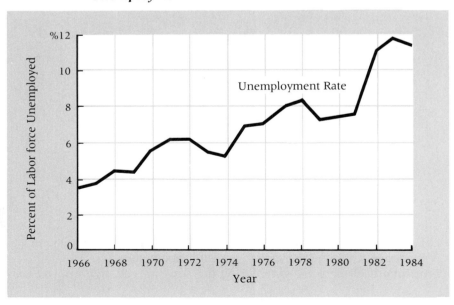

the seasonal elements from the data. The resulting seasonally adjusted unemployment-rate statistics are a better indicator of the actual state of the economy with respect to unemployment. Figure 4-8 shows unemployment rates in Canada from 1966-84.

DEFINITIONS OF NEW TERMS

Gross National Product (GNP)   The market value of the total annual ouput of final goods and services produced in the nation. Also called "GNP at current market prices" and "money GNP."

Real GNP   GNP statistics that have been adjusted to eliminate the effects of price increases, the result being a statistic that measures only changes in real output. Also called "GNP in constant dollars" or "GNP at 1971 prices."

Consumer Price Index (CPI)   A weighted average of the prices of a "basket" of goods and services purchased by a typical urban family.

Inflation   An increase in the general level of prices, usually as measured by the CPI.

Rate of Inflation   The percentage increase in prices, usually measured by the CPI, compared to prices a year earlier.

Unemployment Rate   The percentage of the labor force that is unemployed. Sometimes "seasonally adjusted" unemployment-rate statistics are used, to eliminate fluctuations in unemployment-rate data that occur merely due to seasonal factors.

CHAPTER SUMMARY

1. The Gross National Product, which measures the total output of the economy, consists of four components: consumption (C), investment (I), government (G) and net exports (X-M).

2. The Gross National Product can rise either because the output of goods and services is higher or because their prices have risen. These inflated money GNP statistics can be adjusted to eliminate the effects of increased prices, the result being real GNP statistics that measure only real output.

3. Most people probably overrate the importance of GNP statistics, which are far from perfect measures of the welfare of a society. Nonetheless, GNP statistics are a useful approximation of the overall output of the economy.

4. The Consumer Price Index is the most commonly used and well-known measure of prices. It is a weighted average of the prices of goods and services bought by a typical urban family.

5. While most people think of the CPI as a cost of living index, this is not correct. The CPI is a useful approximation of price changes of consumer goods and services and is used to measure the rate of inflation.

6. The most commonly used measure of the ability of the economy to provide jobs is the unemployment rate.

QUESTIONS

1. If a working couple were married and both decided one should stay at home and renovate their house, what would happen to
   (a) society's output of goods and services?
   (b) the Gross National Product?

2. Can you think of some examples of the "underground economy" referred to in this chapter?

3. From 1947 to 1977, living standards in Canada roughly doubled, rising at an average rate of 2.4 percent per year. What do you think was the basic source of this increased prosperity enjoyed by Canadians?

4. In 1982, the weights given to the various components of the Consumer Price Index were revised from their previous levels established in 1974, as the table shows. What could explain these revisions? If the weights were revised again, which components do you think would gain in importance and which would lose? Why?

	Previous 1974 Weights	Revision 1982 Weights
Food	21.5	20.0
Housing	34.1	38.1
Clothing	10.1	8.4
Transportation	15.8	15.8
Health/Personal Care	4.0	4.0
Recreation/Reading/Education	8.3	8.3
Tobacco/Alcohol	6.2	5.4

5. Over the past year, which components of the Consumer Price Index have increased
   (a) the most rapidly, and
   (b) the most slowly? Why?

6. Over the past year, what change has occurred in the unemployment rate? What might explain this trend?

7. **(a)** If money GNP has increased by 5.3 percent over last year's level, can we conclude that the economy's production of goods and services has risen?

   (b) If the general level of prices has risen by 3.2 percent over the same period, what can we conclude about the economy's production of goods and services?

   (c) If the general level of prices increased by 7.6 percent over the same period, what has happened to the economy's output of goods and services?

8.

Year	Consumer Price Index	Annual Rate of Inflation
1981	100.0	—
1982	110.8	10.8%
1983	117.2	_____
1984	122.3	_____
1985	127.2	_____

   (a) Calculate the rate of inflation for 1983, 1984 and 1985.
   (b) Draw on a graph the Consumer Price Index over the 1981-85 period.
   (c) Draw on a graph the rate of inflation over the 1982-1985 period.
   (d) What explains the different trends shown by the two graphs?

9.

Year	Civilian Labor Force (000)	Employed (000)	Unemployed (000)	Unemployment Rate (%)
1980	11 573	10 708	_____	_____
1981	11 904	11 006	_____	_____
1982	11 958	10 644	_____	_____
1983	12 183	10 734	_____	_____
1984	12 399	11 000	_____	_____
1985	12 639	11 311	_____	_____

   (a) Calculate the number of Canadians unemployed in each of the years shown.
   (b) Calculate the unemployment rate for each of the years shown.
   (c) In 1983, the number of Canadians employed rose; but the unemployment rate also rose. What explains this apparent contradiction?

CHAPTER 5

Sources of economic prosperity: the supply side

Why are some nations so much richer than others? This is a very complex question involving consideration of natural resources, education levels of the population, climate, social attitudes, capital equipment and many other factors. However, societies that have achieved a high material standard of living do tend to have one thing in common: they have what economists refer to as a strong *supply side* to their economies, or the ability to produce goods and services efficiently. The key to a strong supply side is the ability to make efficient use of economic inputs (labor, capital equipment and natural resources) so as to achieve high levels of *productivity*, or output per worker. Such high levels of output per person are a key factor underlying the ability to enjoy high levels of consumption, or a high material standard of living.

> Income and output are intimately related. Real income (that is, income unaffected by inflation) depends on output, so that any growth in real income requires growth in output.
>
> Economic Council of Canada,
> *Twelfth Annual Review*, 1975.

The nature of productivity

Productivity is not a word with a single simple meaning. In its broadest sense, it refers to all three productive inputs (labor, capital equipment and natural resources) and the efficiency with which they work together to produce goods and services. However, the most commonly used definition of productivity—as well as one that is easier to understand and to measure—is labor productivity or **output per worker-hour**.

This definition of productivity is sometimes interpreted as implying that productivity depends on how hard people work. While this is one factor that influences productivity, there are many other more important ones, many of which are interrelated. Some of these factors will be considered later in this chapter. First, we will examine what is generally thought of as the dominant factor determining productivity—the amount of *capital equipment per worker*. Generally, the more capital equipment workers have to work with, the higher their output per person, and the higher the society's standard of living can be. Therefore, a fundamental factor influencing productivity is the amount of *capital investment* done by a society in plants, equipment and machinery.

> . . .another reason why productivity growth is important—it may help to reduce social conflict. When productivity rises, there is a social dividend to be distributed. This distribution eases the tension between groups who are all competing for a share of the income pie. When productivity fails to rise, the struggle over income shares may become more intense.
>
> Economic Council of Canada,
> *Seventeenth Annual Review*, 1980 (page 80).

Sources of productivity: saving and investment

To emphasize the basic economic concepts involved in the process of capital investment, we will use a simple illustration. Suppose you are alone on a desert island and must find food to survive. Since the most accessible food is fish from a nearby stream, you set out to catch some.

The only productive inputs available to you are your labor and the stream and fish (natural resources)—you have no capital equipment at all. So you use your hands, with only limited success, and find that you are able to catch two fish per day. This is just enough to feed you for a day, but to catch the two fish takes the entire day or all your available labor. You have no time available for other productive activities, such as cultivating vegetables or building a shelter. Your low productivity is limiting you to a subsistence level standard of living.

After a few days, you decide one morning to forego fishing for a while and to find something that will help you to catch fish more efficiently. It takes an entire day—leaving you very hungry—but you are able to fashion a spear. Now you have a piece of *capital equipment* to help you catch (produce) fish. Using the spear, you can now catch six fish per day—a significant improvement. This piece of capital equipment has increased your productivity greatly, and by doing so has widened your economic choices considerably. Because you can catch enough fish to feed yourself in less than half a day, you have in effect released your time (or your labor) to do other things. You could produce other consumer products, or you could enjoy some leisure time, or you could further improve the efficiency of your food production (fishing).

Suppose you do the latter, and make a net over a period of four half-days. You could have caught twelve fish in this period of time, but instead you have acquired another piece of capital equipment—a net. Using the net, you are able to catch enough fish to feed yourself for a whole day in about half an hour. Your productivity is now so high that you can use a great deal of your free time (or released labor) to do other things. You then use this available time to fashion some primitive tools—a hammer, a saw, a knife and so on, with which you can construct more capital equipment. After a few weeks, you have a ladder for picking fruit from trees, traps for catching animals, a bow and arrows for hunting, a clearing and a plow for cultivating vegetables, a house for shelter and a boat for transportation, not to mention a couple of hours per day of leisure time and a hammock in which to spend it.

Your standard of living has increased tremendously from its original subsistence level. The key to this process is, of course, the *capital equipment* which you have made and thereby increased your productivity. But how was this capital equipment obtained? To make the spear, you had to forego one day's consumption of fish—the two fish you could have caught instead of working on the spear. Making the net also involved a sacrifice of consumption: twelve fish you could have caught in the two days' time it took to make the net. Similarly, to acquire all the other pieces of your capital equipment, you had to *forego consumption*; that is, *forego present enjoyment*.[1]

You were willing to do this because you expected that the capital equipment, by increasing your productivity, would *increase your future consumption*.

---

[1]This is the concept of *opportunity cost* explained in Chapter 2. The opportunity cost of building capital equipment to increase prosperity in the future is reduced consumption of goods and services in the present.

Thus, you were making a decision to trade off a lower standard of living in the present against a higher standard of living in the future. Each time you made a piece of capital equipment you were in effect saying, "I'll accept less than I could have had today in order that I can have more in the future." At first, this process was quite painful—you had to go a full day without food. Later, as your productivity increased, the sacrifices in the present became less harsh.

Consumption saving and investment

These basic ideas are sufficiently important to be given names and defined carefully. **Consumption** refers to consumer goods and services that are produced to be used up by the consumers for present enjoyment. Consumption includes all such goods and services, from automobiles to manicures. The production of capital goods, which will make possible greater production of goods and services in the *future*, is called **investment**. As we have seen, one key to a society's economic prosperity is the amount of investment it does in capital equipment, which increases productivity.

However, the basic economic problem of scarcity forces upon us a difficult choice: the more of our output we devote to investment (for future prosperity), the less of our output is available for consumption (for present enjoyment). This is the same trade-off decision we faced regarding the building of the spear and net: to gain the future benefits of these tools we had to sacrifice some present consumption.

This basic concept of doing without (foregoing) consumption that could have been enjoyed in the present is known as **saving**. Saving is obviously of great importance, since it is essential if there is to be the investment necessary for economic progress.

The dilemma: consumption vs. saving

Consumption is the end goal of economic activity—the satisfaction of the wants and needs of the consumer. To increase future levels of production and consumption it is necessary to engage in investment, which adds to society's stock of productive capital equipment and increases productivity, while to achieve investment it is necessary to have saving, or the foregoing of some consumption in the present to make productive inputs available for building capital equipment.

These concepts apply to all societies and all economies. Whenever resources are used to construct capital equipment (be it a fishing net or a steel factory) to produce more goods and services in the future, it is true that the resources used to build the capital equipment could have been used to produce more goods and services for consumption in the present. This is true for capitalist and communist economies, and for highly industrialized nations as well as Third World countries.

It is, however, much easier for a wealthy nation, which has high levels of output, to save, invest and grow economically, because it can easily afford to forego some consumption to have more investment. Poor societies are much less fortunate — they may need to consume nearly all of their present output merely to survive. Thus, they may be unable to save and therefore unable to invest. In such a situation, economic progress can be impossible without outside assistance.

How can a society achieve high levels of saving?

Since economic growth requires investment — which requires saving, which in turn involves foregoing consumption — it is likely to be painful, particularly in poor societies. Thus, people may be reluctant to forego consumption (save) today to enable the society's standard of living to be higher in the future, particularly if the future belongs to the next generation. In short, the process of economic development in its early stages may involve very great sacrifices: sacrifices that the people may be reluctant to bear. How can the necessary high levels of saving be achieved in the face of this fact? And who will make the sacrifices?

First, the sacrifices will have to be made mostly by the mass of people. Because of their great numbers, only they are capable of foregoing enough consumption (or generating enough saving) to make possible such high levels of investment. Second, if the society is poor, it is likely that this sacrifice will have to be *imposed* on them — they are unlikely to accept it gladly.

Two interesting examples of this process are the industrialization of Great Britain (during the Industrial Revolution 1760-1830) and the Soviet Union (following the Bolshevik Revolution of 1917).

In Russia, the saving was imposed on the people in a relatively simple way — the Soviet economic planners decided to produce a great deal of capital goods (hydroelectric facilities, roads, factories, steel mills and so on) and relatively few consumer goods (such as appliances, automobiles and housing). Thus, the Russian government decided to divert production away from consumption toward investment. With relatively little available for consumption, the people had no choice — they saved; that is, they did not consume much.

In Great Britain, the process was somewhat different. During the Industrial Revolution, there was a tremendous surplus of labor. As a result, employers were able to force wages to very low levels and profits rose to high levels. Consequently, the working class was not able to consume much (or was forced to save, in the sense of accepting very low levels of consumption) and businesses had high profits which they used to expand their businesses through high investment.

While the process in Great Britain was different from that used in Russia, the results were similar: high levels of investment were made possible by the economic sacrifices (saving) that were essentially forced upon an unwilling public that had no choice. And, of course, both societies subsequently reaped the economic benefits of the investment.

QUESTION   If a group of farmers store some food away to eat during the winter, they could be said to be "saving" that food. Is this the same idea as we have been discussing above, with respect to saving and investment?
(ANSWER ON NEXT PAGE).

Government taxation policies and economic progress

Government policies can contribute to economic progress in many ways; one of the most important ones is by *providing incentives* for the saving and investment that are the key to prosperity. A vital factor here is the government's taxation policies regarding business profits and income from the investment of people's savings. Only if the *after-tax return* on investment income and profits is high enough will individuals and businesses have an incentive to save and invest. While it would seem logical for governments to seek to encourage economic prosperity by providing incentives for saving and investment, it is also possible fo government taxation policies to have the opposite effect, and thus to slow down economic progress. One of the more obvious examples of this involves *income tax rates*: if the tax rate payable on any extra income earned (the "marginal tax rate") is too high, people will be discouraged from doing additional work such as overtime or second jobs.[2]

---

[2]The marginal tax rate is defined as the percentage of any *additional* income (over and above one's present income) that is taken by taxes. If Fred, a musician, earns a salary of $20000 per year for playing in an orchestra and pays $4000 in income taxes on this salary, he is paying a 20 percent tax rate on his income. This, however, is his tax rate on his *total* income, whereas his marginal tax rate is the percentage of any *extra* income that he earns that would be taken by taxes. For instance, if Fred earns an extra $1000 for playing the piano in a marching band on weekends, and he must pay $400 in income taxes on this $1000 of additional income, his marginal tax rate is 40 percent. Because he can decide whether or not to do this extra work, his marginal tax rate will be a key factor affecting Fred's incentive to do such additional work. If the marginal tax rate is too high, Fred will be left with too little after-tax income from such additional work to make it worthwhile to him.

A more subtle but more important problem occurs if high marginal tax rates impair the saving-investment process. If high marginal tax rates make the after-tax returns to investors on income from interest, dividends and capital gains too low, people will be discouraged from saving and less capital will be available for business capital investment. Similarly, high tax rates on business profits can discourage capital investment, not only by leaving business with less funds for capital investment but also by reducing the incentive for businesses to invest in additional production facilities.

Unfortunately, political considerations may lead governments into setting high tax rates which in turn discourage saving and investment. Governments are usually under political pressure to increase their spending and in seeking sources of additional tax revenue, they sometimes turn to business profits, high-income groups and investment income, none of which are particularly sympathized with by the general public. Many economists consider such taxation policies to have been one of the major causes of Great Britain's economic decline following the Second World War. The government financed massive spending programs with extremely heavy taxes on business profits and higher-income people whose savings had contributed much of the funds for capital investment. Thus, the government's own taxation policies contributed to Britain's economic decline by discouraging saving, investment and work.

In a later chapter, we will see another, even more subtle way in which government policies can stagnate the economy by discouraging capital investment. Many economists believe that the severe inflation of the 1970's had the effect of depressing capital investment and thus contributing to economic stagnation in many nations, including Canada.

ANSWER   It is not the same idea. While the farmers are foregoing consumption in the present, their reason for doing so is *not* to build capital goods to increase their production in the future. Rather, their purpose is to consume less in the present so as to keep some food aside for themselves to consume during the winter—they are just changing the *time* of consumption.

Other sources of productivity and prosperity

While we have emphasized the fundamental importance of investment (and saving), productivity and economic prosperity are the result of many factors working together. Several of these factors are examined in the following sections.

During the past 30 years, Canadians have become accustomed to a continuously rising standard of living based on rapid economic growth. Expectations conditioned by this experience demand an awareness of the importance of efficiency, and high productivity, if Canadians are to achieve their economic and social goals. Productivity depends on the role played by all segments of society — business, labour and government at all levels. Increased economic efficiency will require effort from each of these groups.

The Canadian Foundation
for Economic Education,
Understanding Productivity (1977).

Education and skill levels of the labor force

Obviously, the better-educated and more highly-skilled a nation's labor force is, the more likely it is to be highly productive. This is particularly important in an economy with many high-technology industries requiring specialized skills and knowledge. This is why spending on training and education is often referred to as an "investment in human capital." It is estimated by the Economic Council of Canada that our educational advancement has accounted for about one-quarter of the contribution of labor to the growth of Canada's real output between 1946 and 1967. On the other hand, there are real concerns that, due to Canada's lack of apprenticeship programs, economic progress in the future will be hindered by shortages of skilled labor.

Management

The level of managerial ability is an important contributor to productivity, since it is ultimately management that is responsible for the efficiency with which productive resources are combined to produce goods and services. Furthermore, the quality of employer-employee relations, much of which depends on management, influences employee morale and productivity. Many observers believe that Canadian industry is suffering from a shortage of highly qualified managers, and that improved education and training of managers could be of considerable value to the Canadian economy.

Size of market and scale of operations

Generally, as the size of an operation increases, it becomes possible to develop more specialized workers and capital equipment, and thus to achieve higher efficiency through *economies of scale*. This does not mean that bigger is always better, though: beyond a certain size, vast operations become difficult to coordinate and manage effectively, and can become less efficient. Ideally, then, manufacturing plants would be at an *optimum size* at which point their efficiency is maximized.

Generally, Canadian operations are well below this optimum size because of the *small size of the Canadian market* (about 26 million people) and the fact that Canada is not part of a free-trade area such as the European Common Market, which provides tariff-free[3] access to larger markets in other nations. Even Canada's small market of 26 million is not a single market. Geographical factors and a variety of provincial laws that restrict the movement of people, capital and products between provinces have the effect of dividing Canada into several smaller markets. As a result, manufacturing operations in Canada generally tend to be much smaller (and less efficient) than in other industrialized countries.

This problem is not solely one of plant size, however. In some industries, a large plant exists but it must produce several different products. To switch over from one product to another takes time and adds costs, making the operation less efficient than it would be if longer production runs of a single product were made. Recent research indicates that this problem of *short production runs* may be an even greater drag on Canadian manufacturing productivity than small plant size.

International comparisons are important too. If Canada's productivity is not growing as fast as that of other countries, export markets could dry up, and imports may become more attractive than domestically produced goods. Improved productivity growth could make Canadian goods more competitive in international markets. . . .

Economic Council of Canada,
Seventeenth Annual Review, 1980 (page 80)

The state of the economy

Economic activity tends to fluctuate, with rapid growth at some times and sluggish periods (recessions) at others. During recessions, employers tend to keep surplus employees (particularly skilled ones) rather than lay them off, to avoid having to hire and train new workers when the

---

[3]A tariff is a tax (import duty) levied on products imported into a nation from other countries. It has the effect of adding to the price of imported products, making it more difficult for them to compete with domestic products.

economy recovers. With output declining faster than the number of workers producing it, productivity will decline. Conversely, when sales and production pick up again, the same number of workers will be capable of increasing their output (and thus output per person) very rapidly. These short-term fluctuations in labor productivity do not reflect changes in the efficiency of industry; rather, they are the result of fluctuations in the state of the economy itself.

Government policies

As noted earlier, government *tax policies* can have a significant effect on productivity through their impact on incentives to work, save and invest. While it can be argued that some taxes have negative effects in this respect, there are also tax incentives that encourage both saving by householders and capital investment by business. Another way in which governments can influence productivity growth is through their *education policies,* which affect the quality of the labor force. The *size of the market* is also influenced by government policies. Many economists argue that productivity in Canada would be higher if Canada were part of a free trade arrangement with the United States or other nations. Such an arrangement would give Canadian industry access to larger markets; on the other hand, it would reduce the tariff protection from imports that is enjoyed by some Canadian industries, forcing them to become more efficient or to go out of business. Thus, government policies in a variety of areas have an effect on our productivity and prosperity, for better or for worse.

> For eight years now, there has been very little improvement in the efficiency with which the economy uses its resources.
>
> Economic Council of Canada,
> *Seventeenth Annual Review,* 1980 (page 79)

The productivity slowdown

After many years of more or less steady growth, labor productivity stagnated and then declined for several years after the mid-1970's, as shown in Figure 5-1. This phenomenon, which has occurred in all major industrialized countries, and with marked severity in Canada, has serious implications. Unless productivity increases, our standard of living will stagnate or even decline. Furthermore, many Canadians' jobs are dependent upon competing with foreign producers in both world markets and Canadian markets. Poor productivity in Canadian industry means higher production costs, higher prices, and lost sales and jobs for Canadians. From

FIGURE 5-1 *Real GNP per Person Employed 1970-85*

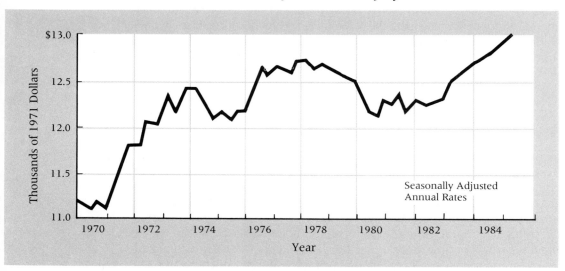

SOURCE   Department of Economic Research, *Canada's Business Climate,*
Toronto Dominion Bank; Statistics Canada.

1970 to 1980, Canada's share of world trade fell from 5 percent to 3 percent; had it remained at 5 percent in 1980, it is estimated that there would have been 1 million more jobs for Canadians. For these reasons, the productivity slowdown is a major concern.

There is a lack of agreement on the causes of the productivity slowdown. Some economists emphasize the weak levels of demand in the late 1970's and especially during the "Great Recession" of the early 1980's, which depressed output and thus productivity. This theory is certainly supported by the fact that real GNP per person employed rose as the economy recovered from the recession after 1982, as Figure 5-1 shows. Indeed, most economists attribute the brisk recovery of productivity growth after 1982 to the fact that total output (and thus output per worker) was able to rise quite rapidly because it was recovering from the far-below-capacity levels of the recession of the early 1980's. This recovery of productivity growth rates was regarded as being most likely a short-term phenomenon reflecting the recovery from the recession, rather than a resumption of the rapid productivity growth of the pre-1974 period. Even with the recovery, the growth of productivity since 1974 remained slower than it had been before, and Canada's productivity performance remained weaker than that of its major international competitors. Obviously, other factors were at work, in addition to the recession, in causing slower productivity growth in Canada.

Canadian productivity performance has been especially weak in the manufacturing sector of the economy, where productivity was at least 25 percent below US levels in the early 1980's. The problem does not appear to be simply one of inadequate levels of capital investment: Canada has the most capital-intensive economy in the world. Rather, the problem seems to be that Canada has not been using its capital and labor effectively. Some economists point to the fact (referred to earlier) that much of Canada's manufacturing industry produces only for the small Canadian market, which limits its productivity; they recommend freer trade with the USA as a road to higher productivity. Others stress the fact that Canadian manufacturers have been slower than their foreign competitors to adopt state-of-the-art production technology such as computer-assisted design and manufacturing (CAD/CAM) and robotics; they recommend tax incentives for research and development (R&D) and capital investment. Still others believe that more emphasis on investment in "human capital", through training and education of workers and managers, could improve productivity significantly.

Finally, some observers believe that the productivity slowdown may be in part due to changes in the composition of Canada's industries and labor force. As the Canadian economy has grown more mature and wealthier, an increasing proportion of consumer demand (and thus output) has been represented by services, such as restaurants, entertainment, travel and so on, as opposed to goods. This trend could have contributed to the productivity slowdown because it is generally more difficult to apply productivity-increasing technology to the production of services than to the production of goods, which lends itself more to automation and mass-production. Also, since the early 1970's, the composition of Canada's labor force has changed due to the entry into the labor force of greater numbers of young people ("baby boomers") and with increasing numbers of women both wanting and needing work. These new entrants to the labor force were often less experienced, and therefore less productive than average. Most of them went to work in the expanding service industries, where productivity was also lower than average and slower to increase, and they often took part-time jobs, where output per worker employed is by definition lower than average due to the fewer hours of work per week.

At present, many explanations of the productivity slowdown are being offered without much agreement on their importance. In its 1980 Annual Review, the Economic Council of Canada noted that only about one-half of the slowdown could be explained by known factors, leaving the causes of half of this very important trend unexplained. Further research into the productivity slowdown is needed, so that its causes may be determined and remedies undertaken for the benefit of Canadians' future prosperity.

Summary of the supply side of the economy

So far we have discussed several factors which have an effect upon the production potential, or supply side, of the economy.

(a) Quantity and quality of capital equipment

To the extent that the economy has large amounts of up-to-date capital equipment, output per worker hour, and therefore the ability to produce, will be greater.

(b) Quantity and quality of labor (including management)

Efficiency of production is also increased by having a greater number of skilled, educated workers and managers.

(c) Incentives to improve productivity by working, saving and investing

The stronger the incentives (such as those from competition or from tax policies) for business and workers to improve efficiency by working, saving and investing, the higher the potential output will be.

(d) Availability and cost of resources

The economy's supply side will be strengthened by readily available, low-cost natural resources, either domestic or imported.

(e) Size of market and scale of operations

Larger markets enable industries to produce on a bigger scale, thereby lowering production costs per unit, and increasing output.

Together, these factors determine not only the efficiency with which the economy can produce goods and services, but also its potential total output: the supply side of the economy.

The concept of "aggregate supply"

The supply side of the economy can be represented by an **aggregate supply curve**, as shown in Figure 5-2, which shows how the level of total output ("aggregate supply") is related to the cost per unit of producing that output.

FIGURE 5-2 *Aggregate Supply Curve*

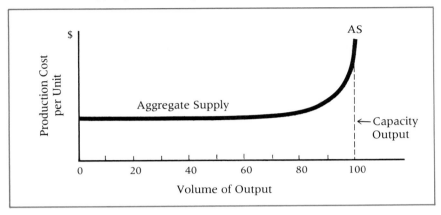

When operating at *capacity* (that is, at its highest production level), this economy is capable of producing 100 units of output per week. The farther we move to the right on the aggregate supply (AS) curve, the closer we get to this capacity output. The higher the curve goes, the more costly it is to produce goods and services. Up to about 80 or 90 units of volume, we can increase output without experiencing increases in production costs per unit, because the economy has plenty of inputs (labor, capital and resources) available, or unemployed. It should, therefore, be possible to obtain more inputs without having to pay higher wage rates or prices to attract them. Beyond this level, however, it is no longer possible to increase output further without some increases in production costs per unit.

In some industries, production *bottlenecks* will occur, due to shortages of production capacity, skilled labor or other inputs. Thus, output can only be increased by means which will also increase production costs per unit: higher wages for overtime or extra shifts, or to attract additional workers, higher prices for increasingly scarce materials or other inputs, and so on. In Figure 5-2, this means that we can move to higher levels of production, but only by accepting higher costs per unit as the AS curve slopes upward.

The closer we get to the economy's capacity output, the more severe these problems of shortages and production bottlenecks become, and the faster the AS curve rises. Finally, at capacity output of 100 units per week, the economy is simply not capable of producing at a faster pace, and the AS curve becomes vertical. The economy is using all of its inputs and the pace of production cannot be increased further, even at sharply higher costs per unit.

Changes in the AS curve

Figure 5-2 represents the AS curve at a particular point in time. If the economy's *potential to produce* were to increase next year as its labor force and stock of capital equipment grew, the AS curve would shift to the right, as shown by AS_1 in Figure 5-3.

FIGURE 5-3 *As Curve Illustrating Increased Production Potential*

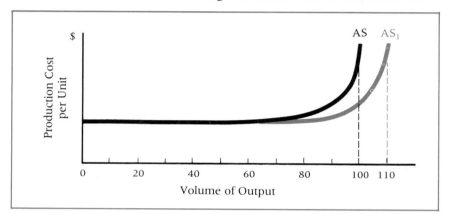

AS_1 reflects the fact that the economy is now capable of producing a higher volume of output (110 units) than last year, at about the same cost per unit. Efficiency (productivity) has not improved, as shown by

FIGURE 5-4 *AS Curve Illustrating Increased Overall Productivity*

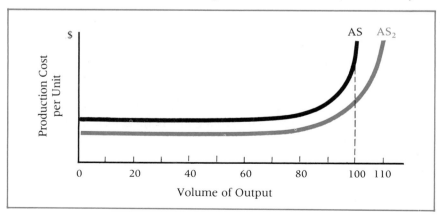

the fact that production costs per unit are the same as last year, but the greater volume of inputs available makes possible a higher volume of total output.

If *overall productivity* in the economy were to improve, so that it was using its inputs more efficiently, not only would its potential (capacity) output rise, but production costs per unit would also fall. This is shown in Figure 5-4, in which AS_2 represents the new situation, with production costs per unit lower than before and capacity output higher than before.

Can saving be too great? A preview of the demand side of the economy

In this chapter, we have stressed the importance of the *supply side* of the economy — its ability to produce goods and services efficiently. Without this ability to achieve high productivity, economic prosperity is not possible. Furthermore, we have stressed the desirability of saving so as to make possible the investment that increases the economy's productive potential. However, productive capability alone is not enough to ensure prosperity. If this productive capacity is to be used, there must be sufficient demand for its output. This raises the possibility that saving could be too high — that excessive saving by households could depress consumption spending (demand), leaving business with low sales and little or no incentive to invest in new plant and equipment.

Ideally, then, there would be a *balance* between consumption spending and saving. Saving would be sufficiently high to finance adequate levels of capital investment, while consumption spending would be sufficiently high to provide business with an incentive to invest in additional plant and equipment. Such a balance between spending and saving is essential for economic progress.

In summary, economic progress and prosperity depend on the inter- action between the *supply side* and the *demand side* of the economy. Not only must the economy have the ability to produce efficiently, but also there must be sufficient demand for its output to ensure that the economy actually produces to its fullest possible capabilities.

Following an examination of consumption, saving and investment in the Canadian economy in Chapter 6, we will consider the demand side of the economy more closely in Chapter 7.

DEFINITIONS OF NEW TERMS

Supply Side   The ability of the economy to use its productive resources efficiently to produce goods and services.

Productivity   A measure of productive efficiency, usually measured in terms of labor, as output per worker-hour.

Consumption   Refers to consumer goods and services that are used up by consumers for present enjoyment.

Investment   Refers to the production of capital goods that make possible increased production in the future.

Saving   Doing without (foregoing) consumer goods; saving is essential if there is to be investment.

Marginal Tax Rate   The percentage of any *additional* income received that goes to taxes; an important factor influencing incentives to work, save and invest.

Economies of Scale   The achievement of increased efficiency as a result of larger-scale productive operations.

Tariff   A tax, or import duty, levied by a nation on products imported from foreign countries.

Aggregate Supply   A representation of the supply side of the economy (usually graphically), showing how production cost per unit changes as the level of output is increased toward its potential.

CHAPTER SUMMARY

1. The key to economic prosperity is high productivity or output per worker-hour.

2. A fundamental factor determining the productivity of a society is the amount of capital investment done by it.

3. While capital investment can increase future prosperity, investment also requires saving, or less consumption, in the present. This process can be very difficult or even impossible for a poor nation, without outside help.

4. Other sources of productivity growth include the education and skill levels of the labor force, the quality of management, the size of the market, the scale of operations and the state of the economy.

5. Government policies regarding factors such as taxation, education and tariffs influence productivity, sometimes positively and sometimes negatively.

6. Since the mid-1970's, productivity growth has slowed in Canada and other industrialized nations. The causes of this trend are not fully understood.

7. Developing the ability to produce efficiently does not by itself guarantee economic prosperity; there must also be sufficient demand for the economy's output to ensure that the economy actually produces to its fullest possible capabilities.

QUESTIONS

1. Because each province has negotiated its own personal income tax rates with the federal government, marginal tax rates vary from province to province. Following is a table of the 1985 marginal tax rates for Ontario. Do you believe that these marginal tax rates provide adequate incentives to work, save and invest?

Taxable Income	Marginal Tax Rate
$ 5 000	25.1%
10 000	28.1
20 000	34.0
25 000	37.0
40 000 to 50 000	44.4
65 000 to 85 000	50.3
90 000 to 130 000	50.3
over 135 000	50.3

2. The Canadian personal income tax system provides for special treatment of income from investments (interest, dividends and capital gains), having the effect of reducing tax rates on such income. What are the special provisions applying to investment income? (Call your District Taxation Office if necessary for this information.) What would the purpose of these provisions be? Do you agree with such provisions?

3. Some people believe that the productivity slowdown that has occurred since the mid-1970's is largely the result of the decline of the "work ethic." Do you agree?

4. If joining with the United States in an economic union (free trade area) would increase living standards (real consumption per person) in Canada by 10 percent, would you support such a change? Why?

5. The graph shows the aggregate supply curve for an economy that can produce a maximum (capacity) output of 100 units per week. Explain how the AS curve would be changed if:
   (a) the economy had 20 percent more of all productive resources, which could be utilized with same efficiency as its existing resources.
   (b) the efficiency with which the economy's existing productive resources could be utilized increased by 20 percent.
   (c) the economy had 20 percent less of all productive resources.
   (d) the efficiency with which the economy's existing productive resources could be utilized decreased by 20 percent.

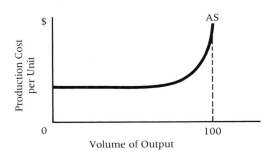

6. Canada's provincial governments have over the years erected various barriers to trade across provincial borders, such as government purchasing policies that favor suppliers from within the province and preferential licensing and hiring practices favoring residents of the province. What effects would such policies have upon the economic welfare of Canadians generally?

7. (a) Donna teaches accounting in a community college for a salary of $40 000 per year, and pays income tax of $10 000. The average percentage of Donna's income paid to income tax is, therefore, ... percent; this is Donna's average tax rate.
   (b) If Donna teaches night school, she will earn an additional $1600. The income tax payable on this additional income will be $600. The marginal tax rate paid by Donna on her additional income is .... percent.
   (c) How would a significant increase in Donna's
      (i) average tax rate
      (ii) marginal tax rate
      probably affect Donna's incentive to work?

8. Fill in the remaining average and marginal tax rates

Income	Income Tax	Average Tax Rate	Marginal Tax Rate	
$20 000	$4000	20.0%	—	
21 000	4300	20.5%	30.0%	($300/$1000)
22 000	4650	—	—	
23 000	5050	—	—	

*Sources of
economic
prosperity: the
supply side*

CHAPTER 6

Consumption, saving and investment in the Canadian economy

In the desert island example of Chapter 5, one person performed all three basic economic functions — *consumption* (by catching and eating fish), *saving* (by foregoing some fish), and *investment* (by making equipment to increase fish production).

The situation is different in a more advanced economy such as ours, where economic functions are much more specialized and money is used. Consumption is done by *households*, which buy and use consumer goods and services, while investment is done by *businesses*, which buy and build the producers' goods (capital goods) that help them to produce goods and services more efficiently. In such an economy, as we will see, the important process of *saving* is carried out by both households and businesses. In this chapter, we will examine consumption, saving and investment in the Canadian economy.

Consumption

This is defined as *spending by households on consumer goods and services*. These can be divided into three categories: *nondurable goods*, such as food and clothing, which are used up quite quickly; *durable goods*, such as cars and appliances, which last considerably longer; and *services*, such as entertainment, medical services and travel. Consumer goods and services are by far the largest single component of the Gross National Product in Canada, representing about three-fifths of all goods and services produced, as Figure 6-1 shows.

Generally, advanced economies such as the USA, Canada and Western Europe are able to devote a relatively high share of their GNP to current consumption because they have already built a strong base of productive capital through past investment. Countries that are in earlier stages of development, such as Japan, Hong Kong, Korea, Singapore and Taiwan tend to devote less of their output to current consumption, and more to investment in building their base of capital.

FIGURE 6-1 *Consumption and Gross National Product 1960–85*

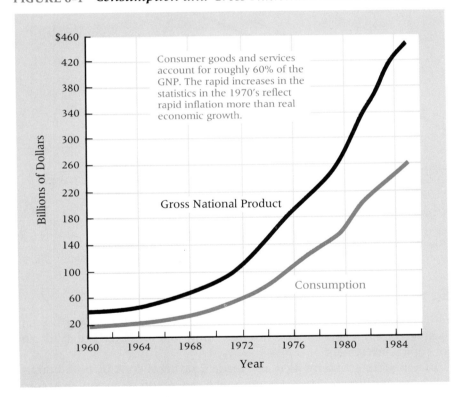

Consumer goods and services account for roughly 60% of the GNP. The rapid increases in the statistics in the 1970's reflect rapid inflation more than real economic growth.

Gross National Product

Consumption

What determines the level of consumption spending?

Many factors may influence the amount of consumption done by individual households. However, when we consider consumption spending in the economy as a whole, it depends mainly on the level of *personal disposable income* (personal income less personal taxes), which is the amount of money households have available to spend. As Figure 6-2 shows, as personal disposable income rises, consumer spending rises.[1]

FIGURE 6-2 *Consumer Income and Spending 1970–85*

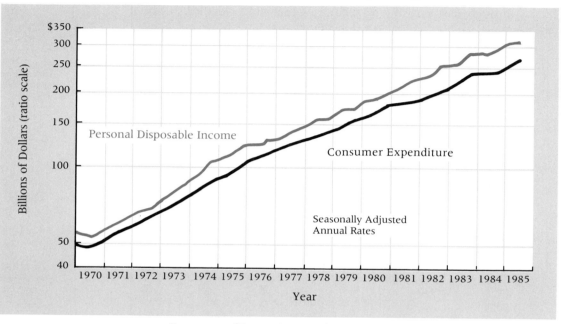

SOURCE Department of Economic Research, *Canada's Business Climate*, Toronto Dominion Bank.

Saving

In Chapter 5, saving was defined as *foregoing consumption*. Saving is vital to an economy's performance because funds that are saved are available for capital investment.

In a modern economy such as Canada's, saving is done by both households and businesses. These savings reflect a decision by society to accept a lower level of consumption in the present than could have been obtained if these funds had been spent on consumer goods. Furthermore, the funds thus saved either are available or could be made available to business to finance capital goods, which contribute to future prosperity.

[1]Also, as personal disposable income rises, *saving* rises. That is, people as a whole do not spend all of an increase in their disposable income; they save some of it.

(a) Personal saving

This is *personal disposable income not spent on consumption.* Saving by households takes many forms. Much of it is done in savings accounts in banks or trust companies. Other people prefer guaranteed investment certificates, bonds or mortgages because they pay higher interest, or corporate stocks because their value may rise.

FIGURE 6-3 *Personal Saving as a Percentage of Personal Disposable Income 1970–85*

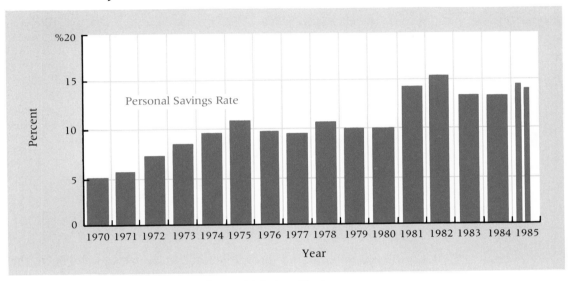

SOURCE   Department of Economic Research, *Canada's Business Climate,* Toronto Dominion Bank.

QUESTION

If Fran's disposable income is $800 per month, and she spends $680 of it on consumer goods and services, puts $60 into a trust company savings account and uses the remaining $60 to buy high-risk "penny-mining" stocks,

(a) How much does Fran save per month?

(b) Does this represent a higher or lower saving rate than the average Canadian?

(ANSWER ON NEXT PAGE)

In the 1960's personal saving in Canada averaged about 5.3 percent of personal disposable income. In the mid-1970's saving rates rose to considerably higher levels, as Figure 6-3 shows. While saving rates of 10 percent of disposable income appear unrealistically high to most Canadians who have little if any money left in the bank by the end of the month, it must be remembered that saving includes two factors not mentioned above. These are *pension fund contributions* which are deducted from paycheques regularly; and *mortgage repayments* (excluding interest).[2] Both of these factors add significantly to saving, although most people do not regard them as such.

ANSWER
(a) $120 — the amount *not spent* on consumption. The fact that some of the savings have been put into a less secure form (stocks) is not relevant here. All of the $120 is saving, and is available for capital investment.
(b) Higher — $120 is 15 percent of $800, as compared to average saving rates of no more than 10 percent or 11 percent (and this doesn't even include Fran's pension contributions).

What determines the level of personal saving?

As with consumption, the most important single factor influencing the level of saving is the level of personal disposable income: as disposable income rises, so does the volume of saving. However, the level of personal saving is also influenced by other factors, including *habit* (many people tend to save a certain amount regularly, for security or for a "rainy day") and *interest rates* (generally, higher interest rates should induce people to save more). Other influences on the saving rate are *people's expectations* and *government taxation policies.* For instance, the high Canadian saving rate since the mid-1970's appears to be the result of a combination of factors: uncertainty among the public about the economic future, government tax incentives to promote saving (such as registered retirement savings plans and tax exemptions for investment income up to $1000) and the unusually high interest rates that prevailed during this period.

[2]Repayments of mortgage principal are counted as saving because they represent income not spent on consumption in that year. Rather, such repayments represent money saved to pay the mortgage on a house purchased in the past. Mortgage *interest* payments, on the other hand, represent a consumption item — payment for the service of loaning money to the homeowner (like rent on the borrowed money).

> The most important change in the behaviour of Canadian households during the 1970's was the increase in personal saving from a range of 5 to 6 percent of personal disposable income to more than 10 percent.
>
> Economic Council of Canada,
> *Sixteenth Annual Review,* 1979 (page 17).

How Canadians invest their savings

While Canadians save a considerable portion of their disposable income, this does not automatically mean that Canadian business has ready access to large amounts of investment capital. Canadians tend to be quite cautious regarding their savings, preferring safe investments such as Canada Savings Bonds, guaranteed investment certificates, term deposits and bank accounts over business shares, which are seen as less secure. In 1985, the federal government introduced additional tax incentives for investment in shares, to encourage Canadians to invest more of their savings in corporations. The most noteworthy of these incentives was a $500 000 lifetime tax exemption on capital gains, such as are earned when shares are sold for a profit. The purpose of the government's policy was to make more savings available for capital investment, as well as to ease the heavy debt burden carried by many Canadian corporations in the early 1980's.

(b) Business saving

Another important source of savings in the economy is saving by the business sector in the form of *retained earnings* or profits retained in the business after taxes have been paid and dividends have been paid to shareholders.

Profits, as Figure 6-4 shows, are quite a variable source of savings, rising rapidly in some years but actually falling in others. While many factors influence the overall level of profits in the economy, the most important factor is the state of the economy itself: in periods of prosperity and rapid economic growth, profits rise rapidly, while economic slowdowns usually bring declines in profits.

Investment

As we have seen, **investment** refers to the building of capital goods such as tools, equipment and so on. In terms of a more advanced economy, it is more precisely defined as *spending by business firms on capital goods* ("producers' goods"). As such, it also refers to additions to society's stock of capital goods, and to replacements for capital goods worn out or depreciated.[3]

FIGURE 6-4 *Corporation Profits 1970–85*

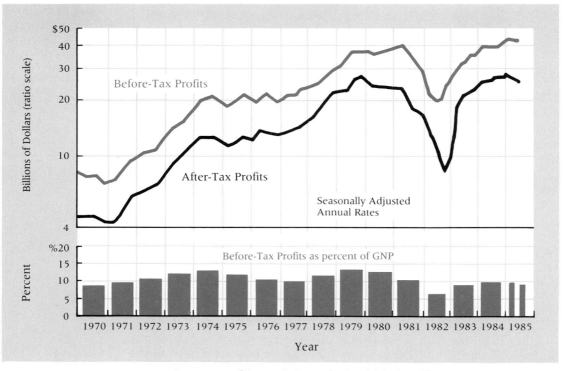

SOURCE   Department of Economic Research, *Canada's Business Climate,* Toronto Dominion Bank.

The nature of investment

Investment refers to all *producers' goods* — products that are used by business firms to help them produce and distribute goods and services. It includes factories, machinery, equipment and tools, ranging from steel mills and

[3]This definition sometimes causes confusion for students because many people associate the word "investment" with purchases of stocks and bonds. The two meanings are obviously related because business often finances its capital-goods purchases (investment) through issues of stocks or bonds to the public (in which the public "invests"). One useful way of resolving this unfortunate — but very important — confusion of terms is to call the purchase of capital goods *real investment,* because it involves real productive assets, and to call the purchase of stocks and bonds *financial investment,* because it involves financial assets, or securities. Most references to investment in the text are to real investment, even if this is not specified. Where confusion may occur, the terms "real" and "financial" will be used.

automobile factories to the chairs and wallpaper in a restaurant. The same product can be classed as either a consumption or an investment item, depending on how it is used. For example, if a consumer buys a car for personal use, this is classified as consumption, while the purchase of an identical car by a business for use by one of its salespersons would be investment.

Investment includes a great deal of *construction* — not only of factories, but also of warehouses, retail stores and offices. Also, residential construction is classified as investment.

When all these types of construction are considered — industrial, commercial and residential — they amount to about one-half of all investment spending. This is without including the great amount of government construction of roads, public buildings, schools and so on. As a result, since investment is a critical type of spending, construction spending and the condition of the construction industry are watched very closely by economists.

While business investment, at 15-20 percent of GNP, is considerably smaller than consumption, investment is a particularly important economic process because the addition of capital goods to the economy increases output per person, thus making possible a higher standard of living.

What determines the level of investment?

While there are many factors influencing the level of investment spending by business, these can generally be classified into two categories.

(a) Expectations regarding future profits

Since most producers' goods typically last a long time and are only bought or built because businesses believe that it will be profitable to do so, the expectations of businesses regarding the future are of great importance. If the outlook for the future is favorable, investment spending will be high; if it is uncertain or unfavorable, investment spending can be quite low.

Expectations are very complex and subjective. Some examples of the types of factors that may affect expectations are: Will there be prosperity or recession in the future? Will the demand for our product rise or not? Will competition (domestic and foreign) increase or diminish? Will our present production facilities have to be replenished or replaced? Will taxes change? Will construction costs and interest rates rise next year? (If so, maybe we should build now.) Will interest rates fall next year? (If so, maybe we should wait, and borrow money then, at lower rates.) Will technological changes occur, making our present facilities obsolete? Do government programs provide tax or other incentives that encourage investment? Because they are so complex, expectations are impossible to analyze with any precision. Still, they are the most important factor influencing the level of investment spending.

> The main source of economic expansion employment growth, and improvement in the quality of life is investment, not only in the manufacturing sector, but also in such areas as education and training, health, protection of the environment, and basic research. Investment also promotes technological advances, without which expectations of an ever-rising standard of living would falter. Traditionally, Canadian industry has counted heavily on infusions of new capital to enlarge its productive capacity and to create the potential for a greater supply of output.
>
> Economic Council of Canada
> *Fourteenth Annual Review*, 1977 (page 45).

(b) Interest rates

Quite frequently, capital investment projects are financed with borrowed money, usually raised by selling bonds to the public. To be profitable, an investment project (say, a plant) must *earn* a higher rate of return on the money invested in it than the rate of interest that the business must *pay* on the borrowed funds. If bond interest rates are 10 percent per year, it would be profitable to borrow money to build a plant that earned a 14-percent-per-year rate of return. It would not be profitable to build a plant that earned only an 8-percent rate of return.

For this reason, when interest rates are lower, investment spending by business would tend to be encouraged, while higher interest rates should be expected to discourage capital investment. For example, a project that looks very attractive if financed with money borrowed at a 9-percent rate of interest may be quite unprofitable should interest rates rise to 13 percent.

Investment in the Canadian economy

Investment has historically played a vital role in the Canadian economy, often amounting to 20-25 percent[4] of GNP. This emphasis on investment has in part been the result of Canada's unusually large investment requirements, which arise from Canada's low population density (which requires proportionately more investment in transportation and distribution facilities), her rapidly increasing housing requirements (due to rel-

---

[4]This figure includes government investment projects, in addition to the private business investment of 15-20 percent of GNP referred to earlier.

atively rapid population growth) and the fact that many of Canada's industries (especially resource industries) are capital-intensive — they use a great deal of capital equipment as compared to labor.

Financing capital investment

Such large-scale capital investment has required great amounts of savings, which have come from various sources. *Personal savings* have been a major source of funds for investment, partly because Canadians, as we have seen, tend to save a relatively high proportion of their disposable income. These savings can be made available for capital investment when they are used to buy stocks and bonds issued by businesses. *Business savings*, or retained earnings, constitute another important source of funds for investment. Canada has also traditionally imported large amounts of *foreign savings*, or foreign capital (mainly from the United States), to finance its capital investment. According to the Economic Council of Canada, "Although Canadians direct a high proportion of their private and business income into savings, Canada has historically needed to supplement its domestic savings with foreign borrowings in order to achieve rates of investment consistent with the desired growth of the economy and employment." When the profits of foreign companies in Canada that are reinvested in Canada are added to the foreign borrowings referred to by the Economic Council of Canada, foreigners have tended to provide nearly 20 percent of the savings used for capital formation in Canada. There are other, less large, sources of funds for capital investment, including *governments* (the federal and Alberta governments provided $500 million of share capital for the Syncrude Athabasca Tar Sands oil project), and *bank credit*, which we will examine more closely in subsequent chapters.

Business investment in Canada in recent years

Figure 6-5 shows business investment in Canada in recent years, in both current dollars and the more meaningful real terms (in 1971 dollars; that is, adjusted for inflation). These statistics show not only that capital investment tends to fluctuate considerably more than consumer spending (compare Figure 6-5 with Figure 6-2), but also that business investment spending has grown only slowly since the mid-1970's. Both of these tendencies have important implications for the economy, which we will examine later.

Canadian investment requirements in the future

Canadian investment requirements are expected to remain high for the remainder of the century, for two main reasons. First, heavy investment will be needed in *energy projects* to ensure future supplies of energy for Canadians. Second, it is anticipated that as *international trade competition* continues to intensify, Canadian industry, particularly manufacturing, will have to engage in substantial capital investment in order to become more efficient and internationally competitive. This has led the Economic Council of Canada to conclude in its *Fourteenth Annual Review*, that, unless governments act to encourage even higher levels of domestic savings than exist now, "the prospect is for continued heavy dependence on foreign lenders to supplement Canadian savings well into the 1980's."

FIGURE 6-5　*Business Investment 1970–85*

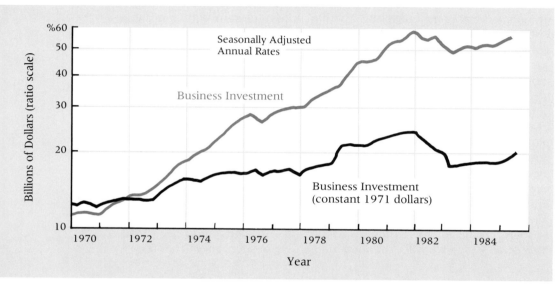

SOURCE　Department of Economic Research, *Canada's Business Climate*, Toronto Dominion Bank.

Investment and potential prosperity

We have stressed the contribution that capital investment makes to output per worker-hour, and thus to the economic prosperity of a society. In the words of the Economic Council of Canada, "there is a tendency for those countries with the highest rates of investment to have the highest rates of economic growth." Thus, nations such as Japan and West Germany, which have stressed capital investment particularly strongly since the Second World War, have achieved rapid economic growth. In comparison, Great Britain, which has not maintained high levels of investment, has tended to fall behind industrially and economically. Canada's investment rate seems to fall into the middle range among western industrialized nations. However, many economists argue that since Canada's capital requirements are unusually high (as noted earlier), in effect, Canada's investment as a percentage of GNP is more like that of the United Kingdom and the United States than that of the high-investment nations such as West Germany and Japan.[5]

It is worth repeating, however, that high levels of capital investment increase a nation's *ability to produce*, but this does not automatically mean that its *actual production* and prosperity will always reach their potential. The most dramatic example of this problem is provided by the Great Depression of the 1930's. During the "Roaring Twenties," capital investment was high and prosperity increased. However, after 1929, levels of actual production (and prosperity) fell spectacularly as the economy slid into a depression. Obviously, the capital equipment that had been built in the 1920's still existed, but something had happened that prevented it — and millions of workers — from being put into production. Similar, although less severe, downturns have occurred periodically. In 1958-61, 1970-71, 1974-75 and 1981-82, when actual output was significantly below the economy's potential output, the economy went into a slowdown, or *recession*.

In Chapters 7 and 8, we will examine the causes of such problems. In doing so, we will shift our attention from saving and investment, which determine the potential output of the economy, to those factors that determine its actual output. This new focus of our attention will be the demand side of the economy: the level of total spending on goods and services.

DEFINITIONS OF NEW TERMS

Personal Disposable Income   Personal income less personal taxes, or after-tax personal income; may be spent or saved.

Consumption   Spending by households on consumer goods and services.

Personal Saving   Personal disposable income not spent on consumption.

Real Investment   Spending by business firms on capital goods.

---

[5]When we describe the USA as a low-investment country, we do not mean that the USA lacks productive capital or has a weak supply side to its economy. The USA has a tremendous stock of capital which has been built up in the past and is the basis for a highly productive economy. However, in recent years, the USA has devoted a relatively high share of current output to consumption and a relatively low share to capital investment; it is in this sense that the USA is considered to be a low-investment economy.

Financial Investment   Purchases of stocks and bonds issued by businesses; through this process business firms raise capital for real investment.

Retained Earnings   Profits retained in a business after taxes have been paid and dividends have been paid to shareholders; another source of capital for real investment.

CHAPTER SUMMARY

1. Consumption, which amounts to about three-fifths of GNP, depends mainly on the level of personal disposable income.

2. Personal savings, which also depend mainly on the level of personal disposable income, rose considerably during the 1970's to more than 10 percent of personal disposable income.

3. Business savings, or retained earnings, constitute another source of saving in the economy, one which rises rapidly when the economy is growing rapidly and often declines during economic slowdowns.

4. Investment, or spending by business on capital goods, usually amounts to 15-20 percent of GNP. Investment, which is vital to prosperity, depends mainly on expectations concerning the future and the level of interest rates.

5. Capital investment has traditionally played a major role in the Canadian economy, often amounting to 20-25 percent of GNP when government investment is added to private business investment.

6. The main sources of funds for investment in Canada have been personal saving, retained earnings and foreign capital. Foreign investment, mainly from the USA, has provided nearly 20 percent of the savings used for investment in Canada.

7. While business investment slowed down in Canada after the mid-1970's, it is generally agreed that heavy investment is needed in the future for major energy-supply projects and to improve the international competitiveness of the Canadian manufacturing sector.

8. Capital investment increases the economy's productive potential, but for actual output to reach its potential, there must also be sufficient demand for the economy's output.

QUESTIONS

1. There has been a long-term tendency for an increased proportion of consumer spending to go to services (as opposed to goods) and to durable goods (as opposed to nondurables). What do you think accounts for these changes in consumer behavior?

2. One of the most variable components of consumer spending from year to year is spending on durable goods, especially new automobiles. Why do you think this is so?

3. Overall consumption spending depends mainly on personal disposable income, but the level of consumption spending by individual households can be influenced by several factors. What are some of these factors that may cause individual households to spend more or less on consumption (and thus save less or more) in any given year?

4. If there were a period of quite rapid inflation, which you expected to continue for some time, would you change your saving habits? Why?

5. During the Great Depression, there was actually *dissaving* by households, as consumption exceeded disposable income (which made saving a negative amount). How can a society have negative saving? Why do you suppose this was done?

6. What characteristics of the British economic and political situation over the past thirty years might account for the fact that Britain has devoted a relatively small proportion of her GNP to capital investment? What are the implications of this for Great Britain?

7. Has the percentage of personal disposable income saved by households changed significantly from the 10-percent level reached in the 1970's? If so, what might account for this change?

8. The text refers to a slowdown in business investment spending during the second half of the 1970's. Has there been any change in this trend in recent years? If so, what might explain such changes?

9. **(a)** In its *Twenty-First Annual Review* (1984), the Economic Council of Canada noted that "The personal saving rate is not expected to fall below 10 percent until mid-decade, and the ratio of investment to gross national expenditure (GNP) as a yearly average is not anticipated to exceed 22 percent during the projection period. This high saving and low investment situation is worrisome."
Why would the Council regard this situation as worrisome?
   (b) Not long after the Council's expression of concern, the Macdonald Royal Commission on Canada's Economic Prospects recommended tax changes which would have the effect of increasing the incentive for Canadians to save.
What could explain the apparently differing views of the Economic Council of Canada and the Macdonald Commission?

10. The economic progress of Japan and West Germany since the Second World War has required, as the text notes, heavy emphasis on capital investment. This, in turn, has involved considerable sacrifices of current

consumption by the people of these countries.

What might a country do to ease the burden of shifting the use of its economic resources away from current consumption and toward capital investment?

11. Following is a list of potential business capital investment projects, showing the expected rate of return on the capital that could be invested in each, and the amount of capital investment for each project, arranged in descending order of expected rate of return.

Investment Project	Expected Rate of Return	Amount of Investment ($100 millions)
A	20%	$5
B	18%	2
C	16%	8
D	14%	7
E	12%	10
F	10%	9
G	8%	6
H	6%	3
I	4%	4

(a) As the rate of interest on funds that must be borrowed for capital investment decreases, more of these potential investment projects become economical. For example, if the rate of interest is 19 percent only project A is profitable, so there will be $500 million of capital investment. If the rate of interest were to fall to 17 percent, both projects A and B would be economical, making the level of capital investment $700 million.

Complete the following table showing the volume of capital investment that will be economical at various interest rates.

Rate of Interest	Volume of Capital Investment
19%	$5 hundred million
17	7 hundred million
15	—
13	—
11	—
9	—
7	—
5	—

(b) Draw a graph showing the relationship between the rate of interest and the volume of capital investment.

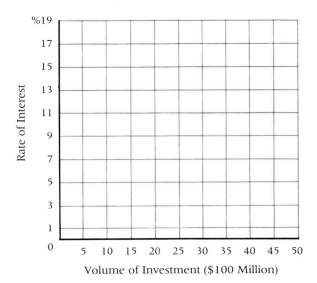

Consumption, saving and investment in the Canadian economy

(c) The graph shows an *inverse relationship* between interest rates and capital investment spending; that is, as interest rates rise, the volume of capital investment spending _____.

(d) If interest rates fell from 11 percent to 9 percent, capital investment spending would _____ by $ _____.

CHAPTER 7

Sources of economic prosperity: the demand side

In Chapter 5, we considered the supply side of the economy — the factors that determine the economy's ability to produce goods and services. Generally, this depends on the amount of the society's economic resources (such as labor and capital equipment) and the efficiency with which they are employed. Of particular importance to an economy's ability to produce is the process of capital investment, which contributes not only to total output but also to output per person, and thus to the society's standard of living.

While these factors determine the *potential* output of the economy, they will not decide its *actual* output. This will depend on the amount of total spending on (or aggregate demand for) goods and services.

Purchasers of the economy's output

Aggregate demand, or total spending in the economy on goods and services, can be divided into four categories.

(a) Consumption spending by households on consumer goods and services, which buys about 60 percent of the economy's output.

(b) Investment spending by businesses on capital goods, which usually amounts to 15-20 percent of GNP.

(c) Government spending on goods and services which purchases approximately 25 percent of the economy's output (the salaries of government employees are included in this category, because they represent the purchase of the employees' services).

(d) Exports A very high proportion of Canada's GNP—approximately 30 percent—is bought by foreign purchasers. While this component of aggregate demand is very important, it depends on factors quite different from the other three types of spending, and will therefore be covered more fully in subsequent chapters. In this chapter, we will cover the role and importance of foreign trade in the Canadian economy only briefly.

Will aggregate demand be sufficient?

An idea that gained some popularity during the Great Depression of the 1930's was the Social Credit Party's theory that there was not enough income received by households, businesses and governments to purchase the entire Gross National Product. The result of such a situation would be a continual tendency toward an economic downturn, or depression, as inadequate aggregate demand caused output to fall far below its potential levels. Unable to sell all they had produced and faced with rising inventories of goods on hand, businesses would reduce production and lay off workers. This, in turn, would reduce householders' total income further, generating worse declines in sales and more layoffs, causing the economy to spiral downward into a depression. According to Social Credit theory, this was a chronic tendency of the economy.

While the Social Credit theory provided an attractive explanation of (and answer to[1]) the perplexities of the Depression, it is not accurate. In fact, there *is* enough income generated in the production of the GNP to purchase the entire GNP. The incomes of households (personal disposable income), businesses (retained earnings plus depreciation allowances) and government (in the form tax revenues) are exactly the same in size as the Gross National Product, as shown in Figure 7-1.

If we regard the value of the GNP as a sort of "super price tag" representing the total of the price tags of all goods and services produced over the year, we can see that each cost item that is covered by or included in that price tag represents an income to someone. Labor costs go to households as wages and salaries, profits and depreciation allowances are income to businesses,[2] and sales and other taxes included in the price tag become income to governments.

[1]The Socreds' proposed solution to the problem was, in effect, for the government to print and distribute more money, to make up the shortfall in aggregate demand.

[2]Depreciation allowances can be regarded as a form of income to business because, while depreciation expenses are deducted from revenues as an expense, no money is actually paid out, so that the business has the amount of money deducted as depreciation expense *in addition to* its reported profit. This was the factor the Social Credity theory overlooked— that depreciation allowances are a form of business income.

FIGURE 7–1 *GNP and Total Incomes*

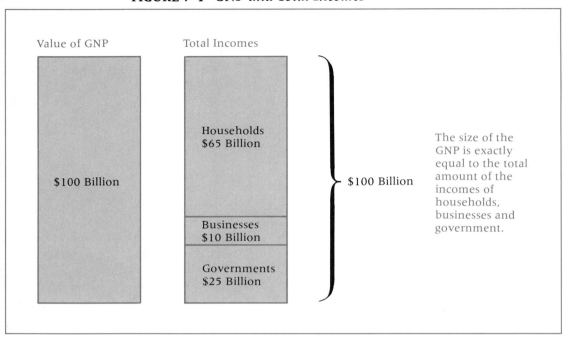

If each of the three sectors of the economy (households, businesses and governments) were to spend all of its income ($65, $10 and $25 billion respectively in Figure 7-1) on goods and services, the entire GNP of $100 billion would be bought. Thus, there is no automatic purchasing-power problem as envisioned by Social Credit theory. The only way the economy could head into a downturn would be if not all these incomes were spent.

The problem of saving

As we have seen, not all income *is* spent — some is saved. Households do not spend all of their disposable income; they save some of it. This *personal saving* can cause problems for the economy, because it creates a *shortage of spending*. If, in Figure 7-1, households saved $5 billion, total spending would amount to only $95 billion, $5 billion short of the value of the GNP, as Figure 7-2 shows.

In addition to personal saving, there may also be *business saving*, in the sense of retained earnings not reinvested in capital goods. The result would be an even larger shortage of demand than that shown in Figure 7-2.

Thus, savings by both households and businesses pose a potential threat to the economy. Money saved by both households and businesses lies

FIGURE 7–2 *The Problem of Saving*

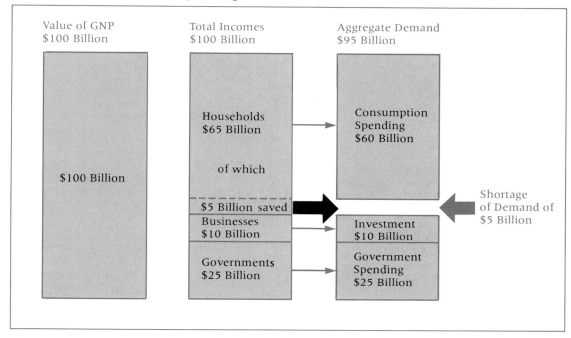

idle rather than purchasing goods and services, dragging the level of aggregate demand down. Because saving reduces the volume of aggregate demand in the economy, there is the risk of an economic downturn (recession) resulting from inadequate total spending on goods and services.

An income-flow diagram of the economy

These flows of income, spending and saving in the economy can be illustrated with a simple[3] income-flow diagram such as Figure 7-3. This diagram shows some of the major flows, or streams, of money in the economy. One major flow is the payment of *incomes* (mostly wages and salaries) to households by the business sector, as shown in the top loop. As the bottom loop shows, households spend most of this income on *consumption* (consumer goods and services). However, the diagram shows that households do *save* some money, and businesses may save, too, in the form of *retained earnings*.

---

[3]This simplified diagram includes only the *business* and *household* sectors of the economy. The *government* and *foreign trade* sectors will be added later in this chapter, and fuller consideration will be given to both of them in subsequent chapters.

FIGURE 7–3 *A Simplified Income-flow Diagram of the Economy*

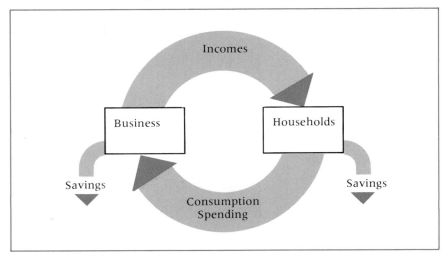

In the economy shown in Figure 7-3, the level of output would fall. The money saved by households and businesses causes a drag on the economy, because it does not buy goods and services. Because of this saving, businesses would be unable to sell all of their output, and would cut production and lay off workers.

Economists use the word **leakage** to describe this effect. If we think of the diagram as an inner tube, with spending and incomes the air, then saving tends to deflate the tube because it *reduces spending*, and thus slows down the whole economy. Thus, saving is described as a leakage from the spending stream.

Offsetting saving: investment

It is possible for the entire output of the economy to be bought, despite saving by households and businesses, if the money saved is used by business to buy additional capital goods. The use of business savings for *capital investment* in this way is simple, as businesses already possess these funds. Indeed, capital investment is the most common use of businesses' retained earnings.

The use of the savings of households to finance capital investment by business is somewhat more complicated, because these funds must first be transferred from the households that have saved them to the businesses that will use them to buy capital goods. In exchange for these savings, businesses issue, or sell, *stocks and bonds*, either directly to households or indirectly. In the latter case, the stocks and bonds are bought by institutions such as trust companies, banks, insurance companies, mutual funds and pension funds into which households have deposited their savings. Such institutions are known as *financial intermediaries* because they act as a go-between to transfer savings from households to businesses.

This is the process referred to as *financial investment* in Chapter 6. Financial investment does not by itself help to offset the shortage of demand caused by saving—it does not buy any of the economy's output. However, by transferring the savings of households to businesses, it sets the stage for the spending of those savings by businesses on capital goods—the process of *real investment*. In Figure 7-4, the dotted lines show how funds that have been removed from the spending stream by saving can be returned to the spending stream as real investment.

FIGURE 7–4 *Offsetting Saving: The return of savings to the spending stream through capital investment by business*

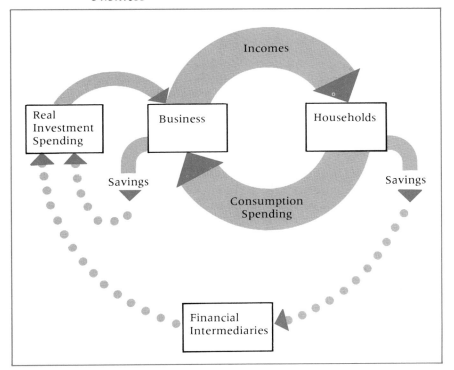

Leakages and injections

The effect of business investment on the economy is just the opposite of the effect of saving. While saving is called a leakage from the spending stream because it reduces spending on goods and services, business investment spending is called an **injection** into the spending stream because it acts as a stimulus to aggregate demand. In effect, the money that was not spent on consumer goods and services can be returned to the economy as spending on capital goods.

The two faces of saving

We have seen how saving can pose a *threat* to economic stability by creating a shortage of aggregate demand, which could cause an economic slowdown. On the other hand, it is also true that saving presents the economy with a great *opportunity*—if savings are used for capital investment, the economy can benefit: not only from the positive effect of investment spending on aggregate demand but also from the positive effect of investment on productivity and living standards. Indeed, economic progress is not possible without investment, and investment requires saving.

To save or not to save? The paradox of thrift

The foregoing suggests that saving alone is less important than the *balance of saving and investment*. Suppose a nation's people decided, for some reason, to increase the amount that they saved substantially, and that this increase in households' savings was not offset by an increase in business investment spending.[4]

Under these circumstances, the public's attempt to save more could actually result in less saving, because it would cause lower levels of aggregate demand, thus generating reductions in output, employment and income—and at these lower levels of income, there would be less saving. This perverse effect, whereby an attempt by the public to increase its saving can actually result in reduced saving, is known as the *paradox of thrift*.

Some observers believe that the Canadian economy suffered from this problem as it entered the 1980's. They argued that Canada's high personal savings rates (about 10 percent of disposable income) were contributing to the sluggishness of business investment spending by depressing consumer demand, and that the economy would benefit if consumers spent more and saved less. Others disagreed with this view, arguing that high savings were appropriate for a country facing Canada's investment re-

---

[4]A large increase in personal saving could itself depress business investment spending, by reducing consumption spending and thus businesses' sales.

quirements in energy and manufacturing in the 1980's, and that the real problem was that capital investment was being depressed by a combination of high interest rates and uncertainty arising from certain government policies. Whatever the causes, there was general agreement that the economy was suffering from an unfortunate combination of high personal saving and sluggish capital investment.

Saving, investment and the performance of the economy

The level of aggregate demand — and the performance of the economy — depend in large part on businesses' plans regarding investment and households' plans regarding saving. If these plans were to coincide, so that businesses were planning enough investment to offset exactly the saving that households were planning, the injections into the spending stream from investment would match the leakages from it due to saving. The level of aggregate demand would remain unchanged; and the economy (and GNP and total incomes) would neither expand nor contract. Rather, it would remain in a state of **equilibrium**[5] as shown in Figure 7-5.

FIGURE 7–5 *The Economy in Equilibrium when Planned Investment equals Planned Saving*

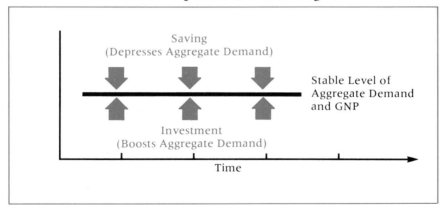

There is, however, no reason to expect that plans regarding saving and investment will always coincide in this way. Personal saving depends mainly on personal disposable income. However, it is influenced by many other factors, including interest rates, the age composition of the population,

[5]It should be noted that the concept of "equilibrium" tends to be a misleading one, since it seems to convey the idea of the economy reaching an equilibrium level and remaining there. In fact, the investment and saving plans of businesses and households are constantly changing and so is the equilibrium level of GNP. Thus, increases in investment will increase the equilibrium level of GNP, and vice-versa.

habit, uncertainty concerning the future and government taxation policies concerning income (interest, dividends and capital gains) from savings. On the other hand, businesses make their investment spending plans largely on the basis of their expectations concerning the future, with the level of interest rates also playing an important role.

With saving and investment plans depending on such different factors, it is very likely that sometimes planned investment will exceed planned saving. At other times, planned investment will be less than planned saving. We will look at each case in turn.

If planned investment is less than planned saving

Suppose that the economic outlook is uncertain at best, unfavorable at worst, and that interest rates are high. Under these circumstances, households may be less inclined to spend freely and more inclined to save, while businesses will likely engage in less capital investment than usual. Thus, planned investment would be less than planned saving, so that injections into the spending stream would be less than leakages from it, *causing aggregate demand to be depressed*. The result would be that GNP would be depressed, for two reasons.

(a) Real output of goods and services will be depressed

Faced with sluggish sales, businesses will reduce their output of goods and services and lay off some workers. Thus, the most direct effect of depressed aggregate demand would be an economic slowdown, or *recession*,[6] as shown in Figure 7-6.

(b) Prices of goods and services will be depressed

Depressed levels of aggregate demand will have a second effect: they will depress the prices of goods and services in general. In response to sluggish sales, business generally will raise prices less rapidly, and may even reduce them, to encourage sales and thus reduce their excessive inventories of goods.

By "depressed," we refer not only to actual declines in output and prices, but also to slower-than-usual rates of growth of these. During a typical economic slowdown, however, even a slower rate of output growth (and employment) will cause higher unemployment rates, as the economy fails to generate enough new jobs for the growing labor force. Thus, a typical economic **recession** is characterized by slow economic growth, rising unemployment and relatively slow increases in prices and wages.

[6]The proper definition of **recession** requires two consecutive quarters of declining real output (a quarter is three months). However, the term is often used to describe economic slowdowns generally, including those less severe than specified in the proper definition.

FIGURE 7-6 ***The Economy in Contraction where Planned Investment is* less than *Planned Saving***

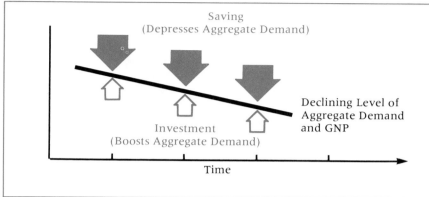

If planned investment exceeds planned saving

Suppose that economic forecasts are encouraging and interest rates are relatively low. As a result, businesses are spending considerable amounts on capital investment, while householders feel less of a need to save and are spending a greater proportion of their disposable income. Under these circumstances, planned investment by business would be greater than planned saving, so that injections into the spending stream would exceed leakages from it, and *aggregate demand would increase*. The result would be an increase in GNP, which could occur for two quite different reasons.

(a) *Increased output of goods and services*

Rising aggregate demand will stimulate businesses to increase their production of goods and services, and to hire additional workers. As these workers spend their new incomes, the demand for goods and services will be increased further. Increases in real output and employment such as these are called *real economic growth*, because they add to society's output of goods and services.

In Figure 7-7, rising aggregate demand is causing rapid increases in output in years 19*1 through 19*4. Such rapid increases cannot occur indefinitely, however, because the potential output of the economy (as shown by the dotted line) is limited by factors such as the amounts of labor and capital equipment available. While these, and the economy's potential output, can increase over time, as the dotted line shows, the economy has reached its potential output by the end of the year 19*4. Further increases in aggregate demand cannot increase output further; they will have quite different effects.

FIGURE 7–7   *The Effects of Rising Aggregate Demand on the
Economy*

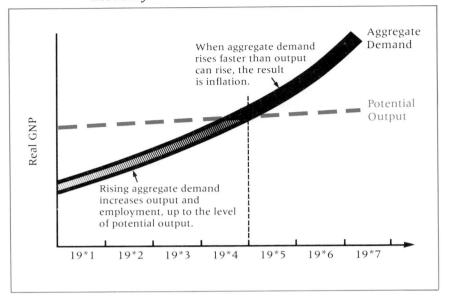

(b) *Increases in the prices of goods and services*

In Figure 7-7, after year 19*4, the output of goods and services is unable
to keep up with the rapidly rising demand. As a result, the prices of
goods and services generally will rise as they are bid up by the excess
of demand over available supply (potential output). Increases in the general
level of prices such as these are referred to as *inflation.*[7]

Thus, increases in aggregate demand may cause increases in output
(real economic growth) and they may cause inflation.[8] In actual fact, the
effects of rising aggregate demand on output and prices are not as separate
as this analysis may suggest. Rising aggregate demand tends to cause
both output and prices to rise simultaneously, with the effect on prices
being stronger the closer the economy gets to its potential output. This
is shown by the grey area in year 19*4 in Figure 7-7: the darker the

[7]While the basic cause of inflation is generally considered to be excess aggregate demand,
its causes are more complex than those considered here, and are considered more fully
in Chapter 12.
[8]At first glance, this may seem like a contradiction: if the output, or supply, of goods and
services rises, should their prices not fall? This would happen if supply increased and demand
did not—if there is a big apple crop without any increase in the demand for apples, the
price of apples will fall. However, what we are discussing here is an increase in output
that was caused by an *increase in (aggregate) demand,* and the same increase in demand that
caused output to rise is also likely to cause prices to rise.

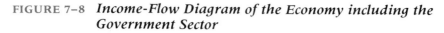

FIGURE 7–8 *Income-Flow Diagram of the Economy including the Government Sector*

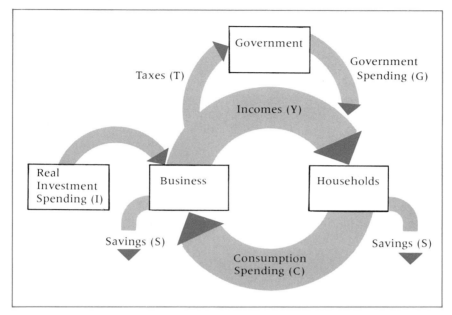

line, the more rapidly prices are rising as higher demand pushes the economy closer to its limits. Thus, *a period of economic expansion tends to be characterized not only by rising output and employment, but also by inflation.*

The importance of saving and investment

The levels of saving and investment are of vital importance to the performance of the economy. If planned investment lags behind planned saving, aggregate demand, output, employment and prices will all be depressed as the economy slumps into a recession. On the other hand, if planned investment exceeds planned saving, upward pressures will develop on aggregate demand, output, employment and prices. However, saving and investment do not constitute the only important leakage from and injection into the spending stream; we must also consider the government sector and the foreign trade sector of the economy.

Adding the government sector

So far, we have omitted the government sector from the picture, so as to develop the basic concepts without unnecessary complications. Now, however, the government sector can be added without any difficulty. As

Figure 7-8 shows, the addition of government (meaning all three levels of government—federal, provincial and municipal) simply adds another leakage (*taxes*) and another injection (*government spending*) to our diagram. The effect of taxes is similar to the effect of saving—by removing money from the spending stream, taxes act as a drag on aggregate demand, or a leakage. The effect of government spending on goods and services is just the opposite—it acts as an injection, stimulating aggregate demand and the economy as a whole.

Figure 7-8 is quite oversimplified—it shows taxes coming out of income alone, while in fact there are taxes on other things (such as sales taxes on consumption spending). Also, it shows government spending going only into the the income flow, while in fact some goes to business and some to households, in various ways. In addition, it does not show how the government sector (as well as business) can borrow and spend the savings of households. Nonetheless, this diagram does show the basic elements of the role of the government.

The addition of the government sector makes no difference to the way in which the levels of GNP and incomes are determined—this still depends on the relationship between leakages and injections. Now we have one more leakage and one more injection.

Figure 7-8 also shows the abbreviations commonly used for various economic terms: **C** for consumption spending, **I** for investment spending, **Y** for income (**Yd** is disposable income), **S** for saving and **T** for taxes.

Adding the foreign trade sector

Finally, we must add exports (**X**) and imports (**M**)—the foreign trade sector—to our analysis. Because they add to aggregate demand in the Canadian economy, exports are considered an injection into the spending stream, and because money spent on imports is removed from the spending stream (in Canada), imports are considered a leakage.

Leakages, injections and the economy

In summary, then, we have considered three leakages (savings, taxes and imports, or S+T+M), and three injections (investment spending, government spending and exports, or I+G+X). While the additional leakages and injections make the situation more complex, the performance of the economy still depends on the balance between leakages and injections, just as it did when we considered only saving and investment.

(a) If leakages exceed injections (S+T+M I+G+X), aggregate demand, output, employment and prices will all be depressed—the economy will go into a slump.

(b) If injections exceed leakages (I+G+X   S+T+M), aggregate demand, output, employment and prices will tend to rise, as the economy experiences a period of expansion.

(c) If injections were equal to leakages (I+G+X=S+T+M), the economy would be in equilibrium, with the levels of aggregate demand and GNP stable.

Aggregate demand and aggregate supply

Figure 7-9 represents the interaction between the supply side of the economy as covered in Chapter 5 and the demand side of the economy as discussed in this chapter.

It is the interaction between the supply side and the demand side of the economy (aggregate supply and aggregate demand) that determines the performance of the economy regarding output (GNP), employment and prices. If aggregate demand is much below the economy's ability to produce, the result will be a **recession**, with output well below capacity,

FIGURE 7-9 *The Supply Side and the Demand Side of the Economy*

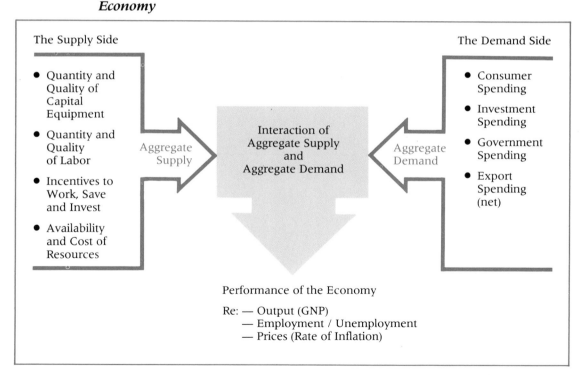

high unemployment and a low rate of inflation, all due to the inadequate level of aggregate demand. On the other hand, if the level of aggregate demand exceeds the economy's ability to produce, the result will be **inflation**, as high aggregate demand drives up not only output and employment, but also prices. Ideally, then, the level of aggregate demand would be between these two extremes: neither so low as to cause high unemployment nor so high as to generate severe inflation.

Aggregate demand graphed

Figure 7-10 shows the relationship between aggregate demand (AD) and the *level of prices* in the economy. At high price levels (in the upper range of the AD curve), aggregate demand is relatively low, while at low price levels (in the lower range of the AD curve), aggregate demand is higher. This is mainly because of the fact that if the prices of Canadian products are higher, foreigners buy fewer Canadian products and Canadians buy more imports, both of which depress the demand for Canadian products. On the other hand, if Canadian prices are lower, the demand for Canadian goods and services will be higher both in Canada and abroad.

We have seen that the level of aggregate demand can fluctuate from time to time, being low in periods of recession and high during periods of boom and inflation. These fluctuations are shown in Figure 7-11. AD is the same curve as in Figure 7-10, while AD_1 represents the low levels of aggregate demand typical of a recession. Note that, at any given price level, AD_1 indicates a lower demand than AD. On the other hand, AD_2 represents a higher level of aggregate demand, with more output being demanded at any given price level.

FIGURE 7-10 *Aggregate Demand*

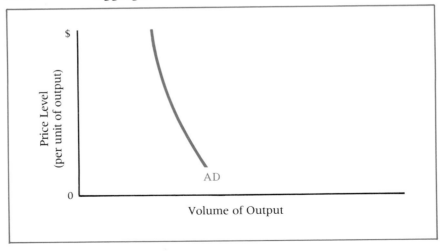

FIGURE 7-11 *Changes in Aggregate Demand*

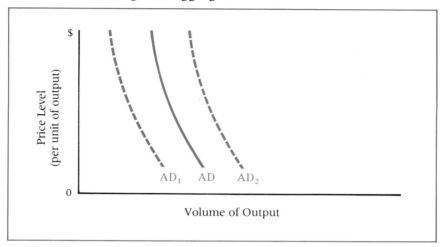

Aggregate demand and aggregate supply combined

Figure 7-12 shows the interaction of the aggregate supply curve from Chapter 5 and the aggregate demand curve from this chapter. With the AD and AS curves intersecting at point E as shown, the level of output

FIGURE 7-12 *Aggregate Demand and Aggregate Supply Combined*

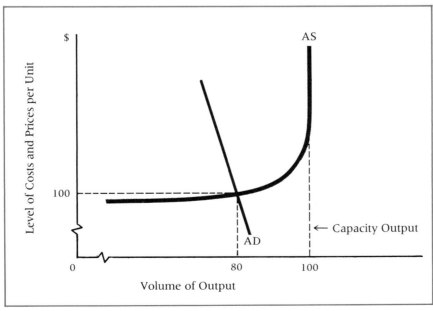

will be 80 and the level of prices will be 100: the economy is in a recession, with output well below its capacity level of 100 and unemployment quite high due to inadequate aggregate demand.

If aggregate demand were to increase to the level shown by AD_1 in Figure 7-13, output would rise to 95 and unemployment would be lower; however, this higher level of demand would also bring more inflation, as the price level on the vertical axis rises to 110. If aggregate demand were to move still higher, to the level shown by AD_2, the economy would be producing at capacity and unemployment would be minimal; however, AD_2 represents an excessive level of aggregate demand. Because demand exceeds the economy's capacity to produce, inflation becomes quite severe, as shown by the movement to a price level of 150.

Thus, increases in aggregate demand can have quite different effects upon the performance of the economy (output, employment and prices), depending on the circumstances. If the economy is operating well below capacity and unemployment is high, increased aggregate demand (up to the level shown by AD in Figure 7-13) will have mainly *beneficial* effects. Output and employment will increase considerably and prices will increase only slightly, as the summary in Figure 7-14 shows.

If the economy is closer to its capacity level of output, a similar increase in aggregate demand (from AD to AD_1 in Figure 7-13) will have *mixed effects* on the economy. Output and employment will increase, but not as rapidly as before, while prices will rise more rapidly than before. If

FIGURE 7-13 *Aggregate Demand and Aggregate Supply Combined*

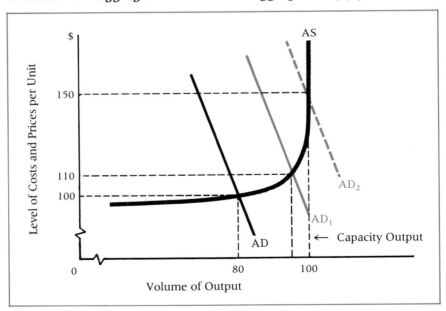

FIGURE 7-14 *The effect of Increases in Aggregate Demand on the Economy Under Different Conditions*

(See Figure 7-13 for graph.)

| | Effect upon | |
Increase in Aggregate Demand	Output and Employment	Prices
Up to AD	Major gains.	Very small increases.
AD to AD_1	Lesser gains.	More rapid increases.
AD_1 to AD_2	Quite small gains.	Quite rapid increases.
Beyond AD_2	No gains.	Very rapid increases.

aggregate demand were to be increased further (from AD_1 to AD_2 in Figure 7-13), there would be only small gains in output and employment at the cost of rapid increases in prices, as the economy is *overheated* by aggregate demand so high that aggregate supply has difficulty keeping up with it. Beyond AD_2, further increases in aggregate demand cannot boost output and employment any higher, and therefore will result only in more severe inflation.

In summary, it is the interaction between aggregate demand and aggregate supply that determines how well the economy functions regarding output, employment and inflation. Aggregate demand can be too low relative to the economy's productive capacity, causing a recession and high unemployment. Higher levels of aggregate demand can bring worthwhile gains in output and employment, although they will also increase the rate of inflation. Excessively high levels of aggregate demand will generate much more severe inflation but only small gains in output and employment. Thus, it is desirable to seek to maintain a rough balance between aggregate demand and the economy's capacity to produce, or between the demand side and the supply side of the economy.

DEFINITIONS OF NEW TERMS

Aggregate Demand   Total spending on goods and services, consisting of consumption spending, investment spending, government spending and net exports (C+I+G+X–M).

Leakages   Factors that reduce aggregate demand in the economy, consisting of savings, taxes and imports (S+T+M).

Injections   Factors that increase aggregate demand in the economy, consisting of investment spending, government spending and exports (I+G+X).

Equilibrium   Condition of the economy in which leakages are equal to injections, causing aggregate demand and GNP to remain stable.

Recession   Formally defined as two consecutive quarters (a quarter being three months) of declining real output; commonly used to describe economic slowdowns of less severity than this.

Expansion   A period of rising output and employment; also called a "boom."

Inflation   An increase in the general level of the prices of goods and services.

CHAPTER SUMMARY

1. The economy's potential output can increase over time, depending largely on the amount of investment and saving which is done.

2. Whether this potential output is actually reached or not depends on the level of aggregate demand in the economy.

3. The level of aggregate demand depends on the balance of leakages (S+T+M) from and injections (I+G+X) into the spending stream.

4. If leakages and injections are equal, the levels of aggregate demand and GNP will remain stable and the economy will be in a state of equilibrium.

5. If leakages exceed injections, aggregate demand, output, employment and prices will all be depressed, and the economy will slump into a recession.

6. If injections exceed leakages, aggregate demand, output and employment will all rise as the economy expands.

7. Economic expansions are typically accompanied by inflation, particularly when aggregate demand rises close to or beyond the economy's potential output.

QUESTIONS

1. To remedy the "purchasing-power problem" which the Social Credit Party saw as the basic problem facing the economy, the party in effect proposed printing additional money and distributing it to the public. In view of the fact that there is already enough income each year to buy the total GNP, what effects would such a policy have on the economy?

2. During an economic boom, when output is rising, why does the rising supply of goods and services not cause the prices of them to fall?

3. During an economic recession, when output is depressed, why does the depressed supply of goods and services not cause prices to rise?

4. Suppose that widespread rumors of a depression caused people to save more, in an attempt to protect themselves against the event. What effect would this have on the economy?

5. Suppose that rapid inflation caused people to reduce their saving and spend more of their income in anticipation of higher prices in the future. How would this affect the economy?

6. This chapter refers to the combination of high personal saving and sluggish business investment spending in Canada at the onset of the 1980's. Has there been any change since then in either personal saving or business investment? If so, what are the reasons for such changes and what effects do you think they would have on the economy?

7. Suppose the economy is in the situation shown below, near its capacity level of output.

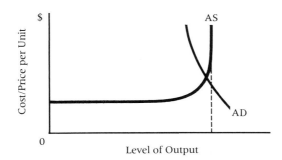

If a major increase were to occur in the price of imported oil which:
  (a) reduced the level of aggregate demand by withdrawing large volumes of funds from the economy to pay for the oil, pushing the AD curve to the left, and
  (b) raised production costs throughout the economy by making energy much more expensive, making it costlier to produce any given level of output, thus pushing the AS curve upwards to higher levels of cost per unit,
draw the new AD and AS curves and explain the effects of the new situation on the levels of output, employment and prices in the economy.

8. In this graph, the AS and AD curves represent the situation in 19*1, with output and prices both at levels of 100. AS_1 and AD_1 represent the situation in 19*3, two years later, when output is 120 and prices are at the same level as in 19*1.

Ordinarily, such a rapid increase in aggregate demand and output would be accompanied by a significant increase in the price level. Why, in this example, has there been no increase in prices?

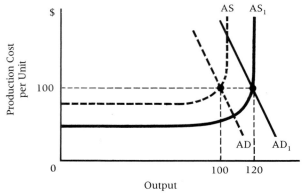

9. (a) At the level of aggregate demand represented by AD_1, the economy is operating at approximately _____ percent of its capacity output (potential GNP), and is in a condition of _____.

(b) AD_2 represents a(n) _____ in the level of aggregate demand that has brought the economy to approximately _____ percent of its capacity output. Describe the effect that this change in aggregate demand has on:

(i) output and employment, and
(ii) the general level of prices
and explain the reasons for these effects.

(c) To get the economy to 95 percent of its capacity output requires a level of aggregate demand as represented by AD_3. How does the effect of this change in aggregate demand differ from the change from AD_1 to AD_2 and why?

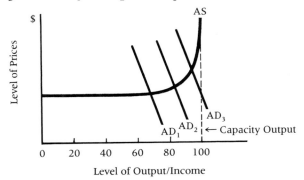

CHAPTER 8

The problem of economic instability

While the Canadian economy has generally grown strongly over the past forty years, Figure 8-1 shows that this growth has not been steady. At times, real GNP has risen very rapidly, but in other years, output has grown slowly, or even declined. While the most famous such economic downturn was the Great Depression of the 1930's, several other slow-downs, or recessions, have occurred: in 1953-54, the late 1950's and early 1960's, 1970, 1974-75 and the "Great Recession" of the early 1980's, which was the worst since the Great Depression of the 1930's. These recessions have been considerably less severe than the depression of the 1930's, but they have nonetheless caused economic and human hardship, as the unemployment rates in Figure 8-2 show.

Phases of the business cycle

The term *business cycle* is used to descibe the fluctuations of the economy between prosperity and recession. A typical business cycle is pictured, and its phases labelled, in Figure 8-3. In the *contraction* phase, which ends in a *trough* when economic activity is at its slowest, output and employment rise more and more slowly, and may even fall: in other words, the economy is in a recession. The *expansion* phase (also known as a "boom") involves rapid increases in output and employment as economic conditions improve until the *peak* (which may involve increasingly rapid inflation) is reached, after which the cycle repeats itself. While such cycles do not repeat themselves on a fixed timetable and may vary in length and intensity, they do tend to follow one another more or less regularly.

Our free-enterprise economic system is successful in many respects, but this tendency toward periodic slowdowns with increased unemployment and hardship for many people has been one of its traditional weaknesses. In fact, Karl Marx predicted that the capitalistic system would eventually collapse in a terrible depression, which would cause a revolution of the working class against capitalism. While Marx's prediction has not come true, it is important for us to try to understand why business cycles tend to occur, so that we can try to take steps to reduce their severity.

FIGURE 8-1 *Percentage Change in Real GNP 1948–85*

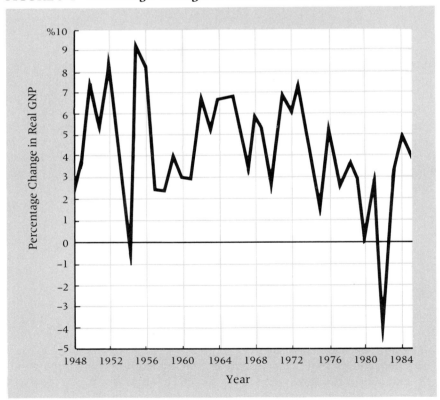

FIGURE 8-2 *Percentage of Labor Force Unemployed 1926–85*

SOURCE   Statistics Canada.

FIGURE 8-3 *A Typical Business Cycle*

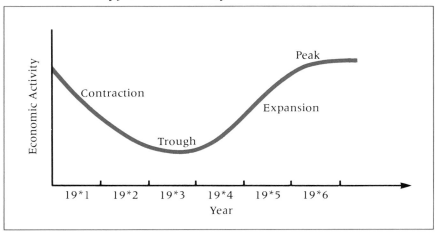

Theories of business cycles

Business cycles have been observed for centuries and many theories have been advanced in attempts to explain them. There are many factors that can stimulate or slow down economic activity. For example, wars cause high levels of government spending, which generate boom-like conditions with very low unemployment, although the military output produced does not add to the prosperity of the people as consumer and capital goods do. Certain inventions, such as the railroad and the automobile, can stimulate the economy by giving rise to surges of capital investment spending. Seasonal factors and variations in weather (such as droughts) can affect the economy, too, although these were regarded as more important in the past, when a greater proportion of economic activity was agricultural. In the past, when gold was used as money, the discovery of new gold mines helped the economy by increasing the money supply. Failure to discover gold for some time could result in economic stagnation. Another theory saw the origin of business cycles in periodically recurring sunspots, which were presumed to affect agricultural production and possibly people's moods and behavior.

While all of these factors may affect the economy, they tend to occur at random intervals and therefore are not a convincing explanation for business cycles, which tend to repeat themselves more or less regularly. For the causes of these economic fluctuations, we will have to look elsewhere.

Fluctuations in aggregate demand

Business cycles involve periodic fluctuations of output and employment across the entire economy. From our analysis of the operation of the economy in Chapter 7, the most likely source of such economy-wide fluctuations would be fluctuations in aggregate demand, or total spending on goods and services, as these will affect, in varying degrees, virtually all sectors of the economy. Untangling the more detailed causes of business cycles is a somewhat complex problem, however, as the answer seems to lie in the dynamics of the economic system itself, and particularly in the interactions between consumption spending and investment spending. In this chapter, we will break the causes of economic instability into the following four types:

(a) fluctuations in business investment spending, the effects of which spread through the economy due to

(b) the multiplier effect, whereby fluctuations in investment spending touch off fluctuations in consumption spending, and

(c) the accelerator effect, through which changes in consumption spending cause changes in business investment spending, and

(d) fluctuations in exports, which are a separate and important source of fluctuations in the Canadian economy.

In the remainder of this chapter, we will examine each of these factors individually. In doing so however, it is important to remember that they are all in fact interrelated, and work together to generate economic fluctuations.

The instability of investment spending

As Figure 8-4 shows, business investment spending tends to fluctuate considerably, rising rapidly in some years and stagnating and even declining sharply in others. In fact, capital investment by business is clearly the

FIGURE 8-4 **Business Fixed Investment Spending (1971 dollars) 1926–85**

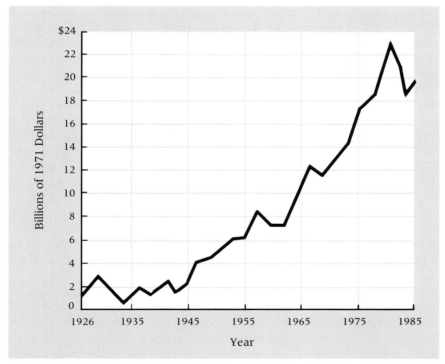

SOURCE Statistics Canada.

most volatile of the components of aggregate demand. Unlike consumption spending, investment does not tend to advance year after year, more rapidly in some years and more slowly in others. Rather, investment tends to surge ahead very rapidly at some times and slow drastically, or even decline, at other times.

The major reason why investment spending by business tends to fluctuate in this way is that investment depends heavily on businesses' *expectations* concerning future profits, which are themselves quite variable from year to year. At times, the economic outlook is favorable and interest rates are low: under these circumstances, business investment tends to rise briskly. At other times, uncertain or poor expectations and/or high interest rates can cause businesses to reduce investment spending, in some cases quite drastically. In fact, investment spending can actually *collapse*, as it did during the Great Depression of the 1930's, when economic conditions were so bad that few businesses were willing or able to consider capital investment projects.

The majority of business investment consists of *equipment* and *construction*, both of which are subject to severe fluctuations, as people who work in the machine-tools industry, the steel industry and the construction industry know only too well. These and other **capital-goods industries** are subject to severe ups and downs in business as investment spending fluctuates. Sometimes they must lay off large numbers of workers, while at other times they cannot keep up with all their orders, despite overtime and extra shifts.

Two other types of investment should also be considered here. The first is *residential construction*—the homebuilding industry. There are times, particularly when mortgage money is readily available and the economy is favorable, when activity in this industry is frantic—buyers want to buy, and they will pay high prices now, because they fear that prices will rise again shortly. Builders and suppliers are barely able to keep up with the demand. But periodically, the situation reverses itself—mortgage money may be scarce, people may expect an economic slowdown in which interest rates and home prices may actually fall, so prospective homebuyers do *not* buy, but rather wait. As a result, the residential construction industry goes into a slump, and experiences bankruptcies and heavy unemployment. Figure 8-5 illustrates the fluctuations in housing starts caused by these fluctuations in demand.

The final category of investment spending to be considered is *additions to businesses' inventories*. When a business buys inventories, this is classed as investment, or producers' goods, because the products have not yet been sold for consumption. This particular type of investment spending—additions to inventories—is the single most variable type of investment spending. This is true because, if retailers and wholesalers expect sales to be strong, they will spend a great deal more than usual on inventory,

FIGURE 8-5   *Housing Starts 1970–85*

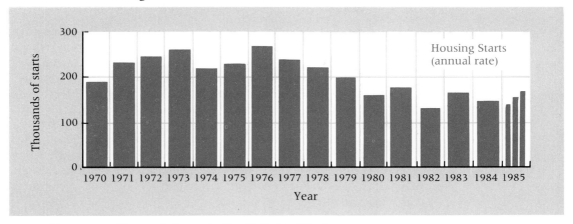

SOURCE   Department of Economic Research, *Canada's Business Climate,*
Toronto Dominion Bank.

and inventories will rise rapidly. On the other hand, if sales turn out
to be unexpectedly slow, many retailers may order virtually nothing for
inventory, so that inventories will actually decline sharply. Thus, investment
spending on additions to business inventories is subject to spectacular
swings, as Figure 8-6 illustrates.

FIGURE 8-6   *Changes in Business Inventories 1974–85*

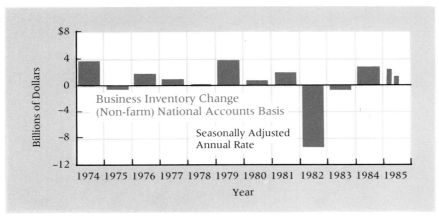

SOURCE   Department of Economic Research, *Canada's Business Climate,*
Toronto Dominion Bank.

How fluctuations in business investment affect the economy

The fluctuations in investment spending that we have been discussing have an important effect on the performance of the entire economy, which can be illustrated by Figure 8-7. As we saw in Chapter 7, saving is a leakage from the spending stream that tends to slow down the economy, because saving involves *not* buying goods and services. Also, investment is an injection into the spending stream that can offset saving and stimulate the economy, by buying capital goods.

We have also seen that saving depends mostly on disposable income, and that in most years, saving tends to be a fairly *steady leakage* from the spending stream—it tends to occur regularly. On the other hand, as we have just seen, investment tends to fluctuate greatly, thus constituting a *variable injection* into the spending stream.

Since saving tends to occur more or less regularly, the key factor is really investment. If investment is high, so that investment exceeds saving, additional spending will be injected into the economy. The effect of this additional spending will be to *stimulate* the economy: output and employment will rise, and so (probably) will prices, and the economy will experience more-rapid-than-average growth.

However, if investment is in one of its periodic downturns, the saving leakage will exceed the investment injection, and total spending will be *depressed*. With total spending depressed, output will rise less rapidly, or even decline, and unemployment will rise as the economy slides into

FIGURE 8–7 *Leakages from, and Injections into the Spending Stream*

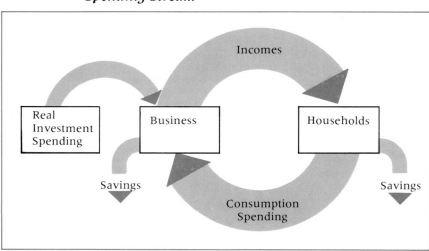

a slowdown, or recession. Wages and prices will also be depressed (rise less rapidly than usual) due to sluggish demand in the economy.

Thus, fluctuations in business investment spending are an important factor in economic booms and recessions. To fully understand the causes of business cycles, however, we must examine how these variations in investment spending interact with consumption spending, through effects known as the "multiplier" and the "accelerator," so as to have a much stronger impact on the economy.

The multiplier effect

We have seen how investment spending by businesses tends to fluctuate, and how this tends to contribute to the economic ups and downs known as the business cycle. But investment is only about one-sixth of GNP, and normal variations in investment amount to only one or two percent of GNP. How can fluctuations of investment cause the entire economy to experience ups and downs?

The answer to this question is suggested by the following illustration. Suppose that a new family moves into a town and builds a $100 000 house, using local labor and materials. Obviously, this will add $100 000 to the incomes of the townspeople involved. While some of this increase in incomes will go to taxes, and some will be saved, a good deal of it will be spent on consumer goods and services, such as cars, movies and restaurant dinners. To those who receive this money, it represents an increase in *their* income. They, too, will respend a large part of it on a variety of goods and services, generating additional income for the suppliers of those items, who, in turn, will increase their spending. This respending effect will continue as increases in income are respent; however, it will grow weaker at each stage because not all of the increase in incomes is respent. It is similar to the ripples on a pond caused by a thrown stone: a series of ripples, each weaker than the previous one, radiates outward. The original $100 000 spent on the new house is the initial splash; the respending of the increases in income at each stage is the ripples spreading out from the center and through the economy.

Thus, the total economic effect of the spending of the $100 000 on the house was much greater than the original $100 000 because the repending of the money caused total spending—and incomes—to rise in a series of stages following the initial spending. In effect, the impact of the original $100 000 was magnified, or *multiplied* by this respending effect. For this reason, the respending effect is known as the **multiplier**.

A numerical example of the multiplier

Suppose investment spending increases over last year's levels, causing the incomes of people in the capital-goods industries to be $100 million higher than last year. Not all of this $100 million will be spent on consumption — part will go to taxes, part will be saved and part will be diverted to foreign nations through purchases of imports. While it is true that each of these leakages can return to the spending stream, it is not completely certain, so we will consider them removed from the spending stream, if only temporarily.

Assuming that these leakages absorb one-half of the increase in incomes, consumption spending would rise by $50 million over last year's level. This increase in consumer spending represents a $50 million increase in GNP and income to those who receive it. Assuming that they will also respend half of it, this will give rise to a further increase in consumption spending of $25 million which boosts GNP and incomes by another $25 million. Of this $25 million of increased incomes, $12.5 million would be respent as the cycle continues, increasing *both GNP and total incomes* at each stage, as shown in Figure 8-8.

FIGURE 8–8 *The Respending Effect underlying the Multiplier*

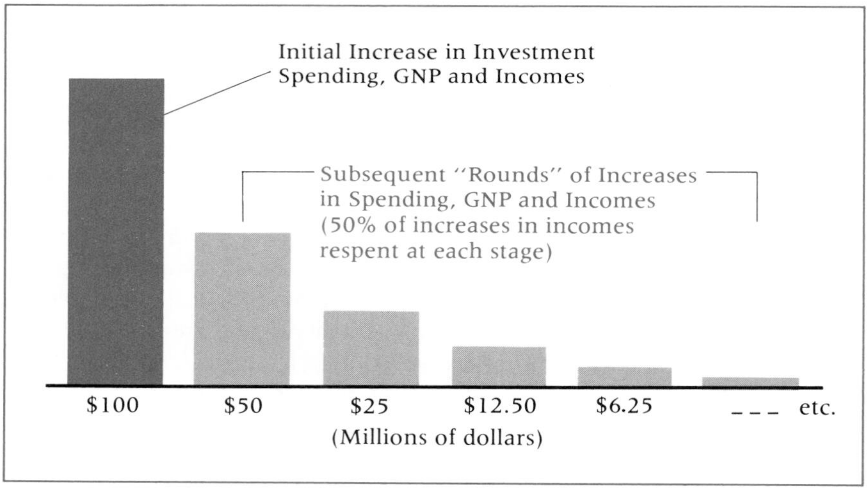

Obviously, the respending effect means that the initial investment project of $100 million has a much more far-reaching effect on the economy (that is, on GNP and total incomes) than its size suggests. To calculate the total impact of the $100 million of investment spending on the economy, we would have to *add together* all of the increases in spending, GNP and incomes at each stage of the process: $100 million + $50 million + $25 million + $12.5 million, et cetera.

If we did this, we would find that the $100 million of investment spending caused GNP and total incomes to rise by $200 million, as shown in Figure 8-9. In this example, the size of the multiplier is two, because an increase in investment of $100 million caused the GNP to rise by $200 million.

FIGURE 8–9 *The Respending Effect with a Multiplier of Two*

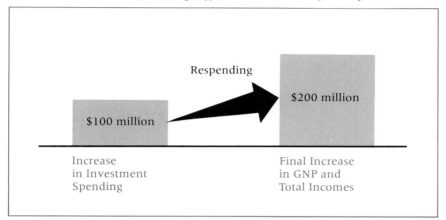

Calculation of the multiplier

So far, we have simply stated that the size of the multiplier in our example was two; next we will see how the size of the multiplier can be calculated.

Obviously, the size of the multiplier depends on how much of each increase in income is respent at each stage. If a greater fraction is respent, the respending effect will be greater, and the multiplier will be larger. Once we know what fraction of increases in income will or will not be respent at each stage, we can calculate the multiplier from the following formula:

$$\text{the multiplier} = \frac{1}{\begin{array}{c}\text{the fraction of } \textit{increases}\\\text{in income that is } \textit{not} \text{ respent}\\\text{at each stage}\end{array}}$$

Using our previous example, since 50 percent of increases in income was respent, 50 percent was *not* respent (or went to leakages), so that the multiplier would be calculated as follows:

$$\text{the multiplier} = \frac{1}{.50} \text{ or } \frac{1}{1/2} = 2.0$$

The size of the multiplier is not fixed; it depends on the proportion of increases in income that is respent at each stage. If 60 percent of increases in incomes were respent, the multiplier would be 2.5, or 1 divided by .40. This larger multiplier reflects the fact that the respending effect is larger in this case (60 percent respent rather than 50 percent). On the other hand, if a smaller proportion of income were respent, the multiplier would be smaller.

The Canadian multiplier

In the Canadian economy, the multiplier tends to be smaller than in the above examples, due mostly to the large proportion of income spent on *imports* (another leakage from the Canadian economy). The Economic Council of Canada has estimated that, for government spending on capital formation (such as public works projects), the size of the multiplier is 1.6 over a one-year period.[1] That is, a $1 million increase in expenditures on public works will boost GNP and total incomes by $1.6 million over the next year.

The downward multiplier

So far, we have applied the multiplier only to *increases* in investment spending. However, the multiplier also works in reverse. Suppose that investment spending *fell* from its previous level. This would reduce incomes by the same amount, with the result that spending would be cut back. These spending cuts would reduce other incomes, which would cause further spending cuts, and so on. This process is known as the *downward multiplier*. Obviously, it can contribute seriously to recessions and depressions, by nearly doubling the economic impact of reductions in investment spending. Thus, with a multiplier of 1.6, a reduction in investment of $3.0 billion would lead to a $4.8 billion decline in GNP.

The multiplier and economic stability

The multiplier effect is a major contributor to economic instability, because it significantly increases the impact of any fluctuation in spending on the economy. For instance, using the Canadian multiplier of 1.6, fluctuations in investment spending (or any other type of spending) of a magnitude of $5 billion will cause the GNP to fluctuate by about $8 billion. Thus, the multiplier effect helps to explain how relatively small fluctuations in investment spending can cause GNP and the economy in general to fluctuate by a considerably larger amount.

The accelerator effect

The multiplier effect which we have just examined shows how an increase in investment spending can generate increases in consumer spending by means of the responding effect. The *accelerator* effect operates in the other

---

[1]Because the responding effect works itself out over a period of time, the multiplier effect tends to be larger after a longer period. The Economic Council of Canada also estimates that if the government spending is maintained at the higher level (which was not assumed in the estimate of 1.6 for the multiplier), the multiplier effect increases to 2.1 after five years.

direction, in that increases in *consumer* spending can also generate increases in *investment* spending, as businesses increase their productive capacity in order to meet the rising level of consumer demand.

Rising consumer spending will not always cause investment spending to rise. During a recession, when a business may be operating at only 80 percent of capacity, an increase in consumer demand will not cause it to invest in new plant and equipment, because it has idle capacity that can be used to increase output. However, when rising consumer demand pushes output to near-capacity levels, further increases in consumer spending will cause an increase in investment spending in order to raise capacity to meet the anticipated demand. When rising consumer spending affects investment spending in this way, the resultant investment is called *induced investment*, and the effect on the economy is called the **accelerator**.

Consequently, when there is an economic boom in which many industries are operating near their capacity levels of output, increases in consumer spending will kick off a *surge* of investment spending, which will create a *great boom* in the capital-goods industries (construction, machinery, steel, building materials, and so on), as shown in years 19*1 and 19*2 in Figure 8-10.

However, this boom in the capital-goods industries may well prove to be temporary. Manufacturers will now have enough capital equipment for their present level of consumer sales, and will not order any more new capital equipment unless *consumer spending* (that is, manufacturers' sales) *increases further*. Year 19*3 of Figure 8-10 illustrates this point: the slowdown of consumer spending has a drastic effect on manufacturers' orders for new capital equipment, so that a mere *slowdown* in consumer spending causes a *drastic decline* in induced investment. Thus, induced investment is a particularly fragile component of investment spending — for induced investment to be merely *maintained*, consumer spending must *keep rising continuously*. And, when consumer spending merely slows down or levels off, induced investment will fall sharply.

Ironically, in year 19*3 of Figure 8-10, consumer spending, while barely rising, is nonetheless at record-high levels, whereas induced investment has declined sharply from its previous levels. This helps explain why, while the economy in general ("consumer spending" on the graph) is prosperous, there can be a serious slump in the capital-goods industries ("induced investment" on the graph). Thus, industries such as construction, steel, and building products can experience serious slumps *simply because consumption spending isn't rising fast enough*. As a result, induced investment is very unstable. This is one reason why capital-goods industries tend to experience feast or famine cycles, and one further reason why the economy tends to experience ups and downs. To aggravate the situation even further, the decline in induced investment can drag the level of consumption spending down with it, via the multiplier effect.

FIGURE 8-10 *The Operation of the Accelerator*

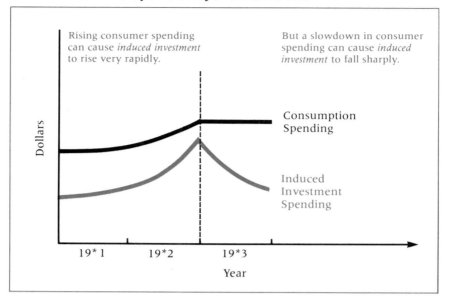

The multiplier and accelerator effects combined

We have seen how the multiplier and the accelerator operate separately. During an economic upswing, however, the multiplier and accelerator can *combine* so as to give even greater momentum to a boom. Suppose that an increase in investment spending, through the respending effect, causes consumer spending, incomes and GNP to rise by considerably more than itself. This is the effect we have called the multiplier.

However, the process may not end here. If the increase in consumption pushes production to near-capacity levels, the increased consumption will induce increased investment, through the process known as the accelerator. This further increase in investment spending will boost the economy to even higher levels, as the multiplier and accelerator effects are combined.

As we have seen, the size of the multiplier alone in the Canadian economy is estimated to be approximately 1.6. However, when the multiplier and accelerator combine in the manner discussed above, their combined size is probably roughly two or three. This effect, then, can be a powerful force when the economy is on the upswing. It could result, under the right conditions, in a $50 million increase in investment spending generating an increase in GNP of $100 to $150 million.

Exports as a source of economic instability

With nearly 30 percent of its GNP sold in export markets (seven-tenths of this to the United States alone), Canada is particularly exposed to international economic fluctuations. When other nations, particularly the USA, have economic slowdowns, their demand for Canadian products (especially resource products) slumps significantly, with serious effects on the Canadian economy.

The effects of such slumps in exports are not, however, confined to regions and industries linked directly to Canada's resource industries, such as forest products and mining. Rather, the effects spread, through the multiplier effect, throughout the economy, and can contribute to a general economic slowdown. On the other hand, economic booms and prosperity in other nations tend to spread almost automatically to Canada, through its large and important export industries.

Thus, economic trends in other countries, especially the USA, are an important source of economic fluctuations in Canada. Unlike the other causes of instability examined earlier in this chapter, the source of this problem lies outside Canada and occurs largely beyond the influence or control of the Canadian government.

Using leading economic indicators to forecast cycles

Obviously, it would be very useful for key economic decision-makers in business and government to have advance warning of changes in the direction of the economy, so that they could make timely preparations for changing economic conditions. To forecast the direction of the economy, economists have developed *leading economic indicators*. These are economic statistics that tend to rise or fall *before* the pace of the economy increases or decreases, and can therefore help to predict future economic trends. Through a combination of theory and experience with statistics, economists have been able to develop several such leading indicators.

One of the better-known tools used for economic forecasting is the Royal Bank's "Trendicator", which is a composite of seven leading economic indicators. The indicators used to compile the Trendicator are:

- the volume of money in circulation (the money supply)

- the ratio of new orders to inventories of consumer durable goods

- primary steel production

- the Toronto Stock Exchange price/earnings ratio (one measure of stock prices)

- the residential construction index (a measure of housing construction activity)

- the ratio of new orders to inventories in export-oriented industries

- the average hours worked (weekly) in manufacturing.

Each of these statistics has tended to give advance notice of economic trends; by combining them into a single statistic such as the Trendicator, a more effective forecasting tool has been developed which is not affected by peculiarities that might make any one (or more) of them ineffective or misleading at any particular time. Figure 8-11 shows both the Trendicator and the trends of the economy since 1956. The bottom graph shows the extent (percentage) by which the growth of real economic activity deviated in each period from the long-term growth trend. Bar graphs above the O axis show periods in which growth was faster than the long-term trend, while bar graphs below the axis show periods in which growth was slower than the long-term trend. Growth slowdowns are indicated by the shaded periods on both graphs.

The upper graph shows the composite of seven leading indicators known as the Trendicator. Note how, in most cases, the Trendicator moved down *before* a slowdown started and moved up again *before* the slowdown had ended. By careful examination and interpretation of leading indexes such as the Trendicator, economists can make better although still not perfect economic forecasts.

The dynamics of business cycles

We have seen how economic fluctuations can result from several factors — fluctuations in investment spending, the multiplier effect, the accelerator effect and fluctuations in exports. In summary, we will take a short look at the actual dynamics of economic instability — how these and other factors interact so as to generate economic instability. No two booms or slumps are the same, but the following will show the typical kinds of interactions that occur in the economy as it swings upward and downward.

The profile of an economic boom

Suppose investment spending by business rises, stimulating the economy. The respending effect of the multiplier will nearly double the impact of that increase in investment spending on the economy. Furthermore, this stimulation of consumer incomes and thus consumption spending may cause still further increases in investment spending, if businesses find they must expand their facilities to meet the increased demand. That is, the accelerator may come into operation.

In periods such as these, the expectations of businesses tend to be very optimistic. This causes spending on capital goods and inventories to rise rapidly. Consumers will be equally confident and optimistic, and will tend to increase sharply their purchases of "big-ticket" consumer durable goods such as appliances, furniture and especially automobiles. Similarly, housing will experience an upswing. To finance these major purchases, consumer credit will expand rapidly, as consumers are eager to borrow and banks are ready to oblige them.

In short, aggregate demand in the economy is at high levels and is rising rapidly—a fact that can lead to inflation. But incomes will be rising rapidly, too, and if consumers and businesses expect prices to continue to rise, they may decide to buy now, before prices rise further. Thus, even the price increases that occur during a boom period may cause spending to rise faster. Thus, there is a strong tendency for an economic boom to feed on itself, and spiral upwards.

The profile of an economic recession

Economic booms do not last forever. Rising prices and high interest rates (the result of high demand for loans during the boom) may breed consumer resistance, particularly with respect to purchases of houses and expensive items such as durable goods. Consumers may increase their purchases of imports, increasing this leakage from the economy. As we have seen, once consumer spending begins to level off, induced investment will decline, dragging the capital-goods industries into a slump, as the accelerator kicks into reverse. Another factor depressing business investment spending will likely be the high interest rates referred to earlier, which typically accompany the latter stages of an economic boom. The effects of reductions in investment spending spread to consumer spending and throughout the economy as the multiplier effect operates in reverse. Businesses' expectations regarding the future become unfavorable, and this lack of confidence causes further reductions in investment spending by businesses. As a result, the capital-goods industries (steel, construction, heavy equipment and so on) experience sluggish sales and lay off workers as they cut production. Similarly, consumer confidence declines as news of bad times spreads, so spending on consumer durables such as automobiles, appliances and furniture slows down or declines. Such purchases are costly, require borrowing (which people may be reluctant to do at this time) and can be postponed. For the same reasons, the housing industry will likely suffer a downturn. Retailers, faced with lower sales, choose to run down their inventories rather than reorder from manufacturers. As a result, the manufacturers cut back production and lay off workers. With rising unemployment and falling consumer incomes, consumption spending falls even further, dragging with it investment plans, and the economy tends to go into a downward spiral.

Conclusion

Whether a particular economic boom or recession was *started* by changes in consumption spending or investment spending often amounts to a question of "which came first—the chicken or the egg?" The causes of business cycles are quite complex, involving interrelationships between consumption spending and investment spending in which variations in investment spending are partly (through the multiplier) the *cause* of economic fluctuations and partly (through the accelerator) the *result* of such fluctuations. Regardless of whether a particular boom (or recession) has its origins in the behavior of consumption or investment spending, however, once a boom (or recession) gets started, it tends to gain momentum for some time, with the result that the entire economy tends to alternate between periods of rapid growth and slowdowns.

The problem of economic instability, and particularly the periodic recurrence of recessions and depressions, has historically been one of the most serious weaknesses of the free-enterprise type of economy. In this chapter, we have examined the causes of this problem; in the next chapter, we will see what governments have been able to do to correct it.

DEFINITIONS OF NEW TERMS

Multiplier   The effect whereby fluctuations in spending (for instance, investment spending) spread by means of the respending effect through the economy, with the total impact on GNP and incomes being considerably larger than the initial fluctuations in spending.

Induced Investment   Capital investment spending undertaken by business in response to increases in sales that have brought production to near-capacity levels and that are expected to continue.

Capacity (Output)   The maximum rate of production of which a plant, or the entire economy, is physically capable.

Accelerator   The effect whereby rising consumption spending causes rapid increases in induced investment, and a slowing down or levelling off of consumption spending causes sharp declines in induced investment.

Leading Economic Indicator   An economic statistic that tends to increase or decrease in advance of increases or decreases in the pace of economic activity, thus giving advance notice of changes in economic trends.

CHAPTER SUMMARY

1. Free-enterprise, or market economies are prone to economic fluctuations, alternating between periods of rapid expansion and slumps, or recessions.

2. These fluctuations occur for various reasons, many of which are complex and interrelated, but which generally generate *fluctuations in aggregate demand*. These include:
   (a) fluctuations in investment spending, which is the most variable major component of aggregate demand,
   (b) the multiplier effect, whereby fluctuations in investment spending, through the respending effect, cause much larger fluctuations in aggregate demand, GNP and total incomes,
   (c) the accelerator effect, through which fluctuations in consumption spending cause much sharper fluctuations in induced investment, and
   (d) fluctuations in exports, an important separate source of fluctuations in the Canadian economy, since exports amount to about 30 percent of GNP.

QUESTIONS

1. In a recession, which *one* of the following industries would likely suffer the greatest percentage decline in its sales, and why?
   (a) Clothing
   (b) Breweries
   (c) Steel
   (d) Agriculture
   (e) Furniture

2. In which *one* of the following industries would you expect annual profits to *vary the most* from year to year, and why?
   (a) Distilling (Liquor)
   (b) Construction equipment
   (c) Banking
   (d) Cosmetics
   (e) Retail food stores

3. Which *one* of the following would be most likely to experience *periodic* unemployment (from time to time)? Do not refer to seasonal factors in your explanation.
   (a) Teachers
   (b) Managers
   (c) Employees of insurance companies
   (d) Bricklayers

4. Suppose that economists state that, due to a $200 million investment project, GNP will be boosted by as much as $500 or $600 million. Outline in detail the processes whereby this might occur.

5. If Canadians imported considerably less from other nations, how would the size of the "multiplier" be affected?

6. What are the most recent trends in Canada regarding
   (a) capital investment by business?
   (b) new residential housing construction?
   What are the reasons for each of these trends, and what effects are they likely to have on the economy?

7. For each of the seven leading economic indicators used to make up the Royal Bank's composite index, consider what that statistic measures and try to determine logically why that statistic could be expected to increase or decrease *before* the pace of economic activity quickens or slows.

8. Suppose that, on average, consumers will respend 50 percent of any increase in income that they receive.
   (a) If business investment spending increases by $6 billion, GNP and total incomes will increase by $ _____ billion.
   (b) Why do GNP and total incomes increase by this amount rather than by $6 billion?
   (c) If consumers respent only 40 percent of increases in income, what difference would this make to the process referred to in (b), and by how much would GNP and total incomes increase?
   (d) If consumers respent 60 percent of increases in income, what difference would this make to the process referred to in (b) and (c), and by how much would GNP and total incomes increase?
   (e) Record the first three stages of the respending process in each of the above cases on the following table, using the same $6 billion increase in investment spending.

Percentage of Income Respent

	40%	50%	60%
Initial Increase in Investment Spending	$6	$6	$6
Stage 1 of respending	—	—	—
Stage 2 of respending	—	—	—
Stage 3 of respending	—	—	—

9. AN ILLUSTRATION OF THE "ACCELERATOR"

Acme Toy Company needs one machine for every 5000 toys it produces per week. In year 1, as the following table shows, Acme has 20 fully-utilized machines producing 100 000 toys per week. We will assume that this production figure exactly matches the number of toys bought weekly by consumers, so that it also represents consumer demand for Acme's toys. In year two, consumer demand and toy output increase to 105 000, so that Acme need 21 machines, as shown in column 2. Since it only has 20 machines (column 3), Acme must buy one new machine (column 4). Since this machine was bought in response to increased consumer demand for toys, we can also regard column 4 as "induced investment" spending.

Year	(1) Toy Sales and Output (000)	(2) No. of Machines Needed	(3) No. of Machines in the Plant	(4) No. of New Machines Bought
1	100	20	20	0
2	105	21	20	1
3	115	—	—	—
4	120	—	—	—
5	120	—	—	—

Now, suppose that, in years 3, 4 and 5, consumer demand (toy sales) and toy production are 115 000, 120 000 and 120 000, as shown in column 1.

(a) Complete columns 2, 3 and 4 in the table.

(b) Summarize the results in the following table.

Year	(1) Consumer Spending (=Toy Sales and Output (000)	% Change From Previous Year	(4) Induced Investment (=Purchases of New Machines)	% Change From Previous Year
1	100	—	0	—
2	105	+5.0%	1	—
3	115	+9.5%	—	—
4	120	—	—	—
5	120	—	—	—

(c) From year 2 to year 3, there was an increase of 9.5 percent in consumer purchases of toys which induced an increase of _____ percent in purchases of new toy-making machines.

(d) From year 3 to year 4, consumer purchases of toys increased by _____ percent, causing purchases on new toy-making machines to _____ by _____ percent.

(e) From year 4 to year 5, consumer purchases of toys remained stable at 120 000; the result of this was that purchases of new toy-making machines _____ by _____ percent.

(f) Show the figures for *consumer spending* and *induced investment* from the table in part (b) on the following graph.

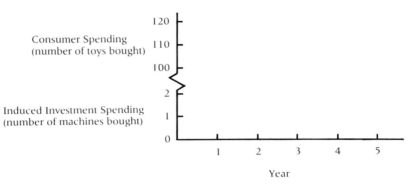

CHAPTER 9

Stabilizing the economy: government fiscal policy

In Chapter 8, we saw that fluctuations in aggregate demand can cause the economy to experience cycles, in which periods of rapid growth are followed by economic slumps. High levels of aggregate demand boost not only output and employment, causing an economic boom, but can also generate inflation, if aggregate demand becomes excessive. On the other hand, when aggregate demand undergoes one of its periodic slow-downs, output and employment are depressed, generating a recession with high unemployment. This tendency to alternate between prosperity and hardship has historically been one of the more persistent and serious problems of free-enterprise economies.

Prior to the 1930's, the tendency for the economy to fall into periodic slowdowns was not a major concern of economists. Recessions were generally regarded as temporary adjustments through which the economy periodically passed, like a retailer cutting its orders to manufacturers temporarily until it had sold off an unexpected accumulation of excessive inventory. Economists believed not only that governments *could* do little about recessions, but that they should not even try. The prevailing view was that, left on its own and given time, a free-enterprise economy would automatically provide full employment, making intervention by the government unnecessary. This belief was based on the elaborate theories that formed the basis for *laissez-faire*: since the economy functioned very well on its own, they asked, why should the government interfere?

However, the Great Depression of the 1930's, in which the economy wallowed for a decade, forced a rethinking of economic theories. The main challenge to the traditional laissez faire theory was advanced by John Maynard Keynes in *The General Theory of Employment, Interest, and Money*, published in 1936. Keynes' basic theory was that the government's

JOHN MAYNARD KEYNES (1883-1946)

The son of two Cambridge University professors, John Maynard Keynes was a child prodigy, working on the economic theory of interest at age four, attending Eton at age fourteen on a scholarship and studying at Cambridge at seventeen. Following graduation, he placed second in a nationwide civil service examination competition. Ironically, he would have finished first if his grade in economics had been higher. He would later comment that this problem had arisen from the fact that he knew more about economics than his examiners did.

Later, while teaching at Cambridge, Keynes served as chairman of the National Mutual Life Assurance Society, editor of the *Economic Journal* and as a director of the Bank of England. He moved in the elite social and cultural circles, organizing Cambridge's Art Theatre and London's Camargo Ballet, and married the celebrated Lydia Lopokova, a prominent Russian ballerina of the era.

In 1936, in the midst of the Great Depression, Keynes completed the most influential of his many writings, *The General Theory of Employment, Interest and Money*, upon which the concept of government fiscal policy is founded. Of *The General Theory, Time* magazine would write thirty years later, "it had more influence in a shorter time than any other book ever written in economics."

Keynes did not live to see the full extent of his influence. As with all new ideas, his met with considerable resistance initially, and were not widely accepted until after the Second World War. Since then, they have become the basis of government economic policy in industrialized market economies. Nonetheless, Keynesian theories remain controversial; their defenders maintain that such policies are the salvation of the free-enterprise system, while their opponents argue that these theories have legitimized spendthrift government spending policies that have fuelled inflation and brought the economy to the brink of ruin.

control over a major injection into the spending stream (government spending) and major leakage from the spending stream (taxes) gave the government the opportunity to influence the level of aggregate demand for goods and services in the economy, and thus to influence the performance of the entire economy. This use of government spending and taxes to influence the level of aggregate demand and the performance of the economy is called *fiscal policy*. By providing this theoretical basis for fiscal policy, Keynes opened the door to a new era in economic thinking. Eventually, he would come to be regarded as perhaps the most influential economic thinker of the twentieth century.

Part A: Fiscal policy

Keynes believed that, during a recession or depression, when the injection of business investment is not sufficiently large to offset the leakage of saving, the government should take steps to correct the situation. One such step could be to *increase government spending*, to create additional injections into the system; another could be to *decrease taxes* so as to reduce that leakage from spending. The common element in both such approaches is that they would *increase the level of aggregate demand* in the economy, with the intention that the increased spending on goods and services would stabilize the economy and avoid serious recessions, as illustrated in Figure 9-1.

FIGURE 9-1 *Keynesian Policies to Stabilize the Economy*

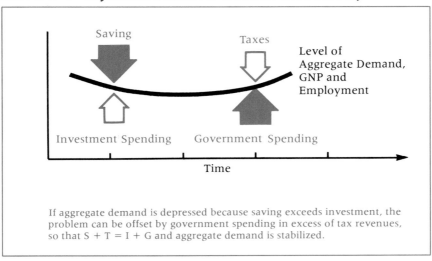

If aggregate demand is depressed because saving exceeds investment, the problem can be offset by government spending in excess of tax revenues, so that S + T = I + G and aggregate demand is stabilized.

Figure 9-1 shows another feature of Keynesian policy: to stabilize the economy in this way the government must spend more than it takes in in tax revenues, or run a *budget deficit*. This was considered unthinkable among orthodox economists, for whom the idea of always balancing the budget (keeping expenditures and tax revenues equal) was sacred.

Keynes' new ideas concerning the role of the government in the economy created a furor in academic, business and government circles. Conservative thinkers saw his ideas as a radical (perhaps even communistic) threat to the free-enterprise system. To others, his theories represented perhaps the only way to save the economic system from its own self-destructive tendency toward depressions.

While controversy and uncertainty prevented Keynes' proposed policies from being used significantly in the 1930's, the outbreak of the Second World War in 1939 *forced* governments to increase their spending dramatically without increasing taxes, a situation which entailed large budget deficits. The economic results were equally dramatic, as the economy recovered quickly from the Depression and unemployment virtually disappeared. For many, the debate had been won—not by theories, but by actual experience.

After the Second World War ended in 1945, a new philosophy concerning the role of the government in the economy developed. *Keynesian economics*, introduced against considerable conservative opposition into university programs, became the basis for the acceptance by government of responsibility for the level of employment in the economy. In its 1945 White Paper on Employment and Incomes, the Canadian government accepted responsibility for maintaining a "high and stable level of employment" in the economy and stated that "The Government will be prepared in periods when unemployment threatens to incur the deficits . . . resulting from its employment and income policy, whether that policy in the circumstances is best applied through increased expenditures or reduced taxation." Laissez-faire had been abandoned; the government had committed itself to influencing the direction of the entire economy.

Budget surpluses and balanced budgets

Keynes, writing during the Great Depression, naturally emphasized the importance of budget deficits, because they help to stimulate the economy. (Figure 9-2 illustrates this approach to fiscal policy.) However, budget deficits to combat recessions are only one of several options governments may choose in planning their budgets. Another alternative is to use a *budget surplus,* with tax revenues greater than government spending, to combat *inflation*. Since inflation is basically caused by aggregate demand rising faster than output can rise, a budget surplus can help to ease inflation by depressing the level of aggregate demand in the economy, as shown in Figure 9-3. This and other anti-inflation policies will be considered in more detail in Chapter 13. The third possibility regarding fiscal policy is a *balanced budget* in which government expenditures and tax revenues are equal. Such a budget (shown in Figure 9-4) would be appropriate when neither unemployment nor inflation was considered unacceptably high, as the economy would not benefit from an adjustment to the level of aggregate demand.

FIGURE 9-2 ***Fiscal Policy to Combat Recession: Budget Deficits Increase Aggregate Demand***

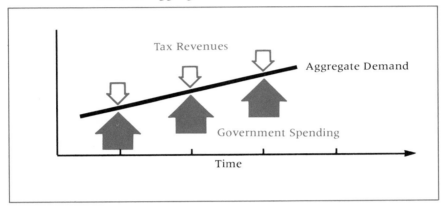

FIGURE 9-3 ***Fiscal Policy to Combat Inflation: Budget Surpluses Depress Aggregate Demand***

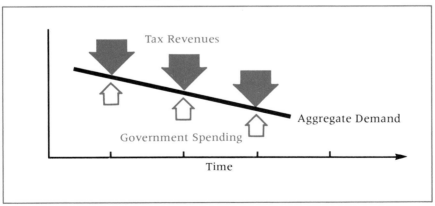

FIGURE 9–4 *A Balanced Budget has a Neutral Effect on Aggregate Demand*

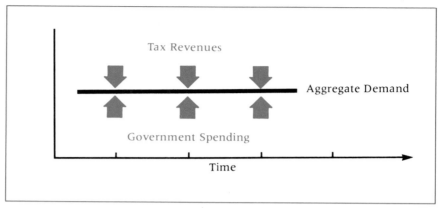

Fiscal policy to stimulate the economy

We will now consider in more detail the two approaches by which fiscal policy can stimulate the economy during recessions: increases in government spending and tax reductions.

(a) Increases in government expenditures

We have seen how increases in government spending can raise the level of aggregate demand and help to lift the economy out of a recession. Traditionally, governments have used *public works* for this purpose, building roads, bridges, parks and public buildings when the economy was slack and the construction industry was particularly depressed. Some programs to increase government spending, such as public works projects or special relief or temporary job programs, must be planned and set up, which creates delays in their implementation. However, there are other types of government spending, such as *unemployment insurance* and *welfare payments,* which tend to rise automatically when the economy slips into a recession, thus providing automatic support to the level of aggregate demand.

(b) Reductions in taxes

While traditional theory would insist that taxes be increased in order to balance the increases in government spending referred to above, Keynesian theory argues that tax increases would only depress spending by consumers and businesses, worsening the recession.

Thus, taxes should not be increased during a recession; indeed, if anything, they should be reduced, so as to help raise the level of aggregate demand. The most popular policy of this type is the *personal income tax cut*, intended to increase personal disposable income and consumer spending, although temporary *sales tax cuts* have also been used for this purpose. To promote higher levels of business investment spending, there are various types of tax reductions, including *cuts in corporate income (profits) taxes* and *increased capital cost allowances*, which permit businesses to depreciate assets more quickly, thus reducing their taxable income and tax liabilities.

Automatic stabilizers

As noted above, certain types of government expenditures, such as unemployment insurance and welfare, tend to rise automatically during recessions, as unemployment rises. In addition to this, many of the government's tax revenues, such as those from income taxes, profits taxes and sales taxes, tend to be depressed by slower economic activity during recessions. With government tax revenues depressed and expenditures rising, there is an automatic tendency for the government's budget to go into a deficit as a recession develops. This budget deficit will then help to counteract the recession automatically, which is why such government expenditures and tax revenues are called *automatic stabilizers*.

The multiplier and fiscal policy

As we have seen, fiscal policy is used to stabilize the economy in recessions by increasing the level of spending on goods and services by government, consumers or businesses. The effect of any such increase in spending will, however, spread through the economy due to the multiplier effect, as increases in income generated by the policy are respent again and again. For example, a government road-building program will increase the incomes of construction workers, who will spend part of their increased incomes on consumer goods and services, starting a chain of respending that will increase total incomes and GNP by about 1.6 times the original increase in government spending. Similarly, personal income tax cuts that boost consumer spending will initiate a respending effect that will ripple through the economy.

Pump priming

Fiscal policy to stimulate the economy can also involve the accelerator effect. Once the level of consumption spending has risen to the point where it is causing induced investment spending by business, the economy should be able to carry on its recovery without further stimulation from government budget deficits. In fact, further deficits at this point would not help the economy; they would only boost demand to excessive levels and cause inflation. This is the concept of *pump priming*. To get a well to work, you have to pour some water into it first; however, after that is done, the well works without further assistance. Similarly, the economy may benefit from a boost to start it on a path to recovery out of a slump, but beyond a point, no further boosts are needed.

The concept of pump priming views budget deficits as a *temporary stimulus* to the economy rather than as a permanent replacement for business investment spending. Indeed, in a basically free-enterprise economy, government spending cannot replace business investment's vital role of adding to the economy's stock of capital goods, and thus to future prosperity. Thus, the key to long-term prosperity lies in private-business capital investment, while temporary expansion of government spending and budget deficits can help to combat periodic recessions.

A note on creating jobs

Often, when the economy is sluggish and unemployment is high, much attention is given to government efforts to create jobs. Many people believe that this simply means direct government hiring of unemployed people, often for *make-work programs* ("digging holes and filling them up again").

In fact, creating jobs is a much more positive concept than this—it refers to government efforts to *stimulate the whole economy* (through budget deficits), rather than merely hiring the unemployed to do work of little value. For example, tax cuts increase consumer spending, which stimulates many industries. Also, the effects of government spending (such as on a public works project) will spread, via the multiplier effect, through the economy, increasing consumer spending, too. By generating a more favorable economic climate, these efforts by the government can result in increased business investment spending as well. Thus, the effects of budget deficits designed to stimulate employment will be felt all through the economy, from the toy industry to the construction industry—not merely in the hiring of the unemployed by the government.

Financing deficits: where will the money come from?

The use of fiscal policy to stimulate the economy during recessions requires that the government have budget deficits, with government expenditures larger than tax revenues. Where will the necessary money come from to finance such deficits? There are two possible sources of funds to finance budget deficits.

(a) *The government can borrow the money*

The government can raise the necessary funds by borrowing them — by selling *government bonds* to individuals, banks, insurance companies, pension funds, investment funds and other financial institutions. By doing this, the government can, in effect, mop up savings that are not being used for capital investment and inject them back into the spending stream as government spending.

(b) *The government can print the money*

Another way to raise the funds for federal budget deficits is to *create new money* (the popular term is *print money*)[1] for the government to spend. While a growing economy requires a larger volume of money in circulation (called the *money supply* by economists), it is dangerous to increase the money supply too quickly. The inevitable result of such a policy would be *severe inflation*, as the excessive amount of money in circulation forces prices up rapidly. Thus, while it may be tempting for the government to simply print money to finance its budget deficits, this should be done only within limits, so as to avoid increasing the money supply by more than the economy can absorb without rapid inflation.

In practice, it is common for budget deficits to be financed by a *combination* of borrowing and printing, a practice that can be economically beneficial as long as the printing of money is kept within reasonable limits.

Part B: The National Debt

We have seen that the use of government fiscal policy to stimulate the economy during recessions requires that the government borrow money (mostly through bond issues) in order to finance its budget deficits. The total amount of federal government debt thus incurred — the amount of money owed by the federal government — is called the *National Debt*. By 1985 the National Debt had passed $200 billion, or $24 000 per Canadian family.

The National Debt has, over the years, been the subject of a great deal of misunderstandings, fears, myths and political hypocrisy. Many Canadians believe, for instance, that the money is owed to other countries

---

[1]The government does not actually physically print new money for itself to spend. The process is more subtle than that, and will be examined in detail in Chapter 11. However, the economic effects of such a policy are such that it can reasonably be described as "printing money."

and that Canada may go bankrupt because of it. Both of these ideas are myths. On the other hand, few Canadians appreciate the real dangers concerning the National Debt. We will examine first the myths, then the dangers.

What is the National Debt?

The **National Debt** is the overall debt of the federal government—the difference between the federal government's *liabilities* (mostly outstanding bonds) and its *net recorded assets* (mostly those assets which yield interest, profits or dividends). Thus it measures, on balance, how much the federal government owes to creditors.[2]

Why does the federal government borrow money?

One reason for government borrowing is to *finance the purchases of "social assets,"* such as roads, hospitals, schools, public buildings and airports. Since these assets are too expensive to be paid out of the current year's tax revenues, the government borrows the money to pay for them—just as households borrow to buy cars and houses, and businesses go into debt to purchase capital equipment or build facilities that are too costly to pay for out of current income. In each of these examples, the benefits of the asset purchased will be received over a period of years in the future, so it is considered appropriate to borrow to buy them and repay the loan in the future.

Another reason for federal government borrowing is *to finance budget deficits to combat recessions*. Thus, the federal government's responsibility for minimizing the effects of recessions sometimes requires it to go into debt. Historically, another major reason for government borrowing and increases in the National Debt has been *the financing of wartime expenditures*. For example, the Second World War added over $10 billion to Canada's National Debt.

Each of the above is generally considered to be a legitimate reason for borrowing by the government. However, ordinary operating expenses of the government, such as its payroll, should be paid for by tax revenues. It is not considered to be good financial practice to borrow (or even worse, print) money to cover operating expenses, or to avoid a necessary increase in taxes for political reasons, any more than it is considered appropriate for households to go into debt to pay their telephone or food bills.

[2]It is important to remember that the National Debt does not include the debt load of provincial or municipal governments nor should it be confused with the federal deficit, which reflects only the *annual increase* in the national debt and not the accumulated total.

To whom does the federal government owe the National Debt?

The vast majority of the National Debt is owed to Canadians—those individual Canadians and Canadian financial institutions such as banks, insurance companies, trust companies and pension funds who have bought the government bonds. The belief that the National Debt represents a claim on our economy by foreign creditors that could cause Canada to go bankrupt is incorrect, because only a small proportion of federal government debt (about 10 percent in the mid-1980's) is owed to foreign lenders.

Isn't any debt bad?

Not necessarily. Most households are in debt, for their cars, appliances, houses, credit card purchases, and so on. And practically every business in the country is in debt, to pay for inventories, equipment and facilities. As consumers and businesses have found, debt can be very useful if it is properly managed. As with debt in general, the dangers associated with the National Debt lie not with debt itself, but rather with excessive debt, as we will see.

> . . . public opinion often tends to judge any deficit as evidence of economic trouble and sometimes as a firm proof of fiscal irresponsibility . . . Government deficits are inherently neither bad nor good. What matters about deficits is their impact on people.
>
> Economic Council of Canada,
> *Seventeenth Annual Review*, 1980.

Government failure to "balance its budget" — why?

Concern about budget deficits and the rising National Debt is often expressed as a complaint that "any business that ran that way would go broke." However, the matter is not that simple. Most successful businesses accumulate more and more liabilities, or debt, reflecting the money that was borrowed to finance their growth in productive assets. Businesses do not regard such a situation as bad management; indeed, the acquisition of the assets can be financially beneficial to the company by increasing its profitability.

Just as a growing economy requires more private productive assets, such as factories and equipment, so it will also require more social assets, such as roads, hospitals and schools. Both private and social assets are typically financed by borrowing, so that the debts of businesses and governments (as well as households) have risen. The simple fact that these debts have risen in no way proves mismanagement on the part of governments, businesses or households in general.

Another problem that contributes to misunderstandings concerning government deficits is that many people confuse a government *budget deficit* with a business *loss*. Some types of government budgets lump together all spending—for current purposes such as payroll and capital purposes such as airports—so that, whenever social assets are bought or built, the government's budget shows an excess of spending over the current year's tax revenues, or a deficit. By contrast, a business' income statement does not include capital expenditures on items such as plant as current expenses, and its balance sheet shows its assets as well as its liabilities (or debt). Governments' budgets generally show the liabilities without showing the corresponding assets.

Furthermore, no business has the responsibility to prevent recessions in the economy, and deficit spending—financed by borrowing—is a proven method of fulfilling that responsibility. Rising unemployment gives the government the choice of either ignoring the problem or using deficit spending to combat it. Considering that the government is responsible for maintaining full employment, it could well be argued that good management sometimes requires the government to have budget deficits.

Hasn't the National Debt been increased recklessly?

While it is true that the net federal government debt rose from about $3 billion in 1939 to over $22 billion by 1975, Figure 9-5 places the question of the growth of the government's debt in better perspective. These statistics portray a much less alarming picture of federal debt. First, they show the dramatic addition to the National Debt caused by the Second World War (1939-45). Second, they show that while the debt has risen since the Second World War, it rose considerably less rapidly than did the GNP, with the result that federal government debt actually *declined* as a percentage of GNP up to 1975. Thus, much of the apparent increase in the National Debt has been an illusion caused by inflation, and the period from 1939 to 1975 in particular does not reflect extravagant spending and borrowing by the federal government. In fact, while from 1947 to 1974 there were five recessions, and in each recession the federal government had a budget deficit, in most other years it had a surplus. In total, the budget surpluses amounted to slightly more than the deficits. After 1975, however the situation changed significantly, a matter which we will examine separately later in this chapter.

FIGURE 9–5 *Federal government debt 1939–75*

Year	Net Federal Government Debt ($ Billion)	Net Debt as a Percentage of GNP
1939	$ 3.15	56.1%
1946	13.42	112.9
1952	11.19	51.7
1957	11.01	34.3
1962	13.23	33.4
1965	15.53	30.9
1968	16.22	24.4
1971	16.59	19.4
1973	19.13	18.2
1975	22.18	15.0

SOURCE: Public Accounts of Canada, *Economic Review*, April 1980 (Department of Finance Canada) page 225.

Reproduced by permission of the Minister of Supply and Services Canada

National Debt on the rise — is Canada headed toward bankruptcy?

Increasing debt does not by itself threaten bankruptcy; what must also be considered is the borrower's ability to carry the debt. We have seen that, for 30 years prior to 1975, the GNP (from which the government derives its tax revenues) rose considerably faster than the National Debt, a fact that indicates that fears of national bankruptcy are based more on emotion than on fact.

There are two other reasons why such fears are unfounded. First, *the National Debt is an internal debt*: it is owed *by* the Canadian public (the federal government) *to* the Canadian public (individuals and institutions owning government bonds). While repayment of the debt would involve removing billions of dollars from the Canadian economy through taxes, it would also involve returning the same amount of money into the Canadian economy, when the bondholders were paid for their bonds. While money would be redistributed by such a transaction, it would involve no net removal from the economy, and thus no danger of bankruptcy or burden on future generations. The same principle applies to payment of interest on the debt: it involves a redistribution of funds within the Canadian economy rather than a withdrawal of funds from the economy.

Of course, the situation would be quite different if the government's whole debt were owed to foreign creditors. In this case, payment of interest and repayment of the debt would involve a withdrawal of wealth from

FIGURE 9-6 *Federal Budget Deficits 1970-85*

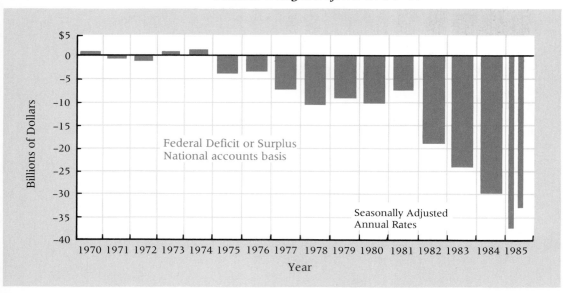

SOURCE Department of Economic Research, *Canada's Business Climate*,
Toronto Dominion Bank.

the Canadian economy and a burden for Canadians. However, since only a small proportion of federal debt has been held by foreigners, this has not been a large concern.

A second consideration concerning the fear of bankruptcy is that *the National Debt need never be paid off,* in the sense of being reduced to zero. As outstanding bond issues become due ("mature") and must be repaid, new bonds can be issued to raise the necessary funds. This process, known as *refunding* a bond issue, is commonplace not only in government finance but also in many large, stable business corporations.

In reality, society can actually benefit from properly managed budget deficits and the resultant National Debt. Depressions can be avoided, economic growth can be maintained and valuable public assets can be built. All of these are left along with the debt to future generations.

Are budget deficits only beneficial, then?

From the foregoing, it would seem that government budget deficits have only beneficial effects on the economy, and that deficits should not be a matter of concern to the public or the government. So far, however, we have been discussing government budget deficits incurred either *pe-*

FIGURE 9-7 *Federal Deficit or Surplus as a Percentage of GNP*

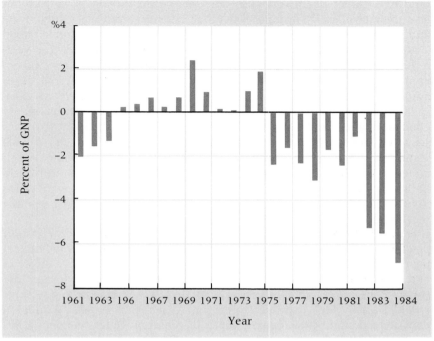

SOURCE   Conference Board of Canada.

riodically, to combat recessions, or for the purpose of *building social assets*.
If the government's borrowing goes beyond these reasonable purposes,
so that it has budget deficits that are *excessively large*, or a *chronic* feature
of government finance, the situation — and the effects — can be quite
different. The remainder of this chapter deals with the possible dangers
associated with government budget deficits.

The dangers of budget deficits: the National Debt since 1975

Until fairly recently, federal budget deficits and debt were of little concern
to Canadian economists. As noted earlier, periodic budget deficits during
recessions were offset by surpluses in other years, and federal debt was
steadily declining as a percentage of GNP.

After 1975, however, the situation changed significantly. The federal
government had exceptionally large budget deficits, not only in dollar
terms, as Figure 9-6 shows, but also as a percentage of GNP, as Figure
9-7 shows.

These deficits were different from the periodic "anti-recession" deficits discussed earlier in this chapter, not only because of their *vast size* but also their *persistence*. Through policy decisions regarding its expenditure and tax programs, the federal government had created a situation in which its spending would exceed tax revenues by a large amount every year, *even if the economy were booming* and a deficit were unnecessary and inappropriate. For instance, the federal government transferred large amounts of funds to the provincial governments to help finance provincial spending on programs such as health care, welfare and post-secondary education, and, until 1985, spent substantial amounts of money to subsidize oil prices. At the same time, the government introduced a wide variety of tax reductions on both personal and business income, which added to the deficit. Because they had become a regular, built-in feature of the very structure of the government's budget, these deficits were called **structural deficits**, as distinct from *periodic deficits* used to combat recessions.

A major contributor to these deficits was the *indexing* of federal transfer payments and personal income tax. To protect the recipients of transfer payments (such as unemployment insurance benefits, family allowances and pensions) against inflation, the government indexed these to the Consumer Price Index. Thus, if the CPI rose by 10 percent, these payments would also, by law, rise by 10 percent. As a result, the rapid inflation experienced until 1983 caused rapid increases in federal expenditures that were indexed.

At the same time, the federal government introduced indexing provisions which had the effect of depressing revenues from the personal income tax. These provisions were intended to protect taxpayers from being forced into higher tax brackets by inflation. Without indexing, taxpayers who were not even keeping up with inflation could be forced to pay higher tax rates because their money income had risen, even though their real income, or purchasing power, had not. To prevent this burden on taxpayers, the federal government in 1974 indexed the personal income tax, so that higher tax rates would be payable only if a taxpayer's income rose faster than the Consumer Price Index. The effect of this provision on the government's tax revenues was similar to an automatic annual tax cut, in that it made federal tax revenues lower than they would have been without indexing.

In summary, the federal government, through a variety of policies regarding its expenditures and tax revenues, created very large budget deficits of a structural, or built-in nature, and was borrowing large amounts of money to cover its expenditure commitments to Canadians and their provincial governments and businesses.

In the first half of the 1980's, the federal budget deficits moved into the $25 to $30 billion range. In part, these deficits were due to the slow growth and high unemployment of the period; that is, they were like

THE PARADOX OF INDEXING

By indexing both transfer payments and the personal income tax, the federal government's policy was to assist financially both households that received transfer payments from the government and households that paid income taxes to the government. Both were to be protected against the effects of inflation. Thus, it was federal policy to *subsidize the consumption of virtually all Canadians.*

The cost of these programs became part of the federal budget deficit, which meant that the government was in effect borrowing large amounts of savings to finance transfer payments and tax cuts. While this supported the consumption spending of Canadians for the time being, there were concerns regarding the longer-term effects of such a policy. Escalating federal budget deficits, pushed higher by the interest payments on the rapidly mounting government debt, would eventually require the government either to cut its expenditures or raise taxes (or both), thereby depressing living standards in the future. In other words, future generations of Canadians would have to pay for the subsidized living standards of Canadians who benefited from indexing.

In the mid-1980's, the government was forced by mounting budget deficits to begin to make such adjustments, cutting back on the extent of indexing and curbing government expenditures while increasing a variety of taxes. Canadians began to pay in the mid-1980's for the benefits they had enjoyed since the mid-1970's.

traditional periodic anti-recession deficits. However, these deficits were partly due to the structural factors referred to above. It was estimated that, even if there were to be an economic boom and minimal unemployment, the federal budget deficit would still be in the $10 to $15 billion range, rather than balanced as in the past.

The hard fact about Canada's deficit is that for more than ten years Canadians have accepted more in services and transfers from the federal government than they have been willing to pay for.

Edward Carmichael,
Tackling the Federal Deficit
C.D. Howe Institute, 1984.

While the business community expressed great concern about the federal government's budget deficits and urged measures to reduce them, organized labor and the New Democratic Party had a quite different view of the matter. In their opinion, the social value of the government's spending programs was too great to be sacrificed on the altar of deficit reduction. In particular, they were concerned about possible cutbacks in spending on the three key elements of Canada's welfare state: *income security programs* (such as unemployment insurance and welfare), *health care* and *education*. In addition, they were resistant to any deficit-reduction measures that would involve higher taxes on Canadians with modest incomes. It was also stressed that with unemployment as high as it was during the first half of the 1980's, it would not be economically appropriate to dampen aggregate demand with government spending cuts or tax increases to reduce the deficit.

FIGURE 9-8   *Canada's Federal Public Debt 1961–91*

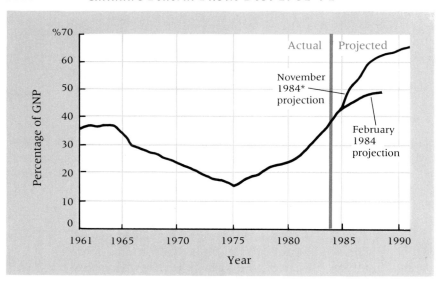

*Includes expenditure cuts announced in the Economic and Fiscal Statement.

SOURCES   Department of Finance, *The Fiscal Plan* (Ottawa, February 1984), p. 62: and Hon. Michael H. Wilson, *A New Direction for Canada: An Agenda for Economic Renewal* (Ottawa: Department of Finance, November 1984).

Concerns regarding federal deficits and debt since 1975

As a result of these massive federal deficits, the National Debt soared from $24 billion in 1975 past $200 billion (in current dollars) in 1985. The long-term decline of the debt as a percentage of GNP was abruptly reversed, as Figure 9-8 shows, and the National debt was projected to surpass $400 billion by 1990.

When budget deficits reach excessively high levels, there are a number of reasons to be concerned.

(a) *Depressing effect on capital investment*

We have emphasized the role of capital investment spending by business in generating economic prosperity, and the importance of saving as a source of funds for such capital investment. Continuing massive federal government budget deficits could undermine business investment spending by requiring the government to borrow such large amounts of Canadians' savings each year that there could be a shortage of funds for capital investment. For instance, in 1984, the federal budget deficit absorbed $30 billion of savings, an amount equal to roughly 70 percent of total personal saving by Canadians in that year. If business investment spending were to be crowded out by government borrowing in this way, economic growth could be depressed over the longer term.

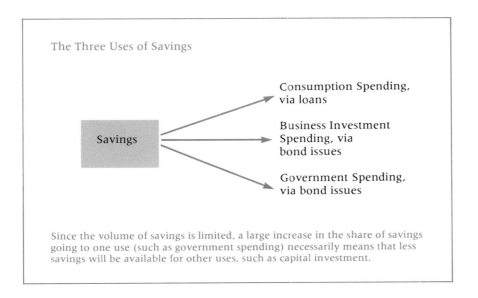

The Three Uses of Savings

Savings →
- Consumption Spending, via loans
- Business Investment Spending, via bond issues
- Government Spending, via bond issues

Since the volume of savings is limited, a large increase in the share of savings going to one use (such as government spending) necessarily means that less savings will be available for other uses, such as capital investment.

A different way of looking at the same problem is to consider that heavy federal borrowing, in competition with business borrowing, could force *interest rates* to high levels. If this were to happen, business investment spending would be curtailed as high interest rates made capital projects unprofitable to undertake.

These were not regarded as very serious concerns during the first half of the 1980's, when business investment spending was low, but by mid-decade, concerns had risen. It was feared that, as the economy recovered and growth resumed, business borrowing for important capital spending would have to compete with heavy federal borrowing to finance government budget deficits. This would force interest rates up, killing off the recovery of both investment spending and the economy.

There was also a more long-term possibility that federal deficits could depress capital investment in Canada's manufacturing sector, where productivity has lagged badly behind that of most of our foreign competitors, and in energy, as our conventional oil reserves deplete. It was thought that the federal government might be diverting large amounts of Canadians' savings away from important long-term capital investment uses and into paying the government's current expenditures; that is, away from investment and into current consumption. Such a situation could, over time, have serious effects on the Canadian economy.

BUDGET DEFICITS AND ECONOMIC STAGNATION

At first, it seems contradictory that budget deficits, which stimulate aggregate demand and thus the economy, could cause slow growth and economic stagnation. However, the problem concerning stagnation would not arise on the demand side of the economy, but rather on the supply side. If continual large-scale government borrowing were to crowd out business investment spending by absorbing too much of the available savings and driving interests rates up, the supply side of the economy — its ability to produce goods and services efficiently — would be impaired. This is a particularly important consideration in an economy such as Canada's, which must compete extensively with foreign producers.

(b) Increasing use of borrowing to finance the government's current expenditures

As noted above, a large proportion of federal borrowing was used to pay for current, as opposed to capital, expenditures. As early as 1980, when the federal deficit was only $10 billion, the Economic Council of Canada expressed concern regarding federal borrowing to cover current expenses. In its *Seventeenth Annual Review*, the Council noted that the result of such a policy is that "greater consumption by the present generation of Canadians is at the expense of future generations."

(c) Increasing indebtedness to foreign creditors

As the federal government's borrowing needs grew, there was an increasing tendency to turn to foreign creditors, by selling federal bonds outside Canada. As a result, the proportion of federal debt held by foreign creditors rose rapidly, from 2.5 percent of total federal debt in 1973 to 10 percent by 1985.

Another factor that contributed much more to Canada's growing international indebtedness was heavy borrowing abroad by Canadian *provincial* governments, and corporations. Many observers believe that this new trend was indirectly the result of the federal government's large budget deficits, which absorbed so much of Canadians' savings that other borrowers were forced to go outside Canada to issue bonds. Unlike the *internal debt* referred to earlier such foreign debt is *external*: the repayment of it, with interest, constitutes a future burden on Canadians.

(d) High interest costs on the debt

In 1974/75, 5 percent of the federal government's tax revenues were spent on the net interest costs of carrying the National Debt. By 1984/85, the figure had grown to over 25 percent. These heavy interest payments on the debt led to fears that the government would be forced to cut its spending on other programs that were considered important, in order to keep the deficit (and the debt and interest payments) from rising further.

Thus mounting interest payments on continually high federal debt can crowd out valued *government spending programs*, much as continued heavy government borrowing can crowd out business investment spending.

(e) Loss of fiscal flexibility

Another possible problem associated with the National Debt is that large deficits can make it difficult for the government to stimulate the economy. Instead of spending money to boost expenditures, or cutting taxes, the government can get tied down by the need to control its deficit. For instance, during the early 1980's, despite the highest unemployment rates in fifty years, the government did not attack the need for job-creation as aggressively as some people would have liked, largely because the deficit was too great to be allowed to increase further.

> The buildup of federal debt, if unchecked, will mean that over the next six years, 33 cents out of every dollar of federal revenue will be spent on servicing the public debt, even if interest rates are cut almost in half. Debt-service costs as a percentage of government expenditures are higher in Canada than in any major industrial country. The reality of compound interest rates is forcing the government to consider program cuts and tax increases to bring the deficit under control.
>
> Edward Carmichael,
> *Policy Review and Outlook, 1985: Time for Decisions,*
> C.D. Howe Institute, 1985.

(f) Fear of renewed inflation

A less immediate, but nonetheless important result of excessive borrowing by government is that it can eventually lead to severe inflation. If the government proves unwilling or unable to get its deficits under control through spending cuts and/or tax increases, the deficits will continue to grow to the point where they are too large to finance by borrowing. At this point, the government may resort to *printing money* to finance its deficits, giving rise to a wave of severe inflation. Such inflation would not only bring hardship to many Canadians, but also reduce the real value of the savings they had placed in government bonds. The government would then be repudiating part of its debt by repaying its bondholders with dollars depreciated by inflation that the government itself had caused.[3]

What to do about the deficits?

By mid-decade, there was widespread agreement that the federal government's budget deficits should be reduced, and that to do so would require some basic changes in the government's spending programs and in the tax system.

However, the agreement ended there. Some thought the problem sufficiently urgent to warrant a massive deficit-reduction program immediately, while others considered a gradual program more appropriate, due to the high level of unemployment. The Economic Council of Canada viewed the problem as a result mostly of past policy decisions that had undercut the government's tax revenues, and believed that *tax increases*

---

[3]One way that bondholders can protect themselves against inflation is to insist upon higher interest rates on their bonds, so that the higher interest income helps to protect them against the risk that their savings will lose real value due to inflation. Ironically, however, the higher interest rates also add to the costs of the federal government, and thus to the budget deficits that gave rise to this concern about inflation in the first place.

> The structural features of the federal government revenue system, particularly the indexation of personal income tax, has reduced its ability to increase federal revenues enough to cover the growing expenses of established programs. Without some changes in structure, as well as changes in fiscal policy, it is difficult to foresee a fundamental change in Canada's fiscal position.
>
> Economic Council of Canada,
> *Seventeenth Annual Review*, 1980.

(rather than cuts in government spending) were the appropriate policy. The government, on the other hand, decided that tax increases "must be avoided if at all possible", and stressed *curbs on spending* instead. However, it proved difficult to make significant cuts into established government spending programs. These programs enjoyed considerable popular support among the Canadian public, only 2 percent of whom viewed the deficit as a major problem, according to a 1985 poll.

By 1985, the government had moved to limit (not eliminate) the indexing of the personal income tax and some transfer payments, to increase a variety of taxes by relatively small amounts and to restrict the future growth of government spending in a variety of ways. Most of these deficit-reduction policies were designed to be phased in during the second half of the decade, when it was hoped that economic conditions would be better. Many observers, however, believed that more fundamental changes would need to be made to federal government spending programs and/or tax revenues in order to reduce the deficit significantly. Even the federal government indicated in its 1986 budget, that its next budget would contain reforms to Canada's social expenditures programs, which had previously been regarded as its highest priority.

Are budget deficits good or bad, then?

There is nothing inherently good or bad about budget deficits in themselves; their effect on the economy depends on their *size*, their *timing* and *how they are financed*. At their best, properly timed and responsibly financed budget deficits can help to lift the economy out of the periodic recessions from which it tends to suffer.

There is, however, an important difference between the periodic deficits described above and excessive and/or chronically large budget deficits, which can have negative effects on the economy.

Excessively large budget deficits financed by printing money will cause severe inflation, while chronically large deficits financed by regular heavy government borrowing can depress capital investment and generate economic stagnation. At their worst, chronically high budget deficits can have both the effects described above, thus contributing to an economic condition characterized by both stagnation and inflation—*stagflation*, which we will consider more fully later.

THE PERILS OF BUDGET DEFICITS

Budget deficits can be likened to drinking liquor, in that, at the appropriate time and used in appropriate quantities, they will not be harmful and can in fact be beneficial. However, as with liquor, excessive budget deficits can have severe side effects, including a "hangover" of severe inflation accompanied by stagnation, or *stagflation*. And, like a hangover, it can be considerably easier to get into this situation than it is to get out of it.

Despite concerns about Canada's large and persistent budget deficits since 1975, deficits remain generally accepted as an appropriate policy for dealing with economic recessions. This approach replaces the older view that the government should balance its budget at all times. It is now recognized that the latter would contribute to, rather than reduce, economic instability. For example, a recession reduces the tax revenues of the government (such as income and sales tax). To keep the budget balanced, the government must either reduce government spending or raise taxes, either of which would make the recession worse. Similarly, if the government spent all of its swollen tax revenues during a period of inflation, or cut taxes, it would stimulate demand excessively and aggravate inflation. Rather, the government should try to keep the level of aggregate demand at a reasonable level, supporting it with budget deficits when it is too low, and dampening it with budget surpluses when it is too high, while avoiding the dangers associated with excessive deficits.

DEFINITIONS OF NEW TERMS

Laissez-faire   The theory that the economy functions best without government intervention.

Fiscal Policy   The use of government spending and taxes (the government's budget) to influence the level of aggregate demand and thus the performance of the economy.

Budget Deficit   A government budget in which expenditures exceed tax revenues.

Budget Surplus   A government budget in which tax revenues exceed expenditures.

Balanced Budget A government budget in which tax revenues and expenditures are equal.

National Debt The overall indebtedness of the federal government, most commonly measured as the difference between the federal government's liabilities (mostly outstanding bonds) and its net recorded assets (mostly those which yield interest, profits or dividends).

Indexing (of Government Expenditures) The practice of increasing government transfer payments (such as pensions) to keep pace with increases in the Consumer Price Index.

Indexing (of Personal Income Tax) The practice of making annual adjustments to the personal income tax system, with the result that taxpayers' income taxes increase only if their real income increases, not if their increases in money income are offset by inflation.

Structural Deficit A budget deficit that is not cyclical (i.e.—anti-recessionary) in nature, but rather is built into the government's finances due to a fundamental imbalance between its revenues and expenditures.

CHAPTER SUMMARY

1. "Fiscal Policy" is the deliberate use of the governments' budget (tax revenues and expenditures) to influence the performance of the economy.

2. A budget deficit will increase the level of aggregate demand, and thereby combat recessions.

3. A budget surplus will depress the level of aggregate demand, and thus help to combat inflation.

4. A balanced budget has a neutral effect on aggregate demand, and is appropriate when neither an increase nor a decrease in aggregate demand is necessary.

5. Budget deficits can be implemented by increases in government spending and/or tax reductions, some of which ("automatic stabilizers") come into effect automatically when the economy slides into a recession.

6. The stimulus to aggregate demand from budget deficits spreads through the economy through the multiplier and accelerator effects, so that a temporary deficit can lift the economy into self-propelled growth again, through an effect known as pump priming.

7. Budget deficits can be financed by borrowing or by printing the necessary funds.

8. Contrary to wide belief, the National Debt is not to any significant

extent owed to foreign creditors, does not threaten the nation with bankruptcy, does not necessarily prove bad management or wasteful spending by government, and has in fact tended generally to decline as a percentage of GNP. In fact, properly managed government debt can be beneficial to a nation's economy and its people.

9. Since 1975, Canada's federal government has had very large and persistent budget deficits, much of which has become structural in nature.

10. These deficits raised concerns that they could force interest rates up, depress capital investment, increase Canada's indebtedness to foreign lenders, impose excessive interest costs on the government, make it impossible for the government to use fiscal policy to stimulate the economy, and in the long run, contribute to renewed severe inflation.

QUESTIONS

1. "Useless make-work programs ('digging holes and filling them up again') run by the government can be of economic value under certain conditions." What is the speaker's reasoning? Do you agree or not?

2. "According to Keynesian economics, taxes are no longer a means of raising revenues for the government." Comment on the foregoing statement.

3. Which of the following do you believe would have a stronger stimulative effect on the economy: a $100 million increase in government spending or a $100 million reduction in personal income taxes? Why?

4. Which of the two policies in (3) above do you believe would have a faster effect on the economy? Why?

5. "The problem with fiscal policy isn't the economics of it, which are reasonable. The problem is the politics of it—democratically elected governments simply can't be trusted to use fiscal policy responsibly." Why does the speaker believe this? Do you agree? Is this a danger in Canada today?

6. Why do you suppose the government indicated a preference for reductions in government spending over increases in taxes as a way to reduce the deficit?

7. If you had to reduce government spending to reduce the deficit, what types of spending would you cut? Why?

8. If you had to increase taxes, which ones would you increase, and why?

9. What is the present size of the federal budget deficit? Has it tended to increase or fall in recent years? Why? Is it still regarded as a serious concern? Why or why not?

10. Does the National Debt seem likely to reach the $400 billion level in 1990 that was projected in 1985? Why or why not?

11. The following table shows the government as having a balanced budget in year 19-1, and no accumulated National Debt from past budget deficits and borrowing.
Given the figures for government spending and tax revenues in subsequent years as shown in the table, fill in the columns for:
(a) the budget deficit or surplus in each year.
(b) the total National Debt at the end of each year.

($ billion)

Year	Government Spending	Tax Revenues	Budget Surplus (+) or Deficit (–)	National Debt
19-1	$100	$100	$ 0̶	$ 0̶
19-2	100	90	—	—
19-3	110	95	—	—
19-4	120	105	—	—
19-5	130	120	—	—
19-6	125	130	—	—

12. (a) At the level of aggregate demand represented by AD_1, the level of GNP and income is $80 billion, or _____ percent below the economy's potential, and the economy is in a state of _____.
(b) What would be the appropriate action for the government to take regarding its budget?
(c) Draw a new aggregate demand curve (AD_2) to represent the new situation that might result from the government's action in (b), and show on the graph how this new AD curve would affect:
(i) the level of incomes and GNP,
(ii) the level of prices.
(d) Explain why the effects referred to in (c) will occur.

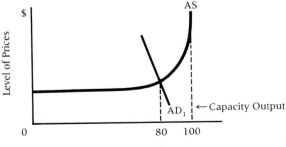

CHAPTER 10

Money and the economic system

In the last few chapters, we have paid much attention to the level of total spending, or aggregate demand, in the economy. A factor that will obviously have a great effect on the level of aggregate demand, and thus on the performance of the economy, is the total volume of money in circulation or the *money supply*. If there is insufficient money in circulation, the result will be inadequate aggregate demand and a recession or depression, while an excessively large money supply will generate excess demand and inflation. In the next chapter, we will examine the question of keeping the money supply at an appropriate level. First, however, this chapter will consider what money is, what it does for us and how it is created.

Part A: The nature and functions of money

The most common definition of money relates to its most basic function, which is a *medium of exchange*. By this, we mean that money is something (indeed, anything, as we shall see) that is generally accepted by people in exchange for (as payment for) goods and services. The simplicity of this function of money should not obscure its importance: without money, transactions would have to be conducted by barter, a system so awkward as to be virtually unworkable. Without an effective means of exchanging goods and services, people would not be able to specialize at producing those goods and services that they produce best and would not be able to exchange these products among themselves. This, in turn, would mean that productive efficiency in general—and society's material standard of living—would be far lower than it could be, because specialization adds greatly to efficiency.

Money is also a *standard of value*, or the yardstick by which we measure the value of a great number of diverse goods and services. Without money, using a barter system, the value of each product would have to be expressed in terms of every other product for which it might be exchanged: a horse might be worth two cows, or four sheepdogs, or forty bushels of apples, and so on. With money, the value of all items can be expressed in terms of one simple standard—the unit of currency, or the dollar. This makes it much easier to compare the values of different goods and services, and thus to make decisions concerning purchases of each of them.

Money also provides us with a *store of value*—a way to store purchasing power. Under a barter system, you must accept another good at the time you sell something; however, if you accept money, you can hold it until some time in the future when you choose to spend it. By thus allowing people to store purchasing power, money adds considerable flexibility to people's economic transactions.

In summary, then, it can be said that money not only adds a great deal of convenience to economic transactions, but also contributes indirectly to specialization and thus to our prosperity.

What can be used as money?

Different peoples, in different societies and at different times, have used as money things that seem quite strange to us, including shells, cattle, and heavy stone wheels. These examples show that money can be anything that people agree to use and accept as a medium of exchange. The one essential quality that something must have in order to function as money is *acceptability*: people must be prepared to accept it in exchange for goods and services. Certain characteristics help to make an item acceptable as money, including *scarcity* (which ensures value), *durability* (money that rots in your pocket is of questionable usefulness), *portability* (so that you can carry it around with you) and *divisibility* (for making change when necessary). However, as some of the above examples show, not all these characteristics are essential as long as the item is acceptable as money—neither heavy stone wheels nor cattle are particularly portable, durable or divisible (at least, not easily), yet they have been used as money because people agreed to accept them as money.

The evolution of money

Notwithstanding the exotic examples of money referred to above, most major currencies have developed in a similar manner, originating with precious metals and evolving into more sophisticated forms of money.

(a) Precious metals

Historically, many currency systems have originated with gold or silver. Because they are naturally scarce relative to the demand for them, gold and silver have a naturally high value. This is sometimes referred to as *intrinsic value*, meaning that people automatically associate such metals with value. It was this value of the money itself that gave the earliest forms of money their acceptability—someone who was asked to accept money in exchange for something of value (say, a horse) had to be confident that the money was as valuable as the horse.

Later, gold and silver were made into coins of standard weights and values. Using these coins was more convenient than weighing pieces of metal of different sizes. A more interesting development occurred, however, with the addition of other metals to the contents of the coinage . . . the *debasement* of the coinage. A king, needing money to finance a war or some other endeavor, would recall all of the currency for reminting into new coins. During the melting and minting, however, substantial amounts of other metals would be added, so that more coins could be minted than had previously existed. Thus, all the coins that had been taken out of circulation could be replaced, and the king could keep the surplus of money for his own purposes—a convenient, if not totally straightforward, way of raising royal revenues.

The debasement of coinage in this way presents an interesting problem—while the face value of each coin remains the same, it contains less gold, and has lost some of its intrinsic value. What will it now be worth? How much will it buy? The answer to this depends on whether people accept the coins at their face value in exchange for goods and services. If they do, the new coins will be worth their face value, and will function as money just as well as the pure gold coins did, because people have faith that they can spend the coinage at its face value. This is the case with coinage today: despite the fact that the metallic content of coins is far less than their face value, they are accepted at their face value in exchange for goods and services. Rather than *possessing* value, they are *representative* of value.

(b) Paper bills (bank notes)

The use of paper bills (bank notes) as money originated with goldsmiths, who performed some of the earliest banking functions. The goldsmith would provide safekeeping facilities for people who would deposit their money (gold) with him. In return, the goldsmith would issue a receipt, or bank note, for the gold as illustrated in Figure 10-1.

At first, people would withdraw their gold in order to buy things, but as they became more familiar with the bank notes, they found it much more convenient simply to exchange the bank notes for goods and services—to use these pieces of paper (bills) as money. Originally, the person to whom the note was issued had to sign it over to another person, but this practice was made unnecessary by the goldsmith making the notes payable "to the bearer"—a more convenient form for bills that would be used as money, and exchanged frequently.

FIGURE 10–1 *An Early Bank Note*

J. R. Goldsmith, Banker
will pay to Fred Flintstone
on demand
Twenty Dollars ($20.00)
in gold

(Signed)

J. R. Goldsmith

J. R. Goldsmith

Thus, paper bills, issued by private banks, came to be used as money. These were very special paper bills, however, because they involved a promise to pay gold to the holder of the notes. This *gold backing* of bank notes established the acceptability of paper bills as money. As we will see in Part B, however, it did not mean that there was $1 of gold for every $1 of bank notes in circulation.

Later, bank notes issued by private banks were replaced by bank notes issued by the government or, more correctly, by government agencies known as *central banks*. Originally, many countries maintained gold backing for the bank notes issued by their central banks.[1] As time passed, however, this practice became unnecessary, as people became completely confident in the paper bills. As well, the original system became impracticable, as the volume of money needed by growing economies far outgrew the available stock of gold. Consequently, there is today no gold backing behind the bank notes issued by Canada's central bank, the Bank of Canada. Bank notes no longer involve a promise to pay, but are instead *fiat money*, meaning that they must be accepted as payment for debts. This fact was given official recognition in the bank note issue of 1971: the new notes issued no longer said "Will pay to the bearer on demand," but rather said "This note is legal tender."

---

[1]The requirement that paper money be backed by gold also had the effect of limiting the amount of paper money that a government could print. Those who feared the tendency of governments to print too much money and cause inflation favored this limitation, while others believed that it would restrict the growth of the money supply too much and thus act as a drag on economic growth.

(c) Cheques (chequable bank deposits)

Are cheques money? Cheques *are* used to buy things; in fact, the vast majority of money transacted — 90 percent by volume — is by cheques. Obviously, then, cheques are widely used to settle transactions.

While many people would say cheques are money, this is not actually correct. If cheques were money, everyone would be able to write their own money without limit. Also, the cheque shown in Figure 10-2 will not stay in Mr. Framish's possession — it will be returned by the bank to Ms. Stuk, for her records. Thus, the cheque itself is not money.

FIGURE 10–2 *A Typical Cheque*

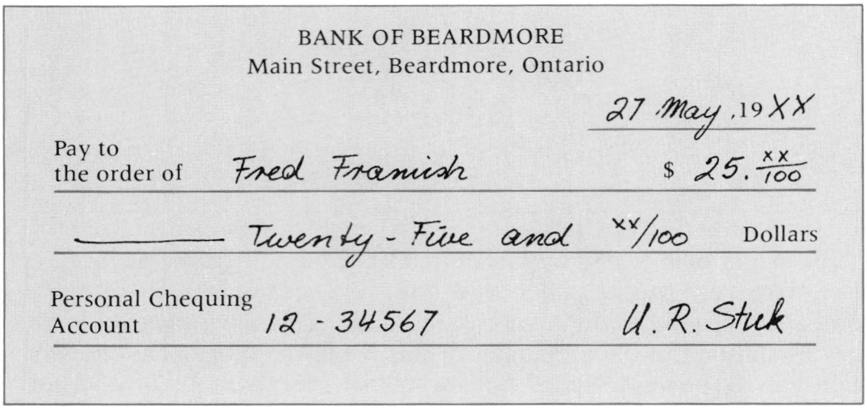

BANK OF BEARDMORE
Main Street, Beardmore, Ontario

27 May ,19XX

Pay to
the order of *Fred Framish* $ 25.$\frac{XX}{100}$

——— Twenty - Five and $^{XX}/_{100}$ Dollars

Personal Chequing
Account 12 - 34567 U. R. Stuk

If you read the cheque carefully, you will see that it is really simply a *letter* to the bank, instructing the bank to pay $25 to Mr. Framish. Figure 10-3 shows the cheque written in letter form.

FIGURE 10–3 *A Cheque is Really a Letter*

Bank of Beardmore   May 27, 19XX
Main Street
Beardmore, Ontario.

Dear Sirs:

Please pay Mr. Framish $25 of mine. You will find it in my account #12-34567.

Thank you,

U. R. Stuk

U. R. Stuk

What, then, is the actual money to be paid to Mr. Framish? He may cash the cheque, in which case he receives bank notes and coins, which we have already discussed. The more interesting case is that he might deposit it into his own account—what does he receive then? He will receive a deposit to his bank account, in the form of *book entries* on the bank's records. When Mr. Framish deposits the cheque, the book entry in his account will be increased by $25 and the book entry in Ms. Stuk's account will be reduced by $25. There is *no cash* involved in this transaction at all—just *book entries*.

Are these book entries in the bank's records money to Mr. Framish? This can be answered simply by asking if he can *spend* them. Of course he can, by writing cheques on them, as Ms. Stuk did.[2] So these chequable bank deposits (book entries) are money, and the banks can transfer it between people's accounts as instructed by cheques.

Many people tend to think that the book entries in bank books represent cash deposits (bills and coins) and that bank deposits are not therefore a separate form of money. In fact, this is not true—total bank deposits (book entries) *far exceed* the total amount of bank notes and coins in the economy. Also, these book entries constitute a separate and very important form of money, through which about 90 percent of the volume of transactions are made.[3] In Part B, we will examine the process by which these deposits are actually created.

Credit cards and the "cashless society"

Credit cards, like cheques, are things that are used to make purchases but that are not in themselves money. Credit cards, in effect, give the card-holder access to instant credit, or instant loans for the purchase of goods and services. However, the actual payment of these accounts is usually done by cheque, with the chequable bank deposit being the actual money involved.

A matter of considerable interest and controversy is the concept of the "cashless society," in which all transactions would be handled through credit cards and computerized book entries, with no cash used whatsoever. For example, a consumer would pay for a $50 item at Eaton's by processing his/her credit card through a computer terminal, with the result that, on the bank's computer, Eaton's bank account would increase by $50,

[2]This raises the question of the acceptability of cheques. Cheques are not acceptable everywhere (such as liquor stores), and not all cheques are acceptable (such as personal cheques of strangers). But, generally speaking, cheques are acceptable, and this makes the chequable bank deposits to which they refer money.
[3]A little thought leads one to suspect this. Sara's cheque for a new suit is covered by her deposit of a paycheque, written on her employer's account into which have been deposited more cheques (from sales), written on accounts into which people deposited their paycheques, and so on, with cash conspicuous by its *absence*.

the Government of Ontario's account would increase by $3.50 (for 7-percent sales tax) and the consumer's account would be reduced by $53.50. While such a process represents the most sophisticated form of money yet devised, there are doubts whether the public is ready to abandon cash totally. As well, there are concerns about the invasion of people's privacy, since all their transactions would be available to anyone with access to the computer containing the bank records.

Some things that are not money

We have said that, in Canada today, coins, bank notes and chequable bank deposits are used as money. To improve our understanding of what money is, we will look quickly at some things that are *not* money.

Stocks (corporate shares) and bonds are transferable financial securities, but they are not money because they are not used as a medium of exchange. This is because their value fluctuates, making their use as money too inconvenient.

Canada Savings Bonds do not fluctuate in value; they can always be cashed in for their face value (plus the interest that has built up to the time they are cashed). However, Canada Savings Bonds are not legally transferable from one person to another, so cannot be used as money. Financial assets such as stocks and bonds are not money: they can be converted into money by simply selling them, but the same thing can be done with any asset, such as a house or car.

Non-chequing bank deposits are not strictly considered to be money for the simple reason that you cannot buy things with them. Unlike deposits in a chequing account, these cannot be transferred to someone else. Of course, you could either shift the money into a chequing account or withdraw it in cash form, but then you would be using these as money rather than the non-chequing bank deposit.

"Near money"

Defining what is and what is not money is not a black-and-white issue. For instance, the non-chequing bank deposits, or *savings accounts* referred to above may not by strict definition be money, but they can certainly be converted into money very quickly. Similarly, *term deposits* (which the depositor has agreed to leave on deposit for longer periods, such as from one to five years) can be readily converted into chequable deposits, or money. These types of deposits, known for obvious reasons as "near money," complicate considerably our attempts to define and measure Canada's money supply.

Canada's money supply defined and measured

In defining and measuring the money supply we must remember that our main concern is that the size of the money supply is closely related to the level of aggregate demand, which is a major factor determining the performance of the economy. Until recently, the most-used definition of the money supply has included only funds that are immediately spendable: *currency* (notes and coins) *outside the banks* plus *demand deposits* (current chequing account deposits). This is shown in Figure 10-4 as **M1**, which is the narrowest definition of the money supply.

FIGURE 10-4   *Canada's Money Supply, December 1984*

	Billions of Dollars
Currency Outside Banks	$ 13.4
Demand Deposits	16.8
Total: M1	$ 30.2
Daily Interest Chequable Deposits and Non-Personal Notice Deposits	17.4
Total: M1A	47.6
Other Notice Deposits and Personal Term Deposits	98.6
Total: M2	146.2

SOURCE Bank of Canada *Review*, February 1985.

It is now agreed, however, that M1 is too narrow a definition, due to the development and rapid growth in recent years of other types of chequable deposits, particularly *daily interest chequing* deposits. Many Canadians now use such accounts in much the same way as they formerly used current chequing accounts — as immediately spendable funds for paying their bills. With a daily interest account, however, they can earn interest on these funds until they are spent. The second definition of money in Figure 10-4 — **M1A** — is defined as M1 plus these daily interest chequable deposits. M1A also includes *non-personal notice deposits*, comprising the interest-earning savings deposits of some businesses and charitable organizations which are often directly connected to chequing accounts. As Figure 10-4 shows, M1A is considerably larger than M1.

However, M1A still does not include a large volume of funds of the "near money" sort: *other notice deposits* (savings accounts) and *personal term deposits* (which people have on deposit for a specified period of time). When these are added to M1A the result is **M2**, which is much larger than M1A, as Figure 10-4 shows.[4]

---

[4]There are still other measures of the money supply, such as **M3**, which is M2 plus non-personal fixed-term deposits plus foreign currency deposits of residents booked in Canada. **M3 plus** adds to this deposits and notes at mortgage loan and trust companies and share capital at credit unions and caisse populaires.

Economists differ on which of these is the most appropriate measure of the money supply. The farther we move away from M1, the more funds we are including in our definition, but the more we are including funds that are more likely to be saved rather than spent, at least in the short run. From 1975 to 1982, the government used M1 as the official measure of the money supply. However, M1 is no longer used for this purpose, because it excludes many readily spendable deposits that have been developed recently, such as daily interest chequing accounts. Thus, the growth of M1 has tended to underestimate the potential level of aggregate demand in the economy. As of 1985, an alternative official definition of the money supply to replace M1 had not yet been developed.

The acceptability and value of money in Canada

As we have seen, only a small proportion of Canada's money supply consists of coins and bank notes; the vast majority of the money supply is in the form of bank deposits. We have also seen that Canada's money supply is not backed by gold—it functions as money because people have faith in it. People accept money in exchange for goods and services because they believe that they will be able to use the money to buy other goods and services of equivalent value. Ultimately, this confidence in money is really confidence in the monetary authorities of the country— that they will not issue an excessive amount of money, causing inflation that will reduce the value of money so that it ceases to be acceptable. This monetary authority—the Bank of Canada—has other and sometimes conflicting responsibilities, though, which are examined in Chapter 11.

While faith is what gives money its acceptability, the actual value of a dollar—what it is worth—depends on its *purchasing power*, or what it will buy. The purchasing power of the dollar, in turn, depends on the general level of the prices of goods and services. If prices in general rise, the value of the dollar will fall, because its purchasing power will be reduced.[5] Conversely, if the price level were to fall, the value of the dollar would rise. Thus, the actual value of the dollar is inversely related to the general level of prices.

Part B: How money is created

We have seen that only a small proportion of Canada's money supply— perhaps 10 percent—consists of bank notes and coins. Of much greater importance and interest is the vast majority of the money supply, which consists of *bank deposits*. Where do these come from? How are they created?

---

[5]The value of the dollar referred to here is its value in use inside Canada. The international value of the Canadian dollar—its value in terms of other nations' currencies—is a different matter, and will be covered in the chapters on international economics.

VARIOUS TYPES OF ACCOUNTS

Demand deposits

These are accounts from which funds may be withdrawn without giving notice to the bank or trust company, usually by cheque but also by cash withdrawal. Often called *current chequing accounts*, these are used as a temporary "parking place" for funds that are soon to be spent. Such accounts pay no interest but provide the service of returning cheques to the depositor for the purpose of record-keeping.

Daily interest chequable deposits

These accounts pay interest (usually monthly) which is calculated on the balance in the account each day. Cheques may be written on such accounts, and withdrawals are normally permitted without notice, although the institution may reserve the right to require notice (usually up to 30 days) of withdrawals. Such accounts are also used as a temporary holding account for funds, but one which pays interest on the money each day until it is spent. Cheques are not returned, however, to the depositor.

Other notice deposits

These are savings accounts, which pay higher interest than daily interest chequing accounts (although interest is usually calculated on the minimum monthly balance and paid twice yearly). These accounts do not carry chequing privileges and the depositor may be required to give notice of withdrawals. Such accounts are primarily used for saving money that is not expected to be spent often or soon.

Personal term deposits

These are deposits in which the depositor agrees to leave the funds on deposit for a fixed period of time (a fraction of a year or one to five years). In return, such deposits earn a higher rate of interest than other accounts; however, there is usually a penalty if the funds are withdrawn from the account earlier than had been agreed.

Non-personal notice deposits

These are savings accounts (used mainly by businesses and charitable organizations) which pay interest rates similar to savings-account rates on deposits.

Such accounts are often linked to chequing accounts, although depositors may be required to give notice of withdrawals.

These bank deposits, which far exceed the volume of cash in circulation, are in fact *created by the banking system, when it makes loans.*

The operation of early banks

To illustrate the process by which banks create money, we will use the early banks of the nineteenth century, operating in a simple situation in which money consisted of various types of coins and bank notes (paper bills) issued by privately owned banks. Like their modern counterparts, these early banks made loans in order to earn interest income. While borrowers could take their loans in the form of coins, they would much more commonly take *bank notes* such as the one in Figure 10-5—paper bills or promissory notes redeemable in coins of gold, silver or other metals considered acceptable.[6]

FIGURE 10–5 *A Typical Early Bank Note*

Bank of Beardmore

Will pay to the bearer of this note, on demand

Twenty Dollars ($20.00)

President

Bank loans create money

The creation of money by these banks arose from this fact: a bank could issue far more bank notes to borrowers than the amount of coinage, or cash, on hand at the bank to back the notes. This was the case for several reasons. First, relatively few holders of the bank notes would want to redeem them for cash. As people became familiar with the bank notes and accepted them in transactions, the notes would be used as money and would seldom be redeemed for cash. Second, while some holders of the notes would redeem them, other people would be making deposits into the bank. Therefore, the withdrawals would be offset by the deposits, enabling the bank to function with relatively little cash to back its notes. As a result, a bank would be able to operate quite smoothly with only a small amount of cash backing up a large volume of bank notes outstanding.

[6]Until the time of Confederation, Canada had no official uniform currency: the nation's currency consisted of a wide variety of coins and notes issued by various banks.

How many bank notes could such a bank issue on the basis of a given level of cash reserves? Obviously, the process is not unlimited: the more bank notes the bank has outstanding, the more notes will be redeemed for cash from time to time. While we have seen that this does not mean that all its notes must be backed by cash, the bank will have to back *a certain percentages* of its notes, to ensure that it is able to meet cash withdrawals by its customers. The cash kept on hand to cover withdrawals is called the **cash reserves** of a bank. The percentage of its bank notes outstanding kept as cash reserves is called its **cash reserve ratio**. Thus, if the banking system had $10 billion of bank notes outstanding backed by cash reserves of $1.2 billion, the cash reserve ratio would be 12 percent ($1.2 billion divided by $10 billion). On the basis of $1.2 billion of cash reserves, the banking system has expanded the money supply to $10 billion, creating money in the process of making loans as shown in Figure 10-6.

FIGURE 10–6 *Creation of Money by Early Banks*

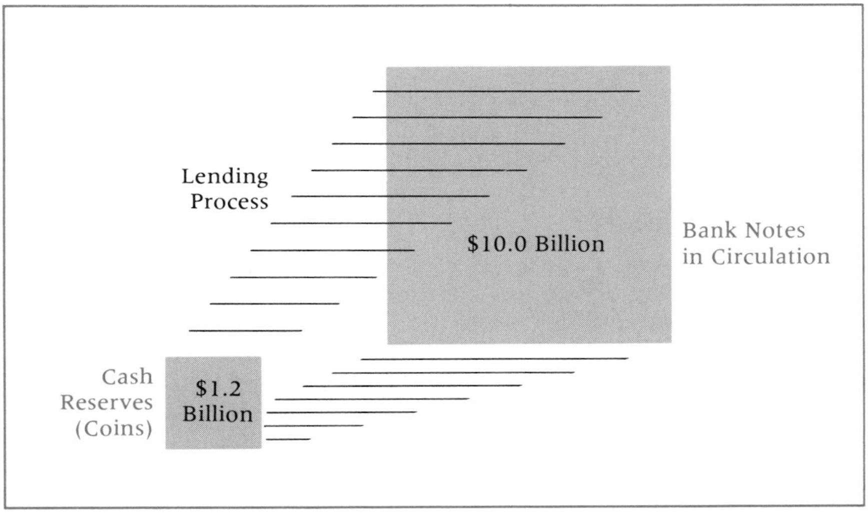

The creation of money by a modern banking system

In a modern banking system, the nature of money is more sophisticated than in our previous example. Bank notes are no longer issued by the banks, but rather by the government, and, as we have seen, roughly 90 percent of the money supply consists of bank deposits, or book entries, which are transferred between accounts by cheques. These bank deposits, however, are created in essentially the same way as bank notes were created by the early banks: through the process of making loans. When a modern bank makes a loan, the borrower does not usually get bank notes or coins (cash). Instead, the bank simply *increases the balance in the*

FIGURE 10–7   *Creation of Money by a Modern Banking System*

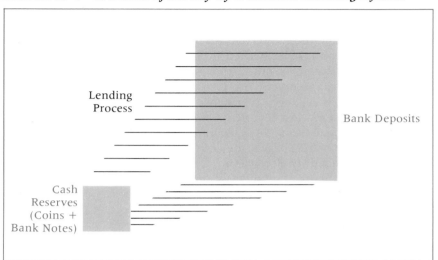

borrower's chequing account, thus giving the borrower more money (book entries) to spend. Using a small amount of cash (bank notes plus coins) as reserves, a modern banking system is able to create a large amount of money (bank deposits) as illustrated in Figure 10-7. Thus, the banking system can, on the basis of a small volume of cash reserves, create a large volume of money.

A formula for calculating the creation of money

How much money can the banking system create in this way? This depends on two factors: The volume of *cash reserves* that the banks have and the *cash reserve ratio* that they maintain. The extent to which the banking system can create money can be calculated from the following formula:

$$\textbf{Potential Total Deposits} = \frac{\textbf{Cash Reserves}}{\textbf{Cash Reserve Ratio}}$$

Thus, if the banking system had cash reserves of $2 billion and a cash reserve ratio of 10 percent, total assets could be as large as:

$$\frac{\$2 \text{ billion}}{.10} = \$20 \text{ billion}$$

Note that this represents *potential total deposits*: it is not certain that total deposits actually will reach $20 billion. For this to happen, the banks would have to make every loan that is mathematically possible — they must carry no excess cash reserves over and above the 10-percent ratio. Since we cannot know whether this will in fact happen, we must remember that our formula only indicates the potential amount of money that can be created by the banking system on the basis of a given amount of cash reserves and a given cash reserve ratio.

The cash reserve ratio and the money-creating process

From our formula, it can be seen that the size of the cash reserve ratio has a large impact on the amount of money that the banking system can create. If the cash reserve ratio had been only 5 percent, total deposits (and therefore the money supply) could have reached $40 billion ($2 billion divided by .05), or twice the level possible with a cash reserve ratio of 10 percent.

The reason for this is simple: because they have to keep *less* cash reserves on hand, the banks are able to loan out *more* money, so that total deposits can rise by much more, creating more money. On the other hand, as we will see, there are dangers in keeping too low a cash reserve ratio.

How can so little cash back up so many deposits?

How is it possible for a bank to operate safely with so little cash to back up its deposits? We have already seen the answers to this question, but it is worth summing them up here. First, people and businesses do make cash withdrawals, but there is a strong tendency for cash deposits to offset cash withdrawals. When a bank has a large number of depositors, it can be confident that while some depositors will be withdrawing cash from the bank at any given time, others will be making deposits of cash that will offset those withdrawals, maintaining the bank's cash on hand. Second, and most important, most transactions — about 90 percent by volume — use cheques, so that no cash needs to be taken out of the bank; all that is needed are changes in book entries. This reduces tremendously the need for cash, not only on the part of the public, but also on the part of the banks.

What size cash reserve ratio should a bank keep?

As we have seen, the lower the cash reserve ratio, the higher the level of loans and deposits can be. And the more loans, the higher the interest income of the bank. Accordingly, there is an incentive for banks to hold as few cash reserves as possible.

However, it is also true that it would not be wise to make the cash reserve ratio too low. Since their deposits far exceed their cash reserves, banks can only function successfully as long as they have the confidence of the public. Obviously, if the public's confidence in a bank were shaken, so that depositors wanted all their deposits out in cash form, that bank would run out of cash, and would *fail*, or go bankrupt. This is known as a *run* on a bank. A run will only occur if public confidence in the bank is shaken, and one way to avoid this is to keep adequate cash reserves so that it can always meet the requests of its depositors for cash. Thus, there is also an incentive for a bank to keep reasonably *high cash reserves,* for safety.

Banks must strike a balance between lower cash reserve ratios for interest income and higher cash reserve ratios for safety. Statisticians estimate that a 2-percent ratio will suffice for a large bank, but banks generally keep considerably higher ratios than that. In Canada, the law requires the banks to keep cash reserves that amount to approximately 4 percent of their deposits, plus another 4 percent in "secondary reserves," which are mostly short-term government promissory notes that are very safe investments and can quickly be converted into cash.

The banking system, the money supply and the economy

We have seen how the banking system, by increasing its lending activities, can cause the nation's money supply to increase. On the other hand, if the banking system were to curtail its lending, the money supply would decline. As outstanding loans were repaid, a decline in deposits, not offset by new deposit-creating loans, would occur.

The creation and destruction of money by the banking system, and the resultant changes in the money supply, are of great importance to the economy. If too much money is created, the result will be *inflation,* as spending is overstimulated and prices rise rapidly. Too small a money supply can slow down spending and economic activity to the point of causing a *recession.* The economy requires the proper money supply and an appropriate rate of increase if there is to be prosperity and economic growth without excessive inflation.

Since banks are privately-owned businesses seeking to make a profit, there is a risk that their lending decisions, while good business from the viewpoint of the banks, may not be suitable for the needs of the economy at certain times. For example, during periods of prosperity, both the banks and borrowers tend to be optimistic. Risks don't look nearly as serious when there are good times, so loans and the money supply tend to increase rapidly, perhaps too rapidly, with inflation the result. On the other hand, during a recession, the situation is reversed. Individuals and businesses are far less ready to borrow money, and banks are far less ready to lend it. Instead, the banks tend to keep some *excess reserves,* for safety's sake, rather than lend them out for interest income. The lack of loans can cause the money supply to shrink and cause a downward economic spiral.

Thus, an unregulated banking system tends to contribute to economic fluctuations and instability. This is because banking is an industry unlike any other. On the one hand, banks are private, profit-making corporations; on the other hand, they have the power to create and destroy money, thereby influencing the volume of money in circulation and the performance of the entire economy. As a result, the banks and the banking system are subject to an unusual degree of government regulation, which will be examined in Chapter 11.

DEFINITIONS OF NEW TERMS

Money Supply   The total volume of money in circulation, defined variously as **M1, M1A** and **M2**.

M1   The narrowest definition of the money supply, including only currency (bank notes and coins) outside the banks plus demand deposits (current chequing account deposits).

M1A   A wider definition of the money supply, including **M1** plus daily interest chequable deposits and non-personal notice deposits.

M2   A wider definition of the money supply, including **M1A** plus "near-money" items such as other notice (savings) deposits and personal term deposits.

Cash Reserves   That amount of cash kept on hand by a bank to cover day-to-day withdrawals of cash.

Cash Reserve Ratio   The percentage of total deposits that a bank keeps as cash reserves.

CHAPTER SUMMARY

1. The size of the money supply is of vital importance to the performance of a nation's economy, as too little money in circulation will cause a recession and too much will cause inflation.

2. Money serves three economic purposes: as a medium of exchange, a standard of value and a store of value.

3. The one characteristic that money must have is acceptability; characteristics that tend to make an item acceptable as money are scarcity, portability, durability and divisibility.

4. Money has evolved through various forms, from pure precious metals to impure metallic coins to paper bills (bank notes) to chequable bank deposits.

5. There are various definitions of the money supply, ranging from narrow ones such as **M1** and **M1A,** which include mainly currency plus chequable bank deposits, to wider definitions such as **M2,** which include savings deposits which, while not immediately spendable, are readily converted into chequable deposits and thus represent a potentially very large addition to the volume of spendable funds.

6. The bank deposits that represent approximately 90 percent of the money supply are created through the lending activities of the banking system.

7. The process of money creation by the banking system is made possible by the fact that banks can operate successfully with cash reserves that represent only a small proportion of their total deposits; thus it is possible to build a large volume of deposits on the basis of relatively small cash reserves.

8. The potential level of total deposits, or money, that can be created through the lending activities of the banks is equal to the banks' cash reserves divided by their cash reserve ratio.

9. Since the banking system's operations can increase or reduce the nation's money supply, they have a strong influence on the performance of the economy and are therefore subject to various government regulations.

QUESTIONS

1. If Canada Savings Bonds were legally transferable, what would be the major obstacle to using them as money?

2. During a war, more of society's scarce economic resources are used for government spending on military activities, leaving less for consumer goods and services. One way to pay for the war spending is to increase taxes, which obviously reduces disposable incomes and consumer spending. Another method, as we saw in this chapter, is to debase the currency, using newly printed money to pay for increased military expenditures. In this case, does the level of consumption fall? Why? Which method—taxation or debasing the currency— might be politically preferable? Why?

3. What objections do you think people might have to the introduction of the "cashless society" as discussed in this chapter? Why might the banks and government favor this idea?

4. In recent years, the prices of precious metals have risen rapidly. What problem could this create for coinage containing these metals, such as silver? What would the government have to do about this?

5. Do you think that "near-money" items such as savings accounts and personal term deposits have increased or decreased in size recently as compared to chequable deposits? Why?

6. What effect would a period of rapid inflation likely have on the role of money as a store of value, and on people's attitudes toward money generally? Why?

7. If, as the government, you wished to control the money supply:
   (a) What would be your objectives?
   (b) What would you have to control in order to control the money supply?

8. Under Canada's present economic conditions, do you think the money supply should be increased more rapidly or more slowly than the present rate of increase? Why?

9. Suppose Canada's money supply increased considerably faster than the USA's, over a period of several years. What consequences do you think this might have for the Canadian economy?

10.
   (a) If the cash reserve ratio were 10 percent and the banking system had $5 billion of cash reserves, the system's total deposits (and thus the money supply) could be as large as $_____ billion.
   (b) How can the banks' total deposits be so much larger than their cash on hand?
   (c) Suppose the cash reserve ratio were reduced to 5 percent. How would this affect the potential level of the money supply?
   (d) Explain the process whereby the size of the money supply would change as in (c).

11. From the data below, calculate:
    (a) **M1**
    (b) **M1A**
    (c) **M2**

Personal Term Deposits	$23 billion
Demand Deposits	8
Daily interest chequable deposits	4
Currency outside the banks	6
Non-personal notice deposits	4
Other notice deposits	24

CHAPTER 11

Stabilizing the economy: government policies to control the money supply

As we have seen, because the banking system is able to create money, it has a very powerful influence on the economic system. The creation of the appropriate amount of money is very important—an excessively large money supply will cause inflation, while too small a money supply will slow the economy down, causing unemployment and recession. We know that our economy has tendencies toward instability, owing partly to the fact that aggregate demand (particularly investment spending) tends to fluctuate, and at the end of Chapter 10 we saw that an unregulated, privately owned banking system can contribute significantly to these economic fluctuations. This occurs because the banks tend to make loans and expand the money supply during economic upswings—thus contributing to inflation and to restrict loans and the growth of the money supply during downswings—thus contributing to recessions and unemployment. In short, a privately owned unregulated banking system is not stable enough to be entrusted with the provision of the nation's money supply, which is a vital and sometimes delicate task.

Government regulation of the banking system

Accordingly, the federal government regulates the operations of Canada's chartered banks in several ways. While these regulations are quite complex,

THE BANK OF CANADA

Canada's central bank, the Bank of Canada, was established in 1934, when the Great Depression caused increased concern regarding economic and monetary management. Part of the central bank's mandate, according to the preamble of the Bank of Canada Act, was to

> ". . . regulate credit and currency in the best interests of the economic life of the nation . . . and to mitigate by its influence fluctuations in the general level of production, trade, prices and employment, so far as may be possible within the scope of monetary action, and generally to promote the economic and financial welfare of the Dominion."

The Bank of Canada is owned by the Government of Canada, and is managed by a board of directors that consists of the governor, the senior deputy governor, the deputy minister of finance and twelve directors. The governor is appointed for a seven-year term by the directors, with the approval of the federal cabinet. The relationship between the federal government and the Bank of Canada will be examined further later in this chapter.

The major function of the Bank of Canada, on which this chapter will focus, is to control the money supply of the nation. Another function is to act as a "bank for banks" — the Bank of Canada accepts deposits from the chartered banks and transfers these funds from the account of one bank to the account of another bank, thus acting as a means of settling debts between the chartered banks. The chartered banks' deposits at the Bank of Canada serve another important purpose: they (along with bank notes and coins held by the chartered banks) count as the cash reserves that the banks are required to hold. Usually, over 70 percent of the banks' reserves take the form of deposits at the Bank of Canada. In addition to these functions, the Bank of Canada, if necessary, will lend reserves to a bank that is temporarily short of reserves. While Canadian banks very rarely use this service, it is available to them from the central bank.

The Bank of Canada also acts as the sole issuer of Canadian bank notes and as the fiscal agent of the federal government. In this latter capacity, the Bank of Canada operates the deposit account through which government revenues and expenditures flow, handles the sale of government securities and acts as financial advisor to the federal government, as well as having other functions.

THE 1980 REVISION OF THE BANK ACT

The legislation governing banking in Canada is the Bank Act, which is revised every ten years. Some of the highlights of the 1980 revision of the Bank Act were as follows:

(a) **A reduction in reserve requirements,** from 4 percent on notice deposits and 12 percent on demand deposits to 3 percent and 10 percent respectively, with the first $500 million of notice deposits requiring only 2 percent and coins to be included as reserves. The effect of this change was to reduce the reserve requirements by about one-fifth, over a period of three-and-a-half years.

(b) **An additional reserve requirement** of 3 percent of foreign currency deposits held by Canadians in bank branches in Canada. In late 1980, these deposits totalled $12.5 billion.

(c) **Several changes affecting foreign banks operating in Canada.** Foreign banks, operating largely outside the requirements of the Bank Act, represented an increasing source of competition for Canadian banks — from 1974 to 1980, their assets had risen from $1.3 billion to $8.2 billion. Under the 1980 Bank Act revisions, the total size of foreign banks in Canada would be controlled by a requirement that their total Canadian assets be limited to 8 percent of "Canadian dollar and foreign assets booked in Canada with Canadian residents." This limitation would be effected through two other regulations: limits on foreign banks' capital (the amount of which must be approved by the governor-in-council) and limits on their assets (which may not exceed twenty-times their authorized capital). Various other regulations were effected regarding many matters, including the establishment of branches, the composition of boards of directors (at least half must be Canadian citizens ordinarily resident in Canada) and investments in shares of non-bank companies.

(d) **Consumer lending** became subject to a new requirement: the terms of a bank loan (with some exceptions) may not deny the borrower the right to repay the loan at any time. The rules for prepayment were to be prescribed later.

(e) **The formation of new banks** became subject to changed requirements. Prior to the 1980 revision of the Bank Act, a new bank could only be formed through the enactment of a private bill in Parliament. Under the revised Act, banks may be chartered through letters patent issued by the minister with the approval of the governor-in-council. One reason for this change was to provide greater flexibility in the granting of charters, as the Parliamentary process is very time-consuming.

they tend to fall into the following categories: limits on the formation of new banks, mandatory insurance on bank deposits, legal minimum cash reserve requirements, and, most important, control over bank lending and thus over the creation of money by the banking system.

(a) *Limits on the number of banks*

It is not as easy to form a bank in Canada as it is to start other types of businesses. Banks are chartered through letters patent issued by the minister with the approval of the governor-in-council. Applications for such letters patent are subject to rigorous standards, and may be subjected to a public inquiry. Alternatively, a bank may be formed by a special act of Parliament. One purpose of these requirements is to prevent the proliferation of a large number of small banks, many of which could be weak and susceptible to failure. Also, a banking system with relatively few banks is more readily influenced by the government than a system with many banks.

(b) *Deposit insurance*

All banks are required by law to be members of the *Canada Deposit Insurance Corporation (CDIC)*, which provides insurance on depositors' deposits of up to $60 000 per account. The insurance of deposits (or, more properly, the knowledge on the part of the public that their deposits are insured) prevents depositors from panicking and starting a *run* on the banks. As we saw in Chapter 10, even the soundest bank could not withstand a run, because it has deposits far in excess of its cash reserves.

(c) *Minimum cash reserve requirements*

The chartered banks are required by law to maintain the following cash reserve levels: 3 percent of *notice deposits*[1] (deposits that are not subject to immediate withdrawal without notice by depositors, such as most savings

[1]For notice deposits up to $500 million, the requirement is 2 percent.

accounts and term deposits), and 10 percent of *demand deposits* (deposits, such as chequing accounts, that may be withdrawn at any time by depositors). Because the banks have more notice deposits than demand deposits, these cash reserve requirements average out to roughly 4 percent of all deposits.

Not even the full amount of these cash reserves is actually kept on hand by the banks in the form of bank notes and coins. In fact, about 70 percent of the banks' reserves take the form of deposits (that is, book entries) at the Bank of Canada, the federal government agency responsible for overseeing the banking system. No interest is paid on these deposits.

In addition to their cash reserves, the banks may be required to keep *secondary reserves* of 0-12 percent of their deposits. These secondary reserves are mostly very short-term government promissory notes called *Treasury Bills*, which can be converted into cash very quickly. Since December 1, 1981 the banks have been required to keep secondary reserves of 4 percent of all deposits.

(d) The control of the money supply

As discussed earlier, it is important that some control be placed on the creation of money by the banking system, so that the money supply grows neither too rapidly nor too slowly for the needs of the economy. The federal government agency responsible for controlling Canada's money supply—the central bank—is the Bank of Canada. We will focus on the most important function of the Bank of Canada: its control of the money supply of the nation through its monetary policy.

Monetary policy

Monetary policy refers to the control of the money supply by the Bank of Canada. In exercising its monetary policy, the central bank has available to it several different approaches, including the following:

(a) open-market operations
(b) changing the secondary reserve ratio
(c) changing the Bank Rate and
(d) moral suasion

Each of these will be examined in turn.

(a) Open-market operations

By far the most important tool of monetary policy is the **open-market operations** of the Bank of Canada, which refer to *purchases and sales by the Bank of Canada of government bonds*. To understand these operations, we must first recall that, to control the money supply, the Bank of Canada must control the lending activities of the chartered banks. With the cash reserve ratio fixed by law, the amount of loans the banks can make depends on their *cash reserves*; thus, the key to controlling the money supply is to control the cash reserves of the banks. Should their cash reserves increase, the banks will be able to make more loans, expanding the money supply, whereas a reduction in the cash reserves would lead to a decline in the money supply, since the banks would be able to support fewer deposits and loans. Open-market operations are directed toward increasing or decreasing the banks' cash reserves and thus the money supply.

(i) **Open-market operations to increase the money supply** require the Bank of Canada to go into the bond market and *buy government bonds*. When the Bank of Canada places an order with a dealer for some bonds, it does not know from whom it will be buying them. Let us suppose, however, that the bonds are bought from private individuals. In exchange for their bonds, these individuals receive cheques from the Bank of Canada, which they deposit into their own chartered bank accounts. When the chartered banks in turn present these cheques to the Bank of Canada for payment, the Bank of Canada pays them by increasing their deposits (with book entries) at the Bank of Canada.

Since these deposits at the Bank of Canada count as their reserves, the banks are now in a position to make more loans, thus increasing the money supply. In fact, as we have seen, the banking system will be able to increase its lending, and thus the money supply, by a far greater amount than the increase in its cash reserves. This process is illustrated in Figure 11-1.

Since the chartered banks invest considerable amounts of their deposits in government bonds, many of the Bank of Canada's bond purchases will be from the banks themselves. In this case, the process is somewhat simpler, as the chartered banks receive funds from the Bank of Canada, and these are then deposited into their accounts with the central bank. As in our first example, the banks' reserves rise, enabling them to make more loans and increase the money supply.

When the Bank of Canada's policies are directed toward increasing the money supply by making loans easier to obtain, it is said to be using **easy money policies**, and the resultant situation is generally referred to as "easy money."

(ii) **Open-market operations to reduce the money supply** are the reverse of the policies described above. To reduce the money supply, the Bank of Canada *sells government bonds* in the open market. If these bonds are sold to the public, the buyers will pay the Bank of Canada with cheques drawn on their accounts in the chartered banks. When the Bank of Canada presents these cheques to the chartered banks for payment, payment is made by simply reducing the chartered banks' deposits (or reserves) at the Bank of Canada.

If this reduction in their reserves pushes those reserves below their minimum level, the chartered banks will have to cut down their deposits to correspond to the new lower level of their reserves. To do this, the banking system must cut back on its lending that gives rise to most of

FIGURE 11-1 *Open Market Operations to Increase the Money Supply*

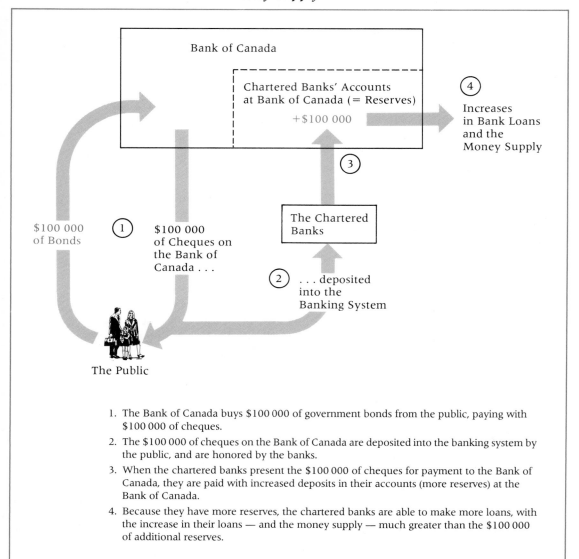

1. The Bank of Canada buys $100 000 of government bonds from the public, paying with $100 000 of cheques.
2. The $100 000 of cheques on the Bank of Canada are deposited into the banking system by the public, and are honored by the banks.
3. When the chartered banks present the $100 000 of cheques for payment to the Bank of Canada, they are paid with increased deposits in their accounts (more reserves) at the Bank of Canada.
4. Because they have more reserves, the chartered banks are able to make more loans, with the increase in their loans — and the money supply — much greater than the $100 000 of additional reserves.

its deposits. The result, as shown in Figure 11-2, is a reduction in the money supply.

Some of the bonds sold by the central bank will likely be purchased by the chartered banks. In this case, payment for the bonds is made simply by reducing the chartered banks' deposits at the Bank of Canada, with the same result: lower reserves and a reduced money supply.

FIGURE 11-2 **_Open Market Operations to Reduce the Money Supply_**

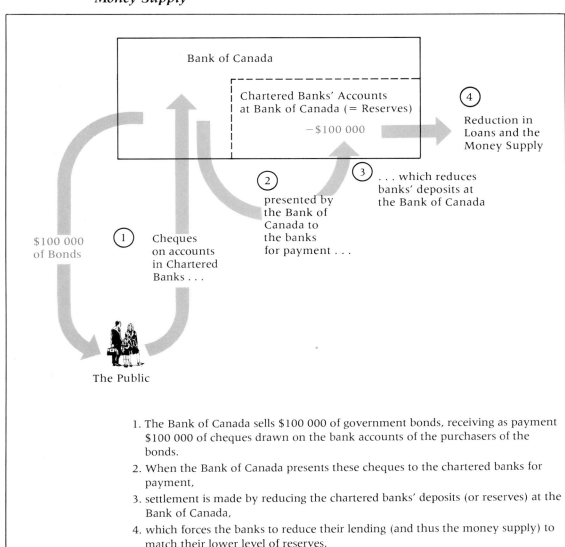

1. The Bank of Canada sells $100 000 of government bonds, receiving as payment $100 000 of cheques drawn on the bank accounts of the purchasers of the bonds.
2. When the Bank of Canada presents these cheques to the chartered banks for payment,
3. settlement is made by reducing the chartered banks' deposits (or reserves) at the Bank of Canada,
4. which forces the banks to reduce their lending (and thus the money supply) to match their lower level of reserves.

THE CANADIAN COMMERCIAL BANK: CANADA'S FIRST BANK FAILURE SINCE 1923

The Canadian Commercial Bank (CCB) was created in the mid-1970's as an Alberta-based "wholesale" bank providing loans mainly to small and medium-sized businesses. The bank started in a promising manner in the West's booming economy of the second half of the 1970's.

However, to expand rapidly in this competitive environment, the CCB pursued lending policies that were overly aggressive. Many of its loans were extended to dubious borrowers, on the basis of inadequate security (often overvalued real estate), out-of-date financial statements and incomplete credit studies.

When the oil and real estate industries in Alberta were depressed in the early 1980's by the combination of the recession and the National Energy Program, many of the CCB's loans became what bankers call *nonperforming*, meaning that borrowers were in arrears on principle and interest payments. The CCB's profits fell precipitously.

Faced with such nonperforming loans, the CCB resorted to some questionable methods of dealing with them. If a debtor had fallen behind on interest payments, the bank would renegotiate the loan, adding the overdue interest to the amount owed, in effect extending further credit to the borrower. It would then charge the borrower a considerable fee for renegotiating the loan, adding this amount to the loan as well. Thus, the bank was including in its reported income, as if they had been earned, fees that the bank itself had loaned to debtors, who were unlikely to ever be able to repay.

At the same time, the CCB began to have trouble with its depositors. Most of these were institutions such as other banks, pension funds and municipalities, which had been attracted by the high interest rates that the CCB paid on deposits. However, as confidence in the bank began to erode, withdrawals increased, forcing the bank to seek replacement deposits even more aggressively.

In retrospect, it is apparent that by this point the CCB had been in serious difficulty for some time. Later, there were questions raised as to whether the situation should have been detected by the regulatory authorities and prompt and strong corrective action taken. There were concerns regarding the experience and capabilities of the regional audit teams that were responsible for monitoring the CCB. These concerns increased when subsequent investigations revealed not only far more bad loans than had been thought to exist, but also a variety of unacceptable banking practices. Doubts were also voiced as to whether the regulatory authorities possessed sufficient resources and staff to adequately monitor the entire banking system. The CCB had been on the "watch list" of the Inspector General of Banks for two years, but no detailed inspection had ever been ordered. It was suggested that the regulatory authorities lacked the powers necessary to perform their function and also that they had been reluctant to take strong action, fearing that an open challenge to the bank's practices might further undermine investors' confidence and make the problem even more severe.

By March 1985, it was apparent that the CCB would go bankrupt (fail) unless some sort of rescue plan was worked out. Finally, the federal government and the governments of Alberta and British Columbia, with the help of the major banks, provided an infusion of funds intended to relieve the CCB of its bad loans and return it to solvency. However, the confidence that is so vital to a successful bank was fading rapidly and by August it had become apparent that the March bailout would not prove sufficient to save the CCB. Investigations revealed that, of the $2.4 billion in loans on the bank's books, about $1 billion was worthless. The CCB did not reopen its doors after the Labor Day weekend.

The position of the CCB's depositors presented a difficult problem for the government. In the view of some people, the depositors (most of whom were institutions which were aware of banking practices) should have known that such high interest rates on their deposits necessarily involved risks. Although the role of the Canada Deposit Insurance Corporation was to insure deposits only up to $60 000, the federal government itself moved to reimburse the CCB's depositors, who were seen by some critics of the government as victims of an inadequate regulatory process.

The failure of the CCB (and the Northland Bank, which also failed at about the same time) raised questions concerning Canada's regulatory system for banking. Following the debacle, the Inspector General of Banks sought increases in its staff (which numbered only 34 at the time) and in its powers, including the power that US authorities have to issue cease-and-desist orders. The Minister of State for Finance indicated that the government planned to increase the powers of bank regulators in Canada, to rebuild confidence in the banking system.

Bank of Canada policies intended to reduce the money supply by restricting the availability of credit are known as **tight money policies**. Because the economy and the appropriate money supply generally grow from year to year, however, it is not often appropriate for the Bank of Canada to actually reduce the money supply, except for quite short periods. The question, is more often *how rapidly* the money supply should be allowed to increase. When the Bank of Canada is seeking to slow down the rate of growth of the money supply by restraining the lending activities of the banks, these policies are also generally described as tight money policies.

Thus, the primary tool of monetary policy is the open-market operations of the Bank of Canada, in which purchases and sales of bonds by the Bank of Canada increase and decrease the banks' cash reserves, and thus the money supply. The Bank of Canada, however, does have other methods of influencing the volume of lending by the banks and thus the money supply, some of which are discussed in the following sections.

(b) Changing the secondary reserve ratio

As noted earlier, the Bank of Canada is empowered to require the chartered banks to maintain secondary reserves of 0-12 percent of their deposits. The more of their funds that they are required to place into secondary reserves (mostly very short-term government promissory notes, or *treasury bills*), the fewer loans the banks will be able to make. Thus, another way in which the Bank of Canada can influence the banks' lending and the money supply is by varying the required secondary reserve ratio: a lower ratio will permit more lending and a higher money supply, while an increase in the ratio will have the opposite effect, creating a tight money situation.

(c) Changing the Bank Rate

We have seen that, in its capacity as "a bank for banks," the Bank of Canada can make loans to chartered banks suffering a temporary shortage of cash reserves. The rate of interest paid by the banks for these loans is known as the **Bank Rate**. In theory, a higher Bank Rate would make the banks keep more excess cash reserves in order to avoid the need to borrow from the Bank of Canada, and would thus restrict the banks' ability to make loans and increase the money supply. In fact, this is not of any real significance, since the chartered banks only very rarely borrow from the Bank of Canada.

Rather, the importance of the Bank Rate to monetary policy has arisen from the use of Bank Rate changes by the Bank of Canada as *signals* to the nation of the direction of the central bank's policies. Until 1980, the Bank of Canada would periodically announce changes in the Bank

Rate. An announcement of an *increase* in the Bank Rate was taken as a signal of tighter money, with loans less available and more costly, whereas an announcement by the central bank of a *reduction* in the Bank Rate was seen as signalling a movement toward easier money, with loans more plentiful and less costly. These periodic announcements of changes in

FIGURE 11-3 *Short-Term Interest Rates*

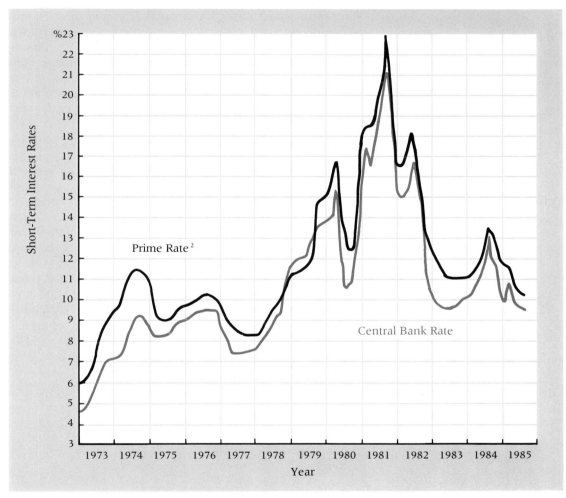

SOURCE   Department of Economic Research, *Canada's Business Climate,*
Toronto Dominion Bank and The Bank of Canada.

[2]"Prime rate" is the lowest interest rate charged by banks, to their most creditworthy borrowers.

the Bank Rate, which were often front page news, served as a way of reinforcing the monetary policy of the Bank of Canada.

In March 1980 the Bank of Canada changed its practice of fixing the Bank Rate at a certain level and periodically announcing changes in it. Instead of a fixed Bank Rate, there would be a *floating Bank Rate* that would change weekly, following fluctuations in the interest rate on federal government Treasury Bills. Each week, to finance its cash needs until tax revenues are received, the federal government borrows quite large amounts of short-term funds[3] through the sale of Treasury Bills. To raise these funds in competition with other borrowers, the federal government has to pay the current rate of interest on short-term funds. The floating Bank Rate was set each week at one-quarter of one percentage point above the rate of interest on Treasury Bills. If the rate of interest on Treasury Bills was 11.25 percent, the Bank Rate for that week would be 11.50 percent. As a result, the Bank Rate would change each week, depending on changes in short-term interest rates in general and in the interest rate on Treasury Bills in particular.

The interest rate on Treasury Bills is determined at the weekly auction of Treasury Bills held every Thursday, in which the federal government borrows the large amounts of short-term funds needed for its operations. These funds are raised through the sale of very short-term (91- and 182-day) promissory notes to the chartered banks (which hold them as secondary reserves) and investment dealers (who resell them, mainly to corporations with surplus cash to invest temporarily). Unlike bonds, these Treasury Bills do not pay a specified rate of interest; rather, *the interest rate (or yield) depends on the price paid* by buyers. For instance, a buyer who pays $965 for a $1000 91-day Treasury Bill will be repaid $1000, thus earning $35 interest on an investment of $965 over a 91-day period. The formula in Figure 11-4 calculates the effective annual rate of interest on this Treasury Bill as 14.55 percent. If this were the average yield on Treasury Bills at the weekly auction, the Bank Rate would be set for

FIGURE 11-4 *Calculation of Annual Interest Rate on a Treasury Bill*

$$\begin{aligned} \text{Annual Interest Rate (Yield)} &= \frac{\text{Interest Received}}{\text{Amount Loaned}} \times \frac{365}{\text{Term of Loan}} \\ &= \frac{\$35}{\$965} \times \frac{365}{91} \\ &= 14.55\% \end{aligned}$$

[3]**Short-term funds** are loans payable in one year or less. At the beginning of the 1980's, the federal government was borrowing over $800 million worth of such funds per week through Treasury Bills, most of which were repayable in 91 days.

FIGURE 11-5 *Higher Treasury Bill Prices Mean Lower Interest Rates*

$$\text{Annual Interest Rate (Yield)} = \frac{\$25}{\$975} \times \frac{365}{91} = 10.28\%$$

the week at 14.80 percent (one quarter of a percentage point higher than the Treasury Bill rate).

Short-term interest rates, and the rate on Treasury Bills, fluctuate with the supply of and demand for short-term funds. If funds are plentiful and not in high demand, interest rates will be lower. Competing for an opportunity to lend funds to the federal government, lenders will *bid up* the price of Treasury Bills at the weekly auction. Figure 11-5 shows that, if the price of Treasury Bills were bid up to $975, the rate of interest on them would fall to 10.28 percent—which would push the Bank Rate down to 10.53 percent. Conversely, if short-term funds are scarce and interest rates are high, lenders will be less anxious to buy Treasury Bills, so their price will be lower, making the interest rate on them higher. Thus, as short-term interest rates fluctuate, so will the Bank Rate.

However, the Bank of Canada can and does influence the level of the Bank Rate. For instance, suppose that the auction process tends to result in lower Treasury Bill prices—and thus higher interest rates and a higher Bank Rate—than the Bank of Canada is prepared to accept, for economic or political reasons. In these circumstances, the Bank of Canada will enter the auction as a buyer of Treasury Bills, bidding their price up and thus pushing the interest rate on them down, so as to keep the Bank Rate down to the level desired by the Bank of Canada. It is because the Bank of Canada is known to be influencing the floating Bank Rate in this way that the weekly movements of the Bank Rate are still regarded as significant by bankers, investment dealers and others who are concerned with interest rates and monetary policy.

The Bank of Canada's move in 1980 to a floating Bank Rate that changed weekly marked a departure from past practice, which had involved infrequent but major announcements of Bank Rate changes by the Bank of Canada. At the time of the change to a floating Bank Rate, interest rates were unpopularly high and expected to rise even higher in the near future. While it was argued that the weekly changes of the Bank Rate were more suited to a situation in which interest rates were changing rapidly, others believed that the reason for the change was political. Under a floating Bank Rate, it would not be necessary to have periodic announcements of major interest-rate increases, which might be blamed by the public on the federal government or its agency, the Bank of Canada.

(d) Moral suasion

Moral suasion refers to attempts by the Bank of Canada to persuade the managements of the chartered banks to voluntarily cooperate with the central bank's objectives regarding lending policies, interest rates or any other aspect of monetary policy. Due to the fact that there are so few banks in Canada, it is relatively simple for the Bank of Canada to discuss its objectives with the banks with a view to enlisting their support, which they are expected to provide.

In summary, the Bank of Canada influences the nation's money supply through various policy approaches including open-market operations, changes in the secondary reserve ratio, changes in the Bank Rate and moral suasion. By using these policy measures, the Bank of Canada can generate easy money, in which lending by the banks and the money supply expand more rapidly, or tight money, in which loans are scarce and the money supply rises slowly or even declines.

Easy money, tight money and interest rates

During a period of easy money, when the banks have plentiful reserves and are ready to make numerous new loans, interest rates tend to fall, to encourage borrowers to borrow additional funds. Thus, easy money tends to involve two characteristics — *increased availability of loans* and *lower interest rates* — both of which tend to stimulate borrowing and spending by consumers and businesses.

During a period of tight money, the scarcity of loans causes interest rates to rise, so that the available loans tend to go to better credit risks and the highest bidders among them. These two characteristics of tight money — *reduced availability of loans* and *higher interest rates* — both tend to depress borrowing and spending by consumers and businesses.

Thus, monetary policy can influence the money supply through either the supply of loans or the demand for them. By increasing or reducing the banks' reserves, the Bank of Canada can influence the availability (or supply) of loans, and by altering interest rates, the Bank of Canada can influence the demand for loans. In its actual operations, the Bank of Canada functions in both ways, influencing both the availability and the cost of credit.

How the Bank of Canada's monetary policies affect the economy

The effects of easy money

Easy-money policies are used to stimulate bank lending and spending by consumers and businesses at times when the economy is in a recession and unemployment is unusually high. If the easy-money policies cause aggregate demand to increase, real output will rise more rapidly and unemployment will decline.

These beneficial effects of easy money are, however, not automatic. If the economy is in quite severe recession and expectations regarding the future are gloomy, consumers and businesses may be reluctant to borrow and spend money. Also, the banks may choose to hold some excess reserves rather than make loans that might prove risky due to poor economic conditions. Thus, easy money merely increases the banks' reserves and makes more loans possible; it does not automatically create money and boost aggregate demand. This problem has been likened to "pushing on a rope," which suggests that easy money by itself may not always be sufficient to lift the economy out of a recession. For this reason, many people believe that easy money should be combined with a *federal budget deficit*, which can provide a more direct boost to aggregate demand and can thereby start the economy on its way toward recovery.

When easy money does generate higher aggregate demand, the results are not totally beneficial: a side effect of the increased total spending may be *more rapid inflation*. While the reduced unemployment from the easy-money policies may make some additional inflation acceptable, this side effect does place a limit on the use of easy money, as excessive use of these policies can result in severe inflation. In Chapter 15, we will examine this trade-off between unemployment and inflation more closely; for now, it is enough to note that while easy-money policies do reduce unemployment, they cannot be pushed too far without causing other problems. Of course, if the economy were already at or near full employment, the added demand could not cause output and employment to rise much further, so it would generate mostly more severe inflation.

In summary, then, easy-money policies can be helpful in lifting the economy out of a slump; however, they may need assistance from fiscal policies (through a budget deficit) and they will likely generate some inflation as a side effect of the higher levels of aggregate demand.

The effects of tight money

Tight-money policies are used to slow down (or even reduce) bank lending and spending by consumers and businesses during periods when excessive aggregate demand is generating unusually rapid inflation. By holding down the demand for goods and services, tight-money policies can help to slow down inflation.

This effect of tight money on the rate of inflation will not always occur automatically, though. If expectations regarding the future are favorable, consumers and businesses may *continue to borrow and spend* despite high interest rates. This is particularly likely to happen if they expect prices to continue to rise and are prepared, therefore, to borrow in order to "buy now, to beat inflation." Despite having their cash reserves reduced by a tight-money policy, the banks may be able to *continue lending*. If they had been carrying some excess reserves before the tight-money policy, they may still have enough cash reserves left to continue expanding their lending, thus frustrating the tight-money policy.

When tight-money policies do succeed in depressing the level of aggregate demand, their effects are not all beneficial. While such policies will help to slow down inflation, a side effect of the depressed level of aggregate demand will be *slower economic growth* and *higher unemployment*. These tend to be costly politically as well as economically. Indeed, it is fair to say that the major limitation on policies to combat inflation is that they tend to increase unemployment — a problem which we will look into further in a later chapter.

This is not the only problem associated with tight-money policies, however. Tight money does not affect all sectors of the economy evenly; it hits some much harder than others. First, *small businesses* are affected considerably more severely by tight money than are big corporations. Because they generally exercise more control over the price of their product, big businesses tend to have higher rates of profit that enable them to finance much of their investment spending out of profits, or retained earnings. Small businesses, on the other hand, tend to have smaller profit margins and therefore be more dependent upon borrowing to finance capital investment projects and less able to afford high interest rates. As a result, the scarcity of credit and high interest rates associated with tight money tend to hurt small businesses more than big corporations.

FIGURE 11-6 *Monthly Payments on a 25-year $50 000 Mortgage at Various Interest Rates*

Interest Rate	Monthly Payment
8%	$385.91
9%	419.60
10%	454.35
11%	490.06
12%	526.61
13%	563.92
14%	601.88
15%	640.42
16%	679.44
17%	718.90
18%	758.71
19%	798.84
20%	839.23

Tight money also affects some industries more severely than others. *Construction* is probably the industry most severely affected by tight money, because high mortgage rates and scarce credit discourage the buying of new homes and commercial and industrial buildings. Because investment spending is depressed by high interest rates, tight money also tends to have bad effects on all the *capital-goods industries*, such as building materials and industrial equipment. In the *consumer-goods sector*, the effects of tight money fall the hardest on the big-ticket items such as cars and appliances, which involve considerable borrowing and are often tied to sales of new houses.

Governments seeking to combat inflation with tight money often encounter political problems due to the *high mortgage interest rates* associated with such a policy, which are especially burdensome to prospective home buyers. As the table in Figure 11-6 shows, rising mortgage interest rates have a dramatic effect upon the monthly payments faced by homeowners. While home buyers are hardest hit, all borrowers are adversely affected by high interest rates. This problem is really a political one more than an economic one, but this political reality places a limit on the level of interest rates and, thus, on the effectiveness of tight money as an anti-inflation weapon.

In summary, then, tight-money policies are used to combat inflation by depressing the level of aggregate demand. While these policies will slow down inflation, they also tend to slow down the economy and increase unemployment, and they have particularly severe effects upon certain industries. While these facts tend to make tight money politically unpopular, we will see in Chapters 13 and 14 that tight money is widely regarded as essential to any successful anti-inflation program. Indeed, some economists believe it to be the only really effective anti-inflation policy.

Monetary policy: who should call the shots?

Obviously, the conduct of monetary policy is extremely important to the nation's economy. A properly conducted monetary policy can be very beneficial, whereas errors in monetary policy can have severe effects on the economy, due to the creation of either too much or too little money.

Who should make such important decisions? Some people believe that the *financial experts* at the Bank of Canada, who possess specialized knowledge of monetary matters, should have the responsibility and the power to decide the nation's monetary policy. Other people argue that such important policy decisions should not be made by the appointed officials at the Bank of Canada, but rather by *the government*, which was elected by (and is ultimately responsible to) the people.

The question of who possessed the final responsibility and authority for monetary policy remained somewhat vague until 1960, when matters came to a head in the celebrated *Coyne affair*. James Coyne, governor of the Bank of Canada, was pursuing a tight-money policy at the same time as the federal government was trying to stimulate the economy with budget deficits. When Coyne refused to alter the Bank of Canada's policies, the government in effect dismissed him by introducing legislation declaring his position vacant. By this act, the government established itself as the final authority in the area of monetary policy. This was given legislative authority in amendments to the Bank of Canada Act in 1967, which stated that in the event of disagreement between the government and the Bank of Canada, the government can direct the central bank in writing as to the monetary policy to be followed.

Supporters of the government's authority over the Bank of Canada argue that, without this authority, the government cannot ensure that the Bank of Canada's monetary policy is consistent with the federal government's fiscal policies, and point to the Coyne affair as evidence on their behalf. Critics of the government's authority over monetary policy fear that political pressures to minimize unemployment will tend to cause elected governments to expand the money supply too rapidly, generating inflation. They point to the exceptionally rapid growth of the money supply and accelerating inflation since the late 1960's, in support of their position.

Thus, for better or worse, the Government of Canada has the final say regarding monetary policy. This should not be interpreted as meaning that the Bank of Canada simply takes orders from the government, however — the expertise of the central bank's staff and officials gives them considerable influence over the government's policies.

Monetary and fiscal policy combined

In Chapter 9, we saw how the federal government's Department of Finance uses fiscal policy to influence the level of aggregate demand in the economy. Since the monetary policy of the Bank of Canada discussed in this chapter also influences aggregate demand, we should review briefly how monetary and fiscal policies can interact so as to affect the performance of the economy.

During a recession, when aggregate demand is inadequate, a *budget deficit* (achieved through increased government spending and/or tax reductions) is usually combined with an *easy-money* policy consisting of lower interest rates and increased availability of loans. The objective of these policies is to increase the demand for goods and services by households and businesses. This increase in spending will be added to by the respending effect of the multiplier, and will be in large part financed by increases in the money supply resulting from increased bank lending. Also, it is possible that increased consumer spending may cause businesses to increase their investment spending (the accelerator effect), a process which would also be financed by the increased money supply through bank lending, encouraged by reductions in interest rates on loans. The overall result would be to stimulate output and employment in the economy.

During a period of inflation, aggregate demand for goods and services is so high that the supply of them cannot keep pace, with the result that prices rise with unusual rapidity. To combat inflation, a combination of a *budget surplus* (tax revenues in excess of government spending) and *tight money,* with loans relatively scarce and interest rates high, is appropriate. The objective of these policies is to depress the demand for goods and services, so as to relieve the pressure of excess demand on the supply and on the prices of goods and services. Government spending will be held down, while tax increases and high interest rates will restrain borrowing and spending by consumers and businesses. With total demand depressed in these ways, the rate of inflation will tend to decrease.

Figure 11-7 shows how the fiscal policy of the Department of Finance and the monetary policy of the Bank of Canada can be combined to affect the economy's performance. By coordinating the two types of policy,

FIGURE 11–7   *Monetary and Fiscal Policy Combined*

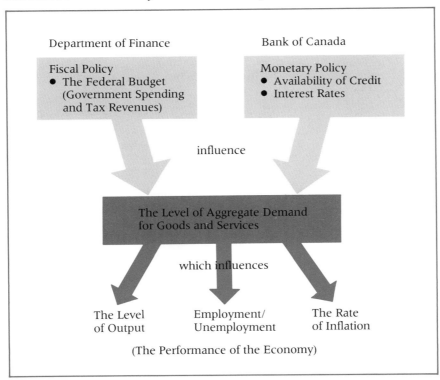

the effect can be made considerably stronger than if either were used by itself.

Financing budget deficits by "printing money"

Until now, we have considered federal government budget deficits and increases in the money supply as separate operations, with fiscal policy the responsibility of the Department of Finance and monetary policy the responsibility of the Bank of Canada. In actual fact, however, these two operations are often closely connected, because federal budget deficits are sometimes partly financed by increasing the money supply, or by "printing money," as referred to in Chapter 9.

Budget deficits do not always lead to an increase in the money supply. In Chapter 9, we saw that the federal government could finance its budget deficits by borrowing the savings of the public. In this case, the government borrows money from the public, deposits it into the government's account at the Bank of Canada, then spends the money, which finds its way back

FIGURE 11-8 *Financing Budget Deficits by Printing Money*

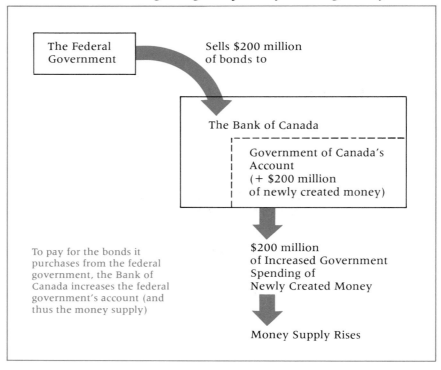

into the banking system as deposits. This operation has no effect on the money supply: while money that was already in existence is transferred around, *no new money is created.*

However, not all federal budget deficits are financed in this way—sometimes the federal government sells bonds *to the Bank of Canada* rather than to the public. To pay for these bonds, the Bank of Canada simply increases the amount of the deposits in the federal government's account at the central bank. Thus, the federal government receives in its account *newly created money* (book entries). When it spends these (through cheques), newly created money will be injected into the banking system, and the money supply will rise as illustrated in Figure 11-8.

When the federal government finances its budget deficits by selling bonds to the Bank of Canada and thus increasing the money supply, it is popularly said to be financing its budget deficits by printing money. Should the government finance its expenditures in this way? There is no simple answer to this question. During a serious recession, increases in both government spending and the money supply can be beneficial, because they boost aggregate demand, output and employment. On the other hand, as we have seen, excessive increases in the money supply can cause severe inflation. Also, there could be a political temptation for governments to resort to printing money to finance budget deficits: it is politically easier than raising taxes (which is always unpopular) or borrowing money (which must be repaid and involves interest costs).[4] True, the increase in the money supply will contribute to inflation,[5] but the public tends to blame inflation on labor unions and business rather than on government policies.

Too great a growth in government debt puts the Bank of Canada in an awkward position. If the market can't or won't pick up the bond issues on the terms offered then the Bank (of Canada) must. The danger is that money may be created at a faster rate than is probably desirable and an increase in inflation becomes inevitable at some point down the road.

Bank of Montreal
Business Review, June 1980.

---

[4]While by printing money in this way, the government still sells bonds, the money is owed and the interest must be paid to the Bank of Canada. Since the Bank of Canada is owned by the federal government, the government, in effect, *owes money and pays interest to itself.* Thus, the only real effect on the government's finances of selling bonds to the Bank of Canada is that the government obtains newly-created money (in the form of new book entries in its Bank of Canada account).

[5]In effect, the public pays for its apparently free government services through higher prices for other goods and services; that is, through inflation rather than taxation.

In summary, it is reasonable to conclude that, while the federal government need not totally refrain from financing its budget deficits by printing money, it should certainly avoid doing this excessively. Such a policy is appropriate only when the economic circumstances warrant it, and not simply to avoid increasing taxes for political reasons.

Monetarism: a new focus for economics?

For many years following the Great Depression of the 1930's, the focus on economics was on *recession*, and the main concern of economic policy was to combat recessions. The key elements of this emphasis were Keynesian fiscal policies, particularly budget deficits to boost aggregate demand and lift the economy out of recessions. Fiscal policy was regarded as the active ingredient of economic policy, whereas monetary policy was seen as playing a secondary role, attracting much less attention.

After the early 1970's, however, the importance attached to the money supply and to the Bank of Canada's monetary policies increased dramatically. This is because the most serious problem of this period was severe *inflation*, associated with exceptionally rapid increases in the *money supply*. This drew critical attention to the Bank of Canada's monetary policies, which its critics saw as having caused severe inflation by allowing excessively rapid growth of the money supply. These critics are often called "monetarists," and their theories monetarism —a term subject to varying interpretations. In its milder forms, it refers simply to an increased emphasis on controlling the growth of the money supply in order to restrain inflation. Its more extreme proponents insist that only excessive increases in the money supply cause inflation, that only curbs on money-supply growth can combat inflation, and that the government should never increase the money supply at rates above a specified limit.

Monetarism in Canada

In Canada in the early 1970's, the money supply expanded at a very rapid rate, and the Bank of Canada continued to allow the money supply to increase rapidly even after inflation became rampant, especially in 1974 and 1975. Critics of the Bank of Canada's policies argued that such a sudden expansion of the money supply would only worsen an already seriously inflationary situation.

By the fall of 1975, inflation was such a severe problem that reassessment of the Bank of Canada's policies seemed necessary. In what was regarded as a landmark speech in September 1975, the Governor of the Bank of Canada, Gerald Bouey, said that, "Whatever else may need to be done to bring inflation under control, it is absolutely essential to keep the rate

MILTON FRIEDMAN (1912-)

Milton Friedman was born the son of immigrant garment workers in New York, and went on to win the Nobel Prize for Economics in 1976. Given this rise from poverty to celebrity, it is not surprising that his theories reflect a strong belief in economic freedom and the virtues of the marketplace.

After receiving his Ph.D. in 1946 from Columbia University, Friedman returned to teach at the University of Chicago, where he had obtained his M.A. There, he became the leader of what has become known as the "Chicago School" — a group of economists which argues strongly for less government intervention in the economy. According to Friedman, such government regulation usually winds up benefiting certain private-interest groups at the expense of the general public interest. The public interest, the Chicago School argues, would be better served by free and open competition than by well-intentioned but counterproductive government regulations which tend to restrict competition and reduce efficiency.

Friedman is most noted for his work on monetarism, which gained prominence during the inflationary 1970's. According to the Chicago School, monetary policy is a large-scale example of how government intervention in the economy can have disastrous results. They point to both the Great Depression of the 1930's, when the authorities reduced the US money supply by about one-third, and the Great Inflation of the 1970's, when the money supply was expanded extraordinarily rapidly, as examples of the harm that can be done by government intervention in the economy. According to monetarists, it would be in the long-run interests of society if the money supply were allowed to increase at only a certain rate each year, as this would avoid the excesses that are possible under the present system. By preventing monetary instability in this way, they argue, a stable financial and economic environment could be established, in which confidence and longer-run decision-making (especially capital investment) could flourish.

While not all economists would agree with the policy prescriptions of Friedman and the monetarists, many regard their views as a healthy counterbalance to those who see increased government intervention and regulation as the answer to all economic problems.

of monetary expansion within reasonable limits. Any program that did not include this policy would be doomed to failure. There is no way of preserving its value if money is created on an excessive scale."[6] In the view of some, the Bank of Canada had undergone a conversion to monetarism; at the least, the Bank had stated an intention to guard more watchfully against excessive increases in the money supply in the future, by keeping the growth of the money supply within publicly stated limits.

Which measure of the money supply to use?

Unfortunately, the matter does not end here. As we saw in Chapter 10, there are different definitions of money supply, ranging from the narrowest (M1), which includes only currency plus demand deposits, to broader definitions such as M2, which includes non-chequing savings deposits and personal term deposits. These definitions and the size of the money supply according to the various definitions are reviewed in Figure 11-9. Due to the great difference in the sizes of M1 and M2, it is obviously

FIGURE 11-9 *The Different Sizes of M1, M1A and M2
December 1984*

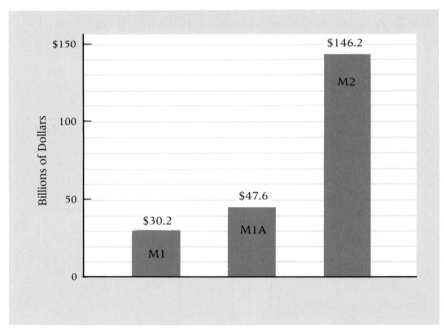

[6]Bank of Canada *Review*, November 1980 (page 9).

important that the Bank of Canada select the appropriate one as its target for its measurement and control of the money supply.

From 1975 to 1982, the Bank of Canada used M1 as its target for monetary policy. In the 1978 Annual Report by the Governor of the Bank of Canada to the Minister of Finance, Gerald Bouey stated that M1 has been chosen because "it moves with the trend of aggregate spending in the economy in a fairly predictable manner and it is susceptible to control by the central bank through the adjustment of short-term interest rates. . . . Our experience to date in using M1 has confirmed in my mind its usefulness as a proximate target in the conduct of monetary policy." In short, the Bank of Canada regarded M1 as the most relevant measure of the money supply because it includes those most immediately spendable funds (currency plus demand deposits) that have the greatest influence on the level of aggregate demand in the economy, and thus on the performance of the economy.

By 1980, however, M1 was no longer viewed as a reliable measure of the money supply. A combination of high interest rates, computer technology and competition among financial institutions had led to the development of new types of deposits, most notably daily interest chequing deposits. These were attracting large volumes of funds out of current accounts that pay no interest (that is, M1) and into M1A, which includes such deposits. Thus, it became accepted that M1 had become a deceptively low indicator of the volume of readily spendable funds and purchasing power in the economy. This is reflected in Figure 11-10, which shows the more rapid growth of M1A and especially M2 as compared to M1.

Most observers would include the daily interest chequing deposits in M1A in their definiton of money, but the notice (or savings) deposits of M2 are a more complicated matter, because some of these funds are likely to be spent soon and some are not.

To the extent that funds are just being "parked" in interest-bearing deposits (M2) for relatively short periods of time before being spent, at least part of M2 is by any reasonable definition money, and should be included in the money-supply figures. Unfortunately, it is not a simple task to determine how much of M2 should be treated as immediately spendable funds: while some of the deposits in M2 will be spent very quickly, others represent longer-term savings with little prospect of being spent for years. Thus, the measurement of the money supply for the purpose of monetary policy is a difficult and complex task.

Because of these problems, the Bank of Canada in November of 1982 abandoned the use of M1 as its official definition and measure of the money supply. In announcing this change, Gerald Bouey, the Governor of the Bank of Canada, noted that "M1 has, for some time — more than a year — been a less reliable guide than it was earlier. It is now clear that there have been major and continuing shifts out of M1 as a result

FIGURE 11-10 *The Growth of M1, M1A and M2 1970-84*

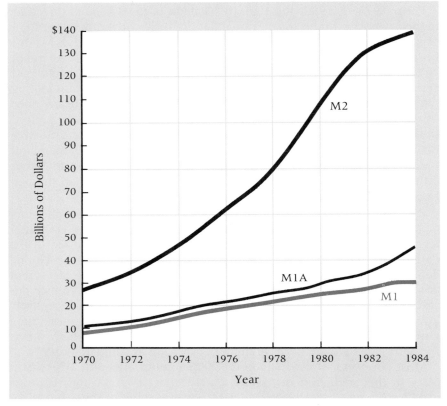

SOURCE   Bank of Canada *Review*, February 1985.

of changes in banking practices. As a result, the recorded M1 series is not a useful guide to policy at the present time. In these circumstances I want to make it known that the Bank no longer has a target range for it (but) . . . the Bank is continuing to search for ways for making more use of a monetary aggregate than it can at the present time."

In conclusion, Canada's recent experience with inflation has led to more widespread agreement on the importance of controlling the money supply. However, there are real difficulties and differences of opinion concerning the vital question of how to actually measure the money supply for purposes of controlling it. Canada's monetary authorities will likely continue to grapple with this problem during the 1980s, as they seek improved approaches to their crucially important responsibility to "regulate credit and currency in the best interests of the economic life of the nation."

DEFINITIONS OF NEW TERMS

Secondary Reserves   Reserves that the chartered banks are required by law to keep in addition to their cash reserves; comprised mostly of Treasury Bills.

Treasury Bills   Very short-term federal government promissory notes of 91 and 182 days maturity sold at weekly auctions to chartered banks and investment dealers.

Monetary Policy   The control of the lending activities of the chartered banks, and thus the control of the money supply, by the Bank of Canada.

Open-market Operations   Purchases or sales of government bonds by the Bank of Canada, the effect of which is to increase or decrease the chartered banks' cash reserves and thereby influence the money supply.

Bank Rate   The rate of interest charged by the Bank of Canada on its infrequent loans to the chartered banks; changes in the Bank Rate are generally interpreted as indicative of the direction of the Bank of Canada's monetary policy.

Moral Suasion   A practice whereby the Bank of Canada seeks to persuade the chartered banks to voluntarily adjust their lending or interest-rate policies so as to support the Bank of Canada's monetary policies.

Easy Money   A situation in which the Bank of Canada's monetary policy is directed toward making loans more available and interest rates lower.

Tight Money   A situation in which the Bank of Canada's monetary policy is directed toward making loans less available and interest rates higher.

Monetarism   An approach to economic theory focusing on the importance of the money supply and of controlling the money supply.

CHAPTER SUMMARY

1. The operations of the banking system are very important to the performance of the economy because it is through the lending activities of the banks that the bulk of the nation's money supply is created.

2. The government regulates the banking system in various ways, the most important of which is monetary policy: the control of the money supply by the Bank of Canada, through its control over the lending activities of the banks.

3. This control is exercised through various means, the most important of which is open-market operations: through these, the Bank of Canada influences the banks' cash reserves and thus their lending activities.

Other ways through which the Bank of Canada can influence the banks' lending activities include changes in the secondary reserve ratio, changes in the Bank Rate, and moral suasion.

4. When the Bank of Canada's policies are directed toward faster increases in the money supply and lower interest rates, an easy money policy is said to be in effect. Tight money refers to the opposite situation.

5. For maximum effectiveness, monetary policy is usually combined with fiscal policy: together, these can influence the level of aggregate demand so as to attempt to avoid the extremes of either recession or inflation.

6. If the federal government finances its budget deficits by selling government bonds to the Bank of Canada, the nation's money supply will increase, a process popularly known as "printing money" to pay the government's debts.

7. The severe inflation of recent years drew increased attention to the Bank of Canada's policies concerning the money supply; such emphasis on monetary growth and the importance of controlling it is known as monetarism.

8. In controlling the money supply, the Bank of Canada sought from 1975 to 1982 to keep the growth of M1 within publicly stated limits. However, many economists argue that M1 growth understates the growth of purchasing power because it excludes daily interest chequing deposits and savings deposits, which are not only large but also have grown rapidly compared to M1 in recent years. In November 1982, the Bank of Canada stopped using M1 as its official definition of the money supply.

QUESTIONS

1. Do you believe that the Bank of Canada's monetary policies should be determined by the federal government or by the Bank of Canada's officials? If the final authority over monetary policy rests with political leaders, how might this affect the conduct of monetary policy? If the final authority were to rest with the Bank of Canada, what kinds of problems might arise?

2. If the Bank of Canada raised the minimum required secondary reserve ratio from 5 percent of deposits to 10 percent, how would this affect the chartered banks, the money supply and interest rates?

3. What effect would a tight-money policy tend to have on
   (a) the stock market (the price of corporate shares)?
   (b) the price of outstanding government bonds (bonds, issued in the past, that have not yet matured and can thus still be bought and sold)?

4. What are the present sizes of M1, M1A and M2, and by what percentage has each of these increased over the past year? Compared to M1, has M2 continued to be as large and increase as rapidly as when this chapter was written? What is the significance of recent trends regarding M1 and M2 for someone concerned with managing the growth of Canada's money supply? (For statistics see Bank of Canada *Review*.)

5. What are the present policies of the Bank of Canada regarding the rate of growth of the money supply, and the availability of credit and interest rates? Why has the Bank adopted these policies at this time?

6. Explain the probable effects of each of the following on the money supply and on the performance of the economy in terms of output, employment and inflation.
   (a) The federal government sells $1 billion of bonds to the Canadian public to finance some of its expenditures.
   (b) The Bank of Canada sells $1 billion of government bonds to the chartered banks.
   (c) The federal government sells $1 billion of bonds to the Bank of Canada to finance some of its expenditures.

7. If the cash reserve ratio were 5 percent and the Bank of Canada bought $50 million of government bonds from the chartered banks,
   (a) by how much could the money supply increase?
   (b) Explain the process whereby the money supply would increase.
   (c) What would be required for the money supply to increase by as much as it could as per part (a)?
   (d) What would be the objective of the Bank of Canada in implementing this policy?
   (e) What problems might make it more difficult for this policy to achieve its objective?

8. Suppose that 91-day $1000 Treasury Bills are selling for $970 this Thursday.
   (a) What is the annual interest rate on these Treasury Bills?
   (b) What would the Bank Rate be for the next week?
   (c) If the Bank of Canada bought Treasury Bills in the weekly auction, bidding their price up to $980 instead of $970, what effect would this have on the Bank Rate?
   (d) What would be the objective of the Bank of Canada in buying Treasury Bills in this way, and how would buying Treasury Bills help to achieve this objective?

CHAPTER 12

The nature and causes of inflation

What is inflation?

Inflation is an increase in the general level of the prices of goods and services, including wages and salaries (the prices of labor services). The yardstick most commonly used to measure prices is the Consumer Price Index, a weighted average of the prices of goods and services bought by a typical urban Canadian household, discussed in detail in Chapter 4.

The upper graph in Figure 12-1 shows that the level of the CPI (1981=100), rose particularly rapidly from the early 1970's to the early 1980's. Over this period, the CPI more than doubled, meaning that the purchasing power of a dollar was reduced by more than half.

More significant, however, is the bottom graph, which shows the actual *rate of inflation*, or how fast the CPI is rising at any particular time. Thus, in the early 1960's, the CPI was rising at less than 2 percent per year, and the rate of inflation remained below 5 percent per year throughout the decade. In the 1970's, the rate of inflation became very high (8-10 percent per year). These rates persisted for about a decade: a time which became known as "The Great Inflation". Then, in 1983, the rate of inflation began a decline that was almost as abrupt as its rise in 1973.

Why the concern about inflation?

While a society can tolerate moderate inflation, rapid inflation such as we experienced in the 1970's is another matter, for several reasons.

FIGURE 12-1 *The Level and the Rate of Increase of the Consumer Price Index 1961–84*

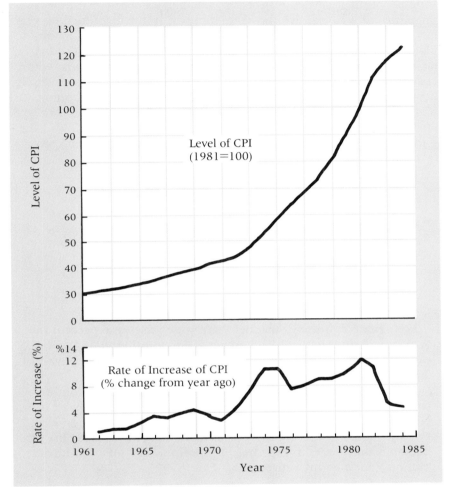

SOURCE Statistics Canada.

(a) Inflation imposes hardship on the economically weak

For those such as professionals, famous athletes and members of strong labor unions, who have the economic power (bargaining power) to increase their incomes, inflation can be more of an irritation than a hardship. For many others, however, such as unskilled, non-union workers and many office workers, it often proves difficult to increase incomes as fast as prices are rising, so that inflation poses a real threat to their standard of living. Generally, it can be said that inflation falls hardest upon those who are the least able to protect themselves—the economically weaker groups in society.

The people most severely affected by inflation are those on *fixed incomes*, that is, people who receive the same number of dollars of income year after year. As the purchasing power of their fixed income falls due to inflation, their standard of living is driven steadily downward. The largest and most seriously affected such group is, of course, *pensioners*, whose pensions are fixed for the rest of their lives. Two other groups adversely affected are *welfare recipients* (whose benefits do not always keep up with inflation) and people living off *investment income*, such as interest. This latter group includes not only wealthy investors, but also widows living off the investment income earned through the investment of their spouse's life insurance.

THE "72" FORMULA

An idea of the impact of inflation on fixed incomes can be gained by using the "72" formula:

> If something (here, prices) is increasing at a compound rate of X percent per year, it will *double* in 72 ÷ X years.

For example, if the Consumer Price Index rises at 6 percent per year, it will double in 12(72 ÷ 6) years. Put another way, a 6-percent annual rate of inflation will slash the purchasing power of a pensioner's fixed income *in half* in 12 years.

Inflation at the 9 percent and 10 percent annual rates common since the mid-1970's has a much more severe impact on fixed incomes, cutting their purchasing power in half in just 7 or 8 years. For a person considering early retirement at age 60, whose life expectancy may be 73, these rates of inflation can ruin a lifetimes's planning for a happy retirement.

Thus, inflation generally tends to redistribute income within a society, with the economically powerful the gainers and the economically weak the losers.

(b) Inflation impairs long-term financial planning

By steadily eroding the value of the dollar, inflation will, over long periods of time, drastically reduce its purchasing power, and thus seriously affect long-term financial planning. One example of this problem is pensions; another is *life insurance* planning. The essence of life insurance is to provide the survivor (say, widow) with enough investment income to live reasonably well. Suppose that a widow, age 32, invests the $200 000 of her husband's life insurance benefits so as to earn $20 000 per year of interest income. While this may seem quite comfortable, inflation of 9 percent per year will reduce its purchasing power to $10 000 by the time she is 40, $5000 when she is 48, and $2500 at age 56 — one-eighth of its original value.

What can be done about this? By planning for far greater pensions and life insurance, this effect can be offset — but few people can afford to put aside that much out of today's income. Consequently, most people cannot protect themselves against this problem, and remain very vulnerable to inflation over the long term. By eroding the purchasing power of money, inflation undermines the role of money as a store of value, making it difficult to plan for the future and to provide for protection against future financial risks. Rather, inflation encourages short-term thinking: "Spend, don't save, and let the future take care of itself."

(c) Inflation can cause economic stagnation

Ordinarily, inflation has been associated with periods of high aggregate demand, brisk economic growth and low unemployment, as we will see later in this chapter. Recently, however, it has become apparent that *very rapid inflation* can actually contribute to economic stagnation and high unemployment, by depressing capital investment spending by business.

Inflation can have this effect for two reasons: first, inflation causes *higher interest rates*. Fearing that continuing inflation will erode the real value of the capital that they loan out, lenders will insist on higher interest rates to offset the declining value of their capital. Would you lend someone $1000 for a year at an interest rate of 6 percent if prices were to rise 10 percent over the year, reducing the real value of your $1000 to $900 by the time it was repaid to you? If you did, your interest income of $60 would be more than offset by the $100 loss on the purchasing power of your $1000, leaving you less well off than before you made the loan. Thus, to induce lenders to invest or lend their money, borrowers will have to offer higher interest rates, to offset the effects of inflation.

This is an important (and often misunderstood) point: *inflation* (or the expectation of inflation) *causes interest rates to rise*. And, the more rapid inflation is, the higher interest rates are likely to be. The high interest rates caused by inflation can, in turn, have certain undesirable effects. For example, they could discourage investment spending and capital formation. Also, high mortgage rates tend to discourage home-buying and dampen new home construction. Both of these effects tend to contribute to economic stagnation and unemployment.

Second, contrary to popular belief, rapid inflation is not generally good for *business profits*. While profits appear to be high during periods of rapid inflation, after allowances have been made for inflation and taxes, real after-tax business profits are for many businesses actually reduced by inflation. Together with the increased cost of capital goods, this can, over a period of time, result in depressed levels of capital investment, slower economic growth and higher unemployment.

Thus, severe and prolonged inflation can contribute to economic stagnation: the uncomfortable combination of stagnation and inflation known as "stagflation". This undermining of the critically important saving/investment process is another example of how inflation discourages long-term economic thinking and planning, at the ultimate expense of future prosperity. The future does *not* take care of itself.

(d) Inflation can affect a nation's foreign trade

For a nation such as Canada, which exports over one-quarter of its GNP, inflation poses another threat to prosperity. By increasing the costs and prices of Canadian products, inflation can impair Canada's *competitiveness* in international trade. Canadian exports to foreign markets could be reduced, and less expensive foreign imports could enter Canadian markets; in both cases, Canadian output and employment would be threatened.

It is important to note that, to adversely affect a nation's exports, its inflation must be more rapid than inflation in other countries; only then will its competitive position be damaged. Obviously, even inflation of 12 percent per year in Canada will not affect Canada's trade if every country Canada trades with also has inflation of 12 percent per year. Just because prices are rising does not automatically mean that our exports are priced out of world markets—the key is our rate of inflation compared to the rate in other countries.[1]

Thus, for a variety of reasons, inflation (and especially rapid inflation) represents a threat to the economic prosperity of society, and governments must seek to restrain it.

What causes inflation?

Inflation is a complex economic process in which various causes are often intertwined and difficult to disentangle. As a result, there is considerable

[1]It can be argued that these problems can be compensated for by a reduction in the international value of the Canadian dollar. For instance, if Canadian prices were 10 percent above our competitors' prices, a 10-percent decline in the international value of the Canadian dollar could occur, leaving our products no more expensive to foreign buyers because the higher prices of the products are offset by the lower price of the Canadian dollar. This, however, is not a painless solution: the lower international value of the Canadian dollar would make the prices of imported products in Canada higher, reducing Canadian living standards. Either way, our excessive inflation would hurt us. Such international matters are covered in more detail in subsequent chapters.

confusion among the public as to the causes of inflation, with blame being attached variously to labor unions, big business, government, high interest rates, low interest rates and excessive lending by the banks, to name a few factors.

Economists agree, however, that there are two basic sources of inflation, one of which originates on the demand side of the economy and the other of which originates on the supply side of the economy. The first of these is known as *demand-pull inflation*, in which aggregate demand exceeds the economy's ability to produce goods and services, causing prices to be pulled up by pressure from the demand side of the economy. A second — and quite different — inflationary pressure can come from the supply side of the economy. If labor unions or businesses with monopolistic powers push their wages and profits higher, the result can be upward pressures on prices. Since this inflationary pressure comes from producers and production costs rather than from demand, it is known as *cost-push inflation*.

The distinction between demand-pull and cost-push inflation is fundamentally important; in one case the problem originates with excess demand from consumers, whereas in the other case it arises from the ability of producers (business and labor) to increase their wages and prices. We will consider each of these two basic types of inflationary pressures in more detail in the following sections.

(a) *Inflation from the demand side: demand-pull inflation*

Suppose bejuniaberries are grown by a large number of small farmers. With many competing producers, there is strong competition in the industry (that is, no monopoly power to raise prices). Under these conditions the price of bejuniaberries last year was $0.40 per kilogram. This year, however, the demand for bejuniaberries has increased greatly. Since the farmers are unable (at least in the short run) to produce enough bejuniaberries to satisfy demand, the price of bejuniaberries rises to $0.60 per kilogram, simply because the demand exceeds the supply. When excess demand causes prices to rise, the result is **demand-pull** inflation.

This example illustrates the classic case of inflation, the situation in which aggregate demand (consumption plus investment plus government plus net export spending) exceeds the capacity of the economy to produce goods and services. The economy is only physically capable at any given time of producing goods and services at a certain (capacity) rate; should total spending exceed this level, the only possible outcome is that prices will rise as a result of the excess demand, as illustrated in Figure 12-2.

It is generally agreed among economists that excess demand is the most basic cause of inflation. The most common examples of demand-pull inflation are periods of wartime, when heavy government spending

FIGURE 12-2 *Demand-Pull Inflation*

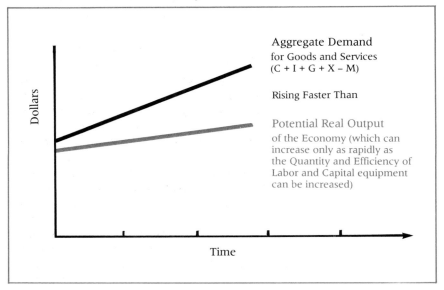

drives prices upward. Another case occurred after the Second World War, when households cashed in their war bonds and went on a spending spree. In the second half of the 1960's, US government spending on the Vietnam War and major domestic social security programs generated increasingly severe inflation, and in the 1972-73 worldwide economic boom—the strongest peacetime economic boom ever—prices rose at record rates as output simply could not keep up with booming demand. Each of these cases of inflation was accompanied by another phenomenon—unusually rapid increases in the volume of money in circulation (the money supply).

The money supply and inflation

Excess aggregate demand is not merely the result of people wanting more: they must also have more money. For society in general (consumers, businesses and governments) to spend more money, there must be more money in circulation—the *money supply* must rise. Any period of rapid inflation is accompanied by rapid increases in the money supply. And, as we have seen, the growth of the money supply is controlled by the Bank of Canada, which is ultimately responsible to the federal government. Therefore, the key factor underlying the rate of inflation—the money supply—is in the final analysis determined by the federal government. In determining its monetary policy, however, the Bank of Canada is not concerned soley with combating inflation. In particular, we have seen that increases in the money supply (easy money) can be used during recessions to boost aggregate demand and reduce unemployment. While easy-money policies can help to lift the economy out of recession, there is a danger that the government will boost the money supply too quickly or for too long a time. Of course, this will result in a new surge of inflation, but only after a time lag.

> The growth rate of the money supply is, over time, the single most important determinant of the inflation rate.
>
> Carl Beigie, President,
> C. D. Howe Research Institute,
> in *Inflation is a Social Malady*,
> British-North American Committee, 1979

Experts in the monetary aspects of economics say that if the money supply is increased excessively rapidly, inflation will probably begin to increase *after about a year* and will continue to work its way through the economy for another two years. Thus, while rapid increases in the money supply may look like a good idea to a government faced with a recession and high unemployment, they are all too likely to cause a much worse inflation problem in the future. An excellent example of this was in Canada, where rapid increases in the money supply in 1972, 1973, and 1974 led to a very serious wave of inflation in 1973 and beyond. Following this experience, the Bank of Canada undertook to keep the rate of increase of the money supply within specified limits.

Generally then, the rate of growth of the money supply and the level of aggregate demand for goods and services are the key factors underlying the rate of inflation. Inflation tends to be most severe during economic booms, when demand is high, and less severe during recessions, when demand is sluggish. While higher aggregate demand is the most basic cause of inflation, the decision to allow the money supply to increase in response to the strong demand for loans associated with an economic boom is an integral part of the inflationary process.

Full-employment policies and inflation

As pointed out earlier, the full-employment monetary and fiscal policies which the federal government has adopted since the Second World War have usually maintained aggregate demand at high enough levels to avoid serious recessions. While such policies keep unemployment rates relatively low, the maintenance of total spending at such high levels tends to generate some inflation. Thus, our commitment to full employment has involved, as a side effect, some inflation of a demand-pull nature.

Government budget deficits and inflation

While it is commonly believed that government budget deficits cause inflation, most economists think otherwise. Budget deficits are generally used during *recessions,* when business investment spending is low and there are unused savings available for the government to borrow. Borrowing existing funds (savings) from Canadians does not increase the money supply or risk boosting aggregate demand to excessive levels.

On the other hand, if the government were to print money to finance its budget deficits (by selling bonds to the Bank of Canada, as in Chapter 11), the money supply would increase and the danger of inflation would be greater.

Demand-pull inflation graphed

Figure 12-3 uses the aggregate demand and aggregate supply curves to show the operation of demand-pull inflation. As the level of aggregate demand rises from **AD** to **AD₁**, and then to **AD₂**, the economy is pushed to its capacity output of 100 at the same time, and the level of prices rises from **p** to **p₁**, and **p₂**, reflecting the increasingly severe inflation that results from the high demand.

FIGURE 12-3 *The Operation of Demand-Pull Inflation*

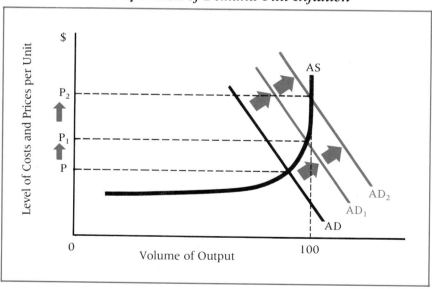

(b) Inflation from the supply side: cost-push inflation

While excessive aggregate demand, fuelled by increases in the money supply, is regarded as the most basic source of inflation, there are other contributing factors on the supply side of the economy that must be considered. To return to the example of the bejuniaberry farms as an illustration, suppose that a large corporation were to buy up all the small bejuniaberry farms and establish a monopoly of the bejuniaberry market. Also, suppose that all of the corporation's employees on these farms were to join a powerful labor union, the United Berry Cultivators. As a result of these two developments, the company's profits and the workers' wages could both rise considerably, with consumers paying the tab through higher prices of \$.60 per kilogram. While sales of bejuniaberries will be somewhat lower due to this higher price, the monopoly producer is in a position to hold down the output (supply) of berries in order to maintain the price at \$.60, or even increase it further.[2] Because in this case the price is being pushed up by cost factors (profits and wages both representing a cost to the consumer), this process is desribed as **cost-push** inflation.

The wage-price spiral

Some people like to blame big business for inflation; others like to blame labor unions. Both of these views are overly simplistic. It seems to be more correct to say that, rather than one or the other, it is most often the *combination* of big business and labor unions that generates large wage and price increases.

In a market economy, the major force holding prices down is *competition* between producers (both domestic and foreign). In some industries, competition is less effective than in others in holding down prices and wages. Some such industries are monopolistic in nature (for example, postal service), while others are dominated by a few large producers who would prefer to "live and let live" rather than compete ruthlessly and perhaps ruinously regarding prices (for example — the petroleum industry). Often, these industries, which are dominated by *large employers* (postal service, telephone service, hydro-electric utilities, steel, automobile manufacturing, petroleum, tobacco, breweries and many others), are also *strongly unionized*.

In bargaining with their unions, such employers may grant above-average *wage increases*, because they are confident that they will be able to pass these on to the consumer in the form of *price increases*, due to the lack of competition. However, if many prices are rising in this way, the resultant increase in the cost of living could cause labor unions to

---

[2]While cost-push inflation originates in the ability of producers to increase prices and wages, it also requires that buyers continue to buy the product rather than switch to substitutes or do without it; that is, that demand be what economists call *inelastic*.

demand more wage increases, creating a **wage-price spiral** in which wages and prices chase each other upwards.[3]

Such a wage-price spiral is most likely when the economy is booming, and employers are anxious to avoid strikes because sales are strong. Also, during a boom it is easier for producers to recover wage increases by raising prices, because demand is high. On the other hand, the cost-push pressures associated with the spiral tend to be less strong during recessions, when weaker demand makes price increases more difficult and employers resist union wage demands more strongly. Recessions, however, are not a complete cure for this cost-push inflation; some producers and some unions possess enough power over their prices and wages to continue to raise them despite sluggish demand. Thus, the wage-price spiral not only aggravates inflation during boom periods, but also helps to keep inflation going (although at a slower pace) during economic slowdowns.

A tax-price spiral?

Another variant of the cost-push theory views the government as playing a more direct role in causing a spiral through taxes. The theory argues that rapidly rising taxes on both wage earners and businesses causes them to increase their wages and prices more rapidly, in attempts to pass on the tax increases to their employers or customers.

The massive federal budget deficits of the 1980's (see Chapter 9) raised concerns regarding a tax-price spiral. If the government moved to reduce its deficits through a sharp increase in taxes, there was the possibility of a tax-price spiral, as wage-earners and businesses scambled to pass the burden on to others by increasing their wages and prices.

Some economists believed that such tax-push factors had, in fact, played a role in the Great Inflation of the 1970's. From the mid-1960's to the mid-1970's, government spending rose from 33 to nearly 43 percent of GNP, financed in large part by rising taxes which in turn were partially passed on into wage and price increases by those who were able to do so.

Cost-push inflation graphed

Figure 12-4 uses the aggregate demand and aggregate supply curves to illustrate cost-push inflation. Essentially, when sellers (producers and workers) are willing to supply their output only at higher prices, the AS curve moves upward to higher cost levels, as shown by AS_1.

---

[3]Only the economically powerful take part in the *wage-price spiral*. Non-union workers and/or workers who lack bargaining power, as well as businesses that are subject to a great deal of competition, are largely left behind by this process—they are unable to raise their wages and prices fast enough to keep up, and suffer accordingly, as noted earlier.

FIGURE 12-4 *The Operation of Cost-Push Inflation*

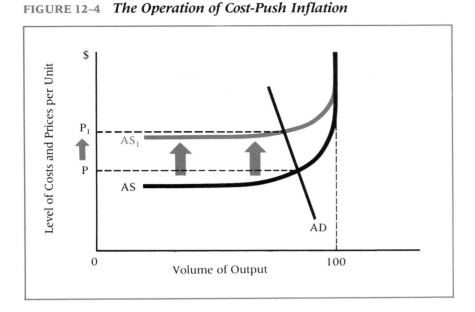

When the AS curve shifts upward to reflect the higher costs, the price level moves from p to p_1, reflecting the inflation which results.

The general public's impressions concerning inflation

While economists emphasize excess demand as the cause of inflation, the general public tends to blame labor unions and big business. This is probably because the activities of unions and big business—wage negotiations, strikes, price increases—are highly *visible*, while the role played by excess demand is *not visible*. Who has seen excess demand bidding up the prices of goods and services? Shoppers are not seen bidding against each other eagerly for roasts or for lumber, thus generating higher prices. Rather, the manufacturers or the stores put higher price tags on them, and explain that their costs are up. Certainly, this looks more like cost-push inflation than demand-pull inflation.

Yet the underlying economics of the situation are often quite different. If, for example, consumer demand for lumber is very high, lumber stores will find their inventories depleting rapidly and will be anxious to replenish their stocks of lumber. With the purchasers for all the various lumber stores bidding actively against each other for a limited supply of lumber from the sawmills, the price will be bid up.

When the lumber reaches the retail stores, it will have a higher price—which store managers describe as an increase in costs. However, the real

JOHN KENNETH GALBRAITH (1908-)

John Kenneth Galbraith, professor of economics at Harvard University, is probably the most prominent Canadian-born economist in the world. Much of his prominence arises from the fact that he disagrees with conventional economists on most matters and writes, not for other economists, but for the mass market. Indeed, his books have often been best sellers. He has had a particularly colourful career in politics, which has included acting as an adviser to John F. Kennedy, and serving as US ambassador to India.

Galbraith is particularly critical of economic theories (such as laissez-faire) that place faith in economic freedom, competition and free markets as the best way to promote economic prosperity. These theories, he claims, are from an earlier time characterized by small, independent businesses. They are made obsolete by the rise of the giant corporation, which manipulates the demand side of the marketplace through advertising and, in concert with its supposed competitors, controls both the supply and the price of its products.

Furthermore, he argues, the modern problem of inflation is linked directly to the economic power of the large labor unions and corporations, which generates a continual tendency toward cost-push inflation. The only way to curb inflation, says Galbraith, is through a permanent system of wage-price controls which will prevent the abuse of the power enjoyed by these large employers and powerful unions.

Galbraith's ideas have been less well-received by the economics profession than by the general public. Economists point out that his criticisms apply to only part of the economy, and that growing foreign competition (such as in the auto industry) has made even that part smaller. They also point out that the rapid growth of the service industries, which are characterized by many small businesses rather than the industrial giants on which Galbraith focuses, has made his criticisms less relevant today than they were twenty or thirty years ago. Nonetheless, he remains one of the most effective critics of the belief that free competition in the marketplace (laissez-faire) can be relied upon to resolve all economic problems.

origin of the price increases lies in high consumer demand; it is really demand-pull in nature rather than cost-push, as it appears.

People tend to blame inflation on what they can see, such as the increases in union wages and business profits that are the most visible aspects of inflation. However, the actions of unions (which represent less than 60 percent of employees) and big business (which produces less than half of the economy's output) cannot account completely for inflation, in which virtually all wages and prices rise rapidly. The wage and price increases of unions and large corporations are simply the most visible symptoms of inflation (or, at most, contributing factors), not its basic cause. In the view of the vast majority of economists, the basic cause of inflation is excessive aggregate demand. Early in a period of inflation caused by excess demand, prices tend to rise faster than wages, many of which are tied to union contracts that have not yet expired; as a result, profits increase rapidly and the public sees profits as the cause of inflation. Later, as union contracts are renegotiated and wages rise rapidly (the catch-up phase), people blame unions for the inflation. In both cases, attention is focused not on the basic cause of inflation, but rather on the more visible symptoms.

The momentum of inflation

Once inflation gets underway, it has a tendency to gather momentum and become more severe. This can occur partly because households and businesses often respond to inflation in ways that make inflation worse, and partly because governments tend to follow policies that accommodate inflation rather than anti-inflation policies that increase unemployment. We will consider each of these problems in the following sections.

Inflation psychology

One complicating factor, which is capable of contributing significantly to inflation, is *inflation psychology*. It refers to a situation in which people, having experienced rapid inflation for some time, come to expect that rapid inflation will continue in the future. They seek to protect themselves against this expected inflation by seeking exceptionally large wage and salary increases and by spending their money now (before prices rise further), reducing their savings or even borrowing money.

While such actions are a logical way for individuals to respond to expected future inflation, when many people behave this way, they actually make inflation more severe, adding not only to cost-push pressures but also to demand-pull pressures on prices. This problem, especially as it relates to wage and salary increases, became a significant factor in inflation in Canada after 1973, as Canadians sought and won very rapid increases in incomes (15-20 percent per year in 1974-75) in attempts to compensate for double-digit inflation. It is ironic that such attempts by people to protect themselves against inflation actually make inflation worse.

The cost-push pressures arising from inflation psychology are partly a *result* of severe inflation, and partly a *cause* of inflation. It was only after two years of rapid inflation (caused by excess demand) that inflation

> But after inflation continues for a while its character changes. It becomes seen as endemic, people act in the expectation that it will continue, and it becomes self-reinforcing. That is when the real trouble starts. If inflation is not resisted, if it is accommodated, it will accelerate.
>
> Gerald Bouey,
> Governor of the Bank of Canada,
> *Annual Report* of the Governor of the Bank of Canada, 1982.

psychology and the associated cost-push pressures broke out in 1974-75. However, from then on it became a strong force that tended to keep the rate of inflation high. Thus, under conditions of strong inflation psychology, cost-push pressures can become a strong factor in maintaining inflation at high rates as well as a major headache for those seeking to curb inflation.

Inflation psychology graphed

Inflation psychology affects both the supply side and the demand side of the economy. On the *demand side*, aggregate demand rises as people increase their current spending in anticipation of price increases; this is shown in Figure 12-5 by the shift of the AD curve to the higher level of AD_1.

FIGURE 12-5 *Inflation Psychology*

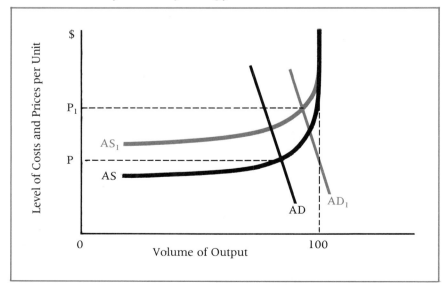

On the *supply side*, the aggregate supply curves moves upward to AS_1, as explained in the section on cost-push inflation. The result is a double impact on prices, which move up from p to p_1. Because people expected inflation, they got inflation.

Cost-push inflation and the money supply

Suppose that (for the sake of round figures) Canada's GNP in 19*1 was $100 billion, and that there was a strong inflation psychology in the nation that caused strong labor unions, big corporations and other groups to increase their incomes and prices quite rapidly. If these cost-push pressures caused prices in general to rise by 10 percent in 19*2, then the same level of real output that was produced in 19*1 would cost $110 billion in 19*2 (10 percent more than in 19*1). Just to support the same level of output and employment that existed in 19*1, at 19*2's higher prices, will require 10 percent more aggregate demand in the economy in 19*2. Viewed differently, to prevent a decline in real output in 19*2, aggregate demand must rise by 10 percent, which means that the money supply must also be increased by approximately 10 percent.

This places the Bank of Canada in an awkward position: if it does not increase the money supply by 10 percent, aggregate demand will be too low to keep output from falling below 19*1's level—there will be a recession, and unemployment will rise. On the other hand, if the Bank of Canada does increase the money supply by 10 percent (or more likely by 12 or 13 percent, to try to stimulate an increase in output), such rapid increases in the money supply, while avoiding a recession, virtually guarantee continued rapid inflation in 19*3 and beyond. Thus, strong cost-push pressures on prices can place the Bank of Canada in the difficult position of having to choose between resisting those pressures at the expense of a recession, or increasing the money supply rapidly enough to avoid a recession, but at the cost of more severe inflation in the future.

In such circumstances, the government and the Bank of Canada could come under strong *political pressure* to avoid a recession by increasing the money supply sufficiently to accommodate the higher prices set by the powerful unions and corporations. While the result will be a rapid increase in the money supply and more severe inflation, the origin of the inflation problem is not simply demand-pull inflation. It is at least in part a cost-push problem, with the government pushed into participating in the process by increasing the money supply to avoid rising unemployment. A government that *accommodates* inflation and inflation psychology by increasing the money supply in this way is likely to find itself faced with *accelerating* inflation, as such a policy feeds not only inflation psychology, but also excess demand. This is the situation that developed in Canada in the mid-1970's.

The causes of inflation in review

The causes of inflation are complex, interwoven and difficult to separate. The most basic factor determining the rate of inflation is the *rate of growth of the money supply*, which in turn determines the degree of *excess demand* present in the economy. However, there are different reasons why the money supply might increase rapidly enough to generate rapid inflation. Some people view the basic cause as excessive stimulation of the economy by government monetary and fiscal policies, while others emphasize that cost-push pressures from big business and labor unions can virtually force the government to increase the mony supply, in order to avoid a recession, by providing the economy with enough purchasing power to buy all of its output at the higher prices caused by the wage-price spiral. While there are elements of truth in both of these viewpoints, most economists tend to place more emphasis on demand-pull pressures originating in government policies as the basic cause of inflation, and view cost-push pressures as a contributing factor to inflation rather than the basic cause.

On a more fundamental level, both the demand-pull and cost-push theories of inflation are related to the *unrealistic expectations* of people and to their attempts — as workers, consumers, business persons and government leaders — to get more out of the economy than the economy can produce. When such unrealistic demands are placed on the economy — either in terms of excessive spending or in terms of excessive increases in incomes — the result will inevitably be inflation. In this sense, inflation is the economy's way of telling people that their expectations and the demands they are placing on the economy are unrealistic and that they can't have everything they want. Instead, what they get is rapid increases in prices and interest rates, which limit their real economic gains to what is economically possible.

FIGURE 12-6 *The Great Inflation*

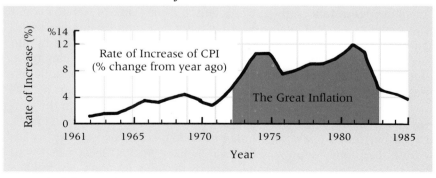

SOURCE   Statistics Canada.

The "Great Inflation"

The decade from 1972 to 1982 saw a prolonged period of severe inflation that was so exceptional that it became known as the "Great Inflation" (Figure 12-6).

Some of the more memorable features of this period were dramatic oil-price increases in 1973-74 and 1979, exceptional increases in wages and salaries, sharp food-price increases and record-high interest rates, followed by the most severe recession since the 1930's. Not surprisingly, the Great Inflation was characterized by unusually strong inflationary pressures from both the *demand side* and the *supply side* of the economy.

Demand-pull forces

While the increases in oil prices, wages and salaries were highly visible and well-publicized, there was another underlying force at work that was less visible but more fundamental. This was an exceptional surge in aggregate demand, fuelled by *very rapid increases in the money supply*. As Figure

FIGURE 12–7   *Money-Supply* Growth in the 1960's and 1970's Compared*

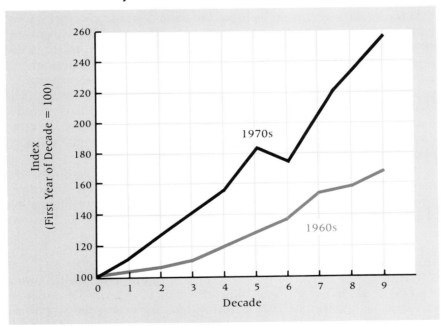

*M1   Cash in circulation and Demand Deposits at Banks

SOURCE   Bank of Montreal, *Business Review*, September, 1979.

12-7 shows, the money supply grew much more rapidly during the 1970's than it had in the 1960's, when inflation rates were much lower. At the same time, there were unusually rapid increases in government spending, which added to aggregate demand.

Why did the money supply increase so rapidly?

(a) The Vietnam War

The origins of the severe inflation of the 1970's go back to the Vietnam War in the 1960's. From the mid-1960's on, the Vietnam War generated excessive demand and inflation in the US economy, as the US government financed the war by massive printing of money rather than tax increases. This led to rapid increases in the money supply of other nations, through the following mechanism.

With the US dollar more plentiful relative to other nations' currencies, the international value of the US dollar tended to fall. Put the other way, the value of other nations' currencies in terms of the US dollar tended to rise—other nations' currencies would become more costly for Americans to buy. For example, from the mid-1960's to the early 1970's, the cost of a Canadian dollar to Americans rose from 92½¢ to over $1.00 US.

This created a serious problem for the nations whose currencies were under upward pressure: if their currencies became costlier to Americans, so would the goods they exported to the vast US market. In short, the rapid increases in the US money supply posed a threat to other nations' exports to the USA and to the jobs associated with those exports. To protect those exports and jobs, many nations undertook to increase their own money supplies at faster rates, making their currencies more plentiful and thus less likely to rise relative to the US dollar. As a result, the rapid increases in the US money supply were matched by other countries seeking to protect their exports to the USA.

While these policies did help to protect exports and employment in the short run, they contributed strongly to inflation in the late 1960's and early 1970's. Thus, the US "Vietnam Inflation" spread throughout most of the industrialized world.

(b) Rapid labor force growth

The exceptionally large number of people born in the decade following the end of Second World War came of working age in the decade from the late 1960's to the late 1970's. During this same period, the proportion of women seeking work increased dramatically. These two factors accounted for an exceptional surge in the number of people seeking jobs, which could only be accommodated if the economy grew with unusual rapidity.

Put the other way, these rapid increases in the labor force caused the unemployment rate to rise, placing pressure on the government to stimulate aggregate demand through fiscal policy and more rapid growth of the money supply, to keep unemployment from rising.

(c) Rapid increases in government spending

The period from the late 1960's to the mid-1970's saw very rapid increases in federal and provincial government spending in Canada, in areas such as health care, education, civil service payrolls, unemployment insurance and transfer payments (family allowances, welfare, old age pensions and so on), many of which were indexed so that they rose automatically at the same rate as the Consumer Price Index. It is widely believed these rapid increases in government expenditures contributed significantly to inflation in the 1970's both by adding to aggregate demand in the economy and by generating *tax-push inflation*, as workers and businesses sought higher wages and prices to offset their rising taxes.

(d) Political factors

The strong performance of the economy in the second half of the 1960's generated among the public *very high expectations* about what was possible economically and about what government economic policies could and should achieve. In particular, strong economic growth with low unemployment and rapidly rising living standards came to be expected by the public. While these expectations can now be seen to have been unrealistic, they placed great pressure on governments to fulfill them, often by stimulating aggregate demand with unusual strength so as to boost economic growth and reduce unemployment. This problem was particularly important in 1972, which, by coincidence, was an election year in both Canada and the USA, as well as in several other nations. Anti-inflation policies that had been applied in 1969-70 had left considerable unemployment in these economies in 1971, so there was heavy political pressure on governments to stimulate their economies before the 1972 elections. The side effects of these policies, which would be extremely severe inflation by late 1973, were considered secondary at the time. The 1972 federal election in Canada resulted in a minority government until 1974, which made it difficult for the government to impose politically unpopular monetary and fiscal anti-inflation policies. Inflation was, therefore, allowed to gain momentum in 1973 and 1974.

As a result of these factors, government spending, the money supply and aggregate demand all rose at very rapid rates from the mid-1960's to the mid-1970's. Government spending rose from 33 percent of GNP to 43 percent, and the money supply, which had risen by 6 percent per year in the early 1960's, rose by more than 15 percent per year from

1970 to 1975. With real output capable of rising only 4 or 5 percent per year at most, such money-supply increases made severe inflation inevitable.

Cost-push forces

The Great Inflation also saw strong cost-push pressures on prices, most notably from *wages and salaries*. By 1974, Canadians were firmly in the grip of inflation psychology: expecting continuing severe inflation, they were seeking — and getting — wage and salary increases of 15-20 percent per year in 1974-75. These attempts by people to protect themselves against inflation made inflation worse, by giving it a momentum of its own: Canadians were suffering from continued inflation in large part because they expected to experience continuing inflation.

Another cost-push factor which contributed to the Great Inflation was *oil-price increases*. While government subsidies kept Canadian oil-price increases well-below world trends during the 1970's, these subsidies only delayed price increases that were inevitable. When the increases finally occurred in the early 1980's, they added considerable cost-push pressures to the later stages of the Great Inflation in Canada. Also, *food prices* rose rapidly in several years in the 1970's, which boosted the Consumer Price Index (of which food is the second-largest component). High food and oil costs also added to wage-push pressures, as people sought large income increases to compensate for these added expenses.

Dealing with the Great Inflation

While some countries sought to curb this severe inflation as early as 1974 (mostly with *tight money* policies), Canada did not do so, as noted earlier. This reluctance continued until late 1975, when the problem had become so severe that something had to be done. Even then, however, the government did not combat inflation with the same determination shown by some nations.

Still fearful of the high unemployment that would result from all-out attack on inflation, the government aimed instead for a *gradual* slowing down of inflation, through three main approaches. First, and most important, the rate of growth of the *money supply* was to be gradually reduced over a period of time. Second, the government stated an intention to curb the growth of *government spending* in the future. And, finally, to reduce cost-push pressures (especially from wages), the government imposed a temporary three-year program of *wage-and-price controls*. We will examine these anti-inflation policies more closely in Chapter 13; however, we should note here that the policies were not as effective as had been hoped. One major obstacle to the success of these anti-inflation policies was the strong inflation psychology that had built up in the 1972-75 period, which continued to exert cost-push pressures on prices thereafter.

In the final analysis, the Great Inflation was curbed by the Great Recession of the early 1980's: a period of severely depressed aggregate demand and high unemployment brought on in large part by very high interest rates intended to combat inflation. Under the pressure of such high unemployment, even Canada's strong wage-push pressures eased, and the rate of inflation declined from about 10 percent per year to less than 5 percent by the end of 1983.

DEFINITIONS OF NEW TERMS

Rate of Inflation   The percentage increase in the Consumer Price Index over a period of one year; a measure of how rapidly the CPI is rising.

Demand-Pull Inflation   Inflation that is the result of excessive aggregate demand in the economy; that is, aggregate demand in excess of the economy's capacity to produce goods and services.

Cost-Push Inflation   Inflation that is the result of the economic power of some large employers and powerful labor unions, which can be used to push up wages and prices.

Inflation Psychology   The expectation of continuing inflation in the future, against which people seek to protect themselves by obtaining large wage and salary increases and by reducing their savings.

CHAPTER SUMMARY

1. Inflation is an increase in the general level of the prices of goods and services.

2. Inflation, especially rapid inflation, has the following negative effects: it imposes hardship on economically weak groups, it impairs long-term financial planning, it can erode capital investment and thus cause economic stagnation, and it can threaten output and employment by reducing exports and increasing imports.

3. The basic cause of inflation is demand-pull pressures arising from excessive aggregate demand. Cost-push pressures are generally regarded as contributing factors rather than the basic cause; however, when inflation psychology is strong, cost-push forces can play an important role in maintaining inflation at high rates.

4. In both the demand-pull and cost-push explanations of inflation, the money supply rises rapidly, but for different reasons. In the demand-pull view, money-supply increases are the direct result of government decisions, while in the cost-push explanation, wages and prices are increased by large corporations and powerful labor unions, forcing the government to increase the money supply to avoid a recession.

5. In the final analysis, inflation is the result of the unrealistic expectations of people, whether these take the form of excess demand (demand-pull) or excessive increases in incomes (cost-push).

QUESTIONS

1. The text notes that inflation psychology can make an inflationary situation considerably worse by causing people to spend more, save less and seek large income increases in order to protect themselves against inflation. What could the government do to attempt to reduce such problems arising from inflation psychology?

2. In conclusion, the text describes the fundamental cause of inflation as "unrealistic expectations of people and . . . their attempts — as workers, business persons and government leaders — to get more out of the economy than the economy can produce." What could be done in order to make people's economic expectations more consistent with economic reality? How much leadership have governments provided in this matter, and why?

3. Suppose that strong cost-push pressures developed in the economy due to the price and wage decisions of economically powerful employers and unions, and that the Bank of Canada resisted this inflationary trend by refusing to increase the money supply sufficiently rapidly to support these price and wage decisions. What would happen in the economy, and upon whom would the burden fall most heavily?

4. Why should the government not attempt to stop inflation by simply passing a law forbidding price and income increases?

5. Interview several people who have not studied economics to determine their views regarding the causes of inflation and appropriate policies for combating it. How accurate are their views? If their views are representative of the Canadian public, do they make it easier or more difficult for the government to come to grips with the problem of inflation?

6. *The Canadian Statistical Review*, published monthly by Statistics Canada, contains in Section 5, Table 2 a breakdown of the Consumer Price Index into its major components (food, shelter, etc.,). Which of these components have increased the *most rapidly* over the most recent pe-

riod, and why? Which components have increased the most slowly, and why?

7. What has the rate of inflation been for the past three years? What are the possible reasons for this trend in the rate of inflation?

8. Is the rate of inflation forecast to decline or increase over the next year? Why?

9. The cumulative, long-term effects of inflation are much greater than its visible impact in any one year. Using the 72 formula, calculate how long it will take prices to double if the rate of inflation is:
   (a) 1 percent per year
   (b) 3 percent per year
   (c) 6 percent per year
   (d) 9 percent per year
   (e) 12 percent per year

10.

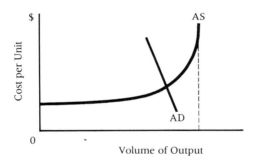

(a) Explain how these aggregate supply and aggregate demand curves (and therefore the rate of inflation) would be affected by each of the following:
   (i) a significant increase in the level of aggregate demand
   (ii) the negotiation of significant increases in wages by labor unions in anticipation of further inflation.
   (iii) reduced saving/increased consumption spending by households in anticipation of further inflation.
(b) Draw new AS and AD curves reflecting (i), (ii) and (iii), to show the cumulative effect of all three of these developments on the rate of inflation.
(c) According to the graph, what are the two basic ways to reduce the rate of inflation from that shown in part (b)?

CHAPTER 13

Government policies to combat inflation

For a variety of reasons discussed in Chapter 12, it is considered important that governments prevent inflation from becoming excessively rapid. Before examining the policies that governments can use to combat and to contain inflation, we should first review the causes of inflation.

The basic cause of inflation is *excessive aggregate demand* for goods and services, which causes prices to rise due to demand-pull pressures. *Cost-push* pressures on prices (arising from the ability of some large corporations and some powerful labor unions to push up prices and wages) are generally regarded as a secondary cause, or a contributing factor to inflation rather than as the primary cause. However, under conditions of strong *inflation psychology*, the expectation of future inflation can generate large wage and salary increases that add significantly to cost-push inflationary pressures, giving inflation a momentum of its own. Related to both the demand-pull and cost-push pressures on prices is the fact that unusually rapid inflation is always accompanied by *rapid increases in the money supply*.

Thus, government policies to combat inflation must attack its basic causes by restraining the growth of the money supply and aggregate demand. Also, depending on the degree of cost-push pressures in the economy, anti-inflation policies may also seek to prevent powerful corporations and unions from increasing their prices and wages as rapidly as they might. Each of these policy approaches, aimed at demand-pull and cost-push inflationary pressures respectively, is examined in more detail in this chapter.

Combating demand-pull inflation

To attack the basic cause of inflation, the government must restrain the growth of aggregate demand for goods and services, by using its monetary and fiscal policies.

Monetary policy

The Bank of Canada can impose a *tight-money* policy to combat inflation, consisting of higher interest rates[1] and reduced availability of credit. By slowing the growth of the money supply, such a policy will ease the pressures of excess demand on prices and help to restrain inflation. It is generally accepted among economists that no anti-inflation policy can succeed unless it includes control of the rate of growth of the money supply. Whatever else is done to curb inflation, monetary restraint is essential, since if money is created too rapidly, its value will decline (because prices of goods and services will rise).

> . . . the fact is that no strategy for dealing with inflation will succeed unless it is well supported by firm and continuing control of the rate of monetary expansion. That proposition is as well established as any general proposition in the whole field of economics, and its acceptance is a basic requirement for any useful debate on how to control inflation.
>
> Gerald K. Bouey,
> Governor of the Bank of Canada,
> in Bank of Canada *Review*,
> November 1980, (page 8).

It was mainly through monetary policy that the Great Inflation of the 1970's was brought under control. Following 1975, the Bank of Canada undertook to keep the growth of the money supply (as measured by M1) within publicly stated limits. Finally, though, it was a period of record-high interest rates in 1981-82 that brought the Great Inflation to an end by depressing borrowing and aggregate demand severely and bringing on the Great Recession of the early 1980's.

---

[1]Because interest payments are one of the costs of doing business, some people believe that the way to curb inflation is to reduce interest rates rather than increase them through a tight-money policy. While lower interest rates would have a slight cost-reducing effect on business, the easy money associated with lower interest rates would more than offset this gain by increasing the money supply and aggravating the problem of excess demand. In short, reducing interest rates is exactly the reverse of what is needed to combat inflation.

Fiscal policy

To dampen aggregate demand in the economy, the federal government can use a *budget surplus,* with government expenditures less than tax revenues. The most likely approach to a budget surplus is for the government to curb the growth of (or even reduce) government expenditures.[2] Such curbs on government spending will be especially helpful in slowing inflation if they reduce the need for the government to increase the money supply to finance its expenditures.

THE IMPORTANCE OF PRICE AND WAGE FLEXIBILITY

Anti-inflation policies that depress aggregate demand will put downward pressure on either *prices and wages* or on *output and employment,* or on both. The more that prices and wages fall in response to reduced demand, the less that output and employment will have to fall. For monetary and fiscal policies to curb inflation by depressing aggregate demand, prices and wages should be flexible: that is, in response to lower demand, they should fall (or at least stop rising). Otherwise, anti-inflation policies will not only be less successful in combating inflation, but will also cause greater declines in output and employment.

Unfortunately, a factor that complicates the problem of combating inflation in Canada is that many prices and incomes are not flexible in this way, but rather are quite resistant to downward pressure from depressed demand. There are various reasons for this lack of flexibility: nearly 60 percent of employees in Canada are unionized; much of the economy consists of large corporations or government enterprises which are not subject to strong competition; and the production of many farm products is regulated by producers' marketing boards, which are intended to support prices. So when aggregate demand is depressed by anti-inflation policies, many prices and incomes do not decline, and the rate of inflation is not curbed by as much as would be ideal. Consequently, the burden of depressed aggregate demand falls more heavily on *output and employment,* and unemployment tends to rise quite sharply in response to anti-inflation policies.

---

[2]Another way to develop a budget surplus would be to increase taxes. In theory, an increase in taxes (for example, personal income taxes) helps to combat inflation by reducing consumer spending and thus aggregate demand. On the other hand, such a tax increase could also prove largely self-defeating, if many wage-earners succeeded in offsetting it by increasing their incomes more rapidly, causing additional cost-push pressures on prices. This idea is explained in Chapter 12 in the section on the tax-price spiral.

Side effects of monetary and fiscal policies

The monetary and fiscal policies described above will slow down inflation, but by depressing aggregate demand they will also slow down the economy, causing *unemployment* to rise. In particular, the high interest rates associated with tight money are likely to depress *capital investment spending* and the capital-goods industries, including housing. Thus, combating inflation with monetary and fiscal policies involves the sacrifice of other important economic goals, such as full employment and economic growth.

As a result, these anti-inflation policies (high interest rates, scarce credit, cuts in government spending) and their side effects (slower growth and higher unemployment) tend to be socially destructive and politically unpopular, making it difficult for governments to persist in using them for long. Despite their problems, these policies, particularly monetary restraint, are generally regarded as essential to combating inflation, because only these policies attack the excessive aggregate demand that is the root cause of inflation.

Combating cost-push inflation

However, curbs on aggregate demand and the money supply may not always in themselves be sufficient. We have seen that, in addition to demand-pull inflationary pressures, there are also cost-push forces, which can be particularly powerful and troublesome if inflation psychology is strong among the public. If output per worker-hour is rising at only 1 percent per year, and workers seek—and get—wage increases of 10 percent per year in their attempts to protect themselves from inflation, production costs (and prices) are bound to rise quite rapidly. While stressing the vital role of monetary policy, Beigie states that "monetary policy alone is unlikely to cure inflationary pressures originating in excessive income expectations . . .", and adds that "it is imperative that expectations be kept in line with potentials."[3]

What is needed, then, is *discipline*, so that people's income expectations do not get so far out of touch with economic reality that they cause severe inflation. How, then, can such discipline be achieved? In some cases, *competition in the marketplace* provides such discipline. Where there is a large labor supply, wages are likely to be lower, and where there are several companies manufacturing a product, prices will be more moderate. Unskilled migratory farm workers, for instance, are hardly in a position to generate inflation through excessive income expectations and demands, because they can easily be replaced. On the other hand, a great many Canadians are sheltered from such competition, either through labor unions or professional associations, or by working for large cor-

[3]Carl E. Beigie, *Inflation is a Social Malady*, British-North American Committee, 1979.

porations or government agencies that are not subject to severe competition. When expectations become unrealistic, one way to dampen them is to use monetary and fiscal policies to create a *policy recession*; people who are worried about their jobs tend to be less aggressive about getting big wage increases. However, such policies are not only politically difficult for a government to pursue for long, they are also not a total solution to the problem, as some economically powerful corporations and unions have demonstrated an ability to continue to push up prices and wages even in the face of a recession.

How else could the necessary discipline be achieved? Some suggest that *better education* regarding economics and economic realities would make people's expectations more realistic, but others argue that all this would produce would be better-educated unrealistically greedy people.

Some nations have attempted a form of economic planning, in which labor, business and government reach some kind of agreement on the division of the economic pie between wages, profits and taxes, so as to avoid an inflationary scramble for larger shares. While such *incomes policies* are interesting, they do not appear to be feasible in Canada in the foreseeable future, since they require a high degree of coordination and cooperation on a nation-wide level between government, business and labor. Even if it were possible to obtain the necessary degree of cooperation, Canada lacks the institutional framework to utilize an incomes policy. There are no central organizations capable of speaking for, much less making commitments for, either business or labor in Canada on a national level. Furthermore, the decentralized nature of Canada's governmental system, with political authority divided among the federal government and the ten provinces (each of which has considerable authority over labor relations) is another major obstacle to this type of planning in Canada. We are left with only two types of government policies for achieving discipline — wage-price *guidelines* and wage-price *controls*.

Wage-price guidelines

The government may adopt a moderate approach to cost-push pressures, and simply set guidelines for wage and price increases: the guidelines might state, for instance, that wages should not rise faster than 5 percent per year and price increases should be limited to 3 percent per year (the other 2 percent being absorbed by rising productivity). Corporations and labor unions are then asked to respect the public interest by following these guidelines in their wage negotiations and pricing decisions.

While this approach seems simple in theory, in practice it encounters several serious problems, the basic one being that wage-price guidelines are *voluntary*. As a result, there is a danger that economically powerful corporations and labor unions will refuse to cooperate with the government and will ignore the guidelines, especially if aggregate demand is high enough to be putting upward pressure on wages and prices. In these circumstances, guidelines ask unionists and businesses to voluntarily refrain from increasing their wages and prices as much as possible, forcing the leaders of these organizations to choose between the interests of their union members or shareholders and some vaguely expressed concept of social responsibility. As a result, experience has been that wage-price guidelines generally prove ineffective as an anti-inflation policy.[4]

Wage-price controls

Under wage and price controls, it is *illegal* to increase prices and wages more rapidly than as specified by the government. Penalties for doing so range from having the excessive increases "rolled back" to the allowable limit, to fines or even (in some countries) death.

The most extreme form of control is a *freeze* on all wages and prices, but most controls systems do allow wages and prices to rise at limited rates. For example, Canada's controls from 1975 to 1978 allowed wages to rise by 10, 8 and 6 percent in 1976, 1977 and 1978 respectively, and allowed prices to rise enough to offset increases in production costs per unit.

A major difficulty with wage and price controls is the detailed task of administering the controls. To enforce a *general* system of controls, which would apply to all prices and incomes in the economy, would require a veritable army of bureaucrats. Furthermore, even such a bureaucracy could not effectively administer such a controls system. Consequently, governments tend to avoid even attempting to implement general wage and price controls.

Instead, on those occasions when they impose controls, governments tend to use *selective* wage and price controls. Such controls apply only to the wages and prices of large corporations and powerful labor unions — those associated with cost-push inflation and the wage-price spiral described in Chapter 12. Because they do not apply to industries with many firms and strong competition or to non-union workers, selective controls are less difficult to administer than general controls. This was the approach used by both the US controls program of 1971-73 and the Canadian program of 1975-78, both of which applied only to those sectors of the economy where competition could not be counted upon to hold down prices and wages.

[4]Some people argue (cynically, but perhaps correctly) that guidelines are introduced by governments that are anxious to be able to say that they tried to stop inflation but that business and labor refused to cooperate. Thus, the blame for inflation can be shifted onto business and labor, and away from the government — even if it was the government's own policies that in fact caused the inflation.

How effective are wage-price controls?

As an anti-inflation policy, wage and price controls enjoy considerable popularity with the public. To the numerous people who believe in the "villain theories" that portray big business and labor unions as the root causes of inflation, controls seem a logical solution to inflation. Also, in controls, many people see an apparently simple solution to the perplexing and frustrating problem of inflation: people don't like rising prices and big wage increases (that other people get), so why not just outlaw them; that is, stop inflation by making it illegal. Other people disagree strongly with controls on the grounds that such a policy involves unwarranted interference by governments in the rights of private citizens.

The vast majority of economists are opposed to the use of wage-price controls as an anti-inflation policy (except in unusual circumstances, as described later) on the grounds that controls are simply *not effective*. More specifically, their opposition to controls is based on two facts: first, controls attack the symptoms of inflation rather than its causes, and therefore cannot succeed; second, controls tend to generate negative side effects on the economy. History abounds with examples of wage-price control programs that have failed because of these problems, which are explained in more detail in the following sections.

> The historical record indicates that controls have had, at best, only a minor impact on inflation over time; that record is one of the main reasons why a strong majority of economists would argue against their use.
>
> Carl E. Beigie,
Inflation is a Social Malady,
British-North American Committee, 1979

Controls attack symptoms rather than causes

As we have seen, the basic cause of inflation is excess demand for goods, services and labor. The rapid price and wage increases that result are merely the symptoms of the problem. Unless the cause is attacked (by policies that restrain spending in the economy), the demand pressure on prices and wages will continue, as willing buyers compete for goods, services and labor.

Under these circumstances, both theory and experience suggest that the controls will not be effective because people will find ways to evade them. For example, some groups (such as professionals and skilled tradespeople) would be able to evade the controls by receiving some of their income in cash or other forms that go undetected by the government's controllers. If the demand for the product is high, a business can find ways to increase prices despite the controls. By making minor changes in the product, it can be introduced as a new product with a new (and higher) price. In the same manner, previously standard features on a product such as an automobile can be made into options, available at additional cost, or a new feature, such as a warranty, can be added. When they believe controls are likely to be introduced, some businesses increase the list prices of their products, while leaving their actual selling prices unchanged. After the controls are imposed, the selling price (the actual price) can be increased as economic conditions permit, while the list price (the official price being watched by the government) remains unchanged. Another technique for evading price controls is to reduce the quality of the product while holding its price constant, thus implementing a *hidden price increase*. Regarding wage controls, employers who have high sales may wish to raise wages in violation of the controls, in order to attract and retain workers. One way to raise wages is to reclassify employees, or create new job classifications. For example, a group of Grade C widget-workers could be upgraded to Grade B (even though they were still really Grade C), and thus given a pay raise in excess of that allowed under the controls.

The result of these evasions of the wage-price controls will be that there will exist a black market for goods, services and labor—reflected in the difference between official (legal) prices, and the considerably higher prices that are *actually* paid. As long as there is excess demand in the economy, people will find a way to charge (and pay) more than the controls allow. Not even the death penalty has prevented the development of such black markets in many instances, because of the difficulties that authorities have in detecting violations of the law.

In 301 A.D., the Roman Emperor Diocletian imposed controls on all important wages and prices. To enforce his controls program, Diocletian used about half the population of Rome. The controls program failed.

The examples described above represent only a few of the types of evasion of controls that are possible. These and other evasion techniques present any wage-price control agency with an impossible task of policing not only wage and price increases, but also whether new products are really new, whether options were standard features last year, whether product quality has been altered in any way, whether reclassifications of workers are really justified and so on. What starts out as an attempt to restrain inflation can broaden into attempts by government to control business decisions concerning new products, product design, product quality, classification of employees, and the like. Whether the government should involve itself in such matters is strongly disputed by many people. However, the overriding reality is that this task is so vast and so complex that it simply cannot be done. For this reason, wage and price controls alone have never proven successful as an anti-inflation policy.

Controls have negative side effects on the economy

Monetary and fiscal policies to combat inflation produce the undesirable side effect of higher unemployment. Many people seem to believe that wage-price controls have no side effects, but this belief is not correct. The most dangerous effect of the imposition of controls is that they could shake business confidence, and thereby result in a *reduction in capital investment*, which would slow down the economy and increase *unemployment*. This danger is particularly great in Canada, because Canadian corporations can readily shift investment to the US, and American corporations are likely to decide to invest in the US rather than in Canada, as actually happened during Canada's controls program of 1975-78.

Controls can also have the side effect of *reducing incentives* to work. for example, if a doctor's income cannot be increased beyond a certain limit imposed by the government, he/she may decide to work only four days per week. These disincentives can result in reduced output of certain goods and services, or even in emigration of skilled people to other countries that do not restrict their opportunities in this way.

Related to the problems of depressed investment and reduced incentives is the problem that controls can cause *shortages* of products. For example, there are numerous examples of price controls causing farmers to refuse to bring their crops to market at uneconomical prices, and, more recently, controls on apartment rents have discouraged construction of new apartments, causing shortages of apartments.

Other side effects of controls are the development of widespread black markets through which the controls are evaded (as described above), a diminished respect for the law and the creation of a vast and expensive government bureaucracy to administer the controls.

For these reasons, wage and price controls alone have never proven effective as an anti-inflation policy, from the days of the Roman Empire to the controls programs in the USA and Canada in the 1970's.

Controls can sometimes be useful

All of this does not mean that controls are useless. Notwithstanding the foregoing criticism of controls, many economists believe that controls can serve a useful (although temporary and limited) purpose as part of an anti-inflation program. Suppose inflation has become quite severe, and inflation psychology is generating very large wage demands that are adding considerable cost-push pressures to the situation. In these circumstances, monetary and fiscal policies will curb inflation only if applied quite severely (and painfully), and even then will only take effect after a year or so. During this period, when the monetary and fiscal policies are taking hold on the economy, controls on wages and prices can be helpful in temporarily holding down the cost-push pressures that are worsening the situation.

> Controls are best used as a relatively temporary 'shock' measure to curb self-realizing rounds of inflationary pressures and expectations arising from a sudden burst of wage or price increases.
>
> Economic Council of Canada,
> *Fourteenth Annual Review*, 1977 (page 19).

An example of an attempt to use controls as a partial, temporary measure is provided by Canada in the mid-1970's: by 1975, inflation rates were in excess of 10 percent per year, incomes were rising at rates of 15-20 percent per year and income expectations had become totally unrealistic. To combat inflation, the government undertook to slow down the growth of the money supply. In addition, it imposed a three-year wage and price controls program intended to curb inflationary expectations until inflation had been slowed down by the curbs on demand. In effect, the controls were used to treat the symptoms of the problem (rapid wage and price increases) while the cure (curbs on demand) was taking effect. In this context, controls can be likened to a wet towel used to keep a patient's fever down while the antibiotics, the real cure, are working on the infection that caused the illness. No one would say that wet towels are a cure for an infection, but they can be of temporary assistance while the cure is being applied. Similarly, wage and price controls are best used as a temporary supplement to, not as a substitute for, real anti-inflation policies. If curbs are not placed on aggregate demand, controls on wages and prices cannot be effective in combating inflation.

Canada's wage and price controls 1975-78

From 1975 to 1978, the federal government imposed a system of wage and price controls on the Canadian economy. The controls were *temporary* (for a period of three years) and were intended to help contain the very strong inflation psychology that had developed until more basic policies such as slower growth of the money supply could take effect. The controls were *selective*, in that they applied only to large corporations (over 500 employees), professionals, government workers and the construction in-

ONE SECTION OF CANADA'S ANTI-INFLATION REGULA-
TIONS, 1976-78

23 (1)   The maximum price that may be charged by a supplier
in a compliance period for a product in a product line to which
this section applies that he commenced to supply more than 182
days before the beginning of the compliance period shall be
computed in the following manner:

(a) determine for the last period that ended before October 14, 1975, or for the first fiscal period that ended
more than 182 days after he commenced to supply the
product line, whichever is later,

   (i) the total revenue received from the sales of the
product line concerned, and

  (ii) the total allowable costs applicable to the product
line in question broken into components, such
components consisting of at least the cost of direct
materials, direct labour and direct and indirect
overhead;

(b) determine, for each cost component referred to in
subparagraph (a)(ii), the percentage, if any, by which
the cost price of the component, expressed as cost per
hour of labour, cost per unit of raw material or cost

dustry: in total, close to 1500 firms and five million people, or about
half the labor force were affected. The allowable increases for wages and
salaries were fairly simple, based on increases of 10, 8 and 6 percent
in 1976, 1977 and 1978 respectively. The rules for prices, as we have
seen, were more complex. To avoid discouraging production and causing
unemployment, the controls allowed prices to increase by the same amount
that production costs per unit rose.

Canada's controls program of 1975-78 illustrates a basic dilemma of
price controls. So that the controls would not jeopardize business incentives
to produce output and employ people, businesses were allowed to increase
prices to the same extent that production costs per unit increased.[5] In
avoiding the danger that the controls would cause production cutbacks
and unemployment, however, the government created another monster:

[5]Suppose the production costs of a product were $100.00 and its selling price was $108.50.
If the production costs rose to $102.13 per unit, the selling price could be increased to
$110.63. Thus, while the controls were intended to prevent profits *per unit* of output from
increasing, they allowed price increases sufficient to keep profits per unit constant.

per unit of other input, has increased or decreased
since the last day of the later of the two fiscal periods
described in paragraph (a);

(c) determine the aggregate of the numbers that result
when there is added to each cost referred to in subparagraph (a)(ii) the result obtained when the cost is
multiplied by the percentage determined under paragraph (b) for that cost;

(d) divide the aggregate determined under paragraph (c) by
the remainder when the target net margin percentage
of the supplier in respect of the product line is sub-
tracted from 100 percent; and

(e) multiply the price of the product on the last day of the
later of the two fiscal periods described in paragraph
(a) by the quotient obtained under paragraph (d),
divide the result by the amount determined under
subparagraph (a)(i) and adjust the amount so calculated
for variations in fixed costs and increases in volume,
where applicable, the result being the maximum price
that may be charged for a product included in the product line.

Anti-Inflation Act Regulations, Anti-Inflation Board.

Reproduced by permission of the Minister of Supply and Services Canada

to administer price controls based on cost increases would require very
detailed analysis of changes in the production costs of all products covered
by the controls. Businesses had to comply with a multitude of regulations
by completing masses of forms for an ever-growing federal bureaucracy
(the Anti-Inflation Board). The following box illustrates the complexity
of these regulations by reproducing less than one page of the Anti-Inflation
Act Regulations; the complete regulations consisted of sixty such pages.
The administration of these rules involved bewildering regulations to be
followed and forms to be completed, which generated considerable opposition from business and made the enforcement process slow, cum-
bersome and of questionable validity.

Thus, price controls present a real dilemma: if they impose simple limits
on prices that ignore cost increases, they are likely to cause production
cutbacks, shortages and unemployment. On the other hand, if the controls
try to avoid these risks by allowing businesses to recover increases in
costs, detailed monitoring is required through a maze of regulations such
as those shown here.

Several products and services were by law specifically *exempt* from the controls, including oil and energy, rents on new apartment buildings, farm prices "at the farm gate" (to the farmer), interest rates and imports. In each case, the exemption was based on legitimate economic concern that the application of the controls would cause shortages of these items. Higher oil prices were needed to finance exploration and development; rent controls have traditionally depressed new apartment construction; controls on food prices cause reductions in agricultural output; if Canadian interest rates fell much below US rates, Canada would be left short of vital capital as funds were shifted to the USA; and, finally, import prices are determined in world markets, so that Canada must pay the world price for imports in order to get them. While exempting these items from the controls undermined the credibility of the controls program in the eyes of the public, the results of applying the controls to these items would have been damaging, as serious shortages would have occurred.

The Anti-Inflation Board was most active in its first year (1976), when unions tested it with large wage increases, most of which were rolled back at the order of the AIB. While a few instances of excess profits and price rollbacks occurred, increasingly slow economic conditions depressed most profits anyway, making such cases rare. By 1977 and 1978, the activities of the AIB were much less noticeable, as the sluggish economy depressed both wage increases and profits. Because of these new economic conditions, the disbandment of the AIB in 1978 was not followed by an outburst of wage and price increases, as some people had expected.

In retrospect, it is now agreed that Canada's wage-price controls were more effective in restraining wage increases than in holding down price increases. Wage increases were subject to clearly stated limits, whereas prices could rise to the extent that production costs per unit rose, and many items (comprising a large proportion of the Consumer Price Index) were exempt from the controls. Supporters argued that controls helped to contain wage and price increases until the monetary and fiscal policies could take effect and ease the demand pressures on prices, while their opponents said that controls had a minor effect on inflation at best, and drove capital funds out of Canada at worst. Certainly, they did not succeed in curbing the Great Inflation: the rate of inflation did not decline significantly until the economy had gone through a period of severely depressed demand in the early 1980's.

What is the answer to inflation, then?

Inflation is one of the most persistent economic and political problems of the modern era, for several good reasons. It is in large part a side effect of government policies that keep unemployment down by maintaining demand at high levels. Also, the economic power of big business and labor unions tends to contribute to inflation. Fundamentally, inflation is the result of everyone—labor, business, government—wanting more out of the economy than the economy is capable of producing. It is not surprising, therefore, that since 1945, the economy has been characterized by a persistent tendency toward inflation.

What, then, should be done about the problem of inflation? It is unrealistic to try to stamp it out, as a few people suggest—to do so would involve such restrictive monetary and fiscal policies that a severe recession would result. Those who say, "What this country needs is a good old-fashioned depression," are definitely a small minority of Canadians. It is unrealistic for the government to focus only on the goal of combating inflation, as this conflicts with other important economic goals such as minimizing unemployment.

At the other extreme is the view that we should accept inflation as inevitable and learn to live with it. The main proposal of this sort is to index everyone's income to the rate of inflation, so that if the Consumer Price Index rose by, say, 10 percent, the government would guarantee that everyone's income rose by 10 percent. (Some people would be able to increase their incomes by more than 10 percent but the government would ensure that those who could not keep up with inflation on their own would not fall behind—their incomes would be supplemented so as to keep up with inflation.)

On the surface, this seems like a sound proposal, as it seemingly would protect everyone against inflation. However, if everyone gets a 10-percent raise, this arrangement becomes self-defeating. With everyone's income up 10 percent, the demand for goods and services increases, driving up prices even further. By boosting demand without doing anything to increase the supply of goods and services, indexing everyone's income would make inflation worse, rather than solve the problem. Thus, while indexing is considered reasonable for some groups (especially pensioners living on fixed incomes), the indexing of all incomes will in no way permit us to live with inflation. In a different sense, though, it is true that we must learn to live with inflation. As noted above, it is not feasible to stop it completely; governments can only keep it within limits. Thus, there will always be a degree of inflation in the economy.

Improving productivity to combat inflation

So far we have discussed inflation in terms of aggregate demand for goods and services outrunning the economy's ability to produce them, and have focused on anti-inflation policies that seek to curb excess demand in the economy. Another approach to this problem (a more positive one) is to take steps to increase the economy's ability to produce goods and services—to increase productivity, or output per worker. Rising productivity can reduce inflationary pressures in two ways: first, by making more goods and services available, demand-pull pressures can be made less severe; second, rising productivity helps to reduce cost-push pressures. For example, an 8-percent wage increase will only boost labor costs per unit by 4 percent if productivity rises by 4 percent, but if productivity only rises by 1 percent labor costs per unit will increase by 7 percent.

> It has become the conventional wisdom to blame inflation on people collectively 'living beyond their means'. While it is imperative that (income) expectations be kept in line with potentials, an economy's potential is a variable. In other words, a supplementary prescription is to increase the 'means' at a society's disposal.
>
> Carl E. Beigie,
> *Inflation is a Social Malady,*
> British-North American Committee, 1979.

The major way in which productivity can be increased is through higher levels of *capital investment,* which in turn require higher levels of saving, both in the form of business profits and personal saving. A society that encourages saving and investment will tend to suffer less inflation than a nation that fails to make provisions for increasing its output in the future. Unfortunately, in many industrialized countries, including Canada and the USA, productivity has lagged badly in recent years, certainly contributing to inflation.

Inflation in perspective

The problem of inflation is a complex and difficult one. Since the only real alternative to inflation is a recession, some inflation must be considered *unavoidable*. An all-out attack on inflation would generate intolerable unemployment. On the other hand, inflation cannot be left unchecked. Prolonged rapid inflation has very serious effects on many people and the economy in general. However, there are no simple solutions to the problem of inflation: wage and price controls and the indexing of incomes may look attractive, but they are essentially quack cures. We are left with the necessity of curbing the growth of aggregate demand and the money supply, and accepting more unemployment than we would like. A more positive approach is to *save, invest and improve productivity*. Only by achieving a closer match between a society's expectations and its potentials can inflation be curbed.

Ultimately, the answer to inflation lies in *discipline*. Governments must practise discipline in their spending programs and in the creation of money, income earners must practise discipline in their income expectations and income increases, and society in general must practise discipline by accepting sufficiently less consumption today in order to provide the capital investment necessary to increase prosperity tomorrow. The fundamental (and unresolved) challenge underlying the problem of inflation is: how can this discipline be achieved in a free and democratic society?

DEFINITIONS OF NEW TERMS

Wage-Price Guidelines   Suggested limits for wage and price increases which unions and employers are asked to follow voluntarily.

Wage-Price Controls   Legal limits on wage and price increases imposed by government.

Black Markets   The buying and selling of goods and services in violation of the law; in this case the law that sets limits on their prices.

CHAPTER SUMMARY

1. The most basic anti-inflation policies aim at reducing excessive aggregate demand through budget surpluses and, especially, tight money.

2. Such policies have the side effect of causing slower economic growth and higher unemployment.

3. For short-term purposes, particularly when inflation psychology is generating strong cost-push pressures, wage-price controls can make a temporary contribution to combating inflation.

4. Unless accompanied by restraints on aggregate demand, controls cannot succeed for more than short periods. Because they attack the symptoms rather than the causes of inflation, controls can be evaded in a wide variety of ways. Also, controls tend to have negative side effects on the economy by impairing incentives to work and invest.

5. It is not feasible to simply stamp out inflation; the result would be a serious recession. Thus, it is necessary to accept some inflation.

6. Indexing all incomes to ensure that everyone's income rises at least as fast as prices would be self-defeating, since such income increases would fuel further inflation.

7. While most anti-inflation policies are aimed at reducing demand, another beneficial approach would be to increase productivity.

8. Ultimately, the answer to inflation lies in discipline: by governments in their spending and creating of money, by the public in its income expectations and by society in general in doing enough saving today to finance the investment necessary to allow the future to meet our expectations.

QUESTIONS

1. In 1979, the New Democratic Party proposed a cost-of-living tax credit. Under this plan, families would receive personal income tax cuts (up to a maximum of $358 for a family of four) to offset the effects of inflation on their living standards. Do you believe that such a plan would be an effective way of dealing with the problem of inflation? Why?

2. The text states that the most positive approach to the problem of inflation is probably to improve productivity. What obstacles might a government experience in introducing policies intended to achieve more rapid increases in productivity?

3. Suppose that the incomes of all Canadians were indexed to ensure that they would always rise at least as rapidly as inflation, and that there was a sudden sharp increase in inflation in Canada due to major increases in the prices of imported items.
   What would happen?

4. Suppose that all prices in Canada were frozen by law, and that the international price of various commodities imported into Canada rose.
   What would happen?

5. Suppose that, in an attempt to keep interest costs down during a period of severe inflation, the federal government imposed legal limits on how high interest rates could rise.
   What would happen?

CHAPTER 14

The nature of unemployment

There is no economic problem that has a more devastating impact on people than unemployment. While economists consider costs of unemployment mainly in terms of lost income and output, there are human costs associated with unemployment that cannot be measured by economic statistics. According to the Canadian Mental Health Association,

> One of unemployment's most devastating effects is its erosion of self-respect. This is a nearly universal phenomenon. It not only darkens the unemployed individual's image of life, but also puts great stress on the quality of family relations.
>
> Our association's studies have cited numerous investigations that indicate a strong positive correlation between increased rates of unemployment and various manifestations of loss of self-respect, such as increases in depression, anxiety, self-deprecation, fatalism, anger, spouse abuse, child abuse, mental hospital admissions, homicides, rape, property crimes, racism, youth alienation, children's problems in school, and divorce. Almost every painful social consequence known to humankind is related to unemployment. Just as a physically unhealthy society is costly, so too is one that is socially and psychologically destructive.[1]

Since the Great Depression of the 1930's, the single most basic goal of economic policy-makers has been the minimization of unemployment, mainly through the use of monetary and fiscal policies. As a result, the thirty years following the end of the Second World War in 1945 were, with some relatively brief exceptions, characterized by lower unemployment rates than in the past. However, in the second half of the 1970's,

[1]"Economic Policy and Well-Being.' Submission to the Macdonald Commission, Toronto 1984.

the unemployment rate drifted upwards again, and when the Great Recession struck in the early 1980's, Canada experienced its highest unemployment rates in a half-century, with nearly one in eight Canadians jobless, and nearly one in five young Canadians out of work. Throughout the first half of the 1980's, unemployment was regarded as Canada's most serious economic problem.

> When somebody asks me what I do, I usually say, "I don't." As far as society is concerned, I don't contribute anything. I'm not a productive member of society.
>
> Unemployed university graduate, quoted in "The real costs of unemployment", by Richard Spence, *Financial Times*, March 19, 1984.

Causes of unemployment

On a macroeconomic scale, unemployment arises from an imbalance between the *supply of labor* (or the number of people seeking jobs) and the *demand for labor* (or the number of jobs available). Therefore, unemployment can be affected by developments on both the supply side and the demand side of labor markets.

The demand side

By far the most important factor influencing the level of employment (and therefore unemployment) is the level of aggregate demand for goods and services, which in turn determines employers' demand for labor. During economic booms, when aggregate demand is high, the demand for labor is also high, and unemployment is low. On the other hand, when aggregate demand is depressed, such as during recessions or when the government is pursuing anti-inflation policies, unemployment rises.

Aggregate demand is the most basic factor influencing unemployment for another reason: whatever the reason why people *become* unemployed, the absence of other job opportunities caused by inadequate aggregate demand is the main reason why they *remain* unemployed. While the government can reduce unemployment by using budget deficits and easy money policies to stimulate aggregate demand, it can only do this within limits, because such policies have the side-effect of making inflation more severe.

The supply side

Most discussions of unemployment focus on aggregate demand and the demand for labor; but changes on the supply side of the labor market can also be important. Unemployment can increase not only because lower demand means fewer jobs, but also because there are *more people seeking jobs*, or a greater supply of labor in the job market.

For instance, the labor supply can grow because of an increase in the proportion of the working-age population who want to work (the *participation rate*), or because of an unusually large number of young people who are seeking their first jobs. In both cases, the number of job-seekers — the labor supply — is increased. In Canada in the recent past, both of these factors have played a significant role in labor markets, as the postwar "baby boomers" came of working age and participation in the labor force by women increased considerably.

Aspects of unemployment in Canada

Wide *fluctuations* in unemployment rates from year to year are a characteristic of the Canadian economy. As Figure 14-1 shows, the unemployment rate has fluctuated greatly since the 1920's, with unemployment ranging from less than 2 percent to nearly 20 percent of the labor force.

FIGURE 14-1 *Percentage of Labor Force Unemployed 1926–85*

SOURCE   Statistics Canada.

The main reason for this instability is fluctuations in aggregate demand in the economy: unemployment increases whenever the economy experiences a recession, most recently in the 1930's, the late 1950's to the early 1960's and the early 1980's.

Seasonal variations

Seasonal variations are the source of shorter-term fluctuations in unemployment. Mainly because of the seasonal nature of economic activity in industries such as agriculture and fishing, unemployment is highest in the winter months of January through March, and lowest from June through October. Such seasonal factors probably add about 200 000 people to the ranks of the unemployed during the winter.

Types and duration of unemployment

The duration of unemployment varies greatly from case to case. The briefest type of unemployment is **frictional unemployment**, which arises from people being temporarily out of work because they are changing from one job to another. Frictional unemployment is considered to be a normal process in a free and dynamic economy, and probably averages about one percent of the labor force, being higher in periods of prosperity when job opportunities are more plentiful, and lower during recessions, when fewer people are able to change jobs. **Seasonal unemployment** usually lasts a few months, during which unemployment insurance benefits reduce the economic costs for many of the seasonally unemployed.

Cyclical unemployment, which arises from periodic recessions, is a more serious matter for many workers. Depending on one's seniority, a layoff due to cyclical forces may be short or long, and may exceed the one-year time limit on unemployment insurance benefits, forcing the unemployed worker into a very difficult position. During the recession of the early 1980's, the average duration of unemployment increased to 21.8 weeks, and many of the unemployed were out of work for much longer. The risk of cyclical unemployment is higher in industries that are strongly affected by recessions, including capital goods, construction and consumer durables, such as automobile manufacturing. An even more serious problem is **structural unemployment**, the major sources of which are changes in product demand or technology. Changing technology can not only cause layoffs, but also leave laid-off workers with inadequate or outdated skills. The result can be a mismatch of the training and skills of the unemployed and those required by employers, making it considerably more difficult for some unemployed people to find work. A related additional problem in Canada is the inadequacy of apprenticeship programs administered by labor unions and industry, which has contributed to shortages of some skills even when unemployment in general has been quite high. Changes in product demand (sometimes themselves related to the development of new technology and products) are another source of structural unemployment. For instance, the decline of industries such as coal mining, shipping and shipbuilding in Atlantic Canada has created whole communities that are characterized by very high unemployment. Structural unemployment can become very long-term in nature, forcing the unemployed — and in some cases whole communities — to fall back on welfare.

Demographic variations

The impact of structural unemployment on communities is reflected in the regional distribution of unemployment in Canada. Figure 14-2 demonstrates some regional differences in unemployment rates, with the highest rates found in Quebec and Atlantic Canada, where they are well above the national average.

FIGURE 14-2 *Unemployment Rates by Region 1966–85*

			Unemployment Rates			
	Canada	Atlantic region	Quebec	Ontario	Prairie region	British Columbia
1966	3.4	5.4	4.1	2.6	2.4	4.6
1967	3.8	5.3	4.6	3.2	2.3	5.1
1968	4.5	6.0	5.6	3.6	3.2	5.9
1969	4.4	6.2	6.1	3.2	3.3	5.1
1970	5.7	6.2	7.0	4.4	4.9	7.7
1971	6.2	7.0	7.3	5.4	5.2	7.2
1972	6.2	7.7	7.5	5.0	5.3	7.8
1973	5.5	7.8	6.8	4.3	4.7	6.7
1974	5.3	8.4	6.6	4.4	3.4	6.2
1975	6.9	9.8	8.1	6.3	3.9	8.5
1976	7.1	10.9	8.7	6.2	4.1	8.6
1977	8.1	12.6	10.3	7.0	4.9	8.5
1978	8.4	12.5	10.9	7.2	5.2	8.3
1979	7.5	11.7	9.6	6.5	4.3	7.7
1980	7.5	11.1	9.9	6.9	4.3	6.8
1981	7.6	11.7	10.4	6.6	4.5	6.7
1982	11.0	14.3	13.8	9.8	7.6	12.1
1983	11.9	15.0	13.9	10.4	9.7	13.8
1984	11.3	15.2	12.8	9.1	9.8	14.7
1985	10.5	16.0	11.8	8.0	9.2	14.2

SOURCE: Statistics Canada, "The Labour Force;" *Canadian Statistical Review* (Section 4, Table 5); Bank of Canada *Review.*

The age and sex distribution of unemployment is also noteworthy. As Figure 14-3 shows, unemployment rates are particularly high among *young people* (ages 15-24). During the recession of the early 1980's, the unemployment rate for males age 15-24 peaked at 22.4 percent, or nearly one in four jobless. When the economy slows down, employers tend to reduce or cease hiring, leaving many young people who are trying to enter the labor force unable to find work. Also, layoffs are most commonly done by seniority, and, therefore, hit the young hardest. Another factor underlying Canada's high rate of youth unemployment is believed to be Canada's minimum wage laws, which require minimum wage rates for younger workers that are not much less than those for more experienced workers, making it relatively less attractive to employ young people.

FIGURE 14-3   *Unemployment Rates By Sex and Age Groups 1966–85*

	Unemployment Rates			
	Age 15-24		Age 25+	
	Male	*Female*	*Male*	*Female*
1966	6.3	4.8	2.6	2.7
1967	7.2	5.5	3.0	2.8
1968	8.7	6.5	3.5	3.3
1969	8.3	6.5	3.2	3.7
1970	11.2	8.5	4.1	4.4
1971	12.1	9.8	4.3	5.0
1972	11.9	9.5	4.1	5.7
1973	10.1	9.2	3.4	5.4
1974	9.6	8.9	3.3	5.1
1975	12.6	11.4	4.3	6.5
1976	13.3	12.0	4.2	6.6
1977	15.0	13.8	4.9	7.4
1978	15.1	13.9	5.2	7.7
1979	13.3	12.7	4.5	7.0
1980	13.8	12.7	4.8	6.5
1981	14.2	12.3	4.9	6.7
1982	21.1	16.1	8.1	8.8
1983	22.4	17.0	9.2	9.6
1984	19.4	16.2	8.9	9.7
1985	18.2	14.6	8.3	9.4

SOURCE   Statistics Canada, "The Labour force;" *Canadian Statistical Review* (Section 4, Table 4).

For the 15-24 age group, the unemployment rate for *females* is regularly lower than for males, while for the 25-and-over age groups, the female unemployment rate is usually somewhat higher. This, however, has not always been the case. The recession of the early 1980's reduced employment more sharply in the male-dominated goods-producing industries than in the service industries where many women are employed, making the unemployment rate at times higher for men in the 25-and-over group than for women.

This uneven distribution of unemployment in Canada among different age groups, industries and regions creates problems for governments seeking to reduce unemployment by increasing aggregate demand. Even if aggregate demand in the Canadian economy as a whole were high enough to reduce the overall nationwide unemployment rate to the full-employment level (or even lower), there would still be substantial pockets of unemployment in certain regions and high unemployment rates among certain groups, especially the young.

Technological unemployment

There has always been controversy over whether technological change creates unemployment. While no one disputes that new technology displaces *some* workers from their jobs, the real question is whether new jobs are created in sufficient numbers to prevent unemployment in general from rising. Generally, economists have found that (at least so far) technological change has not caused unemployment rates to rise. As technology has raised living standards and disposable income, aggregate demand has risen, generating new jobs to replace those eliminated by technology. Also, government monetary and fiscal policies have usually maintained aggregate demand at levels high enough to prevent unemployment from rising to high levels. The comments of the Macdonald Royal Commission on Canada's Economic Prospects (1985) are worth noting here:

> "There is no significant evidence that the massive unemployment of . . . the present day resulted from technological change. Most . . . would agree that the sharp rise in unemployment resulted from the fact that total demand for goods and services in the economy fell considerably short of the economy's ability to produce them. Over the period for which we have reasonable data on the composition of unemployment, there is no evidence that structural unemployment caused by technological change has ever accounted for a major share of total unemployment over a large geographic area and during extended periods of time. Structural unemployment caused by technological change can be significant in smaller regions and for certain groups of workers (especially older workers), but it has not been a major contributor to the long-term pattern of national unemployment in Canada or in other comparably *industrial* countries."

Thus, there is no evidence that technological change has been the cause of the high unemployment rates of the 1980's. This is not to say that technological change does not have strong effects on unemployment among specific groups of people, especially when depressed aggregate demand makes alternative jobs scarce. The main factor determining the unemployment rate, however, is still the level of aggregate demand.

Measuring unemployment

There is probably no economic statistic that is more politically sensitive than the unemployment rate. A high and rising unemployment rate over a considerable period of time is more dangerous to a government's prospects for re-election than any other economic trend. For these reasons, we should examine the way in which unemployment is defined and measured.

As described in Chapter 4, unemployment-rate statistics are the product of a monthly survey of about 56 000 households across Canada, which is intended to determine whether respondents are employed or unemployed (and available for work). The *labor force* is the total of the employed and the unemployed, and the *unemployment rate* is the number of unemployed expressed as a percentage of the labor force. Thus, if there were 9 million people employed and 1 million unemployed, the labor force would be 10 million and the unemployment rate would be 10 percent.

In the labor force survey, a person will be counted as unemployed if, during the survey week, he/she was:
(a) without work, had actively looked for work during the past four weeks and was available for work, or
(b) had not actively looked for work in the past four weeks but had been on layoff for 26 weeks or less and was available for work, or
(c) had not actively looked for work in the past four weeks but had a new job to start in four weeks and was available for work.

There has been considerable debate in recent years over the *accuracy* and the *significance* of these unemployment-rate statistics. Some observers argue that the official statistics underestimate the extent of unemployment, while others assert that they overestimate it.

Hidden unemployment

Those who believe that the official statistics underestimate unemployment base their argument on what is called **hidden unemployment**. According to their argument, large numbers of Canadians can be described as "discouraged workers" — people who have given up looking for work, mainly because they believe jobs are not available. As a result, such people are excluded from the unemployment and labor force statistics altogether, and are missed when the jobless data are gathered.

Some critics have claimed that by excluding these people, Statistics Canada is underestimating unemployment by a large amount, perhaps by a third or more. In the early 1980's, these claims prompted Statistics Canada to defend its statistics (a highly unusual move). It argued that the unwillingness of the hidden unemployed to hunt for work shows that they have little attachment to the labor market, or little desire to work. The agency also noted "the labor force survey counts as 'active job search' anything done to find out about jobs in general, to collect information about particular jobs, or to attempt to obtain a specific job." People who had not done any of these things, StatsCan said, should not be counted as unemployed.

While there is disagreement over the nature and extent of hidden unemployment, it is generally agreed that it is greater in regions of chronically high unemployment (such as the Atlantic provinces) and during recessions. In such circumstances, even people who want to work may give up looking for work, and thus not be counted among the unemployed.

Voluntary unemployment

Other people argue that the official unemployment statistics have become a misleadingly high indicator of the number of Canadians who are unemployed, because the statistics include a considerable number of people who will not take jobs that are available. According to this view, the availability of unemployment insurance benefits for up to a year encourages some recipients to be more selective regarding the jobs that they will take, prolonging their period of unemployment and adding to the unemployment rate. This type of **voluntary unemployment** is more likely to occur in households that have more than one income, a situation that became increasingly common after the early 1970's. It is difficult to measure the extent of voluntary unemployment, but those studies that have been done estimate it to be between 1 and 1.5 percent of the labor force. Viewed from another perspective, this would be between 10 and 15 percent of total unemployment in Canada in recent years, or up to 200 000 people.

To the extent that voluntary unemployment exists, it would make it more difficult for the government to reduce the unemployment rate. As a result, it would become necessary to accept a higher unemployment rate than would otherwise be acceptable.

Why has unemployment increased?

The statistics in Figure 14-1 show not only periodic fluctuations in the unemployment rate, but also a general upward drift since the late 1960's. This upswing has occurred due to various developments related to both the supply side and the demand side of labor markets.

On the supply side, two developments have caused the labor force, or the supply of labor, to grow at more rapid rates. First, the "baby boomers" born in the decade after World War Two came of working age in large numbers during the 1970's. This influx of young people caused the labor force to grow exceptionally rapidly, so that even in years when employment grew strongly, not all these new job-seekers could find work. Secondly, changes in the role and status of women led to a significant increase in the number of *women seeking work* outside the home. Married women, in particular, began looking for jobs, to provide a needed second income for households. From 1961 to 1980, the *participation rate* for women more than doubled, rising from 23 percent to 50 percent, as women sought work in unprecedented numbers. This move toward fuller economic participation by women added substantially to the growth of the labor force — and thus to *both* employment and unemployment.

> Perhaps the most important labor force development in this period (the 1970's) was the increase in the proportion of married women in the labor force.
>
> Industrial Relations Centre,
> Queen's University,
> *The Current Industrial Relations Scene in Canada,* 1980.

Another factor affecting the supply side of labor markets was the 1971 revisions to the *Unemployment Insurance Act.* As noted earlier, it is believed that the improvements to UI benefits added to voluntary unemployment by encouraging prolonged and selective job searches by some UI recipients. A study for the Economic Council of Canada estimated that the UI revisions had added as much as 1.5 percentage points to the unemployment rate.[2] This finding was supported by the fact that even in the exceptionally strong economic boom of 1973, with aggregate demand at highly inflationary levels, the unemployment rate did not go below 5.5 percent. On the basis of past experience, an unemployment rate of less than 4 percent could have been expected under such conditions.

On the demand side, as the growth of the economy slowed from 1975 to 1978, the unemployment rate moved upwards, reaching 8.4 percent in 1978. Better economic conditions over the next three years brought the rate down into the 7.5 percent range, which, while high by the standards of the previous decade, at least represented a trend toward improvement. Then the Great Recession struck with unexpected severity in 1982, driving employment down by 362 000, unemployment up by 416 000 and the

[2] C. Green and J. -M. Cousineau, *Unemployment in Canada: The Impact of Unemployment Insurance* (Ottawa; Economic Council of Canada, 1976)

unemployment rate went from 7.5 percent to 11 percent in a single year. The unemployment rate peaked in 1983 at 11.9 percent, the highest since the Great Depression of the 1930's.

> The combination of unemployment insurance and the existing tax system also discourages many unemployed people from accepting available jobs. In many cases, UI benefits exceeded what could be earned for part-time work. Furthermore, part-time workers do not currently qualify for UI benefits, so acceptance of a part-time position can lead to a loss of entitlement to benefits.
>
> Edward Carmichael,
> *Policy Review and Outlook, 1985: A Time for Decisions,*
> C. D. Howe Institute.

Following the recession, unemployment decreased only gradually as the economy recovered, not falling below 10 percent until the summer of 1985. Most forecasters expected only a gradual trend toward lower unemployment rates for the rest of the decade, mainly because only modest economic growth was anticipated.

Is the unemployment rate an accurate measure of hardship?

In the past, an unemployment rate of 10 percent would have been regarded as intolerably high, compelling the government to attack the problem with strong monetary and fiscal policies to stimulate aggregate demand. In the 1980's, however, this was not the case: the government was willing to accept such high unemployment rates, partly because the unemployment rate was no longer regarded as the accurate measure of the extent of economic hardship in society that it once was. In the past, when the unemployed were almost all the sole supporter of their family, the unemployment rate came to be regarded as a real indicator of the degree of economic hardship in society. Now, however, the significance of unemployment statistics is much less clear. Studies conducted during the 1970's reported that unemployment was no longer an adequate indicator of family or individual economic hardship, because well over half the unemployed were not sole family supporters, but rather one of two or more incomes in a family.

The studies also found that in half the families in which one member was unemployed, the average family income was higher than that of families with no unemployment. This finding reflected the fact referred to earlier that many of the unemployed were not the only earners in the family. Furthermore, even as the unemployment rate increased during the 1970's, average family income rose by about half in real (after-inflation) terms, from 1967 to 1981. Thus, while the social and psychological hardship caused by unemployment remains, the unemployment rate is no longer viewed by some as the accurate indicator of economic hardship that it was in the past.

How low can unemployment go?

The government can use budget deficits and easy money policies to stimulate aggregate demand and reduce unemployment, but these policies will have the side-effect of making inflation more severe. At some point— determined as much by political as economic considerations—the rate of inflation will be considered too high to warrant attempts to reduce unemployment further. This brings us to the question of economic policy trade-offs between the conflicting goals of reducing unemployment and avoiding inflation, which will be considered in Chapter 15.

DEFINITIONS OF NEW TERMS

Frictional Unemployment   Unemployment arising from people being temporarily out of work because they are in the process of changing jobs.

Cyclical Unemployment   Unemployment caused by periodic slumps in industries that are strongly affected by recessions.

Structural Unemployment   Unemployment arising from shifts in the demand for products or from changes in technology.

Hidden Unemployment   Those unemployed who are not counted in the official unemployment statistics because they have given up looking for work.

Voluntary Unemployment   Unemployment resulting from people's decisions not to take jobs that are available, due to personal preferences and/or the availability of Unemployment Insurance benefits.

Participation Rate   The percentage of the population of working age participating in economic activity (or included in the labor force; that is, working or seeking work). Participation rates are also calculated for subgroups of the population, such as men, women, and young people.

CHAPTER SUMMARY

1. Unemployment, which involves major costs to society in both economic and human terms, became Canada's most serious economic problem in the first half of the 1980's.

2. The main cause of unemployment is inadequate aggregate demand in the economy, which depresses the demand for labor.

3. Factors which affect the supply of labor can also influence the amount of unemployment.

4. Unemployment fluctuates considerably from year to year, depending on economic conditions.

5. The duration of unemployment varies widely, depending on the circumstances. Frictional unemployment is very short-term in nature, seasonal unemployment is relatively short-term, cyclical unemployment may be of quite short or longer duration and structural unemployment is often quite long-term in nature.

6. Unemployment is higher in certain regions of Canada, especially the Atlantic provinces and Quebec, and among young people.

7. There is no significant evidence that technological change was the cause of the high unemployment of the early 1980's, the main source of which was weak aggregate demand.

8. There is disagreement regarding the accuracy of Canada's unemployment-rate statistics. Some argue that the statistics understate the extent of unemployment because they exclude hidden unemployment, while others argue that they overstate the extent of unemployment because they include voluntary unemployment.

9. Since the late 1960's, the unemployment rate has generally drifted upwards, due to a variety of developments on both the supply side and the demand side of the labor market.

10. Mainly because many of the unemployed are members of multi-income families, the unemployment rate is no longer regarded as the accurate indicator of the extent of economic hardship that it once was.

QUESTIONS

1. Why do unemployment rates in Canada tend to be higher for
   (a) young people (age 15-24)?
   (b) women age 25 and over?
   (c) the Maritime provinces and Quebec?

   What could be done about the high unemployment rates in each of these cases?

2. What could be done to reduce structural unemployment, and what obstacles would such attempts encounter?

3. Has the distribution of unemployment among different age and sex groups changed since the last statistics in Figure 14-3? If so, what factors might account for these changes?

4. Has the distribution of unemployment among Canada's regions changed since the last statistics in Figure 14-2? If so, what factors might explain these changes?

5. Have any changes been made in Canada's unemployment insurance program recently? If so, what are they and why were they made?

6.

Year	Population of Working Age (millions)	Partici- pation Rate (%)	Labor Force (millions)	Em- ployed (millions)	Unem- ployed (millions)	Unemploy- ment Rate (%)
19-1	20.0	60.0	12.0	10.8	1.2	10.0%
19-2	21.5	61.5		11.2		

In 19-1, the population of working age is 20 million, 60 percent of whom participate in the labor force, making the labor force 12 million. Of these, 10.8 million are employed and 1.2 million, or 10 percent of the labor force are unemployed.

Suppose that, in 19-2, the following developments occur:
(i) Employment grows quite rapidly (by 4 percent), to 11.2 million.
(ii) The population of working age increases to 21.5 million.
(iii) The participation rate increases to 61.5 percent.
Calculate the unemployment rate for 19-2.

CHAPTER 15

Economic policy in perspective

We have examined the major macroeconomic problems of recession and inflation, and the policy tools available to the government for dealing with them—monetary policy, which is the responsibility of the Bank of Canada, and fiscal policy, which is conducted by the Department of Finance. In short, a combination of easy money and a budget deficit can be used to lift the economy out of recessions by increasing aggregate demand, while tight money and a budget surplus can combat inflation by depressing aggregate demand.

While the *theory* of monetary and fiscal policy is quite straightforward, the *application* of this theory in practice involves certain practical problems and limitations. In this chapter, we will consider these problems and limitations, so as to place the matter of government macroeconomic policy into perspective.

Part A: Conflicting objectives of monetary and fiscal policy

We have seen how the government uses monetary and fiscal policies to influence the level of aggregate demand for goods and services and thus steer the economy toward desired goals. Three goals that the government seeks to achieve with these policies are:

(a) Full Employment

Probably the dominant objective of economic policy since the Great Depression has been "full employment"—the lowest possible rate of unemployment.

(b) Economic Growth

Another major objective of economic policy is a growing economy, which will provide not only jobs for a growing labor force, but also a rising standard of living for the population.

(c) Stable Prices

Economic policy-makers seek the lowest possible rate of inflation, for the reasons outlined in Chapter 13.

Unfortunately, it is not possible, in a basically market type of economy such as ours, to reach all three of these goals simultaneously. A conflict between goals occurs because the high levels of aggregate demand necessary to stimulate the economy toward full employment and growth also generate inflation. Beyond a certain point, it is not feasible to pursue the goals of full employment and growth further, because inflation would become intolerably rapid.

To see why this conflict between our economic goals arises, we will examine how the economy responds to increases in aggregate demand under each of the three following conditions:

(a) when unemployment is unusually high,
(b) when unemployment is below average, nearing "full employment," and
(c) when the economy is operating at its capacity (with production at its maximum possible pace and unemployment at a minimum).

(a) When unemployment is high

Suppose the economy is in a recession, with unemployment unusually high and output far below its potential. Assume also that with aggregate demand so depressed there is little inflation in the economy, and little is expected in the near future, so that inflation psychology and cost-push pressures are minimal. In these circumstances, if the government uses its monetary and fiscal policies to increase aggregate demand in the economy, the results should be quite favorable. Output and employment should increase, but without a large increase in prices. This increase in output can be achieved without much of an increase in prices, for several reasons. First, businesses should be able to hire unemployed labor at existing wage rates—they should not need to raise wages to attract additional workers. Second, as output increases, production costs per unit will fall, as production facilities are used more efficiently and fixed costs are spread over more units of output. Third, with the economy still sluggish, businesses and unions will be reluctant to seek large price and wage increases, for fear of jeopardizing their sales and jobs.

In short, then, during a period of high unemployment, government policies that increase aggregate demand will have *beneficial* effects on the economy by causing quite large increases in output and employment with quite small increases in prices. Such a situation is shown in Figure 15-1 by the increase in aggregate demand from AD to AD₁.

FIGURE 15-1 *How Increases in Aggregate Demand Affect the Economy Under Various Conditions*

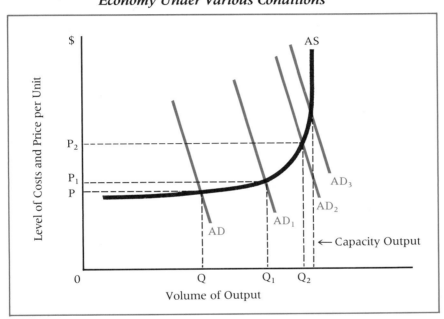

(b) When the economy is nearing full employment

As such expansionary monetary and fiscal policies bring unemployment down, however, their effects on the economy will change. With output nearing its potential (capacity) level and unemployment falling to near full-employment levels, further increases in aggregate demand will have *mixed* effects on the economy. While output will still rise (although less rapidly), prices will begin to rise more rapidly, as inflation speeds up. There are several reasons why inflation appears in the economy before unemployment has disappeared. Despite the fact that unemployment is still quite high in some regions such as the Atlantic provinces and Quebec, demand will be sufficiently high to generate full employment and inflationary pressures in other regions, such as Ontario and the West. Also, as demand rises, shortages of certain productive inputs (such as skilled labor and certain raw materials) will develop, causing their prices to rise despite the fact that the national economy is not yet operating at its capacity output. The price increases resulting from these production bottlenecks will force up production costs, contributing to more rapid inflation. Furthermore, as economic conditions improve, those business firms that are in a position to raise prices will begin to do so, and labor unions will take advantage of the improved bargaining position that low unemployment rates bring, negotiating larger wage increases that add to cost-push inflation.

Thus, as the economy nears full employment, increases in aggregate demand will cause increases not only in output and employment but also in prices, with inflation becoming more severe the closer the economy gets to full employment. In Figure 15-1, this is illustrated by the shift in the aggregate demand curve from AD_1 to AD_2.

(c) *When the economy is at full employment*

Once the economy has reached full employment, further increases in aggregate demand will bring no economic benefits. Producers as a group cannot respond to increases in spending by expanding real output, because the economy is already operating at capacity. Thus, increases in total spending will cause prices to rise very sharply, as aggregate demand in excess of society's productive capacity pulls prices upward. Higher levels of total spending will simply bid up the prices of a fixed real output. Thus, at full employment, increases in spending will cause pure inflation to set in: *Prices* will rise sharply but *real output* will not rise at all. Increases in aggregate demand beyond AD_3 will have this effect.

Depending on the circumstances, increases in aggregate demand can cause increases in output and employment, increases in prices, or both. As the economy moves closer to full employment, increases in aggregate demand become less beneficial, generating smaller gains in output and employment and more rapid inflation, as shown in Figure 15-1. The result is that it is *not possible* to achieve full employment and rapid economic growth simultaneously with stable prices. Therefore, our major economic goals conflict with each other.

Economic policy trade-offs

The conflict between various economic goals forces difficult choices upon the government in regard to its monetary and fiscal policies. If the government pursues full employment and economic growth by stimulating aggregate demand, more rapid inflation will occur. On the other hand, if the government seeks to combat inflation by restraining aggregate demand, economic growth will slow down and unemployment will rise. Economic policies, then, which are directed toward achieving beneficial results, will also have negative side effects.

The government is faced with a problem of economic policy *trade-offs*—the closer it approaches one of its goals, the farther it gets from another. Under these circumstances, the only practical course of action for the government is to seek a *politically acceptable balance* between its conflicting goals—a situation in which neither inflation nor unemployment is unacceptably severe. In the following sections, we will consider how much inflation and how much unemployment are considered to be tolerable.

How much inflation is "too much?" How much is "acceptable?"

As Figure 15-2 shows, the rate of inflation has varied widely, from less than 1 percent in 1961 to over 10 percent in the mid-1970's and early 1980's. While there is no official target for the rate of inflation, the rates of 4 percent per year that were experienced in 1985-86 seemed to be generally regarded as satisfactory, at least in the light of the double-digit inflation that had preceded them. To try to reduce the inflation rate much below this would risk worsening an unemployment problem that was already regarded as the nation's most serious economic problem.

FIGURE 15-2 *Rate of Inflation 1961–85*

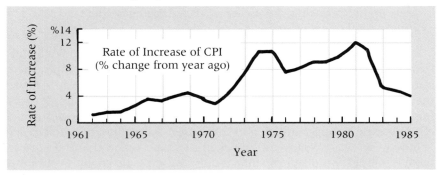

SOURCE   Statistics Canada.

How much unemployment is "too much?" How much is "normal?"

Because of the hardship and human costs associated with unemployment, these are controversial questions. There is considerable disagreement over the answers to them, with some people insisting that we can and indeed must reduce unemployment to about 4 percent of the labor force and others asserting that we cannot expect to do better than an unemployment rate of 8 percent—a difference of about 500 000 jobs.

As we have seen, unemployment can be reduced by policies that stimulate aggregate demand; however, the lower the unemployment rate becomes, the higher the inflation rate becomes. At some point, inflation becomes so severe that it threatens the performance of the economy— including employment itself in an economy as dependent as Canada's is on its ability to compete internationally. Beyond this point, it is not advisable to push aggregate demand higher in an attempt to reduce unemployment further; therefore, *full employment* is considered to have been reached.

What unemployment rate actually represents full employment? In the 1960's, it was thought that a 4 percent unemployment rate was a reasonable full employment target for policy-makers. In more recent years, however, the task of reducing unemployment has been made more difficult by at least two factors:

(i) a greater degree of voluntary unemployment, arising largely from the combination of many more multi-income households and the unemployment-insurance system's encouragement of more prolonged and selective job searches by some UI recipients, and

(ii) inflationary expectations: to the extent that inflation psychology exists, government policies to stimulate aggregate demand are likely to touch off larger wage demands and price increases, making inflation more severe and reducing the ability of rising aggregate demand to boost output and employment.

By the early 1980's, economists believed that this combination of factors had increased the realistically attainable (full employment) unemployment rate to as high as 7 or 8 percent of the labor force. That is, it was believed that if unemployment were at this level, increasing aggregate demand further would not only fail to reduce unemployment by much, but would also generate stronger inflationary pressures, as inflation psychology led people to increase wages and prices in the expectation that the government's policies would prove inflationary. As a result, many economists in the early 1980's came to the belief that the underlying unemployment rate or NAIRU (Non-Accelerating Inflation Rate of Unemployment) was nearly 8 percent of the labor force, and that attempts to reduce unemployment much below this level would generate strong inflationary pressures.

By mid-1986, this view had not yet been tested by experience, as the unemployment rate remained well above even this full employment level and the inflation rate remained quite stable at about 4 percent per year. To the extent that inflationary expectations can be reduced by the less inflationary environment that followed the recession of the early 1980's, it could well prove possible to achieve unemployment rates of less than 7 or 8 percent without generating excessive inflation.

Part B: Further problems and limitations concerning monetary and fiscal policies

Since the economic collapse of the 1930's, the government has taken a much more active role in economic matters. Of particular importance has been the government's use of monetary and fiscal policies to influence the level of aggregate demand, supporting demand during recessions and dampening it during periods of inflation. Unfortunately, as we have seen, the major goals of monetary and fiscal policy—full employment and price stability—conflict with each other, presenting the government with trade-offs between these goals and forcing the government to accept some of each in order to avoid excessive amounts of either. The existence of these trade-offs imposes certain limitations on the government's use of monetary and fiscal policy.

This conflict, however, is not the only limitation on the effective use of monetary and fiscal policies in Canada. In this section, we will examine several other factors that tend to make economic policy-making a complex, difficult and uncertain process.

There are no quick cures to economic problems

While everyone would like government policies to bring a quick end to inflation or recession, this is not possible, due to the problem of *time lags*.

To illustrate this problem, suppose the economy is expanding rapidly, with unemployment low and nearing full-employment levels. The rate of inflation is rising, causing some people in business and government to warn that anti-inflationary policies are in order. However, the situation is not yet completely clear—in some months, the Consumer Price Index barely rises. Other people argue that inflation is not a serious problem yet, and that the government should permit the economic boom to continue rather than slow the economy down. By the time the picture becomes clear enough for those responsible for economic policy to recognize and agree that anti-inflation policies are necessary, a considerable period of time will have passed. This, then, is the first of the lags: the *recognition lag*, or the time between the existence of a problem and the recognition of it.

The policies to attack inflation cannot all be put in place immediately. While the Bank of Canada can move quite quickly to change its monetary policy, changes in fiscal policy involving taxes and government spending can take considerably longer, as they may involve budget or legislative changes. The time lag between the recognition of the problem and the actual implementation of policies designed to remedy it is called the *policy lag*.

Once the government's economic policies are in place, there will be a further time lag before they take effect on the economy. As noted in Chapter 12, changes in the rate of growth of the money supply do not affect the rate of inflation for about a year. Similarly, changes in taxes and government spending do not affect the economy quickly. Higher taxes do not depress consumer spending immediately — despite lower disposable incomes, many consumers will continue for some time (often estimated at about six months) to spend as they have become accustomed to doing. Corporations will complete investment projects that they have started, and the multiplier effect of previous high levels of spending will continue to operate. After a while, the economy will slow down and the rate of inflation will fall. The period between the implementation of policies and the feeling of the effects of those policies is called the *impact lag*.

Together, time lags create serious problems for economic policy-makers. Because of the lags, the problem being attacked (inflation or recession) can grow considerably more severe and difficult to remedy by the time the government's policies take effect, which makes it particularly important for the government to have accurate economic forecasts so that it can decide its policies as early as possible. Unfortunately, economic forecasting is an imprecise process at best, making governments understandably reluctant to base policy decisions on forecasts that may well be inaccurate.

In the mid-1960's, many economists were quite optimistic about the effectiveness of government policies, and talked about "fine-tuning" the economy with small shifts in policies intended to achieve small and specific policy goals. The economy was likened to a sports car, in that it was seen as being very responsive to subtle directions from its driver (the government). Now, however, it is recognized that managing the economy is more like handling an oil supertanker which will continue in the same direction for nearly two kilometres before *beginning* to respond to its wheel being turned.

Political problems: overstimulation and overreaction

In managing the economy, as in steering a supertanker, it is important to avoid sudden or excessive changes in speed or direction, as these will be impossible to correct quickly. However, in deciding economic policy, governments are sometimes more responsive to political considerations than to economic ones.

In particular, governments may be motivated by political considerations to *overstimulate* the economy so as to reduce unemployment, generating severe inflation in the process. Considering the time lags involved, such severe inflation is likely to gain momentum, eventually becoming a political issue itself and forcing the government to impose harsh anti-inflation policies. These policies will throw the economy into a recession from which it will take considerable time to recover. Recent history provides good examples of these tendencies: during the second half of the 1960's, the government overstimulated demand, causing such rapid inflation that by 1969, harsh anti-inflation policies were considered necessary. However, fighting inflation caused quite high unemployment in 1970-71, and the government, facing an election in 1972, reversed the direction of its policies dramatically once again. The result was a very rapid increase in both government spending and the money supply, and the worst inflation in years. By late 1975, the government was again forced to reverse the thrust of its policies, imposing anti-inflation policies that would depress growth for years.

The irony of the situation, of course, is that the monetary and fiscal policies designed and intended to moderate economic fluctuations were being used in ways that actually *caused* economic instability. Our bad experience with such *stop-go policies* presents a strong argument for a steady hand in the application of monetary and fiscal measures: the government should not allow short-term political considerations to prevail over longer-term economic considerations.

Some people regard these political obstacles to sound economic policy-making as a failing of political leadership, while others blame the public's ignorance of or unwillingness to accept economic realities. If the public will elect politicians who promise to reduce unemployment and provide more and more public services while reducing taxes (and later print money to pay for their promises), who is at fault—the public or the politicians? If the public possessed a better understanding of economic realities, sound economic policy-making by governments would be much more likely. However, as long as the public remains relatively uninformed or misinformed on such matters, there is a risk that economic policy questions will be debated and decided more to gain political support than to solve real economic problems.

Limitations on fiscal policy

The effective operation of fiscal policy requires a central government with strong powers, to adjust tax revenues and government expenditures as economic conditions require. In Canada, however, the economic role of the 10 *provincial governments* has expanded tremendously over the past 20 years, to the point where the provinces control much of the tax revenues and government expenditures in the country. Provincial governments are responsible for large expenditures in many areas, including health, welfare and education; and control many tax revenues, including resource taxation. By 1979, provincial and municipal governments employed approximately 800 000 people, compared to the federal government's 583 000 employees.

Many Canadians believe that the erosion of the federal government's fiscal power has gone too far—so far that the federal government's relatively small share of total tax revenues and government expenditures in the nation impairs its ability to use fiscal policy effectively.

Another limitation on the effectiveness of fiscal policy in Canada arises from the high level of *imports* into the country. The result is that much (probably as much as 30 percent) of the increased demand for goods and services created by budget deficits is siphoned off into imports, reducing the stimulus to output and employment within Canada. This process is explained more fully in the section dealing with limitations arising from international factors.

Limitations on monetary policy

Monetary policy is a vitally important but imprecise art. The money supply and monetary conditions are difficult to measure accurately, there is disagreement on which definition of the money supply (M1, M1A or M2) should be used as the target for monetary policy, and the Bank of Canada's policies affect the economy in ways that are difficult to predict precisely, especially in view of the long time lags (one to two years) involved. As a result of these problems, the conduct of monetary policy remains an uncertain operation. These problems are, however, not the only ones limiting monetary policy in Canada—other major limitations are imposed on the Bank of Canada's freedom by international considerations, discussed in the following section.

International limitations on Canadian policies

The Canadian economy has an unusually large exposure to international economic forces, which inevitably have a major influence on its performance. In the first place, Canada is heavily involved in world trade, exporting nearly 30 percent of our GNP and importing a similar amount. Of the almost 30 percent of Canada's GNP that is exported, seven tenths goes to the vast US market alone. Furthermore, Canada has historically received large inflows of foreign capital, mostly from the USA. This inflow of foreign capital has not only financed a significant proportion of Canada's capital investment, but also has provided Canada with the considerable amounts of foreign currencies (mostly US dollars) needed to pay for large-scale imports of goods and services. To attract a continued inflow of foreign capital, the Bank of Canada has traditionally kept Canadian interest rates somewhat higher than US interest rates. In the process of its international dealings, then, Canada places significant limitations on its own monetary and fiscal policy decisions. Some of these limitations are explained further in the following paragraphs.

Probably the major international influences on Canadian policies concern monetary policy, particularly *interest rates*. If Canadian interest rates are not high enough compared to US rates, the inflow of capital into Canada could slow or stop (or, worse yet, capital could flow out of Canada seeking higher returns in the USA). Such a development would have negative effects on the Canadian economy, as it would reduce capital investment and provide fewer US dollars for Canadians to buy imports. Another effect of reduced capital inflows would be a decline in the international value of the Canadian dollar. An important factor influencing the international value (or price) of the Canadian dollar is the buying of Canadian dollars by foreigners for the purpose of investing in Canada; should this foreign investment decline, the reduced demand for the Canadian dollar would cause its international value to decline. Canadian living standards would, in turn, be reduced, because the prices of imported goods and services would rise due to the reduced purchasing power of the Canadian dollar internationally.

These international considerations significantly limit the freedom of the Bank of Canada in deciding Canadian interest rates—to a large extent, Canadian interest rates are determined in the USA. For example, over the 1978-81 period, despite a sluggish Canadian economy, the Bank of Canada repeatedly increased interest rates in order to match increases in US rates.

Canadian authorities are also generally reluctant to allow Canada's *rate of inflation* to significantly exceed US inflation rates for long. If they did, Canada's prices would be significantly higher than US prices, Canada's exports to the USA would decline and imports from the USA would rise. Not only would many jobs in Canada be threatened, but the international value of the Canadian dollar would also decline, due to reduced US demand for Canadian dollars with which to buy Canadian goods. In the 1974-75 period, Canadian authorities did, in fact permit inflation rates in Canada to remain well above US rates. The result was much as has been described: sluggish Canadian exports, a dramatic increase in imports and an 18-percent decline in the Canadian dollar relative to the US dollar after late 1976.

The presence of the vast US economy to the south limits the freedom of Canadian authorities to decide *taxation policies*, as well. If Canadian taxes on profits, interest income or dividend income become too high relative to US taxes, there is a risk that the flow of investment capital into Canada will be reduced, and that Canadian businesses will invest in the USA instead of in Canada.

Finally, Canada's high level of imports limits the effectiveness of *policies intended to stimulate the Canadian economy.* Because so much (about 30 percent) of the responding effect of the multiplier is drained off by imports when Canadian authorities inject additional demand into the economy, the multiplier effect is quite small. As a result, these policies have less impact on output and employment in Canada than Canadian authorities would like.

In summary, the heavy exposure of the Canadian economy to international economic forces creates special difficulties for Canadian economic policy-makers. In particular, the importance of exports and of foreign capital inflows places significant limitations on Canadian authorities in deciding monetary and fiscal policies, forcing them to consider not only domestic Canadian problems, but also international factors, when formulating policies.

The problem of expectations

A relatively new problem for governments seeking to stimulate a sluggish economy is that, since the experience of the 1970's, people have become much more aware of the possible inflationary consequences of such policies. If the government were to move aggressively to boost aggregate demand to combat unemployment, people would anticipate renewed inflation. If inflation psychology sets in, people will seek to protect themselves, mainly by increasing their incomes and prices as quickly as possible. As a result, much of the increased aggregate demand from the government's policies may be dissipated in price and income increases, and output and employment would increase only slightly. If this theory (sometimes referred to as *rational expectations*) is correct, it could place significant limitations on the ability of government to reduce unemployment by stimulating aggregate demand.

Part C: How inflation affects capital investment

In Chapter 9, we saw how excessive government budget deficits could, over time, depress business investment spending by competing for capital funds and by driving interest rates up. There are similar concerns regarding easy money policies—that the inflation that results from excessive easy money could also depress capital investment.

Applied *periodically* and *temporarily* to combat recessions, budget deficit and easy money policies are generally regarded as beneficial. There is some concern regarding the trade-off of higher inflation, but this side effect is a major problem only if they are used excessively.

However, there is reason for concern if either, or both of these policies are applied excessively over considerable periods of time. Both theory and the experience of the 1970's suggest that if severe and chronic inflation is generated, the trade-off of higher output and employment can worsen or even disappear. Instead, the result can be not only severe *inflation*, but also *stagnation* — slow economic growth, high unemployment and weak business investment spending. The uncomfortable combination of stagnation and inflation, which are ordinarily not supposed to occur together, came to be known in the 1970's by the appropriately unattractive name of **stagflation**. The stagflation of the 1970's was a complex phenomenon, involving many factors. In the following section, however, we will focus on one of the more important — although less noticed — ones: the depressing effect that severe inflation has on capital investment spending by business.

> The idea, once rather popular, that high employment and output could be more readily achieved and sustained by being relaxed about inflation has surely now been demonstrated to be clearly wrong. Inflation and unemployment are not alternatives between which we can choose. Inflationary policies lead to poor economic performance, including high unemployment.
>
> Gerald Bouey,
> Governor of the Bank of Canada,
> *Annual Report of the Governor of the Bank of Canada,* 1983

The three basic sources of capital investment funds

The ways in which inflation can depress capital investment are quite complex and subtle. In considering this problem, attention must be given to the effect of inflation on all three basic *sources of funds* for capital investment:

(a) Bond issues
(b) Stock issues
(c) Retained earnings

(a) Bond issues: how inflation affects borrowing as a source of capital

A major source of funds for capital investment is long-term borrowing, through the issue of bonds that are usually repayable after ten or more years. However, severe inflation makes it much less attractive to corporations to engage in long-term borrowing, by forcing interest rates to high levels. Inflation causes high interest rates in two ways: first, lenders demand an interest *premium* to compensate them for the declining value of their capital, and, second, the *policies* used by the government to restrain inflation involve increases in interest rates. In particular, the very high interest rates associated with the severe inflation of the 1970's made many corporations reluctant to raise capital through bond issues that would commit them to paying very high interest expenses for many years.

It seems logical that such high interest rates should at least increase the amount of capital available by increasing the incentive for people to *save*, but this is not so, either, due to the effects of inflation and taxation. Figure 15-3 shows the return on $100 of savings invested at a 15-percent rate of interest for one year during which the rate of inflation is 12 percent. Although 15 percent seems like a high rate of interest, the figures in the chart are misleading. While $15 of interest income is received, the purchasing power of the lender's capital declines by $12 (12 percent of $100) due to inflation, leaving a real return of $3. Assuming that income tax is payable at a rate of 40 percent on the interest income,[1] taxes will amount to $6 (40 percent of $15), leaving a net after-tax return of –$3, or a rate of return of –3 percent . . . hardly a great economic incentive to save and invest. The combination of severe inflation and high interest rates discourages not only capital investment, but also the saving upon which much capital investment depends.

In summary, rapid inflation tends to discourage borrowing and bond issues as a source of funds for capital investment by forcing interest rates to high levels. Furthermore, rapid inflation can lessen the use of borrowing as a source of capital by eroding the economic incentive to save, thus undermining the saving-investment process.

FIGURE 15-3   *Inflation, Taxes and Incentives to Save*

Interest Income on $100 Invested at 15%		$15
Less:		
Loss of purchasing power of capital due to inflation (12% of $100)	$12	
Income tax (40% of $15)	<u>6</u>	<u>18</u>
Net return to investor after inflation and taxes		<u>–$3</u>

[1]In Canada, no income tax would be payable on interest (and other investment income) below a total of $1 000 per year. On the other hand, a tax rate of 40 percent on interest income above this exemption would not be unusual. While personal savings rates in Canada were very high in the 1970's, the high rates were more the result of economic uncertainty and special tax incentives for savings than of the apparently high interest rates available on savings. In the USA, personal savings rates were sharply reduced by the factors discussed above.

(b) Stock issues: how inflation affects the ability of corporations to raise capital by selling shares

Borrowing, however, is not the only way of raising capital for investment. Another important source of capital is the selling of shares (stocks) by corporations to the public. Traditionally, stocks have been regarded as a good investment during periods of inflation because they represent ownership of real property, the value of which should increase along with prices in general (as opposed to bonds, which have a fixed value, the purchasing power of which is reduced by inflation). However, this theory has not been borne out, when one considers the actual performance of the stock market over the inflationary period since the late 1960's, as shown in Figure 15-4.

According to the blue graph, the TSE 300 (an index, or average value of 300 stocks traded on the Toronto Stock Exchange) rose only about 70 percent through the 1970's. Since the Consumer Price Index rose by about 100 percent over the same period, stock prices failed to keep up with inflation. That is, the real value of stocks fell.[2] While there are several possible explanations for the poor performance of stock prices, a fundamental reason is that the severe inflation of the 1970's could have depressed stock prices, for two reasons. First, rapid inflation has

FIGURE 15-4 *Stock Prices 1965–85*

SOURCE   Department of Economic Research, *Canada's Business Climate*, Toronto Dominion Bank.

[2]The rapid increase in the TSE 300 during 1980 was the result of heavy speculative buying of oil and energy stocks, which pulled up the entire index. Generally, however, the stocks of companies in other industries did not perform nearly so well.

an adverse effect on real after-tax business profits. Second, if inflation forces interest rates to very high levels, as happened during the 1970's, these high interest rates can attract investors' capital into interest-earning securities such as bonds, mortgages and guaranteed investment securities, rather than stocks. As savings are attracted to these investments, the demand for stocks is depressed, resulting in depressed stock prices, and making it more difficult for corporations to raise capital through stock issues.

Rapid inflation, then, makes it more difficult for businesses to raise capital not only through bond issues, but also through stock issues. Finally, we must consider how inflation affects the third source of funds for capital investment — retained earnings.

(c) Retained earnings: how inflation affects business profits

If issuing stocks and bonds to raise capital presents difficulties during periods of rapid inflation, shouldn't businesses be able to get the required funds from their own profits?

The public believes that rapid inflation is good for business profits; indeed, the statistics in Figure 15-5 seem to confirm this, as they show rapid increases in profits in the inflationary 1970's, especially in the highly inflationary 1972-74 period. However, the profit picture is not as simple or as rosy as the reported profits of corporations suggest. In short, much of these apparently large increases in profits was not available for capital investment; rather, the profits were required to replace inventories and depreciated capital equipment at the much higher prices caused by inflation. The reported profits in Figure 15-5 are *exaggerated*, for the following reasons:

  (i) the reduced purchasing power of profits due to inflation,

 (ii) the inclusion of inventory profits in the figures, and

(iii) the inadequacy of depreciation allowances.

     Each of these factors will be examined in some detail in the following sections.

(i) Reduced purchasing power of profits due to inflation

While profits rose in the 1970's, so did the cost of capital goods which are bought with those profits. In fact, the cost of capital goods increased in the 1970's far more rapidly than the costs of goods and services generally. According to one study, "A fundamental reason for (slow investment in basic industries) is the exceptionally high cost of new projects when measured in terms of units of output. For a group of ten basic industries surveyed, these costs were growing on average at over three times the (general) rate of inflation during the 1970's."[3] Thus, much of the apparently rapid increase in profits in the 1970's was an illusion, as inflation eroded their purchasing power exceptionally fast.

FIGURE 15-5 *Corporation Profits 1970–85*

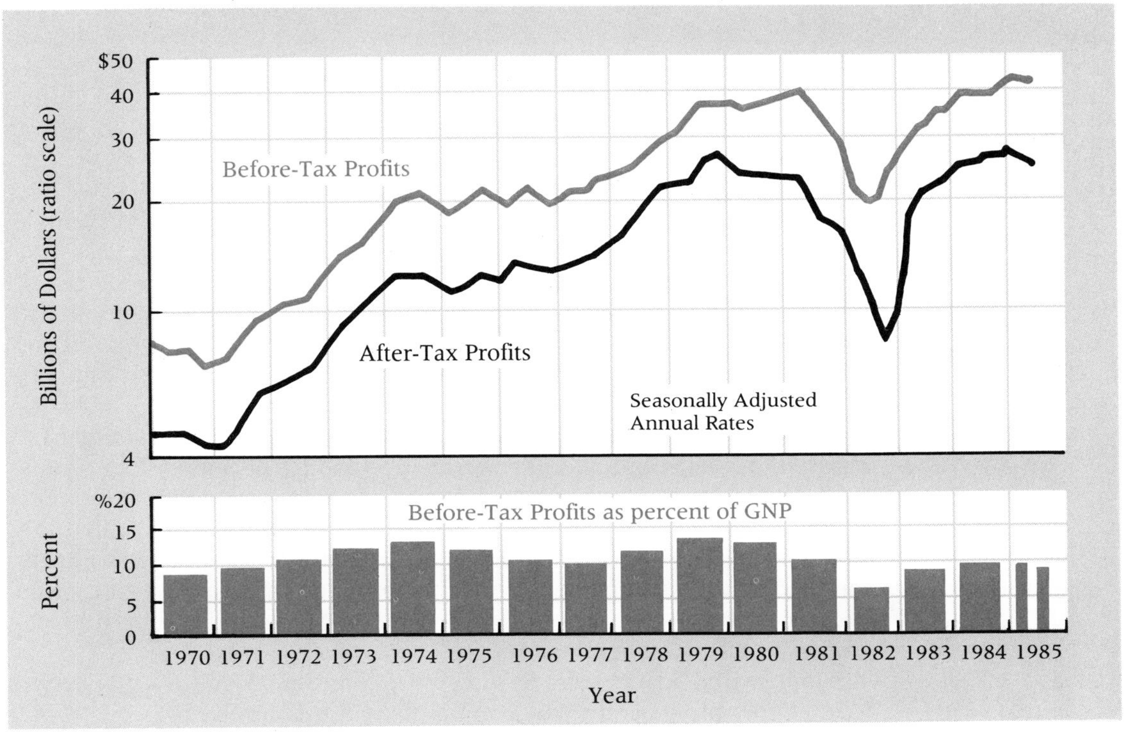

SOURCE Department of Economic Research, *Canada's Business Climate*, Toronto Dominion Bank.

(ii) *Inflation and inventory profits*

As noted earlier, a good deal of the apparently large increases in profits in the 1970's was required to replace inventories at higher prices, a problem that requires further explanation. The effect of inflation on the value of inventories is to generate *artificial* increases in reported profits. For example, consider the effect of rapidly rising lumber prices on the apparent profits of the furniture manufacturer shown in Figure 15-6.

[3]British-North American Committee, *New Investment in Basic Industries,* an Occasional Paper by a Committee Task Force Montreal, 1979 (page 13).

FIGURE 15-6

Year	Cost of Wood	Processing Costs	Selling Price	Reported Profit
19*1	$100	$90	$210	$20
19*2	$100	$90	$220	$30

In 19*1, wood is bought for $100 and made into a table, the processing costs being $90. The table, which cost $190 to produce, is sold for $210, making the profit on the table $20. In 19*2, another $100 of wood is bought and processed into a table at the same total cost of $190 (the processing costs are assumed to be unchanged in order to keep the example simple). However, during 19*2, there is rapid inflation, which causes the value of the $100 of wood bought by the company to increase by 10 percent ($10) *while it is in the company's inventory*. This rapid inflation also makes it possible for the company to increase the selling price of the table by $10 in 19*2—which it does, because it will have to pay $10 more to replace the wood next year.

The result, however, is a dramatic 50-*percent increase* in the company's reported profit, from $20 in 19*1 to $30 in 19*2. This increase in profits, however, is an *illusion*, because the entire $10 of extra profit is required to replace the inventory (wood) at its new, higher price of $110 in 19*3. Thus, this $10 increase in profit is *not available for capital investment* (or for dividends to shareholders) and is therefore not truly profit—it is given the name *inventory profit*, to indicate that it is an illusion arising from increases in the value of inventories.

Suppose that, in 19*3, wood prices stopped rising. What would happen to inventory profits and to the company's reported profits?

With no further price increases in 19*3, the company's reported profits would fall back to the $20 level of 19*1, as shown in Figure 15-7. Once wood prices stop rising, the inventory profits simply vanish. Inventory profits are solely the result of rising inventory prices, and the faster those prices rise, the more the reported profits of businesses will be exaggerated.

The degree to which reported profits are overstated because of inventory profits depends on several factors, particularly the rate of inflation. Research shows, however, that inventory profits caused significant exaggerations of profits in the 1970's—in some years, they have caused total corporate profits to appear as much as 30 percent higher than they really were. For individual firms and industries carrying large inventories that were increasing rapidly in price, the overstatement of profits was much larger.[4]

[4]This was particularly true of the oil industry. In 1973, the after-tax rate of return on shareholders' equity of the US petroleum industry was 11.6 percent. As a result of the dramatic Arab oil-price increases of 1973-74, "inventory profits" nearly doubled their rate of return to 21.1 percent; however, when oil prices stabilized again, their rate of return fell back to 12.4 percent.

FIGURE 15-7

Year	Cost of Wood	Processing Costs	Selling Price	Reported Profit
19*1	$100	$90	$210	$20
19*2	$100	$90	$220	$30
19*3	$110	$90	$220	$20

(iii) Inflation and depreciation allowances

As with inventories, much of the apparently large profit increases of the 1970's were needed simply to replace depreciated capital equipment at prices made much higher by inflation. In theory, funds are provided by *depreciation allowances* (capital cost allowances) to replace depreciated equipment, but inflation makes these provisions inadequate.

For example, suppose in 1970 a business buys a $50 000 machine that is expected to last 10 years, and charges $5000 depreciation expense each year against its income to reflect the annual cost of the machine over its lifespan. Since this $5000 expense is only a book entry and is not actually paid out each year, it represents $5000 per year of funds available to the business *in addition to* its reported profits as per the income statement. Theoretically, this money could be accumulated over the 10-year period so as to provide $50 000 for the replacement of the machine.

However, to replace the machine in 1980 will cost over $150 000, meaning that $100 000 of profits (which should be available for new investment to expand productive capacity) will have to be used to merely *replace* depreciated equipment. Put differently, since the business has not charged enough depreciation to cover the cost of replacing its assets, its profits have been *overstated* — they have included funds that are required to replace assets as they depreciate. Thus, the reported profits are misleadingly high.

> . . . there is now wide recognition within the accounting professions and among financial analysts that reported profits are badly distorted by inflation. In particular, there is little serious dispute as to whether depreciation expense and cost of sales computed by conventional methods overstated reported profits. . . . We are disturbed that Canadian reporting practices have not yet evolved in more realistic directions, as has occurred in many other industrialized countries. . .
>
> Economic Council of Canada,
> *Sixteenth Annual Review,* 1979 (page 33, 34).

> **PRECISION VERSUS USEFULNESS**
>
> The irony of accountants preparing distorted income statements with great care and precision is perhaps best illustrated by the story of the balloonist who became totally lost in a great storm. Upon landing, the disoriented aerialist asked a man where she was, and was told, "You, madam, are in the gondola of a balloon." "I take it, sir, that you are an accountant," said the balloonist. "You are right, but how could you have known that?" asked the man. Because your information, while absolutely precise," replied the balloonist, "was totally useless."

The effect of inflation on reported profits

Inflation distorts the reported profits of business by making them appear to be much higher than they really are, partly because the purchasing power of each dollar of profits is severely eroded by rapidly rising capital-goods costs. Another problem is the accounting practices used by business (and required by the government), which overstate retained earnings by including substantial amounts of funds that are not truly profits—rather, they are required to replace inventories and depreciated assets at prices made much higher by inflation.

In conclusion, highly inflationary periods such as the 1970's do not really generate excessive profits, in the sense of funds available for dividends to shareholders or, more important, for new capital investment. The reported profits of business during the 1970's were largely an illusion created by inflation, and capital investment lagged despite an apparently strong profit picture.

The tax implications of overstated profits

The problem of overstated business profits has important implications for capital investment, because businesses *pay taxes* on the exaggerated reported profits, not on more realistic inflation-adjusted figures. Because taxes on profits are calculated on overstated figures, the taxes are also inflated—they are higher than the real situation warrants. As a result, the combined effect of *inflation plus taxation* is to reduce the ability of business to finance expansion out of retained earnings. Figure 15-8 shows the extent of this problem by presenting both reported profits and inflation-adjusted profits after taxes, expressed as a rate of return on shareholders' equity. Note that not only were the inflation-adjusted profits far lower than the reported profits, but also that the exaggeration of reported profits became much worse in the inflationary 1970's, as the reported rate of return increased while the real (inflation-adjusted) rate of return declined.

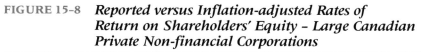

FIGURE 15-8 *Reported versus Inflation-adjusted Rates of Return on Shareholders' Equity – Large Canadian Private Non-financial Corporations*

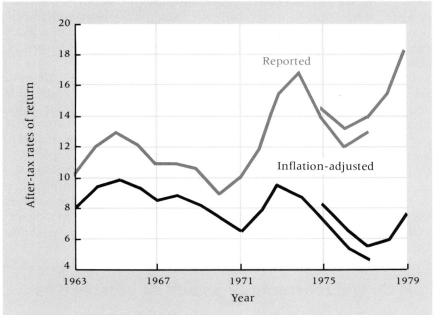

(1) The break in the series is attributable to the incorporation of benchmark revisions and changes in sampling procedures. 1979 data correspond to the average of the first three quarters.

SOURCE Department of Finance, *Economic Review: A Perspective on the Decade* (Ottawa: April, 1980) p. 83. Reproduced by permission of the Minister of Supply and Services Canada.

One oft-cited reason for the reduction in the rate of capital growth is inflation. This has worked in numerous ways. Capital investment becomes less attractive in an inflationary environment because, using traditional accounting methods, corporate profits are overstated and hence taxes are overassessed. This is because the value of capital stock is based on the cost of the asset when it was purchased and not on what it would cost now to replace it. Thus, in inflationary periods the true replacement cost is underestimated and hence depreciation on the firm's capital is understated, resulting in an overstatement of the firm's profits and an overpayment of taxes. In addition, the higher that inflation rates are in the current period, the more uncertainty is generated about future inflation. Thus, capital expenditure is further discouraged because of a perceived added risk.

Bank of Montreal
Business Review,
September 1980.

In Chapter 5, we saw that there are two basic uses for society's economic resources: consumption, for *present* enjoyment, and investment, for increased *future* prosperity. Since economic resources are limited, the more resources that are devoted to one of these purposes, the fewer resources are available for the other.

In this chapter, we have seen how rapid inflation can tend to depress *capital investment*, by raising interest rates, depressing stock markets and eroding real after-tax business profits, thereby causing a smaller share of society's economic resources to be devoted to capital investment. That is, rapid inflation (in combination with the tax system) can cause a shift in the allocation of society's economic resources toward current consumption for short-term purposes and away from capital investment for longer-term benefits. In the short run, the results of this process can appear favorable, as strong aggregate demand brings an economic boom; however, over the longer term the results of weakened capital investment gradually become evident. Productivity growth and the growth of living standards slows, and the economy shows signs of stagflation.

Part D: Macroeconomic policy in perspective

Before the Great Depression of the 1930's, the prevailing economic philosophy was *laissez-faire*, which held that the economy automatically moved toward full employment and that there was therefore no need for government intervention in the economy. The experience of the Great Depression and the war that followed it ushered in a new era of economic policy, based on the *Keynesian* idea that the government should use its fiscal and monetary policies to support the level of aggregate demand, and lift the economy out of downturns. The new ideas seemed radical at first, and were only used timidly by governments in the 1950's. However, they received a big boost from John F. Kennedy's successful application of them during the 1960's. By openly discussing and using Keynesian policies, Kennedy gave them — and the economists who proposed them — public acceptance and respectability. In many ways, the 1960's were the golden years of Keynesian economics.

Following the late 1960's, however, experience with government monetary and fiscal policy was much less satisfactory. Excessive stimulation in the late 1960's led to rapid inflation; in response, strong anti-inflation policies were applied, causing unemployment to rise to high levels. Again in the 1970's, excessive stimulation generated very severe inflation, followed by anti-inflation policies and a recession.

Clearly, something had gone wrong: the monetary and fiscal policies that were supposed to be used to reduce economic instability were being applied in a *stop-go* fashion that actually created instability, wrenching the economy from rapid inflation to recession and back again. The bad economic effects of these policy decisions have led some economists to argue that the government should not actively manage the level of demand in the economy with its monetary and fiscal policies. They believe that, due to political pressures and the problems of time lags, government attempts at demand management tend to become mismanagement, with negative effects on economic stability and prosperity.

These economists argue that governments should be required to follow *fixed rules* for monetary and fiscal policy rather than be allowed to adjust the federal budget and rate of growth of the money supply as they see fit. In particular, the money supply should be allowed to grow at only a certain rate and the federal budget should always be balanced. Such rules, it is said, would prevent governments from making major errors in economic policy, especially in the direction of overstimulation.

Other economists disagree with this view. They point out that our economic system has a history of instability, culminating in the Great Depression of the 1930's. They argue that the government can and should actively intervene in the economy with monetary and fiscal policies to steer the level of demand, stimulating it during recessions and dampening it during periods of inflation. They point to the fact that generally, since such policies came into use after the Second World War, economic growth has been more rapid and recessions less frequent and less severe than before. They also argue that, if mistakes were made in the use of these policies, we should learn from those mistakes rather than abandon the policies altogether in the blind hope that it will all work out somehow.

Which view is correct? There seem to be elements of truth in both views. Management of demand by government can have either beneficial or negative effects on economic stability and prosperity, depending on whether the policies are used with the proper timing and strength. For such policies to benefit the economy, the government must base its decisions on the longer-term *economic* effects of such policies rather than their short-term *political* attractiveness. During the late 1960's and first half of the 1970's, this was not done, and the results were severe instability. Whether this experience has made governments wiser in the use of their policies remains to be seen.

The debates are not likely to be resolved in favor of either the Keynesians or their critics. While governments are extremely unlikely to give up the use of policies to manage demand in the economy, their own errors of the 1970's have provided them with a strong lesson that such policies must be used carefully and moderately, and not for short-term economic or political goals.

Supply-side policies

Since the 1930's, government economic policy, and debates over policy, have focused on monetary and fiscal policies and the management of aggregate demand. Now, a new element is being added to the policy debate because, notwithstanding the importance of the *demand side* of the economy, there has been increased concern regarding the *supply side*. Sluggish business investment spending, poor productivity performance and difficulties competing with foreign producers whose productivity has improved more rapidly, have all drawn more attention to the supply side factors (Chapter 5) that affect our productivity and prosperity.

The need for balance: Perspectives on prosperity

In summary, economic prosperity is the result of a *balanced interaction* between the two sides of the economy:

(a) the supply side through which saving and investment make higher productivity and living standards possible, and

(b) the demand side because only if aggregate demand is sufficiently high will the economy's potential levels of output, productivity and prosperity actually be reached

Until recently, government economic policy has emphasized the demand side of the economy, and the use of monetary and fiscal policies to combat recessions by stimulating aggregate demand. It has been more or less assumed that the supply side would take care of itself, as high levels of consumer spending would generate sufficient business investment spending, higher productivity and greater prosperity. However, recent experience indicates that this cannot be taken for granted, particularly under conditions of severe inflation. A combination of high interest rates and the taxation of overstated profits can impair both the ability and the incentive of business to invest.

The inflationary period from the early 1970's to the early 1980's was a period of weak capital investment. According to one point of view, it would be beneficial if the 1980's were to be a period of renewed capital investment, in order to build for long-term prosperity. However, an increased emphasis on capital investment necessarily means a temporarily reduced emphasis on current consumption. Whether the public is prepared to make short-run sacrifices of consumption in exchange for the longer-run economic benefits of increased capital investment will be an important factor in Canada's economic performance for the rest of this century.

DEFINITIONS OF NEW TERMS

Full Employment   The minimum possible rate of unemployment that can be achieved without generating unacceptable inflation in the economy.

Non-Accelerating   Inflationary   Rate   of   Unemployment (NAIRU)   The unemployment rate that is consistent with a low and stable rate of inflation.

Stagflation   The coincidence of high unemployment with rapid inflation; also characterized by slow growth of output and productivity.

Inventory Profits   Illusory increases in the reported profits of businesses arising from increases in the value of materials held in inventory; such profits being illusory because they are required to replace the inventory at higher prices.

Supply-Side Policies   Government policies aimed at increasing the economy's ability to produce goods and services, or productivity (as opposed to demand-side policies which influence the level of aggregate demand for goods and services).

CHAPTER SUMMARY

1. The economic goals of full employment and economic growth conflict with the goal of stable prices, forcing the government to accept trade-offs between these goals.

2. Because of these trade-offs, full employment cannot mean an unemployment rate of zero. In the early 1980's, it was believed that it was not possible to reduce the unemployment rate much below 8 percent without generating considerable inflation.

3. Economic policies cannot solve problems quickly, due to the existence of various time lags in their implementation and operation.

4. There are serious dangers in overstimulation of the economy by government policies, including severe inflation and subsequent severe recessions.

5. The effectiveness of fiscal policy in Canada is limited by the fact that the federal government lacks control over large volumes of government spending and tax revenues which are controlled by the provinces.

6. Despite its importance, the effectiveness of monetary policy is limited by problems of defining and measuring the money supply, and by long time lags in its operation.

7. Economic policy in Canada is limited by international factors, particularly the need to keep Canadian interest rates high enough to attract foreign capital.

8. The effectiveness of monetary and fiscal policy in recent years has been limited by inflation psychology, which makes anti-inflation policies less effective and adds inflationary risks to any policies intended to stimulate the economy.

9. Excessive stimulation of aggregate demand by government policies generates severe inflation, which can in turn depress the level of business investment spending.

10. During the 1960's, Keynesian policies were unchallenged. However, the experience with government economic policies since then has led to criticisms of these policies; in particular, there has been a new emphasis on the money supply and on avoiding excessive stimulation of the economy through government policies.

11. The problem of stagflation emphasizes the fact that economic prosperity is the result of the successful performance and interaction of *both* sides of the economy: the supply side and the demand side.

12. Severe inflation reduces both the ability and the incentive for business to spend on capital investment by:
    (a) causing interest rates on bonds to rise to levels that business borrowers find unattractive,
    (b) depressing stock prices, thus making it more difficult to raise capital through share issues, and
    (c) causing reported profits to appear significantly higher than they really are, which inflates taxes payable and depresses real after-tax business profits.

QUESTIONS

1. In 1986, the federal government proposed tighter "policing" of the unemployment-insurance system, with the objective of enforcing stricter requirements that UI recipients engage in serious job searches and take suitable jobs that are available. What effect would such a policy have on the unemployment rate that represents full employment?

2. In 1986, it was reported that only 4 percent of all unemployment insurance exhaustees (those whose benefits had expired) were falling back on welfare. What might such a statistic suggest?

3. What is the present unemployment rate, and what has been the trend in the unemployment rate over the past two years? Does the present rate of inflation and the trend in inflation over the past two years suggest that the economy is at or approaching a condition of full employment?

4. Suppose you are the Minister of Finance. Prepare a statement:
    (a) explaining to a group of unemployed young people why the government has decided to implement anti-inflation policies that will have the side-effect of increasing unemployment, especially among young Canadians.
    (b) explaining to a group of senior citizens why the government has decided to stimulate the economy to reduce unemployment in spite of the fact that inflation is already unacceptably rapid in the view of pensioners.

5. Why would businesses use accounting methods for inventories and depreciation which overstate their profits and therefore increase their tax liabilities?

6. What is the recent trend in real output per worker employed (productivity) in Canada? What might explain this trend?

7. Have the 1980's turned out to be the decade of strong business capital investment that had been hoped for? Why or why not?

8. Do you believe that the inflation psychology that was so strong among Canadians as recently as 1983 has ceased to be a factor in people's expectations? Why or why not?

9. What has been the trend over the past year in the Toronto Stock Exchange "300" composite index of stock prices? What might explain this trend?

10. The text states that the high interest rates caused by rapid inflation make long-term borrowing, such as bond issues, unattractive to businesses, because they are reluctant to commit themselves to paying high interest payments for many years. What changes in the terms on which funds are borrowed could be made in order to reduce this problem?

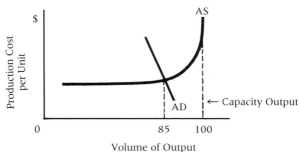

11. With aggregate demand at the level represented by AD, the economy is operating at only 85 percent of its capacity.
    (a) Suppose the government wanted to increase aggregate demand sufficiently to bring the economy up to 90 percent of capacity. Draw a new aggregate demand curve (AD_1) and show on the graph the effect of the new situation on output and prices. Explain why these effects occur.
    (b) Suppose the government increased the level of aggregate demand further, bringing output up to 95 percent of capacity. Show this new situation on the graph, labelling the new curve AD_2. Explain the effects on output and prices.
    (c) If the government increased aggregate demand sufficiently to bring output up to 100 percent of capacity what would happen? Draw another aggregate demand curve (AD_3) to represent this situation.

CHAPTER 16

International trade

With nearly one-third of Canada's national income earned by exports and one in five jobs directly dependent on exports, international trade is a matter of great importance to Canadians. While the United States and Japan export 7 and 13 percent of their GNP respectively, Canadian exports amount to nearly 30 percent of GNP,[1] making Canada more dependent upon trade for its prosperity than most nations in the world. This high exposure to international economic trends is of particularly vital concern to those specific regions and communities of Canada that produce products for export, such as the grain of the prairies and the natural resources and resource-related products of British Columbia and of countless industries and communities all across the country. Many of these experience *boom and bust* cycles due to world economic fluctuations totally beyond their control.

However, the effects of world economic trends are not confined to export industries — they affect all Canadians, as the effects of fluctuations in Canada's exports spread throughout the economy due to the *multiplier effect*. Thus, a bad year for prairie wheat farmers means not only lower incomes for farmers, but also reduced incomes for Ontario manufacturing employees, as Massey-Ferguson's sales of farm machinery are reduced. There will also be lower sales of consumer goods and services, as a result of reduced incomes in the manufacturing sector. Exports are vital to our prosperity in another way: they are our main means of earning *foreign currency* (mostly US dollars) with which Canadians buy the vast array of

---

[1]If only goods (not services) are considered, Canada exports nearly 50 percent of what it produces.

imported goods and services that make our standard of living so high. In short, by increasing our exports, we increase our ability to enjoy imports.[2]

While international trade is a major source of Canadians' prosperity, it is also a matter of some concern. Canada's share of world trade fell from 5 percent in 1970 to 3 percent in 1980, and Canada slipped from fourth to eighth place among trading nations. It has been estimated that if Canada had maintained in 1980 the share of world trade it held in 1970, there could have been up to one million more jobs for Canadians. In this chapter, we will examine the nature of Canada's international trade and the basic principles underlying trade between nations; in Chapter 17 we will consider some of the specific problems and opportunities facing Canada in world trade.

Patterns of Canadian trade

As Figure 16-1 shows, Canada's exports consist heavily of *natural resources and resource-related products*, such as food, natural gas, lumber, wood pulp, metal, mineral and chemical products, with manufactured goods comprising a relatively small share of exports.[3] Figure 16-1 also shows that Canada's imports consist largely of *finished products*, both capital goods and consumer goods. Generally, then, Canada's foreign trade consists of an exchange of resources and resource products for finished products.

On *merchandise* trade, Canadian exports exceed its imports. However, on transactions in *services* (such as travel, tourism and interest on debts to foreign lenders), Canada spends much more than it earns internationally.

From Figure 16-2, it can be seen that Canada's trade is overwhelmingly conducted with one nation—the USA. The strong linkage between the two economies is probably an inevitable result of their geographical proximity. Despite attempts by the Canadian government to diversify Canadian trade by increasing ties with Europe during the 1970's, the proportion of Canadian exports going to the USA actually increased over that period, from 65 to 70 percent. While nationalistic Canadians bemoan this dependence on the US market, it appears to be an inescapable economic reality.

---

[2]"Imports" includes services bought from foreigners, a major one of which is the travel and tourism enjoyed by Canadians.

[3]A major exception to its concentration on natural resources is Canada's large exports of *motor vehicles and parts*. This case is an exceptional one, however, as the automobile industry operates under a special arrangement between the Canadian and US governments (the Auto Pact), whereby the two governments have encouraged and supported continent-wide specialization of auto plants, for increased efficiency. Canadian auto plants specialize in the production of a few cars, most of which are exported to the USA. On the other hand, many cars bought in Canada are imported from similarly specialized plants in the USA. This fact is reflected in the statistics in Figure 16-1 showing Canada's *imports* of motor vehicles and parts.

FIGURE 16-1   *Canada's Top Exports and Imports 1983*

Exports			Imports		
Commodity Grouping	Value (millions of dollars)	Percent	Commodity Grouping	Value (millions of dollars)	Percent
Road motor vehicles	$14 055.2	15.5%	Motor vehicle parts	$9 333.2	12.4%
Motor vehicle parts	5 752.6	6.3	Road motor vehicles	7 904.4	10.5
Wheat	4 647.7	5.1	Crude materials, inedible	7 201.1	9.5
Newsprint paper	4 005.1	4.4	Machinery	6 805.7	9.0
Lumber	3 969.1	4.4	Food, feed, beverages and		
Natural gas	3 958.2	4.4	tobacco	4 870.3	6.4
Crude petroleum	3 456.9	3.8	Miscellaneous end products	4 330.3	5.7
Wood pulp	3 057.6	3.4	Personal and household goods	3 421.7	4.5
Machinery	2 918.8	3.2	Communication and related		
Other equipment and tools	2 761.3	3.0	equipment	3 315.1	4.4
Chemicals	2 173.6	2.4	Crude petroleum	3 274.0	4.3
Non-metallic minerals	2 082.6	2.3	Office machines	3 109.5	4.1
Non-ferrous metals and alloys			Aircraft and parts	1 814.5	2.4
(excluding aluminum, copper,			Measurement and scientific		
nickel, zinc)	1 977.3	2.2	equipment	1 507.0	2.0
Miscellaneous end products	1 800.8	2.0	Plastics and synthetic rubber	1 361.4	1.8
Aluminum	1 744.2	1.9	Organic chemicals	1 265.8	1.7
			Metal fabricated basic products	1 169.9	1.6
Total Exports	$90 963.9	100.0	**Total Imports**	$75 586.6	100.0

SOURCE: Statistics Canada, *Canadian Statistical Review.*

Tariffs and other barriers to trade

As any Canadian who has returned from a trip outside the country knows, there are special restrictions on the importation of goods into nations. The most visible of these are tariffs (or custom duties), which are taxes levied on goods imported into a country. The effect (and, indeed, the intent) of a tariff is to increase the price of imported goods, making it more difficult for them to compete in domestic markets, and thus to protect domestic producers against foreign competition.

In addition to tariffs, there are other, often more subtle, restrictions placed on imports by governments. These **non-tariff barriers** to trade include *quotas* on imports, which restrict the quantity of a particular product that may be imported, and *licences and bureaucratic procedures*, which can involve so much red tape that would-be importers are discouraged. Sometimes, governments practice *preferential purchasing policies*, through which

FIGURE 16-2   *Canada's Trade by Nation*

Canada's Exports by Destination (excludes re-exports)				Sources of Canada's Imports			
	1983 $ million	Percent	1983 vs 1973 (% change)		1983 $ million	Percent	1983 vs 1973 (% change)
US	64 461	72.9%	+287%	US	54 203	71.6%	+228%
Japan	4 734	5.4	+162	Japan	4 410	5.8	+336
Britain	2 446	2.8	+54	Britain	1 811	2.4	+80
Soviet Union	1 762	2.0	+506	West Germany	1 576	2.1	+160
China	1 605	1.8	+487	Mexico	1 079	1.4	+1 196
West Germany	1 156	1.3	+162	Venezuela	1 014	1.3	+94
Netherlands	953	1.1	+239	Taiwan	926	1.2	+465
Belgium/Luxembourg	696	0.8	+146	France	841	1.1	+157
France	627	0.7	+197	Hong Kong	821	1.1	+647
Brazil	598	0.7	+420	Italy	798	1.1	+225
South Korea	555	0.6	+789	South Korea	791	1.0	+774
Italy	546	0.6	+86	Iran	527	0.7	+300
Algeria	448	0.5	+1529	Brazil	499	0.7	+473
Australia	438	0.5	+105	Sweden	416	0.5	+150
Mexico	375	0.4	+216	Switzerland	409	0.5	+247
Other	7 026	7.9	+225	Other	5 573	7.4	+158
Total (customs basis)	88 426	100.0	+256	**Total** (customs basis)	75 694	100.0	+225

SOURCE   *The Financial Post,* March 31, 1984.

they buy only domestically-produced products, or provide subsidies for domestic producers, such as tax treatment that makes it easier for them to compete with foreign firms. Another non-tariff barrier to trade is *contingent-protection* measures, which allow a government to counter unfair or disruptive trading practices by foreign competitors, such as "dumping" goods at exceptionally low prices. Finally, there are *voluntary export restraints*, under which one nation agrees to restrict its exports to another. An example of this is the 1985 Japanese agreement to limit automobile exports to Canada so that the Japanese share of the Canadian market would not increase and disrupt the market.

Government attitudes toward trade

Notwithstanding all the restrictions they place on imports, governments are generally *officially* in favor of *free trade*, that is, the reduction and eventual removal of barriers to trade between nations. Later in this chapter we will examine the economic reasoning behind free trade, but it is only fair to note that, while many governments advocate free trade in theory, what they seem to want in practice is greater access to export markets for their own industries while continuing to protect domestic industries from foreign imports. There are obvious contradictions in these positions that make the issue of trade barriers and their reduction or removal a very complex and controversial one. In short, the matter of international trade is a source of many myths, misconceptions and misunderstandings. In order to deal with these myths, our examination of the topic will take the form of a discussion between a curious citizen and an eminent economist.

How does international trade benefit nations?

CURIOUS CITIZEN: The government is talking about further reductions in tariffs, but most people seem to think that, with all the imports coming into Canada, we need higher tariffs, not lower ones. Why do economists and governments tend to favor reducing tariffs?

EMINENT ECONOMIST: Tariffs tend to reduce the volume of international trade between nations because they make it more difficult for imported products to compete with domestically produced products. But international trade is beneficial to all nations, in that it permits nations to specialize their production. Instead of trying to be self-sufficient and produce all sorts of products, nations can specialize in what they can make most efficiently. The result is greater efficiency of production throughout the world, and a higher material standard of living for all concerned.

Anything that interferes with this process, such as tariffs or other barriers, tends to reduce our productivity and our material prosperity. That is why economists and governments believe that barriers to trade should be reduced, and there should be freer trade between nations.

To turn the argument around, if you believe that Canada should have tariffs to keep out foreign goods, then why shouldn't Ontario or Alberta seek to keep out outside goods through tariffs, too? But then why should Toronto or Calgary or Halifax import any goods from "outsiders" . . . shouldn't they seek to be self-sufficient, too? And why should your family buy anything not produced by a member of the family? Finally, why should you as an individual have any dealings with other people . . . why shouldn't you seek to be totally self-sufficient?

The answer lies, of course, in the fact that it is economically beneficial for people to specialize in something that they do well, to sell it to others, and to buy from others those things that they produce better than you do. This system runs on the principle of specialization, and it does increase efficiency and living standards . . . the most economically advanced nations are those with the highest degree of specialization.

CURIOUS CITIZEN: I can see some cases where this would apply. The prairie provinces are best suited to wheat production, and southern Ontario specializes in manufacturing—obviously the most efficient arrangement at present. Also, some countries specialize in manufacturing, at which they are very efficient, while others produce raw materials more efficiently. It's obviously beneficial to both Canada and Brazil to specialize in wheat and coffee, respectively, and to trade their products, rather than to try to be self-sufficient.

EMINENT ECONOMIST: Those examples are accurate enough, but it goes further than that. Surprisingly, the greatest volume of world trade today is not between dissimilar countries, but rather between countries that are on the surface quite similar—the highly developed and industrialized nations such as the USA, Japan, Canada, Britain, Germany, France and other western European countries.

CURIOUS CITIZEN: That seems rather odd. How do you explain that?

EMINENT ECONOMIST: These industrially advanced countries have pushed specialization to the nth degree. For example, the USA exports Cadillacs to Germany but imports Volkswagens from Germany. These high degrees of specialization create a greater incentive for trade.

CURIOUS CITIZEN: But the USA is so advanced technologically that it is more efficient than other countries in the production of most products. Why, then, should the USA trade with other countries—what has the USA to gain through trade?

EMINENT ECONOMIST: That can be explained by what economists call the *theory of comparative advantage*. It is best illustrated by a simple example on a personal level. Suppose the best lawyer in town is also the best typist in town—should she therefore do her own typing?

CURIOUS CITIZEN: Not at all. She may be a faster typist than her secretary, but she can use her time more efficiently by doing legal work. By doing her own typing, she would gain a little on the typing but lose a great deal by not using the time for legal work.

EMINENT ECONOMIST: In other words, she can increase her efficiency, her output and her income by specializing in that which she does best of all?

CURIOUS CITIZEN: Right. By trying to do something else, she loses more than she gains. She has better uses for her time.

EMINENT ECONOMIST: That's right—and the same principle applies to the way nations use their productive resources (labor, capital equipment and natural resources). Suppose the USA is 30 percent more efficient than other nations in producing machinery, and 10 percent more efficient in producing shirts. Then the USA should concentrate on producing machinery—it would not make sense to divert scarce productive resources from producing machinery, where they are most efficiently used, to producing shirts, where they are less efficiently used.

CURIOUS CITIZEN: But then the USA would have to buy its shirts from foreign nations.

EMINENT ECONOMIST: That's right, but by selling shirts to Americans, foreign nations can earn the US dollars they need to buy American machinery. And with both the USA and foreign nations specializing in products in which they are relatively better at producing, productivity, total output and general living standards are increased. This theory of comparative advantage, then, provides a logical reason why a country such as the USA should import even certain products that it could produce more efficiently than foreigners can. Like the lawyer, it is best for the USA to specialize in what it does best of all.

CURIOUS CITIZEN: Okay—I can see how, in theory, international trade permits increased specialization, greater efficiency and a higher standard of living. But, in practice, I see foreign imports causing a lot of trouble for Canadian producers, in areas like cars, clothing, appliances and so on.

EMINENT ECONOMIST: That's competition, which is what free enterprise is suppose to be all about. Sure, it causes problems for producers, but it keeps them on their toes, and benefits consumers through lower prices. Also, international competition works both ways—Canadian producers sell a great deal abroad, you know—about 30 percent of our Gross National Product is exported.

Unfair competition?

CURIOUS CITIZEN: I can see how competition can be beneficial in the ways you say, but I also think competition should be fair—and much foreign competition is not fair.

EMINENT ECONOMIST: What do you mean?

CURIOUS CITIZEN: Cheap foreign labor. How can Canadian producers compete with foreign producers using low-wage labor?

EMINENT ECONOMIST: That's a common viewpoint but it's not supported by the facts. If low wages guaranteed an industry the ability to compete internationally, you would expect the lowest-wage industries in any country to be its most successful exporters. In actual fact, the opposite tends to be true—it's usually the higher-wage industries that export the most. So higher wages do not necessarily mean that an industry or nation cannot compete internationally, nor do low wages necessarily provide a competitive advantage.

CURIOUS CITIZEN: That seems odd. Why is that so?

EMINENT ECONOMIST: The key to the whole thing is the productivity of labor—output per worker per hour. Suppose a foreign worker receives $3.00 per hour for making pencils and, using simple hand tools, produces 150 pencils in an hour. The labor cost per pencil is obviously $.02 ($3.00 divided by 150). Now suppose a high-wage Canadian worker receives $10.00 per hour for producing pencils, but, using modern machinery, produces 500 pencils per hour. The labor cost of each Canadian-made pencil will be $.02 ($10.00 divided by 500). So, just because Canadian wages are higher doesn't necessarily mean that Canadian production costs per unit must be higher and Canadian producers unable to compete internationally. (See Figure 16-3.)

FIGURE 16-3 *Productivity and Labor Costs*

	Canadian Worker	Foreign Worker
Hourly Wage	$10.00	$3.00
Hourly Output	5.00	1.50
Labor Cost Per Unit	$.02	$.02

CURIOUS CITIZEN: So high productivity can more than offset high wages.

EMINENT ECONOMIST: Right. North American workers worry about competition from low-wage foreign workers, but those same foreign workers feel that they cannot possibly compete with North American workers — they talk about the "cheap capital" in North America, and the great efficiency of North American workers.

CURIOUS CITIZEN: Your example was rigged to come out in a tie, with the pencils costing the same in both cases. In the real world, who does have the competitive advantage?

EMINENT ECONOMIST: It depends on the product. Where production lends itself to mechanization, the North American worker usually has an advantage. For more manual tasks, lower-wage labor is often more efficient. Some companies produce parts in North America, using mechanization, export them to be assembled by hand by lower-wage foreign labor, and bring back the assembled product to be sold in North America.

CURIOUS CITIZEN: So some nations are better at some things, and others at other things.

EMINENT ECONOMIST: Yes — and that's why it pays economically to specialize at what you do best, and then trade. Then, everyone can be better off.

But what about unemployment?

CURIOUS CITIZEN: So far, what you have said makes sense, but I don't see why we should reduce tariffs right now, when a lot of Canadians are unemployed.

EMINENT ECONOMIST: Why not?

CURIOUS CITIZEN: Imports would come in, causing more unemployment in Canada, because Canadians would not have jobs producing those imported goods. To protect jobs, shouldn't we raise our tariffs, so as to keep out foreign goods and reserve the Canadian market for Canadian-produced goods?

EMINENT ECONOMIST: Is that all there is to it—to solve unemployment, raise our tariffs on foreign products?

CURIOUS CITIZEN: Well, now that you mention it, it seems kind of logical.

EMINENT ECONOMIST: If it were that easy, we'd have solved our unemployment problems long ago. Let's look into this a little further. If we did raise tariffs to try to protect Canadian jobs, what would other nations do?

CURIOUS CITIZEN: I see . . . they'd retaliate by raising their tariffs on Canadian goods that we export to their countries. Then our exports to them would fall, and unemployment would increase in those industries.

EMINENT ECONOMIST: Right. What we would gain in employment in some industries by raising tariffs, we would lose in other industries (our export industries) because of similar retaliatory action by other nations. What many people forget in this connection is that Canada sells about 30 percent of its GNP to other countries.

CURIOUS CITIZEN: So if you have an unemployment problem, you shouldn't try to solve it by reducing foreign imports.

EMINENT ECONOMIST: That's right. In fact, that sort of action makes things worse. In the 1930's, governments tried to *export unemployment*, by raising tariffs like this. By the time that everyone had taken such action, tariffs were so high that international trade had been severely reduced, and as a result, unemployment had been made much worse than it would have been if tariffs had been left alone. You simply cannot export your economic problems by tossing them off onto other nations. . . . if they depend on you for something, then you depend on them for something else.

CURIOUS CITIZEN: So international trade is a two-way street—you can't just be an exporter, you have to be an importer, too.

For a country as dependent on trade as Canada, matching foreign trade restrictions with domestic ones is not a winning strategy. Canadians would be denied access to an international market large enough to sustain efficient scale production, and an important source of improved productivity and living standards would be foreclosed.

Edward Carmichael,
Policy Review and Outlook, 1985: A Time for Decisions,
C. D. Howe Institute.

EMINENT ECONOMIST: Yes, and that's true for another reason, too. There's the problem of earning foreign currencies. For example, Japan can't buy Canadian goods (our exports) unless Japan has Canadian dollars. But to get Canadian dollars, the Japanese have to sell goods to Canada (our imports). So we must import if we want to be able to export.

Who pays for tariffs?

CURIOUS CITIZEN: I can see why international trade is economically beneficial to everyone who takes part in it. Still, taxing foreign imports seems to be a nice way of raising revenue for the government. Canadians already pay so many taxes that it's nice to have some paid by foreigners.

EMINENT ECONOMIST: Just a minute. Who pays the taxes on imports?

CURIOUS CITIZEN: The foreigners . . . it's their products we're taxing, isn't it?

EMINENT ECONOMIST: Hold on. Why do we tax imports, anyway? To raise revenue for the federal government?

CURIOUS CITIZEN: Not really. We tax imports to protect our domestic producers from foreign competition.

EMINENT ECONOMIST: And how do tariffs do that?

CURIOUS CITIZEN: By making the price of the imported product higher than it would otherwise have been.

EMINENT ECONOMIST: And how will that affect the price of the same product that is produced by Canadians?

CURIOUS CITIZEN: With less severe competition, Canadian producers will be able to charge higher prices.

EMINENT ECONOMIST: So who really pays, in the final analysis?

CURIOUS CITIZEN: It's the Canadian consumer who pays, through higher prices.

EMINENT ECONOMIST: Right. It is difficult to determine *how much* tariffs cost Canadian consumers, but a 1980 study estimated that quotas on clothing alone cost Canadians $327 million a year, or $43 for every Canadian household. For 1983, the Canadian Import Tribunal estimated the cost to consumers of protection of the footwear industry at $85 million. The Consumers Association of Canada was particularly critical of the import situation, pointing out that the heaviest burden of import taxes such as these falls upon low-income families.

In a broader sense, you could say that eveyone pays in the sense that tariffs reduce international trade, interfere with the process of specialization that increases productivity, and therefore cause us all to have a lower material standard of living than we could have had without tariffs. And the cost of tariffs goes further than that, too.

CURIOUS CITIZEN: In what way?

What about Canadian export industries?

EMINENT ECONOMIST: Suppose the Canadian widget industry, which is not very efficient, gets a tariff to protect itself against imports from Europe, which are of equal quality but less expensive. This tariff will benefit the Canadian widget industry and its workers, who will be sheltered from the effects of foreign competition, but it will hurt the Canadian public, as we have seen, because the price of widgets will be higher than it would have been. However, an equally important effect of the tariff, and one which most people do not see, is its effect on the Canadian fradistat industry, which is a very efficient industry that exports a large proportion of its output to Europe.

CURIOUS CITIZEN: Because the Europeans are likely to retaliate by placing higher tariffs on Canadian products sold in Europe.

EMINENT ECONOMIST: Quite likely. Furthermore, because they can sell fewer widgets to Canada, Europeans will have fewer Canadian dollars with which to buy Canadian-made fradistats.

CURIOUS CITIZEN: So tariffs serve to reward the inefficient producer who can't compete with imports, and *penalize* the efficient producer who is able to compete in world markets.

EMINENT ECONOMIST: Yes — and this explains why some industries (such as resource industries, and large and efficient agricultural and manufacturing industries) are strongly in favor of free trade, while other industries (such as textiles) are in favor of continued or even increased restrictions on imports. To some, free trade is an opportunity, while to others, it represents a threat.

CURIOUS CITIZEN: In summary, then, tariffs and other barriers to trade have a negative effect on our economic prosperity.

EMINENT ECONOMIST: Yes, as a general rule that is true. If you were to summarize what we have said, it would be as follows:

(a) Tariffs do benefit economically the protected industries and their workers. By protecting them against foreign competition, tariffs permit them to have higher output, employment, profits and wages than otherwise would have been possible.

(b) Because of tariffs the Canadian public as a whole pays *higher prices* for products that it buys. In effect, a tariff takes money from the public in general and gives it to particular industries and their workers, being very similar in its effect to a *subsidy* that is paid by the government out of tax revenues to an industry, except that a tariff has another effect.

(c) It also hurts Canadian industries that *export* to other nations, for the reasons outlined earlier. These industries will have lower output, employment, profits and wages than they otherwise would have had if there had been no tariffs on imports.

CURIOUS CITIZEN: You could say, then, that point (a) is offset by point (c), leaving on balance point (b) as the net effect of tariffs.

IT'S ALL IN HOW YOU LOOK AT IT

As with all things, there are different ways of looking at tariffs. If the government proposed legislation intended to "tax consumers so as to raise funds to pay subsidies to inefficient Canadian industries, the subsidies to be larger the more inefficient the industries are," the public would be in an uproar.

If, on the other hand, the government proposed legislation, the purpose of which was "to protect Canadian businesses and their workers against low-price foreign-made products," many Canadians would quietly accept this as a valid policy.

Both statements are valid descriptions of the effects of tariffs on the Canadian economy.

EMINENT ECONOMIST: Yes, on balance, their effect is higher prices . . . or, if you prefer, a lower material standard of living than we could have had.

THE PETITION OF THE CANDLE MAKERS

The following was written more than 100 years ago by Frederic Bastiat, a brilliant French proponent of free trade.

To the chamber of deputies: We are subjected to the intolerable competition of a foreign rival, who enjoys such superior facilities for the production of light that he inundates our national market at reduced prices. This rival is no other than the Sun. Our petition is to pass a law shutting up all windows, openings and fissures through which the light of the Sun is used to penetrate our dwellings, to the prejudice of the profitable manufacture we have been enabled to bestow on the country.

Signed: Candle Makers

CURIOUS CITIZEN: I can see now that, economically, tariffs do not always benefit society as a whole. Rather, they benefit some people at the expense of others. Why, then, do we have tariffs and other barriers to free trade?

EMINENT ECONOMIST: Many tariffs are probably most readily explained by the fact that certain industries have the political influence to convince the government to continue to give them tariff protection (a subsidy at the expense of the consumer). However, there are other reasons for tariffs, too . . . cases where, in particular instances, a tariff could be argued to be in the best interests of the society as a whole (rather than just to the advantage of a few).

CURIOUS CITIZEN: Such as?

Tariffs as a stimulus to industrial development

EMINENT ECONOMIST: The most important is the *infant industry* argument. This is based on the idea that certain manufacturing industries could grow in Canada to become fully efficient and competitive with other nations if they were protected by tariffs from well-established foreign competitors during their early years, so that they could become established and efficient themselves. This argument in favor of tariffs could be particularly important if a nation desired long-term industrial growth. Both Canada and Mexico have used tariffs to promote the growth of the manufacturing sector of their economies, with Canada's tariff policy dating back to Sir John A. Macdonald's *National Policy* in 1879.

CURIOUS CITIZEN: I can see why . . . they don't want to be merely suppliers of raw materials to industrialized nations forever. Industrial development can benefit them economically.

EMINENT ECONOMIST: There's a second important effect of these tariffs. If a US firm finds that the tariff prevents it from exporting to Canada, for example, it may decide to establish *branch plants* in Canada. By setting up branch plants, the company can avoid having its products taxed by the tariff, because these products are no longer imports; they are produced in Canada. The foreign firm can, "jump over" the tariff. There are many actual examples of industrial development through branch plants, from the development of the automobile industry in Canada to the existence of similar breakfast food plants in Niagara Falls, New York and Niagara Falls, Ontario.

CURIOUS CITIZEN: So, by protecting domestic producers and by attracting branch plants, tariffs can contribute to a nation's industrialization, diversifying its economy away from a dependence on resource extraction and agricultural products, and boosting productivity and employment. All this makes tariffs look like a good thing economically, rather than a bad thing as you have suggested.

EMINENT ECONOMIST: It's not that simple . . . you don't get something for nothing. Tariffs can stimulate the manufacturing sector of the economy, but this development comes at a cost—the consumer must pay higher prices for the products of these industries. In effect, the public is *subsidizing* the protected industries.

CURIOUS CITIZEN: But the situation should be temporary, shouldn't it?

Once the infant industries have matured and become efficient, the tariff protection will be removed.

EMINENT ECONOMIST: In theory, yes, but in fact, it usually doesn't work out that well. The tariff protection removes the competitive incentive to become more efficient, with the result that protected industries usually mature slowly and the tariffs are maintained longer than they really should be. Removal of tariff protection is made more difficult by the fact that, once protected industries become established, they can become strong political lobbyists for continued tariff protection. For instance, the Canadian textile industry, which is besieged by import competition, employs about 200 000 people — about 10 percent of Canada's manufacturing jobs — most of whom have little education and limited job opportunities, and about half of whom are in Quebec and 30 percent in Ontario. The industry constitutes a strong, well-organized political lobby group in favor of import restrictions. Consumers, on the other hand, who would benefit from tariff reductions, are not well organized into a political lobby, and therefore lack political influence. As a result, some infant industries tend to have a prolonged and sheltered childhood, and become a drag on the nation's economy.

CURIOUS CITIZEN: So tariffs tend to cause inefficiency.

EMINENT ECONOMIST: Yes, but not just because they shelter industries from foreign competition. Another problem is that the branch plants established in Canada by foreign companies to get behind our tariffs are intended to produce for the Canadian market only, which is very small by international standards. Consequently, much of Canada's branch-plant manufacturing sector consists of small-scale operations that are less efficient than those in other nations. For example, to be fully efficient, a plant producing television sets should produce between 300 000 and 700 000 sets per year. However, in Canada in the late 1970's, there were ten companies producing an average of only about 60 000 each. Such small-scale operations make it difficult for producers to become internationally competitive, which in turn requires continued subsidization by the public through tariff protection. One of Canada's basic economic problems — a branch-plant manufacturing sector that is generally not competitive internationally — is, therefore, largely a consequence of Canada's own tariff policies.

CURIOUS CITIZEN: So tariffs can help to stimulate industrial development, but there are costs and dangers in doing this. How can we tell if it's worth protecting an industry from foreign competition or not?

EMINENT ECONOMIST: There's no simple answer to that question; it's a question of trade-offs, or *costs versus benefits*. How much extra is the public willing to pay in order to maintain a protected industry and the jobs of its workers? For instance, in 1979 it was estimated that import restrictions cost Canadian consumers $24 000 for each job saved in the clothing industry—more than double the $10 000 average earnings for the industry's workers. It would have been considerably less costly to pay the workers their salary but leave them unemployed. When an industry requires heavy protection, and fails to become more competitive, the public becomes increasingly less willing to continue bearing the burden of subsidizing it, and the government may have to reconsider its tariff protection. At some point, the question has to be faced whether, economically, the country ought to have certain industries or not. In the future, Canada faces some tough decisions in this regard. (More on this in Chapter 17).

The evolution of tariff policy

CURIOUS CITIZEN: I see. Does that mean that Canada is committed to the reduction of tariffs?

EMINENT ECONOMIST: Over the long haul, that has been the trend. Perhaps it would be a good idea to run through a brief history of tariff policy, to put the matter in perspective. Sir John A. Macdonald's National Policy adopted in 1879 used tariffs to promote the growth of manufacturing, especially in central Canada. These tariffs established a pattern of east-west trade in Canada, rather than the north-south trade with the USA which would have developed without tariffs. This policy was (and still is) controversial, with the Maritime and Western provinces arguing that they were being forced to subsidize the industrialization of central Canada. However, supporters of the National Policy, mainly in Ontario and Quebec, argued that tariffs were necessary not only to foster industrial development in Canada, but also to preserve Canada's independence from the USA, as it was feared that economic union with the USA would eventually lead to political union.

During the Great Depression of the 1930's, many nations, especially the USA, increased tariffs to very high levels. While each country was trying to protect the jobs of its people in the face of the depression, the overall result of such very high tariffs was a sharp decline in world trade, and higher unemployment in all nations.

The General Agreement on Tariffs and Trade (GATT)

Following the bitter lesson of the 1930's, 23 countries, including Canada, signed the *General Agreement on Tariffs and Trade* (GATT) in 1947. The basic purpose of GATT was to prevent a recurrence of the 1930's experience by agreeing to the principle of negotiating reductions in tariffs among participating countries, with the objective of increasing world trade and prosperity for all concerned. This agreement represented a major shift in policy and began a long trend toward freer international trade, with members of GATT meeting several times to negotiate reductions in tariffs. In 1979, they concluded the *"Tokyo Round"* of negotiations, which not only reduced tariffs but also paid increased attention to non-tariff barriers to trade.

Recently, however, with sluggish growth, high unemployment and an increasing need to earn US dollars to pay for costly imported oil, many nations have shown increased resistance to further reductions in barriers to imports. A tendency toward increased *protectionism* has been observed, especially in the USA and Europe. The new protectionism has caused some observers to wonder whether GATT's success in reducing tariffs was largely the result of the buoyant economic conditions of the 1947-77 period, and whether the trend toward freer trade has been halted by the slower economic growth of recent years. Economists will watch future rounds of GATT negotiations with considerable interest to see whether the recent trend toward protectionism can be halted or reversed.

CURIOUS CITIZEN: How does Canada fit into all this?

> . . . by early 1977, it was apparent that there had been an interruption to the reduction of protectionism that had characterized the commercial policy of the industrial countries over the post-war period.
>
> International Monetary Fund,
> *28th Annual Report on*
> *Exchange Restrictions,*
> Washington, IMF, 1977.

EMINENT ECONOMIST: As a major trading nation, Canada's long-run interests lie in the direction of freer international trade — wider access to world markets would be of great benefit to Canada. Many Canadian industries are still protected by tariffs that are high by international standards (see Figure 16-4), but Canadian exports face non-tariff barriers, especially in the USA and Japan, which are considerably higher than those imposed by Canada on imported goods. However, even if the trend toward freer trade has slowed, much of Canada's manufacturing sector will come under increasingly severe foreign competition in the future, especially industries such as textiles, clothing and footwear.

CURIOUS CITIZEN: And attempts by the Canadian government to provide increased protection for such industries would come at ever-increasing cost to the public, and would risk retaliation from foreign nations against Canada's own export industries.

EMINENT ECONOMIST: Right — so the pressure of competition will continue, and, in all likelihood, intensify. Hopefully, many of Canada's threatened industries will be able to respond by increasing their own productivity and competitiveness.

FIGURE 16-4 *Average Canadian Tariff Rates 1979*

	Importer's Cost Price (Percentage)
Machinery	14.9
Clothing:	
Textiles	19.6
Footwear	24.7
Forest products	14.7
Minerals:	
Iron and steel	9.8
Non-ferrous metals	7.6
Chemicals and plastics:	
Rubber products	14.8
Chemicals and paints	13.5
Whiskey and gin	50¢/gal.

SOURCE Financial Post, July 21, 1979.

Adjusting to reduced tariffs

CURIOUS CITIZEN: Still, not all will succeed in doing so. What are the implications of some of these international economic forces for the Canadian economy? Where *do* Canada's comparative advantages lie?

EMINENT ECONOMIST: Canada's traditional strength in *natural resources* will continue, along with products linked to our resource base. However, Canada is quite capable of competing internationally in many other areas as well, as shown by companies such as Northern Telecom and Spar Aerospace. Generally, Canadians' manufacturing successes tend to be in *high technology* or specialized fields, in which output per worker (productivity) is high enough to make Canadian products competitive despite our high wage rates. However, if past trends continue, *labor-intensive* industries (those that require a lot of labor, such as clothing and footwear) will experience difficulty competing with imports, and production of such products will tend to relocate in lower-wage countries such as Hong Kong, Singapore, Taiwan and Korea.

CURIOUS CITIZEN: But wouldn't free trade involve some pretty serious problems for the Canadian economy, too? Some of our industries would expand greatly with access to foreign markets, but others would contract severely due to foreign competition. This would be a tremendous adjustment for our economy to have to make—in the process, many workers might be laid off, businesses go bankrupt, and so on. I know that's only the dark side of the story, but layoffs and bankruptcies would likely happen if free trade became a fact.

EMINENT ECONOMIST: That's true, which is why it is generally agreed that governments should *reduce tariffs gradually,* and provide advance notice of planned tariff reductions to industries that will be affected by them. The gradual approach would give these industries time to make adjustments, in either their production methods and efficiency, or in their actual product lines. In some cases, it makes more sense to switch to new products rather than to try to compete with the imports.

. . . it seems clear that the growth of the developing nations will call for a substantial increase in trade and offer opportunities for Canadian exports of agricultural and other primary and semiprocessed products, as well as some heavy equipment and capital-intensive manufactured goods. In return, Canadians must expect to import increasing amounts of manufactured items with a relatively high labor-intensive content. Enhancing the competitiveness of the economy will require substantial capital to modernize existing plants and modify the industrial structure in line with the nation's advanced technological know-how and natural resource base. It may also require more specialization in somewhat fewer products, in order to gain wider access to export markets. These developments will also necessitate measures to minimize and to distribute the costs of adjustment to low-productivity firms in such areas as textiles, footwear and electronic products, which will likely have difficulty competing and which are often the sole or major employer within a community.

Economic Council of Canada,
Fourteenth Annual Review, 1977 (page 78).

CURIOUS CITIZEN: Those things would certainly help, but the fact remains that some industries and workers in all countries would be very adversely affected economically—shouldn't something be done for them?

EMINENT ECONOMIST: Many people would agree—tariff reductions are undertaken for the economic benefit of the majority, so it seems unfair to sacrifice the minority that is hurt by tariff cuts. There is a logical, moral argument for government assistance of some sort to those industries and workers that are hurt—the basic idea being that the majority that benefits economically from tariff cuts should in some way assist the minorities that are hurt economically.

CURIOUS CITIZEN: You say "assist in some way"—but surely you don't mean subsidies to keep them producing the same products that were proving uncompetitive and unsuccessful.

EMINENT ECONOMIST: No—generally, the proposed assistance would take the form of *retraining allowances* for workers, and *loans and technical advice* to help businesses to convert to other lines of production. The idea is not just to help those who are adversely affected by tariff cuts, but also to promote more rational and efficient specialization of production among countries, for the general economic benefit of all concerned, which is what international trade is all about. There is little doubt that freer trade involves significant long-term economic benefits for all. The transition period would be difficult, as long-established industries declined or vanished, but the economics of the situation dictate freer trade as the long-run approach, as the government says.

> For a trading nation like Canada, which already generates one-third of its national income from the sale of exports, obtaining secure and growing markets abroad is essential to its investment prospects and to raise individual living standards.
>
> Edward Carmichael,
> *Policy Review and Outlook, 1985: A Time for Decisions,*
> C. D. Howe Institute

CURIOUS CITIZEN: What you say is logical, but it all sounds so difficult. Wouldn't it be easier to continue as we have in the past, with our natural resource exports earning our way in the world, and our manufacturing industries protected against foreign competition?

EMINENT ECONOMIST: Circumstances are changing. Canadians can no longer count on their natural resources to carry them economically for an indefinite period of time. There is growing competition from Third World countries anxious to sell their resources as a base for their economic development. Also, many forecasters believe that world demand for natural resources will not grow as it has in the past, as the direction of economic growth shifts from physical products toward services, information processing and more sophisticated manufactured products such as electronic equipment. To succeed in these fields, Canada needs access to larger markets, which means export markets. Attracting export markets would, in turn, mean opening Canadian markets more to foreign producers, and accepting the kinds of adjustments we have been discussing here. The world is changing—Canada can choose to resist change, by sheltering its established industries indefinitely, or to adapt to change by looking outward to new markets and opportunities.

YOU DECIDE

Import quotas on footwear, which have been in effect for eight years, are scheduled to expire in one month. The Canadian Import Tribunal (a government agency) has recommended that the government should drop import quotas on all footwear except women's and girls' casual footwear, and that quotas on these should be phased out over the next three years. The Import Tribunal bases its recommendation in part on estimates that shoe import quotas are costing Canadian consumers $100 million annually, and that perhaps 350 to 700 jobs have been saved by quotas at an annual cost to consumers of $120 000 to $240 000 per job saved. The Consumers Association of Canada and the Canadian Shoe Retailers Association have both argued that the quotas should be removed, pointing out that even without quotas, footwear imports are subject to a tariff of approximately 20 percent—the highest Canadian tariff.

The Shoe Manufacturers Association of Canada claims that domestic manufacturers' share of the market has declined over the past four years from 47 percent to 33 percent. It has asked the government to extend the quotas for a minimum period of five more years and to reserve 50 percent of the Canadian market for Canadian producers. The industry employs about 15 000 people, mainly in Ontario and Quebec. Over the past few years, the federal government has invested quite heavily in financial support for the industry. Political support for the government in Quebec and Ontario, which was crucial to its success in the last election, has been weakening lately. The labor union movement has clearly stated its opposition to any move that would threaten jobs, and a recent public opinion poll indicates that Canadians are nervous about free trade.

Finally, the European Economic Community has warned that if the Canadian footwear quotas are extended, it will retaliate against Canadian exports, including methanol, styrene, polyethylene, acetate, kraft paper, wire rod, steel coils and cold-rolled sheets and plates. The value of these exports is about $170 million per year.

If you were the government of Canada, what would you decide?

DEFINITIONS OF NEW TERMS

Tariff   A tax, or import duty, on goods imported into a country, the effect of which is to increase the prices of those imported goods.

Non-Tariff Barriers   Other methods (besides tariffs) of restricting imports, including quotas and licences for imports, preferential purchasing policies and subsidies for domestic producers.

Import Quotas   Legal limits on the volume of particular types of goods that may be imported into a nation.

Theory of Comparative Advantage   The theory that even if one nation is more efficient in the production of all items than another nation, it can still be to the economic advantage of both nations to specialize in what they produce most efficiently (items in which each has a "comparative advantage"), and trade with each other.

Subsidy   Government financial assistance, through measures such as grants, loans or special tax treatment, to an industry.

Branch Plant   A manufacturing plant established in a nation by a foreign-owned firm in order to avoid tariffs on imports by producing its products inside that nation.

General Agreement on Tariffs and Trade (GATT)   An international agreement under which many nations have since 1947 negotiated reductions in tariffs in order to promote freer trade.

CHAPTER SUMMARY

1. International trade is of great importance to Canada, which exports about 30 percent of its GNP.

2. Free trade between nations promotes international specialization and higher productivity, making a higher standard of living possible for all concerned.

3. The results of tariffs and other barriers to trade are higher prices, reduced specialization, lower productivity and lower living standards.

4. Canada has, for more than a century, used tariffs to promote the development of the manufacturing industry in Canada. Consequently, much of the nation's manufacturing sector consists of relatively small-scale plants (including many branch plants of foreign firms) which produce for the small Canadian market only and are inefficient by international standards.

5. Since 1947, Canada has been one of many nations which, through GATT, have negotiated reductions in tariffs in order to promote freer

trade among nations. However, the trend toward freer trade appears to have slowed significantly since the late 1970's.

6. Canadian manufacturing faces strong international competition in the future, the likely result of which will be the decline in Canada of some (mostly labor-intensive) industries, and the expansion of industries in which Canada has the greatest natural advantage.

QUESTIONS

1. Since the 1979 "Tokyo Round" of GATT negotiations, have any further tariff reductions taken place?

2. What would be the attitudes toward Canada's tariff policy in
   (a) British Columbia?
   (b) the Prairies?
   (c) Ontario?
   (d) Quebec?
   (e) the Maritimes?

3. What steps could Canada's textile industry take to compete more successfully with imported goods?

4. "$43 per family per year is a small price to pay for the preservation of jobs in Canada's textile industry." Do you agree or disagree? Why?

5. Have there been any further meetings of GATT recently? If so,
   (a) what agreements were reached regarding tariffs?
   (b) what agreements were reached regarding non-tariff barriers?

CHAPTER 17

Canadian international trade policy

Since Sir John A. Macdonald's National Policy of 1879, Canada has basically relied upon natural resources to provide export earnings, while seeking to develop a domestic manufacturing sector by protecting it behind quite high tariffs. The benefits of this policy were the development of a larger manufacturing sector, particularly in Ontario and Quebec, than would otherwise have been possible. The benefits were achieved, of course, at the cost of higher prices for Canadian consumers, due to the tariffs. However, the policy remained basically intact despite periodic challenges, because Canadians generally viewed its benefits as greater than its cost.[1]

Recently, however, there has been considerable concern regarding Canada's manufacturing sector. The first concerns were over the *foreign ownership* of Canadian industry, in the guise of foreign-owned branch plants, established only for the purpose of getting behind Canada's tariffs. During the 1970's, foreign ownership and control became a significant political issue in Canada.

More recently, however, attention has shifted toward the *economic performance* of Canadian manufacturing. Particular attention has been focused on the problems the industry has competing with foreign producers, not only in export markets but also in protected Canadian markets, as the extensive penetration of imports into Canadian markets indicates.

---

[1]Canada's tariff policy has had much stronger political support in Ontario and Quebec, where the protected manufacturing industries are mostly located, than in other parts of the country, particularly the resource-exporting West. However, the concentration of population and political power in central Canada has been the deciding factor politically.

By the beginning of the 1980's, the weaknesses of Canadian manufacturing were of growing public concern. While Canada's manufacturing sector employed roughly 2 million people, or 20 percent of the nation's labor force, this proportion had been gradually shrinking. Plant closings, particularly in Ontario, led to warnings that unless the recent trend was altered, during the 1980's Canada would become the first major nation to *de-industrialize* its economy. The Canadian economy, it was said, would evolve into a "warehouse economy," the primary function of which would be to store and distribute imported manufactured products, rather than produce its own.

In this chapter, we will consider first the question of the ownership of Canadian industry, then the more basic economic issue of its performance.

How much Canadian industry is foreign-owned?

As Figure 17-1 shows, foreign ownership of Canadian industry is an important feature of the Canadian economy. Foreign ownership, about 80 percent of which is American, tends to be concentrated in certain sectors of the Canadian economy, particularly manufacturing, petroleum and natural gas, and mining and smelting. In general, these are the more dynamic and rapidly growing sectors of the Canadian economy. While foreign-owned firms are few in number (less than 5 percent of all business firms in Canada), they tend to be very large, comprising about 30 percent of the sales of non-financial firms in Canada and 49 percent of manufacturing sales.

In Figure 17-1 we see that there has been a definite overall decline in the percentage of foreign ownership over the 1970-81 period. For the manufacturing sector the figures are higher, but they do show a decline, from 57 percent in 1974 to 49 percent in 1982. Despite these declines, however, the degree of foreign ownership in Canada remains very high by international standards.

What forms does foreign investment in Canada take?

Most people think of foreign investment in terms of foreign corporations controlling firms in Canada, but in fact the concept is much wider than that. First, foreign investment can come in two distinctly different forms: debt and equity. **Debt** refers to loans made by foreigners to Canadian businesses or governments, usually through bond issues. Many major projects in Canada, including the Quebec Hydro James Bay project and the Ontario Hydro expansion, have been financed in this way. Such investments by foreigners are in effect loans to Canada, and as such involve

FIGURE 17-1 *Foreign Ownership of Canadian Industry 1970 and 1981*

Industry	Percentage of Sales	
	1981	1970
Tobacco	100%	82%
Rubber	89	91
Transportation equipment	84	89
Petroleum & coal products	78	99
Chemicals	76	83
Electrical products	62	66
Nonmetallic mineral products	59	53
Oil and gas	58	91
Machinery	56	77
Textiles	52	49
Mining extraction	37	68
Beverages	35	30
Metal fabricating	34	42
Paper & allied	28	47
Food processing	25	33
Wholesale trade	25	27
Leather	22	20
Knitting mills	17	18
Community, business and personal services	16	19
Primary metals	15	41
Furniture & fixtures	14	19
Wood	14	23
Retail trade	13	21
Communications	12	n.a.*
Clothing	11	11
Printing & publishing	11	13
Construction	10	14
Transportation	7	13
Agriculture, logging & fishing	4	7
Storage	3	n.a.
Public utilities	3	8
Total	30%	37%

*Not available.

SOURCE Statistics Canada

no foreign ownership or control. **Equity** investment, on the other hand, refers to ownership of the shares of Canadian businesses, and often does involve foreign control. Most US investment in Canada is of this type.

Second, foreign investment funds may be used in different ways. They may be used to build new *productive facilities* (capital equipment—plants, machinery and equipment) which did not previously exist. Or they may be used to buy (take over) existing *Canadian businesses*, by purchasing a controlling interest in their stock. Or they may be used to buy *Canadian resources* such as real estate, mineral rights, natural gas, or timber rights.

Third, foreign investment may come from different sources. The funds may come, say, from the USA, to be invested in Canada—in effect, then, Americans would be making their savings available for use in Canada. Or the funds may come from profits earned in Canada and reinvested by US-owned corporations. In recent years, foreign firms in Canada seem to be expanding more through *reinvestment* of Canadian-earned profits than through additional *imports of capital* from abroad.

The varieties of foreign investment indicate that foreign investment is not the simple thing that many Canadians perceive it to be. For instance, the same person may welcome to his or her community a new US-owned plant and the jobs it brings, yet feel uneasy about Canadian firms being taken over by foreign companies, and oppose strongly the development and exportation of Canadian resources by foreign corporations.

Why so much foreign ownership?

The most basic reason for the large flows of foreign investment into Canada over the years has been that Canadians wanted it, and sought to attract it. We wanted it because we wanted industrialization and the economic benefits—higher productivity and a higher standard of living—which it brings. Industrialization required capital investment in excess of our own ability and willingness to save and invest, so we imported savings (capital) from more developed countries, especially the USA.

It is not unusual for a country to rely on capital from other countries during the earlier stages of its development, since it is often impossible to generate domestic savings in the amounts required. In its earlier stages, the USA relied on extensive amounts of British capital; later the USA became a supplier of capital to other countries, including Canada.

To attract foreign capital, Canada used three basic approaches. First, Canada has the *least restrictive policy* toward foreign investment of any nation in the western world. Until quite recently there was scarcely any legislation impeding foreign capital inflows. Second, since 1879, Canada has imposed *high tariffs* on imported goods, which have been a major cause of much foreign investment. These tariffs have created a strong incentive for foreign firms to build branch plants in Canada rather than export into the Canadian market. A third measure to attract foreign funds has been Canadian *interest rate policy*: the government has consistently kept Canadian interest rates above those in the USA, with a view to attracting investment funds to Canada.

Other factors have contributed to the high levels of foreign investment in Canada. The very nature of the Canadian economy — geographically spread out over large areas and concentrating on resource development — has made high levels of *capital investment* necessary. Furthermore, Canadian investors have not been particularly willing to provide *risk capital* for Canada's industrial growth, preferring safe, low-yield investments instead, such as residential property, public utilities, and agriculture. The expanding, or *growth sectors* of the economy — mining, chemicals, electrical apparatus, energy and so on — secured much of their investment capital from foreign sources. Thus, the tendencies of Canadian investors themselves have played a role in the inflow of foreign capital.

From the viewpoint of US corporations, Canada has been a logical place to invest quite heavily. Geographically proximate, with a similar culture and language, Canada presented after the Second World War a relatively untapped market, a skilled but lower-paid labor force and access to great natural resource wealth. In summary, high levels of US investment in Canada were considered beneficial by all concerned.

Canadian attitudes toward foreign investment

Canadians are ambivalent toward foreign investment — they want the economic benefits it brings, but many feel uneasy about the degree of foreign ownership and control associated with foreign investment, as well as the dependence which it implies. As a result, Canadians have tended to be quite critical of foreign investment but have generally been reluctant to take action that would discourage it.

Probably, the most basic concern of Canadians regarding foreign investment is that foreign-controlled firms will not act in accordance with *Canada's best interests*. This argument, however, is disputed by many people. They point out that it is based on an assumption that, because a firm is foreign-owned, it behaves differently than it would if it were Canadian-owned. They argue that corporate executives are loyal above all else to the corporation, regardless of nationalistic considerations, and challenge opponents of foreign investment to provide examples of Canadian-owned companies that have acted in the national interest at the sacrifice of their profits. Also, they point out, the Canadian government has the power (indeed, the responsibility) to set down rules for corporations — both foreign-owned and Canadian — to follow when the public interest requires it.

Another common criticism of US ownership of Canadian industry is the payment of *dividends and interest* to the parent company in the USA. Of course, dividends and interest are paid to the US parent company, just as they would be if the parent company were in Canada. However, foreign-owned firms have also engaged in substantial reinvestment of their profits in Canada, as the rapid growth of many of these firms indicates.

A frequently expressed criticism of American investment in Canada is that, through US-owned corporations, *US law* is extended into Canada. Perhaps the best example of such an extension is the application of the Trading with the Enemy Act to Canadian subsidiaries of US firms — the law has prevented these firms from exporting to nations such as Cuba and Russia. While the volume of exports in question is undoubtedly small, the principle is important to many Canadians. On the other hand, the effects of US law have not always been harmful. American antitrust law prevented Schlitz Brewery from taking over Labatt's, and forced the establishment of a separate Aluminum Company of Canada. Nonetheless, some Canadians feel that such decisions should be made in Canada.

Some of the other criticisms of foreign control are that the parent company may interfere with exports by the Canadian subsidiary, that key corporate officers may tend to be non-Canadians sent in from the parent company, that research and development is done by the parent firm rather than in Canada — to the disadvantage of Canada's scientific community — and that Canadian subsidiaries may be required to buy supplies from the US. In the latter case, the Canadian subsidiary may buy parts from the US parent at unusually high prices. The result is lower profits for the Canadian operation, higher profits for the parent company and a reduction in corporate income taxes payable to the Canadian government.

Other Canadians see in US ownership of industry threats that are not economic, but rather *social and political*. They fear that Canadian society will become Americanized through US television, movies, magazines, sports and advertising, or even that US ownership of industry will lead

---

The main source of economic expansion, employment growth, and improvement in the quality of life is investment, . . . Although Canadians direct a high proportion of their private and business income into savings, Canada has traditionally needed to supplement its domestic savings with foreign borrowings in order to achieve rates of investment consistent with the desired growth of the economy and employment.

Economic Council of Canada
Fourteenth Annual Review, 1977 (page 45).

to US control of Canada politically. This argument, too, is very difficult to assess — in theory, at least, Canada need not surrender her sovereignty. It is true that Canada, like most other countries, is subject to considerable political influence from the USA — inevitably, given the vast economic power of the USA. Whether US ownership of much of Canadian industry would tend eventually to translate this influence into political control is impossible to assess.

While these criticisms tend to upset many Canadians, it is only fair to note that objective studies have failed to develop evidence that foreign ownership and control have resulted in significant negative effects on the Canadian economy. Perhaps because of this lack of evidence, Canadian governments have generally tended to voice concerns and complaints about foreign investment, but to do little to actually restrict it, because by doing so Canada would lose the benefits associated with it.

Government policies

The basic attitude of Canadian federal and provincial governments over the years has been to *encourage* foreign investment, through tariff and interest-rate policies as well as a lack of restrictions, as noted earlier. While there has been some legislation intended to protect Canada's interests, this legislation has been quite mild by international standards.

Until 1974 the most important approach which the federal government used was the *key sector* tactic — an across-the-board foreign ownership restriction in sectors of the economy deemed to be essential to Canada's political and economic integrity. Through various key sector legislative acts, foreigners have been effectively excluded from control of chartered banks, loan, trust and securities companies, radio and television broadcasting, cable TV companies, magazine publishing and book distribution. In addition, provincial governments regulate foreign investment in certain ways. For example, there are restrictions on sales of land to foreigners in several provinces, and Ontario requires that a majority of the directors of all provincially incorporated companies be Canadian.

In 1974, the federal government passed Canada's most extensive and controversial legislation regarding foreign investment — the *Foreign Investment Review Act* (FIRA). Under this legislation, a federal agency would screen (approve or reject) foreign investment proposals for either the takeover of Canadian businesses over a certain size or for the establishment of new businesses. In making its decisions, the agency was to assess whether or not such investments would be "of significant benefit to Canada". FIRA was quite controversial. It was criticized both for being ineffective in regulating foreign investment and for discouraging valuable investments, due to the red tape involved and the subjective and political nature of the agency's decisions.

In 1985, faced with a sluggish economy and the need for more investment spending, the new federal government replaced FIRA with *Investment Canada*. While Investment Canada was still to review major foreign takeovers of Canadian businesses, it would do so on a greatly reduced scale.[2] Also, foreign investment creating new businesses in Canada was no longer to be subject to review, but would be required only to provide notification to Investment Canada.

Perhaps more importantly, Investment Canada's basic orientation was to be quite different from FIRA's. While FIRA played the role of *watchdog* to prevent harm to Canada from foreign investment, Investment Canada's role was to be to *promote* both foreign and domestic investment, and to attract foreign investment to Canada. In introducing the new agency, the Prime Minister, Brian Mulroney, said, "Canada is on the march to new projects and new prosperity. We have put behind us fears and self doubts that created the National Energy Program[3] and the Foreign Investment Review Agency. Our objective is an economy that is open to new ideas and not afraid of competition."

On balance, what have been the economic effects of foreign investment in Canada?

No one doubts that foreign investment has played a large role in developing Canada economically and in providing the prosperity and high standard of living enjoyed by Canadians. If we had had to rely for investment funds on savings generated solely within Canada, our economic development would have been much slower. Furthermore, along with foreign capital have come managerial and technological expertise, both of which have been of substantial value to Canada. Canadians have gained economically from foreign investment in another way: when foreign firms invest in Canada, they must buy Canadian dollars with their own currency, providing Canada with foreign currencies (mostly US dollars) with which to buy large quantities of imported goods. This process has added substantially to Canadians' living standards. The typical pattern of Canada-US trade has involved heavy purchases of US goods and services by Canadians, paid for partly by Canadian exports and partly by funds provided by US investment into Canada.

Over the longer term, the effect of foreign investment in Canada has been that the manufacturing sector of the Canadian economy has grown larger than it otherwise would have, which has provided employment

[2]Exceptions are the publishing industry, where controls were more strict, and the oil and gas industry, where Canadian ownership was to continue to be pushed toward the goal of 50 percent set by the National Energy Program in 1981.

[3]The National Energy Program was to increase Canadian ownership of the oil and gas industry to 50 percent, partly by policies favoring the growth of Canadian companies and partly by takeovers of foreign firms by PetroCan, the federally-owned oil company.

for many Canadians. On the other hand, this manufacturing sector consists largely of foreign-owned branch plants which have been sheltered from foreign competition, and are not competitive internationally. Rather than becoming the dynamic force that it was intended to be, the sector has tended to become a drag on the economy. Continued protection of manufacturing industries from imports burdens Canadian consumers with higher prices. It also limits the growth of more successful Canadian firms and industries by encouraging the imposition of retaliatory trade restrictions by other nations. What to do about this situation is one of the most important economic questions facing Canada.

Why not just buy back Canada from the foreign investors?

Some economic nationalists would like to deal with the foreign ownership question by "buying back Canada" from foreign investors. One way to do this would be to require foreign parent companies to sell their shares of their Canadian subsidiaries to Canadians over a period of time until controlling interest had passed into Canadian hands. While their plan may seem attractive, the matter is not that simple. First, the cost of doing so would be staggering—not just in dollar terms, but also in terms of the opportunity cost, or the forfeited alternative uses for such vast amounts of money, including job-creating capital investment. More importantly, however, buying back the country would not solve the basic economic problem of making Canada's manufacturing sector efficient enough to be competitive internationally. All that a "buy back Canada" campaign would achieve (even if it were feasible) would be that Canadians rather than foreigners would own an uncompetitive sector of the Canadian economy.

While the productivity and export performance of many of the foreign-owned branch plants that comprise much of Canada's manufacturing sector has been disappointing, their problems have not arisen merely because of foreign ownership. The underlying economic problems of the Canadian manufacturing sector are considerably more subtle and complex than the simple question of who owns and controls it.

Weaknesses of the Canadian manufacturing sector

There are various reasons why much of the Canadian manufacturing sector is not competitive internationally. Due to Canada's tariffs and her lack of a free-trade arrangement with other nations, Canadian manufacturers and foreign-owned branch plants are geared mostly to the Canadian market, in which inefficiency is generated not only by *tariff protection*, but also by the *small size of the market*.

By the mid-1980's, Canada was the only high-income country in the northern hemisphere that did not have something approximating free-trade access to markets of 100 million people or more, either domestically or through trade.

The relatively small market available to many Canadian manufacturers restricts their use of modern mass-production technology. Since the average Canadian manufacturing plant is significantly smaller than plants in the USA, the United Kingdom, France, Sweden and West Germany, it is less able to develop the productive efficiencies associated with large-scale operations (economies of scale) that plants in many other nations possess.

However, the problems of Canadian manufacturing go beyond small plant size. Because many plants are geared to the Canadian market only, they are *unable to specialize* in producing one or a few products; rather, they must produce an entire range of products for a market of only 25 million people. The switchovers from one product to another are costly and reduce the plants' efficiency. According to recent studies, the problem of *short production runs* could be a greater source of inefficiency in Canadian manufacturing than the problem of small plant size.

According to a 1984 study by Canadian economist Don Daly,[4] Canada pays wages second only to those in the USA, but does not generate the productivity (output per worker-hour) to support such high wage levels. Consequently, Canada's labor costs per unit of output were the second highest (after the United Kingdom's) of all countries studied by Daly — roughly 30 percent above those of the USA and double Japan's. These high labor costs, Daly concluded, led to the low profits, low investment, plant closures and high unemployment that have characterized much of Canada's manufacturing sector. It is interesting to note that a basic cause of both this inefficiency and foreign ownership has been Canada's tariff policy: rather than foreign ownership causing inefficiency, as some people think, both are the result of another factor — restrictions on imports.

We have seen that much of Canadian manufacturing consists of relatively inefficient, small-scale branch plants, and of Canadian firms in various industries such as textiles and clothing, footwear, electrical machinery and equipment, furniture and consumer products. While these Canadian-owned industries are not competitive internationally, they have grown behind their tariff protection into *major employers*; for instance, the clothing and textile industry provides nearly 200 000 jobs. These industries — and jobs — require protection from imports that is quite costly to consumers — from $25 000 to over $200 000 per job saved, according to various studies.[5]

[4]Donald J. Daly, *Cost Competitiveness in Canadian Manufacturing: The Challenge and Some Policy Options*, York University, Toronto, October 1984.
[5]See for example the study by Glenn Jenkins (Harvard University) cited in *Canadian Consumer* Oct., 1985.

Despite protection, many such firms have had and will continue to have considerable difficulty competing with imports. On the one side, the newly industrialized countries such as Taiwan, Mexico, South Korea and Malaysia have low labor costs that enable them to compete very

WORLD PRODUCT MANDATING

We have seen that one problem with foreign-owned branch plants is that they are often inefficiently small replicas of their parent operations. Ideally, they would be able to specialize in the production of one or a few products; however, the small size of the Canadian market precludes such specialization.

An interesting approach to making branch plants more efficient is *world product mandating*. Under such an arrangement, a Canadian branch plant acquires a mandate to design, manufacture and market a particular product for the world market on behalf of the parent company. That is, branch plants would no longer produce, on an inefficient scale, the full range of their parents' product lines, but rather would concentrate on a few selected products for a wider market. With greater specialization and longer production runs, Canadian manufacturers could become more efficient and internationally competitive. Ideally, the Canadian plant would be responsible for all operations associated with its product lines, including research and development, design, production, marketing and exporting, the result being a much more complete industrial structure than the present branch-plant structure. According to the Science Council of Canada, world product mandating has been successful in companies that have tried it, including Black and Decker Canada Inc., Garrett Manufacturing Ltd., Westinghouse Canada Inc., and Litton Systems Canada Ltd.

While world product mandating now applies to only a small proportion of the activities of Canadian foreign-company subsidiaries, it is an interesting approach that could have considerable potential. For a nation facing increasing outside competition, it is a way to channel the great economic resources of foreign multinational corporations into the development of a competitive Canadian manufacturing sector, which would be better able not only to survive competition, but also to thrive in it.

A major attraction of world product mandating is that it can make Canadian plants more competitive without creating a sink or swim situation, such as that created by free trade.

strongly in labor-intensive industries such as clothing and footwear, and in assembly activities such as electronics. On the other side, Canada faces strong competition in high technology industries such as communications and transportation equipment, from the advanced western economies such as the USA, Japan and western Europe. Manufacturing employment accounted for barely 20 percent of Canada's jobs at the start of the 1980's, a percentage that had been steadily declining.

In the past, the relatively weak part of Canada's manufacturing sector has been carried by subsidies from consumers in the form of higher prices, and by natural resource exports, which have paid Canada's way internationally. However, Canada cannot rely on resource exports as in the past, due to slower growth of world demand for resources and increased competition from less-developed nations with resources to sell.

Consequently, it is generally agreed that Canada would benefit greatly if manufacturers could improve their competitiveness. However, great improvements have not generally come about, and part of the manufacturing sector continues to seek protection against foreign competition.

What those who talk about "structural adjustment" to meet low-wage competition never tell you is there is no end to it. There'll always be some other country . . . where the wage rate is 40 cents an hour — with which we'll never be able to compete.

> Robert White,
> United Auto Workers,
> *Toronto Star*, May 9, 1984.

White is absolutely right. But his answer, of protectionism, is wrong. What we have to do is move out of making the kinds of things that can be made cheaper in underdeveloped countries and develop new products.

> David Culver,
> Chairman, Alcan Aluminum Ltd.,
> *Toronto Star*, May 9, 1984.

The manufacturing sector has not withered, and is not withering, in the face of international competition . . . Canada is far from de-industrializing; there is no evidence that this process is even beginning.

> Economic Council of Canada,
> *The Bottom Line*, 1983

Strengths of Canadian manufacturing

The Canadian manufacturing sector also includes a quite different group of firms — efficient, competitive, outward-looking firms which support freer trade because they see it as an opportunity, rather than a threat. This group includes successful *Canadian firms* (such as Northern Telecom, Moore Corp., Spar Aerospace and Magna International) and about one in five of Canada's *branch plants* (usually those which have specialized in the production of one or a few products under a *world product mandate*).

FIGURE 17-2 *Canada's Twenty Multinationals 1983*

	Percentage of Foreign to Total Sales
Alcan Aluminum Ltd.	84%
Nova Corp.	29
Hiram Walker Resources Ltd.	42
Northern Telecom Ltd.	79
Noranda Inc.	63
Moore Corp. Ltd.	90
Seagram Co. Ltd.	92
MacMillan Bloedel Ltd.	79
John Labatt Ltd.	n.a.*
Massey-Ferguson Ltd.	91
Genstar Corp.	60
Domtar Inc.	29
Abitibi-Price Inc.	63
Amca International Ltd.	78
Molson Cos. Ltd.	32
Inco Ltd.	85
Consolidated-Bathurst Inc.	54
Cominco Ltd.	73
Bombardier Inc.	67
National Sea Products Ltd.	71

*not available.

As Figure 17-2 shows, Canada has some companies that fare very well in international competition. In Fortune magazine's 1983 list of 500 international giants, 39 were Canadian as compared to 41 for France and 59 for West Germany.

Indeed, many Canadian firms have grown to the point where they find the Canadian market too confining. As a result, successful Canadian firms support moves toward freer trade, which would give them access to larger export markets. In the words of David Slater, chairman of the Economic Council of Canada, "We are not a basket case, but a mixed bag of some good and some bad things." There are two distinct aspects of the Canadian manufacturing sector. One is strictly *domestic*, with low productivity and high costs, and wants and needs continued protection against international competition. The other is efficient, competitive and *internationalistic*, and supports freer trade because of the larger markets it would open up. The question is what should Canada's trade and tariff policy be: — protection or freer trade?

What trade policy for Canada?

Some *economic nationalists* would have Canada seek to develop a full-fledged manufacturing sector that is protected by tariffs and intended mainly to serve the Canadian market. The economic realities, however, run strongly against such self-reliance. The Canadian market is simply too small to support an efficient manufacturing sector,[6] and the economic costs to Canadians of a lower standard of living would be too great. Rather, Canada must look outward, seek access to larger markets in other countries, and specialize in those areas in which Canadians enjoy the greatest advantages.

Other economic nationalists would have Canada attempt to force countries to lower their tariffs by making it a condition of selling them vital Canadian natural resources. This approach, however, counts upon other nations (especially the USA) being sufficiently dependent upon Canadian resources to submit to Canada's demands — and it is by no means clear that this is the case.

A completely different approach (to trade) is favored by some *internationalists*. They recommend that Canada move toward freer international trade as a means of shaking up Canadian manufacturers that have grown inefficient and complacent behind high tariff walls. Freer trade would result in a major restructuring of Canadian industry; labor-intensive operations (such as textiles) would largely cease, to be replaced by high-technology industries with high enough productivity to offset Canada's steep labor costs. If all went well, Canada would wind up with a more specialized and efficient manufacturing sector, capable of competing internationally. This "sink or swim" approach assumes that enough of Canadian industry could become internationally competitive to avoid large-scale increases in unemployment — an assumption which may or may not be valid. Another obstacle to the wide-open free trade approach is

[6]For instance, while the concept of a Canadian automobile industry producing a Canadian car (The "Can-car") appeals to nationalists, the economic realities of such a proposal are that, to be reasonably efficient, such an industry would have to produce only a single model of one car, and that Canadians would have to be prevented from buying any other (imported) cars — only the totally standardized "Can-car" would be available to Canadians.

that most of the world's industrial nations belong to *trading blocs* or *free-trade areas*, such as the European Common Market, the European Free Trade Association and the Latin American Free Trade Association. While members of such groups engage in free trade among themselves, they often maintain common tariffs against non-members such as Canada. Canada, which is not a member of any such group, is left with one major prospective partner for a free trade deal — the United States.

Free trade with the United States?

One variant of the general free-trade concept consists of a proposed North American trading bloc or free-trade area between Canada and the USA. Many Canadians object to the idea emotionally, but a strong case can be made on economic grounds that Canada's future lies with closer economic integration with the USA.

> Canadian business has reached a stage where our domestic market can no longer assure our continued growth, and where our access to foreign markets is no longer perceived to be secure enough to stimulate long-term, job-creating investment.
>
> Report of the Macdonald Royal Commission
> on the Economic Union and
> Development Prospects for Canada

The USA is Canada's largest trading partner by far, buying nearly 75 percent of Canada's exports. In 1984, those exports accounted for 1.7 million jobs and $3000 in per capita income in Canada. The USA is a nearby market that is not only large (ten times the population of Canada), but also very wealthy, with similar consumer tastes and language. With Canadian population growth slowing, the US market looks all the more attractive to many Canadian businesses.

By the mid-1980's, another factor was pushing Canada toward a freer-trade arrangement with the USA. Faced with rising imports far in excess of its exports, the USA was increasingly turning toward protectionist measures against imports — measures that could have particularly severe effects on Canada. US protectionism would not only hurt Canadian exports, but also cause Canadian firms to invest in the USA instead of Canada, in order to avoid actual or anticipated US laws limiting imports.

By 1985, the government of Canada was expressing considerable interest in freer trade with the USA. The idea received a substantial boost in September 1985, when the Royal Commission on the Economic Union and Development Prospects for Canada (more commonly known as the

THE CANADA-U.S. AUTO PACT

The Canada-United States Automotive Products Agreement ("Auto Pact") is an example of what is known as *sectoral free trade* — an arrangement in which nations agree to free trade for specific products only.

Before 1965, US auto companies faced a 15 percent tariff at the Canadian border, which led them to establish branch plants in Canada. The branch plants were essentially miniature replicas of the large US plants, built to produce all models of cars for the Canadian market. Because of their size, they were quite inefficient, with the result that Canadian autoworkers' wages were lower and Canadian car prices higher than in the USA.

The Auto Pact of 1965 provided for free trade in automotive products, vehicles and parts across the border. As a result, Canadian plants could specialize in the production of certain models, and enjoy longer production runs and economies of scale. Canadian autoworkers' wages rose and Canadian car prices moved closer to US levels. Canada's auto exports rose sharply, and now represent Canada's largest manufactured export.

The Auto Pact represents a type of world product mandating, which can bring economic advantages to all concerned.

Macdonald Commission) made free trade with the USA its centerpiece proposal. Stating that "Canadians can be first class in any field they choose if they set their mind to it", commission chairman Donald Macdonald emphasized the economic opportunities of free trade rather than its dangers. The commission's report stated that "The long-term gains from bilateral free trade would almost certainly heavily outweigh the short-term adjustment costs", estimating those gains at 25 to 30 times the costs. The gains in real income for Canadians were estimated at between 3 and 8 percent, mainly due to higher investment, productivity and exports, totalling $13 to $34 billion for the Canadian economy as a whole.

One concern raised by proposals for free trade is the fact that Canadian industry's productivity is considerably lower than US productivity — 25 percent lower in many cases. However, the inequality was offset by the fact that the Canadian dollar had by the mid-1980's declined to about $.73 US, which reduced the cost of Canadian goods and services to US buyers. Nonetheless, there were fears that if the Canadian dollar were to rise again to, say, $.80 US or higher, Canadian products would become too costly to compete in the US market.

Another concern raised was that, even if free trade would bring long-term economic benefits for Canadians, the short-term adjustment process could prove difficult. While Canada's stronger industries would grow, the weaker ones would decline in the face of tariff-free US competition. To reduce these transitional problems, the Macdonald Commission recommended a gradual phasing-out of tariffs. US tariffs would be eliminated over a period of five years, as compared to ten years for the higher Canadian tariffs, in order to provide time for firms and workers to make adjustments. Furthermore, the commission proposed a transitional adjustment assistance program to help finance retraining, relocation or early retirement for workers adversely affected by free trade. Depending on the pace at which a move to free trade took place, the adjustment problem could well prove to be less severe than many Canadians fear. Studies suggest that free trade would likely involve a shift of about 7 percent of the

Manufacturing accounts for only 20 percent of total employment. The sectors most vulnerable to competition from developing countries are leather goods, textiles, hosiery and knitted goods, clothing, and selected electronics products. Many of the enterprises in these industries are located in or around Montreal, Hamilton, Toronto and Winnipeg. They represent a substantial proportion of manufacturing employment — about a third in Quebec and a fifth in Ontario — but only about 7 percent of total employment in Quebec and less than 5 percent in Ontario. The situation appears to be particularly acute in Montreal, where a large proportion of the work force consists of married women with relatively poor education, who would likely find it difficult to readapt to either other locations or other occupations. It is rather less severe on the other hand, in the Toronto-Hamilton-Niagara region and southwestern Ontario in general, where the proximity of many small and medium-sized towns to a large number of industrial firms facilitates movement to better jobs in more promising industries.

The situation is very critical in some of the smaller cities in Quebec and Ontario where, in general, alternative employment opportunities are less readily available. Many small towns and villages are threatened because of their greater dependence on the economic viability of one or a few firms. These communities are scattered all over the central provinces but are also numerous in other parts of the country. Their heaviest concentration, however, is in Quebec, especially in the Eastern Townships and the central and western regions of the province, as well as in the Ottawa Valley and other areas of eastern Ontario.

Economic Council of Canada
Fourteenth Annual Review, 1977 (page 43).

labor force from one industry to another, and that most workers laid off due to import competition would succeed in finding other jobs. While the adjustment process would undoubtedly be severe for some workers and communities, these problems would likely not be as widespread as feared.

By 1986, the movement toward free trade with the USA seemed to be losing momentum. Rising protectionist sentiment in the USA, coupled with high unemployment and rising political opposition in Canada, particularly from Ontario and the union movement, seemed to be making a major, formal free-trade deal less likely.

Behind all this, however, lies a less-noticed reality: Canada is gradually moving toward freer trade with the USA, as a result of gradual mutual tariff reductions. Given the need for larger markets for Canadian industry, and given Europe's continued resistance to tariff reductions, Canada has little choice. Increasingly, Canada has been relying on the USA for export markets, and increasingly, Canada-US trade is occurring without tariffs, as Figure 17-3 shows.

FIGURE 17-3 *Average Canadian Tariff on Industrial Imports from the USA, 1979 and 1987*

	1987	1979
Clothing	24.4%	25.4%
Footwear	22.3	24.8
Primary textiles	19.1	22.7
Furniture	14.3	19.3
Plastics	13.4	17.2
Drugs	9.0	15.0
Synthetic resins	8.9	11.2
Chemicals	8.4	14.7
Musical instruments	8.3	17.0
Nonelectrical machinery	8.1	14.8
Earthenware/stoneware	8.0	13.1
Electrical apparatus	7.9	15.2
Paper	7.8	14.9
Rubber products	7.6	13.8
Iron & steel	7.1	10.6
Photographic equipment	7.0	14.8
Wood products	7.0	14.0
Consumer electronics	6.7	14.7
Nonferrous metals	3.1	9.2
Office equipment	2.5	13.1

SOURCE: Federal Department of Finance.

Under previously-signed agreements, tariff rates on 95 percent of Canadian industrial exports to the USA were to be set at 5 percent or less by 1987, and the same rule would apply to 81 percent of US industrial exports to Canada by the same year.[7]

> We are backing into this. We know our trade with the U.S. continues to grow and that most remaining tariffs are coming down. But I can tell you that nobody wants to confront the topic head on.
>
> Unidentified federal official, quoted in the *Financial Post*, March 17, 1979.

Because of the political opposition, especially in Ontario, to free trade with the USA, federal officials have been reluctant to discuss the trend. However, it seems inevitable that freer trade with the USA, whether by an overall deal, or by sectoral arrangements, or by gradual tariff reductions combined with various forms of world product mandating, represents the future trend for Canada's trade policy.

> The Canadian nation is not a weak and fragile plant doomed to disappearance merely because we trade more freely and securely with our American neighbor.
>
> Report of the Royal Commission on the Economic Union and Development Prospects for Canada

Afterword: free trade versus freer trade

Much of the controversy over free trade with the USA arises from the fact that the debate over the issue has often involved confusion between "free trade" and "freer trade".

Freer trade would simply mean reductions in tariffs and non-tariff barriers between Canada and the USA. As such, it would represent little more than a continuation of the long-term trend toward lower trade barriers between the two countries. While less protection against imports would be threatening to some Canadian industries, it would provide others with expanded opportunities in the US market.

[7]These figures do not take into account non-tariff barriers to trade, which had been increasing in the first half of the 1980's.

Totally free trade could be quite another matter. In order to ensure that firms on both sides of the border compete from an equal starting point, a free trade agreement might require the modification or even elimination of some Canadian government programs to assist firms and workers, since these might be considered as subsidies providing their recipients with an unfair competitive advantage. For example, laws to protect Canadian culture and related industries such as television, radio and publishing might have to be abandoned, as an unfair restriction on imported programming and books. Similarly, it could be argued that Canadian income-support programs such as farm marketing boards and unemployment insurance for workers in seasonal industries amount to subsidies to Canadian producers that give them a competitive advantage. Regional development grants to encourage production and employment in less advantaged regions constitute subsidies that might very well be considered unfair to their US competitors. (On the US side, a major problem area would be American government purchasing policies that give preference to US suppliers.)

Another concern is whether Canada would be free to determine its own monetary policy. For instance, if the Bank of Canada thought it appropriate to let the Canadian exchange rate fall to stimulate employment in Canada, might the USA be able to prevent such a policy because it gave Canadian firms an unfair advantage in competing with US firms?

These questions go well beyond the concerns associated with freer trade, which are basically restricted to whether Canada's economic gains would outweigh its losses, or vice-versa. Rather, free trade would bring into question not only whether long-standing Canadian policies and programs could be maintained, but also whether Canada's national sovereignty — our right to determine our own policies — would be threatened. As a result, the question of completely free trade with the USA is much more controversial than the question of freer trade. Even if one assumes economic gains for Canada under a free trade agreement (as most economists do), would they be worth the changes described above? According to Jack Gibbons, a Toronto economist, "The response of the majority of Canadians for more than 100 years has been quite simply that material riches are not everything. Canadians have wished to remain masters in their own house so that they can create a unique society in the northern half of North America" (Financial Post, February 15, 1986).

DEFINITIONS OF NEW TERMS

Debt Investment Investment in which the investor lends capital to a corporation, such as by purchasing its bonds.

Equity Investment Investment in which an investor buys shares representing ownership (equity) in a corporation.

Trading Bloc   An association of nations that have removed trade barriers between themselves, also called a "free-trade area."

World Product Mandating   An arrangement whereby a branch plant acquires a mandate from its foreign parent company to design, manufacture and market a particular product for the world market on behalf of the parent.

CHAPTER SUMMARY

1. A basic objective of Canada's tariff policy has been to foster the development of the manufacturing sector in the Canadian economy.

2. The high degree of foreign ownership of the Canadian economy is largely due to the fact that Canada has generally encouraged foreign investment, partly through its tariff policy, which has led to the establishment of branch plants.

3. Canada's manufacturing industry consists of two quite different components: one which is inefficient and produces for the Canadian market only, needing considerable protection against imports, and another which is efficient and internationally competitive, and supports freer trade as a means to gain access to larger markets.

4. The efficiency and potential of Canadian industry is limited by the small size of the Canadian market and the fact that Canada does not have secure and open access to larger markets.

5. It is considered important to Canada's economic future to gain access to larger markets; however, to do so would require Canada to open its markets more, and expose its protected industries to increased foreign competition.

6. The most likely partner for Canada in a free trade arrangement is the USA, which already buys nearly three-quarters of Canada's exports.

7. By 1985, the Canadian government was expressing interest in a free trade deal with the USA, partly in response to increased protectionism in the USA.

8. Whether or not Canada reaches a formal free-trade agreement with the USA, the gradual trend toward lower tariffs on Canada-US trade seems likely to continue.

QUESTIONS

1. "Regardless of Canadian attitudes and government policy, Canada's destiny lies in economic union with the United States." Do you agree or disagree? Why?

2. "Canada might as well negotiate reductions in tariffs on textiles and footwear now, in exchange for reductions in foreign tariffs on Canadian products, because in ten or twenty years, those industries will be gone no matter what Canada does, and we'll have nothing to negotiate with." Do you agee or disagree? Why?

3. Has the degree of foreign ownership in the Canadian economy increased or decreased since 1981? What are the reasons for such trends?

4. Has any kind of a free-trade arrangement been worked out between Canada and the USA?
   If so, what is the nature of it?
   If not, why do you think this has not happened, in view of the Canadian government's interest in freer trade as of 1985?

5. Has the percentage of Canadian exports going to the USA continued to increase, or is Canadian trade showing a tendency to diversify toward other markets?

6. Is Investment Canada viewed as a success? Why or why not?

7. Has the value of the Canadian dollar in terms of the US dollar risen or fallen over the past few years? How has this trend affected Canada's ability to compete in US markets?

8. In the interests of preserving Canadian culture and identity, Canada has placed restrictions on foreign activity in fields such as television and radio programming and publishing. Such regulations limit the choices available to Canadian consumers but expand the opportunities for Canadians in these fields. With which of the following views do you agree?
   (a) Without these protections, Canadian culture will be swamped by an influx of mass-produced American competition and will eventually disappear. This would be too great a loss for Canada to risk for the supposed economic benefits of free trade, which are only estimated to lie in the range of 1.3 to 7 percent of GNP.
   (b) Culture is no different from other inefficient Canadian industries that want consumers' choices to be restricted so that they may continue their protected survival. If Canadian culture is as worthwhile as the nationalists say, it will be able to survive in open competition; if it can't survive, it will be because most Canadians liked something else better. Why should Canadian consumers be forced to support something just because it's Canadian?
   If a free-trade agreement would increase your family's income by 3 percent, would you be willing to sacrifice our protection of Canadian culture?

CHAPTER 18

The Canadian dollar in foreign exchange markets

We have seen that international trade and Canada's competitiveness in world markets play a vital role in Canada's prosperity, and have stressed the importance of industrial efficiency in improving Canada's competitive position. Another factor that has a very strong bearing on Canada's international competitiveness is the *exchange rate*, or international value of the Canadian dollar. It was much more difficult for Canadian exporters to sell to the USA during the first half of the 1970's, when Americans had to pay up to $1.03 of US currency to buy $1.00 Canadian, than it was after 1976, when the international price of the Canadian dollar began to fall steadily, reaching the $.73 US range by the 1980's.

International financial matters and movements in the values of currencies, such as the devaluation of the US dollar and the revaluations of the Japanese yen and West German deutschemark, are intriguing, but mysterious and confusing to many people. To a trading nation such as Canada, however, it is a matter of great importance when the international value of the Canadian dollar (the exchange rate) fluctuates. Why does the value of the Canadian dollar fluctuate so much, and what are the effects of these movements on the prosperity of Canadians? In this chapter, we will examine the forces influencing the Canadian exchange rate.

Markets for currencies

International transactions such as trade, investment and tourism between nations require that there be some mechanism for converting currencies, or for exchanging various nations' currencies for each other. For example, a Canadian importer of French wine must be able to exchange Canadian dollars for French francs to pay for the wine, and a Japanese corporation buying Canadian lumber must be able to convert its Japanese yen into Canadian dollars to complete the purchase.

These transactions take place in *foreign exchange markets* in which various nations' currencies can be bought and sold. For instance, the Canadian importer of French wine is really selling Canadian dollars and buying French francs, while the Japanese importer of Canadian lumber is in fact buying Canadian dollars and selling Japanese yen. These transactions are conducted through banks, in each country, that have arrangements with each other for exchanging various nations' currencies. The markets for currencies, then, are the banks, where currencies are bought and sold. On any given day, vast amounts of various currencies are bought and sold, for a wide variety of purposes, including imports and exports, investment, tourism and the payment of interest and dividends between nations. Most people have participated in this market at least in some small way at one time or another—for example, before travelling to the USA, by converting Canadian dollars to US dollars. While we describe such a transaction in terms of exchanging or converting currencies, the reality is that we are selling Canadian dollars and buying US dollars.

International exchange rates

If currencies are to be bought and sold, there must be *prices* for them. For instance, when the Canadian tourist exchanges Canadian dollars for US dollars, will he or she get $1.00 US for each Canadian dollar? Or $1.10? Or $.90? Similarly, how much is a Canadian dollar to be worth in terms of French francs, German deutschemarks, Japanese yen or British pounds? The international values of currencies, which are called *exchange rates*, tend to fluctuate, usually on a day-to-day basis. Figure 18-1 shows the international price (or value) of the Canadian dollar on November 29, 1985.

FIGURE 18-1 **International Price (Value) of $1.00 Canadian, November 29, 1985**

```
$1.00 Canadian = $.725 US dollars
               = 5.60 French francs
               = 146.18 Japanese yen
               = 1.835 West German deutschemarks
               = 0.491 British pounds
```

The figures can be interpreted in two ways:

(a) If you were a foreigner who was *buying* Canadian dollars on Nov. 29, 1985, the price you had to pay for each Canadian dollar was $.725 US, 5.60 francs, 146.18 yen, 1.835 marks or 0.491 pounds.

(b) If you were a Canadian who was *selling* Canadian dollars on Nov. 29, 1985, the value which you received was $.725 US, 5.60 francs, and so on.

What determines exchange rates?

Thus, on Nov. 29, 1985, it took $.725 US to buy $1.00 Canadian. What actually decided this value of the Canadian dollar? Why was it not $1.03 US, as it had been in 1976, or $.925 US, as in the 1960's?

Simply stated, the international price of the Canadian dollar, like the price of anything, depends on *supply and demand*. Supply in this case means the volume of Canadian dollars being offered for sale in foreign exchange markets, and demand refers to the volume of offers to purchase Canadian dollars. It is the balance between the supply of and the demand for the Canadian dollar in foreign exchange markets that determines its value, or price.

For instance, in the early 1970's, strong foreign demand for Canadian exports generated increased demand for the Canadian dollar, which rose significantly in value from $.925 US to over $1.00 US. Conversely, after 1976 the international price of the Canadian dollar declined sharply for a variety of reasons, including increased selling of Canadian dollars to buy foreign imports and to pay increased interest payments on foreign loans.

Receipts and payments

A useful way to summarize a nation's international transactions (and thus the demand for and supply of its currency) is to classify transactions as either *receipts* or *payments*. For example, Canadian exports of lumber to Japan cause Canada to receive foreign currency, so exports are classified as a receipt to Canada. Conversely, the winter vacations spent by Canadian tourists in Florida are classified as payments, because they involve payments from Canadians to a foreign nation. Receipts generate a *demand for the Canadian dollar*, because foreigners must buy Canadian dollars in order to pay Canada, whereas payments generate a *supply of Canadian dollars*, or offers by Canadians to sell Canadian dollars in order to pay foreign nations.

In summary, Canada's international transactions can be classified as receipts, which increase the demand for and the price of the Canadian dollar, and payments, which depress the price of the Canadian dollar by causing increased selling (a greater supply) of it on foreign exchange markets. A summary of Canada's major receipts and payments is presented in Figure 18-2; as the balance of Canada's receipts and payments fluctuates, so should the international value of the Canadian dollar tend to rise and fall.

FIGURE 18–2 *A Summary of Canada's Major International "Receipts" and "Payments"*

CANADIAN RECEIPTS
(Transactions generating **offers to buy** Canadian dollars, and thus increasing the international price of the Canadian dollar.)

1. **Exports of Merchandise**
   (Foreigners must buy Canadian dollars to pay for Canadian goods.)

2. **Foreign Tourists Visiting Canada**
   (Foreigners must buy Canadian dollars to spend while in Canada.)

3. **Interest and Dividends Received**
   (Foreigners must buy Canadian dollars to pay interest and dividends to Canadian lenders and investors.)

4. **Foreign Investment in/Loans to Canada**
   (When foreign funds are invested in or loaned to Canada, they must first be converted into — that is, used to buy — Canadian dollars.)

CANADIAN PAYMENTS
(Transactions generating **offers to sell** Canadian dollars, and thus depressing the international price of the Canadian dollar.)

1. **Imports of Merchandise**
   (Canadians must sell Canadian dollars to buy foreign currencies to pay for imports.)

2. **Canadian Tourists Visiting Other Countries**
   (Canadians must sell Canadian dollars to buy foreign currencies to spend abroad.)

3. **Interest and Dividend Payments**
   (Canadian businesses and governments must sell Canadian dollars to buy foreign currencies to pay interest and dividends to foreign lenders and investors.)

4. **Investment by Canadians in Foreign Countries**
   (Canadian citizens and businesses investing in other countries must first sell Canadian dollars in order to buy foreign currencies with which to make such investments.)

Canada's Balance of Payments

The Balance of Payments is an annual summary of all of Canada's international financial transactions, classed as receipts or payments. These items, as Figure 18-3 shows, are divided into *current account* and *capital account* transactions, with current account including mostly day-to-day transactions in goods and services, and capital account referring to flows of investment funds, both long-term and short-term, into and out of Canada.

Canada's international receipts of funds come from earnings from the various current account items shown, plus inflows of capital into Canada, including foreign direct investment[1] into Canada, foreign purchases of Canadian stocks and bonds (including corporate bonds and bonds issued by governments), and foreign purchases of short-term Canadian securities (such as Treasury Bills) and bank deposits. Canada's payments internationally are comprised of payments for the various current account items, plus outflows of capital from Canada, as Canadian businesses and citizens invest funds in other nations.

FIGURE 18–3 *Major Categories of Canada's Balance of Payments*

RECEIPTS	PAYMENTS
Current Account	**Current Account**
Merchandise Exports	Merchandise Imports
Travel and Tourism	Travel and Tourism
Interest and Dividends	Interest and Dividends
Freight and Shipping	Freight and Shipping
Inheritances and Immigrants' Funds	Inheritances and Emigrants' Funds
Capital Account	**Capital Account**
Foreign Direct Investment in Canada	Canadian Direct Investment Abroad
Foreign Purchases of Canadian Stocks and Bonds	Canadian Purchases of Foreign Securities and Deposits
Foreign Purchases of Canadian Government Bonds	
Foreign Purchases of Canadian Short-Term Deposits and Securities	

[1] **Direct investment** is defined by Statistics Canada as "those investments in business enterprises which are sufficiently concentrated to constitute control of the concern." More specifically, such investments include new plants and equipment built by foreign firms, as well as provision of working capital for Canadian subsidiaries by foreign parent firms and mergers in which the assets of Canadian firms are purchased by foreign firms.

The Balance of Payments and the exchange rate

As we have seen, foreign exchange markets, in which the currencies of various nations are bought and sold, resemble a tug of war between each nation's receipts (which push the international price of its currency up) and its payments (which push the international price of its currency down). There are three possible situations regarding a nation's Balance of Payments and the international value of its currency, which are:

(a) a Balance of Payments **deficit**, when payments exceed receipts,

(b) a Balance of Payments **surplus**, when receipts exceed payments, and

(c) **equilibrium** in the Balance of Payments, with payments equal to receipts.

Using Canada as an example, we will examine the results of each of these situations.

(a) A Balance of Payments deficit

If Canada has a Balance of Payments deficit, Canada's payments (offers to sell Canadian dollars) exceed her receipts (offers to buy Canadian dollars). As a result, the supply of Canadian dollars in foreign exchange markets will exceed the demand for Canadian dollars, and the international price of the Canadian dollar will *fall*, as shown in Figure 18-4. An example of such a situation is 1974-75, when Canadian exports slumped and a large deficit developed in trade in goods and services, leading to declines in the international value of the Canadian dollar. Also, from 1977 to 1981, deficits arising mainly from outflows of interest payments and direct investment contributed to further declines in the dollar.

(b) A Balance of Payments surplus

If Canada has a Balance of Payments surplus, Canada's receipts will exceed its payments, so that the demand for the Canadian dollar will exceed the supply of it, causing the international price of the Canadian dollar to rise, as shown in Figure 18-5. Such a situation occurred in the early 1970's, when strong exports boosted the international value of the Canadian dollar.

(c) Equilibrium in the Balance of Payments

If Canada's Balance of Payments were in equilibrium, with receipts equal to payments, the supply of and demand for the Canadian dollar would be in balance, and the international value of the Canadian dollar would tend to remain stable, until an imbalance developed between receipts and payments.

FIGURE 18-4 *Balance of Payments Deficits and the
Exchange Rate*

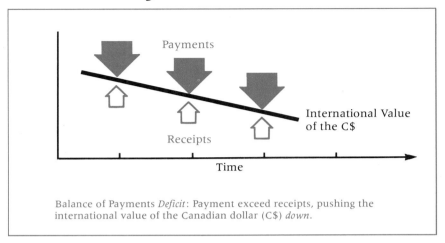

Balance of Payments *Deficit*: Payment exceed receipts, pushing the
international value of the Canadian dollar (C$) *down*.

A floating exchange rate system

We have been looking at how the international prices (values) of currencies
can rise and fall in response to changes in international receipts and payments. When a nation permits the international value of its currency to
move (float) up and down as the supply of and demand for it change,
it is said to be operating on a floating *exchange rate* system.

In the following, we will examine how a system of floating exchange
rates, or currency prices, operates, under conditions of (a) a Balance of
Payments surplus and (b) a Balance of Payments deficit.

(a) *How a floating exchange rate operates with a Balance
of Payments surplus*

Suppose Canada is operating on a floating exchange rate system, with
the international value of the Canadian dollar at $1.00 US, when Canada
develops a Balance of Payments surplus (say, due to increased exports
of natural resources). As noted earlier, the Balance of Payments surplus
will cause the international price of the Canadian dollar to rise, say, to
$1.04 US.

The increase in the price of the Canadian dollar will set into motion
an automatic *adjustment mechanism*, which will tend to eliminate the Balance
of Payments surplus. Because the Canadian dollar is more costly to foreigners, *Canada's receipts will fall*: foreigners will buy fewer Canadian goods,
travel less to Canada, and invest less in Canada. Also, because the in-

FIGURE 18-5 *Balance of Payments Surpluses and the Exchange Rate*

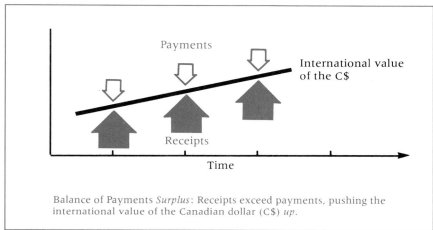

Balance of Payments *Surplus*: Receipts exceed payments, pushing the international value of the Canadian dollar (C$) *up*.

ternational value of the Canadian dollar has risen, it will buy more foreign currency than before, making it less costly for Canadians to buy, travel and invest in other nations. As Canadians increase their purchases of imports and their traveling to and investing in other nations, *Canada's payments will rise*. With receipts falling and payments rising, the original Balance of Payments surplus will tend to disappear, with the international value of the Canadian dollar having moved to a new, higher equilibrium level which is more consistent with the high demand for Canadian exports.

This tendency to move automatically toward equilibrium is illustrated in Figure 18-6. It shows a Balance of Payments surplus causing an increase in the price of the Canadian dollar, which in turn tends to eliminate the surplus.

(b) How a floating exchange rate operates with a Balance of Payments deficit

In a deficit situation, the adjustments are the opposite of those described above. Suppose Canada develops a Balance of Payments deficit (say, due to increased imports of foreign goods). The increase in offers to sell Canadian dollars will cause the international value of the Canadian dollar to fall, say, to $0.98 US from its original level of $1.00 US.

This decrease in the price of the Canadian dollar will cause the automatic adjustment mechanism referred to earlier to operate in the opposite direction, as shown in Figure 18-7. With the Canadian dollar less costly to them, foreigners will buy more Canadian goods and travel to and invest in Canada more; as a result, *Canada's receipts will rise*. Also, *Canada's payments*

FIGURE 18-6 *Adjustment of a Floating Exchange Rate
to a Balance of Payments Surplus*

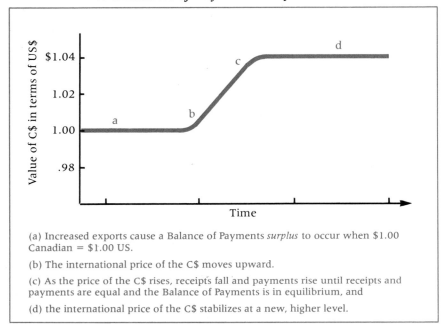

(a) Increased exports cause a Balance of Payments *surplus* to occur when $1.00 Canadian = $1.00 US.

(b) The international price of the C$ moves upward.

(c) As the price of the C$ rises, receipts fall and payments rise until receipts and payments are equal and the Balance of Payments is in equilibrium, and

(d) the international price of the C$ stabilizes at a new, higher level.

will fall: with the Canadian dollar worth less, other nations' currencies will cost Canadians more, making it more costly for Canadians to buy foreign goods and services. Consequently, Canadians will buy fewer foreign imported goods, travel less and invest less in other countries, causing Canada's international payments to decline. As a result of the increased receipts and reduced payments, Canada's Balance of Payments deficit will tend to disappear, and the Balance of Payments will move toward an equilibrium situation with the Canadian dollar at a new, lower equilibrium level.

Thus, a Balance of Payments deficit will cause the international price of the Canadian dollar to fall, which will increase receipts and reduce payments, moving the Balance of Payments toward equilibrium.

Summary

Under a system of floating exchange rates, a nation's Balance of Payments will always tend to return to equilibrium, because of the relationship between the Balance of Payments and the exchange rate (or international price of the currency). While the Balance of Payments affects the exchange rates, so also does the exchange rate affect the Balance of Payments.

FIGURE 18-7 *Adjustment of a Floating Exchange Rate to a Balance of Payments Deficit*

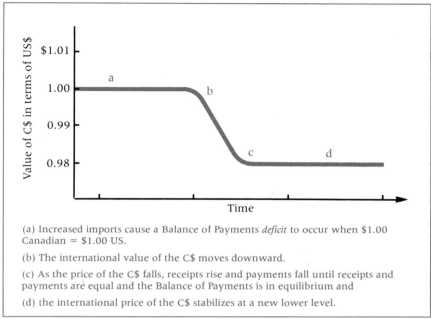

(a) Increased imports cause a Balance of Payments *deficit* to occur when $1.00 Canadian = $1.00 US.

(b) The international value of the C$ moves downward.

(c) As the price of the C$ falls, receipts rise and payments fall until receipts and payments are equal and the Balance of Payments is in equilibrium and

(d) the international price of the C$ stabilizes at a new lower level.

The Canadian dollar in foreign exchange markets

Specifically, if a Balance of Payments deficit develops, it will tend to be removed by a reduction in the exchange rate, which will increase receipts and reduce payments. Conversely, a Balance of Payments surplus tends to be eliminated by an increase in the exchange rate, which reduces receipts and increases payments. In both cases, the Balance of Payments tends to return to equilibrium through changes in the international price of the currency.

There is not, however, a natural or fixed level which represents *the* equilibrium price for the Canadian dollar, toward which the exchange rate will always tend. Nor, having *reached* its equilibrium level, will the price of the Canadian dollar *stay* at that level. As international trade and investment patterns change, causing shifts in payments and receipts, the supply of and demand for the Canadian dollar—and its equilibrium value—constantly change. The equilibrium price of the Canadian dollar is a moving target, toward which the value of the dollar will tend to move. When a nation allows the international value of its currency to fluctuate according to supply and demand in this way, it is said to be operating on a floating exchange rate. Figure 18-8 presents a summary of the operation of a floating exchange rate in the three contexts we have discussed.

FIGURE 18–8 *Summary of the Operation of a Floating Exchange Rate*

Situation	Effect on foreign exchange markets	Effect on the balance of payments
1. Canada's PAYMENTS exceed RECEIPTS (a Balance of Payments deficit)	The supply of C$ exceeds the demand for C$; the price of the C$ falls.	As the C$ falls, receipts will increase and payments decrease until they are equal and the C$ stabilizes at a new, lower equilibrium level.
2. Canada's RECEIPTS exceed PAYMENTS (a Balance of Payments surplus)	The demand for C$ exceeds the supply of C$; the price of the C$ rises.	As the C$ rises, payments will increase and receipts decrease until they are equal and the C$ stabilizes at a new, higher equilibrium level.
3. Canada's PAYMENTS and RECEIPTS are equal (the Balance of Payments is in equilibrium)	The supply of and demand for C$ are equal; the price of the C$ remains stable.	Payments and receipts remain equal; C$ remains at equilibrium level until payments or receipts change.

Dirty floats and exchange rate policy

So far, we have spoken as if governments allow the international value of their currencies to fluctuate according to supply and demand, doing nothing to prevent increases or decreases in their exchange rates. In actual fact, however, governments are often reluctant to allow the international value of their currencies to rise (appreciate) or fall (depreciate) too quickly. A rapid increase in the international value of the Canadian dollar could damage the competitive position of Canadian producers by making Canadian exports more expensive and foreign imports cheaper. On the other hand, a sharp decline in the value of the Canadian dollar would cause import prices to rise quickly, which could add significantly to inflationary pressures in Canada. For these and other reasons, governments often seek to moderate the fluctuations associated with floating exchange rates; when they do so, the situation is referred to as a *dirty float*, because while the exchange rate is floating it is also being manipulated by the government.

> ### CAN A NATION FLOOD ANOTHER NATION'S MARKETS WITH GOODS?
>
> Sometimes, nations fear that they will be unable to compete with goods imported from foreign countries, with the result that entire large segments of domestic industry will be wiped out by imports. During the 1960's and 1970's, the increasing export success of Japan caused such fears in the USA and Canada.
>
> Under a system of floating exchange rates, could one nation flood another nation's markets to this extent?
>
> (ANSWER ON NEXT PAGE)

Exchange rate management

To influence the international value of currencies, governments simply *buy and sell currencies* in foreign exchange markets. By buying a currency, a government can increase, or support, its price by adding to the demand for it, while sales of a currency by a government will depress its value by increasing the supply of it on foreign exchange markets.

In Canada, exchange rate management is handled by the Bank of Canada. If the Canadian dollar is under strong upward pressure due to heavy foreign demand, the Bank of Canada may prevent excessive increases in the exchange rate by *selling Canadian dollars* to foreign buyers in foreign exchange markets. In the process of selling Canadian dollars to foreign buyers, the Bank of Canada also *buys foreign currencies*, which the Bank of Canada holds as part of its *foreign exchange reserves*, or official international reserves. In 1980, Canada held approximately $4 billion of such reserves, consisting mainly of US dollars and gold.

These official international reserves are useful (indeed, essential) when the Bank of Canada wishes to prevent an excessively rapid decline in the exchange rate. When the exchange rate declines, the Bank of Canada must *buy Canadian dollars* in foreign exchange markets, a process that requires that the Bank of Canada *sell foreign currencies* from its official international reserves.

By selling and buying Canadian dollars (and adding to and decreasing its official international reserves in the process), the Bank of Canada can, within limits, prevent excessive fluctuations in the exchange rate and their possibly disruptive effects on the economy.

Another way in which the Bank of Canada can influence the exchange rate is through its *interest-rate policies*. By increasing rates in Canada, the Bank of Canada can attract short-term investment funds from foreign nations, seeking the higher interest rates. To invest these foreign funds in Canadian-dollar deposits or securities, however, their owners must use them to *buy Canadian dollars*, which will increase the international value of the Canadian dollar. Conversely, by allowing Canadian interest rates to fall relative to foreign rates, the Bank of Canada can induce the exchange rate to fall, as Canadian dollars are sold in order to buy those currencies paying higher interest rates.

ANSWER

No, it could not. Under a system of floating exchange rates, the relative values of the two nations' currencies would change so as to make this impossible. In the case of the Japanese exports, North Americans would have to buy vast amounts of yen (and sell vast amounts of US and Canadian dollars) to buy such large volumes of Japanese goods. As a result, the international price of the yen would rise sharply relative to the US and Canadian dollars, making Japanese goods significantly less competitive in North America.

For instance, from 1954 to 1980, the price of the yen in Canadian dollars rose by 80 percent, and the price of the West German deutschemark rose by 191 percent, reflecting in large part the export successes of those nations.

By increasing Canadian interest rates, the Bank of Canada can support the international value of the Canadian dollar, and by holding Canadian interest rates down, it can depress the exchange rate. Such changes in interest rates represent another tool for the Bank of Canada for influencing the exchange rate, in addition to purchases and sales of currencies.

Objectives of exchange rate policy — more trade-offs

In managing the exchange rate, should the Bank of Canada seek to increase or reduce the international value of the Canadian dollar? The answer to this question is quite complex: while some Canadians believe that a higher exchange rate is automatically better, largely because it sounds better, the situation is not nearly so simple.

To Canadian *consumers*, an increase in the international value of the Canadian dollar is good news. Because the Canadian dollar buys more foreign currencies, imported goods and trips outside Canada will cost less. However, to Canadian *businesses that export or compete with imports*, an increase in the exchange rate is bad news. The higher-priced Canadian dollar will reduce export sales by making Canadian exports more expensive, and the relatively lower value of foreign currencies will encourage Canadians to buy imports instead of Canadian products. Conversely, a reduction in the exchange rate would be welcomed by businesses that export or compete with imports, but would mean higher prices for consumers.

The answer, however, goes beyond a conflict between producers and consumers. In a broader sense, it is the trade-off between *unemployment* and *inflation* which we saw in Chapter 15. Declines in the international value of the Canadian dollar will stimulate employment in industries that export or compete with imports—but at the cost of increased inflation, as the prices of imports rise. On the other hand, increases in the exchange rate will help to combat inflation by holding down import prices (which amount to roughly 30 percent of the Consumer Price Index), but at the cost of higher unemployment in Canadian industries that export or compete with imports.

Exchange rate policy, like monetary and fiscal policy, boils down to choosing trade-offs between the conflicting objectives of full employment and stable prices. By increasing the exchange rate, the Bank of Canada can combat inflation, while reductions in the exchange rate will combat unemployment. As with monetary and fiscal policy, exchange rate policy must be directed toward striking a reasonable balance between these conflicting objectives.

Limits on exchange rate policy

In determining its exchange rate policy, a government cannot ignore the fact that there is an *equilibrium international value* for its currency. If a government tries to maintain the value of its currency too far below its equilibrium level, to assist its exporters, it would have to sell vast amounts of its own currency in foreign exchange markets. To sell such quantities of its currency, it would have to borrow or print such large volumes of money that it would damage its own economy, through high interest rates and severe inflation. While Japan and West Germany resisted the upward movement of the values of the yen and deutschemark in the 1960's for fear it would depress their export industries, both nations finally found it impossible to prevent their exchange rates from rising.

Similarly, a nation that seeks to keep its exchange rate too far above its equilibrium level will encounter difficulties. Continual large-scale sales of its foreign exchange reserves will be required in order to buy its own currency, which will eventually deplete its reserves and force it to allow the value of its currency to decline. As Great Britain's competitive position in world trade declined after 1945, and severe chronic Balance of Payments deficits developed, the British government tried to maintain the international value of the pound at unrealistically high levels, and failed because of shortages of foreign exchange reserves.

A nation can manage its exchange rate, but only to prevent excessively rapid fluctuations around its equilibrium level—it cannot succeed for long in keeping its exchange rate much above or below its equilibrium level.

Foreign exchange speculation

As Figure 18-9 illustrates, the international values of currencies, including the Canadian dollar, fluctuate considerably over time, sometimes quite suddenly and dramatically. These fluctuations introduce the possibility of making profits through *speculation* in currencies—that is, buying a currency when its value is low and selling it after its value has risen. For instance, a person who anticipated the rapid decline of the Canadian dollar relative to the US dollar after late 1976 could have bought $10 000 US in late 1976 for $9700 Canadian, then sold those $10 000 US for $10 600 Canadian a few days later, making a profit of $900 virtually overnight.

The problem with such exchange-rate speculation is, of course, that while you might make a killing, you might also get killed. The risk, however, does not deter speculators, who will often move considerable volumes of short-term capital out of currencies seen as weak (likely to fall in value) and into currencies believed to be strong (likely to rise), hoping to make a quick profit by anticipating economic trends or political developments, or just by being lucky. Such speculative purchases and sales of currencies can cause their values to fluctuate more severely, by forcing strong currencies higher and weak currencies lower. For instance, the upward movements of the Japanese yen and West German deutschemark referred to earlier were both preceded by considerable speculative buying of those currencies, and the downward plunge of the Canadian dollar after late 1976 was preceded by widespread speculative selling, which made it considerably more difficult for the Bank of Canada to manage the exchange rate during that period. To offset such heavy speculative selling of the Canadian dollar, the Bank of Canada would be forced to engage in heavy purchases of the Canadian dollar, using up large amounts of its official international reserves to do so.[2]

The fluctuations associated with a floating exchange rate make currency speculation inevitable; however, such speculation can cause difficulties for governments seeking to manage their exchange rates by placing strong upward or downward pressure on currency values.

---

[2]Another way to offset speculation against the Canadian dollar would be to *increase interest rates* in Canada to the point where speculators would be reluctant to sell Canadian dollar deposits because of the high interest rates they paid. However, such a policy would increase interest rates throughout the economy, depressing economic activity generally, which may be considered more undesirable.

FIGURE 18-9 *The International Value of the Canadian Dollar 1970–85*

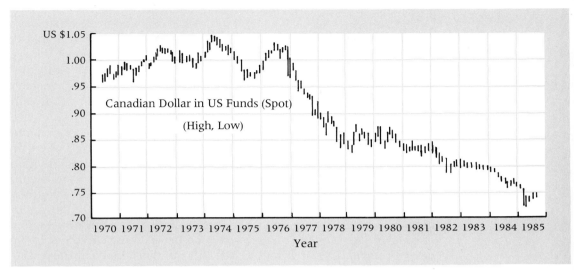

SOURCE   Department of Economic Research, *Canada's Business Climate,* Toronto Dominion Bank.

The Balance of Payments and the Canadian dollar in recent years

(a) The 1950's and 1960's

Figure 18-10 shows Canada's Balance of International Payments for 1961, a year that was fairly typical of the 1950's and 1960's. Generally during this period, Canada had a deficit on current account which was offset by inflows of foreign capital, or a surplus on its capital account. More specifically, a surplus on merchandise trade of $173 million (mainly due to resource exports) is more than compensated for by deficits in other areas, especially travel ($160 million), and interest and dividends ($551 million paid out on the considerable amount of foreign capital invested in Canada). The result is a current account deficit of $928 million. The current account deficit was financed mainly by an inflow of long-term foreign capital ($930 million), over half of which took the form of direct investment, usually involving investments and foreign loans to Canada. In the view of some, Canadians were living high on foreign imports, paid for by "digging up Canada and exporting it," selling out control of Canadian industry to foreigners and going into debt to foreigners. Others disagreed:

they saw Canada as being in a stage of development in which large capital investment requirements exceeded the capacity of the economy to generate savings, so that it was natural and beneficial to import capital from foreign nations, especially the USA. Inflows of capital provided Canadians with an inflow of US dollars, which Canadians used to buy imported goods and services. Regardless of one's viewpoint, however, it was indisputable that Canadians were enjoying greater economic prosperity than would otherwise have been possible, and that both foreign ownership of Canadian industry and Canada's indebtedness to foreign nations were increasing.

The increase in foreign ownership was not widely regarded as a matter of serious concern. In the process of industrialization, nations often use foreign capital quite extensively in the early years when capital requirements are high. However, after a point, the economy will grow and mature enough that domestic savings become sufficient to finance investment requirements, and the dependence on foreign capital ends. Eventually, the nation will likely become sufficiently wealthy that it will be a supplier of capital to (or lender to, or investor in) other nations. The US economy went through just such a process, with British capital financing the original development.

(b) The early 1970's

In the early 1970's, Canada's dependence on foreign capital appeared to be coming to an end. Figure 18-11 shows that Canada's deficit on current account, inflows of foreign direct investment, long-term borrowing abroad and general reliance on foreign capital of all sorts decreased significantly compared to the GNP. These trends were consistent with the process of economic development described earlier, and it was expected that they would continue as Canada's prosperity increased and its dependence on foreign capital decreased. However, after 1975, Canada incurred a large and unexpected increase in foreign indebtedness, as we will see in the following sections.

(c) After 1975

Figure 18-12 shows Canada's Balance of International Payments from 1975 to 1984. There are several features of Canada's international transactions over this period that we should examine in detail.

Current account

As noted earlier, a nation's current account includes day-to-day transactions in goods and services, such as merchandise trade, travel and tourism, interest and dividends and the like.

FIGURE 18-10 *Canada's Balance of International Payments 1961*

	Receipts (+)	Payments (−)	Balance Surplus (+) or deficit (−)
		(millions of dollars)	
Current Account			
Merchandise	$5 889	$5 716	+$173
Travel	482	642	−160
Interest and Dividends	213	764	−551
Freight and Shipping	486	568	−82
Other			−308
Balance on Current Account			−928
Capital Account			
LONG-TERM			
Direct Investment	$560	$80	+$480
Canadian Stocks and Bonds			
Sold (Net[1])	307		+307
Government Bonds Issued			
(Net[1])	40		+40
Other	103		+103
Balance on Long-Term Capital			
Account			+$930
SHORT-TERM			
Balance on Short-Term Capital			
Account			+$133

[1]After deduction of repayments (retirements) of issues that have matured.

SOURCE Bank of Canada *Review*, November 1981.

FIGURE 18-11 *Canada's Decreasing Dependence on Foreign Capital in the Early 1970's*

	Current Account Deficit	Net Inflow of Foreign Direct Investment	Long-Term Bond Issues Abroad (net)	Total Capital Inflow (Long-Term and Short-Term)
	(all figures expressed as a percentage of GNP)			
1950–59	2.5%	1.3%	0.8%	2.6%
1960–69	1.5	0.8	1.3	1.8
1970–74	0.04	0.3	0.7	0.4

SOURCES Department of Finance, *Economic Review*, April 1980; Bank of Canada *Review*.

FIGURE 18-12 Canada's Balance of International Payments 1975-85

(millions of dollars)

	1975	1976	1977	1978	1979	1980	1981	1982	1983	1984	1985
Current Account											
Merchandise	$ -451	$+1 559	$+2 975	$+4 315	$+4 425	$+8 778	$ +7 328	$+17 813	$+17 705	$+20 668	$+16 817
Travel	-727	-1 191	-1 641	-1 706	-1 068	-1 228	-1 116	-1 284	-2 204	-2 126	-2 144
Interest and Dividends	-2 202	-3 178	-4 218	-5 575	-6 685	-7 119	-10 559	-11 752	-11 202	-13 910	-15 004
Freight and Shipping	-433	-150	-26	+131	+304	+513	+440	+585	+539	+668	+191
Other	-479	-1 149	-1 424	-2 082	-1 816	-2 058	-2 158	-2 697	-3 152	-2 747	-1 439
Balance on											
Current Account	$-4 757	$-4 109	$-4 334	$-4 917	$-4 840	-1 114	$-6 065	$+2 665	$+1 686	$+2 553	$-2 648
Capital Account											
(A) LONG TERM											
Direct Investment	$ -190	$ -890	$ -265	$ -2 190	$ -1 800	$-2 350	$-11 300	$ -2 075	$ -2 775	$ -1 650	$-7 350
Canadian Stocks and Bonds Sold (Net)	+1 089	+3 067	+1 521	+708	+1 541	+3 912	+3 845	+2 301	+1 961	+4 554	+7 038
Government Bonds Issued (Net)	+3 405	+5 512	+3 653	+4 289	+2 472	+1 160	+7 113	+9 144	+3 876	+3 283	+5 862
Other	-369	+332	-625	+414	-102	-1 609	+517	-1 057	-1 242	-3 339	-1 677
Balance on Long-Term											
Capital Account	$+3 935	$+8 021	$+4 284	$+3 221	$+2 112	$+1 112	$+175	$+8 314	$+1 819	$+2 848	$+3 873
(B) SHORT TERM											
Balance on Short-Term Capital Account	$+1 620	$+377	$+890	$+1 523	$+7 049	$-171	$+15 780	$-10 065	$+1 861	$-93	$+676
Statistical Discrepancy	$-1 203	$-3 767	$-2 261	$-3 126	$-2 630	$-1 323	$-8 675	$-1 610	$-4 818	$-6 396	$-3 253

SOURCE   Bank of Canada Review.

One outstanding feature of the current account was Canada's large *merchandise trade surpluses.* This strength in trade in goods was largely due to the decline of almost 30 percent in the value of the Canadian dollar against the US dollar from 1976 to 1985, which made Canadian exports more competitive in the US market and US products more expensive in Canada.[3] The large decline in the Canadian dollar had two quite different effects on Canadians: by boosting Canadian sales and production of goods, it increased employment in Canada, and by making imports much more expensive, it reduced Canadians' real incomes. In effect, Canadians as a whole were taking a pay cut in order to make their products more competitive and protect their jobs, much as employees sometimes do when their employer is in difficulty.

FIGURE 18-13   *Canada's Deficit on Interest and Dividends 1970–85*

	Millions of Dollars	Percentage of GNP
Average, 1970–74	$ 1 205	1.1%
1975	1 953	1.2
1976	2 829	1.5
1977	3 841	1.8
1978	4 905	2.1
1979	5 369	2.0
1980	5 557	1.9
1981	6 701	2.0
1982	9 125	2.5
1983	8 953	2.3
1984	11 253	2.7
1985	12 812	2.8

SOURCE   Bank of Canada *Review.*

Another noteworthy aspect of Canada's current account is the large and growing *deficit on services,* particularly on interest and dividends. The deficit on interest and dividends (especially interest) grew rapidly after 1975, not only in dollar terms but also as a percentage of GNP (see Figure 18-13). The rapid growth of interest payments reflected two developments: this was a period in which Canadian governments and corporations engaged in *heavy borrowing abroad,* and the resulting interest payments on

[3]Other factors generating large trade surpluses were the greater severity in Canada of the Great Recession of the early 1980's (which reduced Canadians' purchases of imports) and the USA's faster and stronger recovery from the recession (which added considerably to US purchases of Canadian goods).

the large foreign debt were heavy because of the unusually *high interest rates* that prevailed at the time. Figure 18-14 summarizes the highlights of Canada's current account from 1975 to 1984.

FIGURE 18-14   *Features of Canada's Current Account 1970–84*

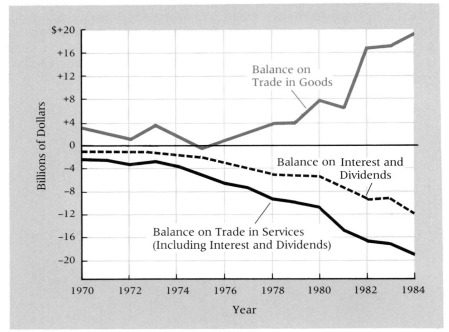

SOURCE   Bank of Canada *Review.*

Capital account

A nation's capital account records the flows of investment capital into and out of the country, including direct investment by business and purchases and sales of stocks and bonds, as well as short-term deposits. Canada continued to have considerable *inflows of foreign capital* after 1975, but there was a significant change in the composition of these inflows. Until 1974, there had been inflows of both direct investment and borrowed funds, whereas after 1974 there were *outflows of direct investment* and *large inflows of borrowed funds*. We will consider each of these developments in turn.

The outflows of direct investment are shown in Figure 18-15. While some of these outflows are due to specific causes (particularly the National

Energy Program in 1981-82), there is a general tendency toward not only less foreign direct investment coming into Canada, but also toward more Canadian direct investment going out of Canada. In part, this trend reflects the fact referred to in Chapter 17: that many successful Canadian corporations have reached their limits within the small Canadian market and have been expanding into other countries (particularly the USA) where markets are larger and costs are lower.

FIGURE 18-15 *Flows of Direct Investment Into and Out of Canada 1970–85*

Year	Foreign Direct Investment in Canada	Canadian Direct Investment Abroad	Balance
1970	$ 905	$ –315	$ +590
1971	925	–230	+695
1972	620	–400	+220
1973	830	–770	+60
1974	845	–810	+35
1975	725	–915	–190
1976	–300	–590	–890
1977	475	–740	–265
1978	135	–2 325	–2 190
1979	750	–2 550	–1 800
1980	800	–3 150	–2 350
1981	–4 400	–6 900	–11 300
1982	–1 000	–1 075	–2 075
1983	200	–2 975	–2 775
1984	2 150	–3 800	–1 650
1985	–2 450	–4 900	–7 350

Inflows into Canada are shown by +
Outflows from Canada are shown by –

SOURCE: Bank of Canada *Review*.

Offsetting these outflows of direct investment have been large inflows of borrowed capital. Since 1975, Canadian corporations and governments (especially provincial governments) have borrowed large amounts of capital abroad, mainly by selling bonds in the USA. Figure 18-16 shows the extent of this borrowing, which has made Canada's debt to foreign lenders one of the world's largest on a per capita basis.

It is not completely clear why Canadian governments and corporations turned to foreign lenders on such a scale after 1975. One apparent reason was the greater availability of funds at lower interest rates in the USA.

FIGURE 18-16   *Net[1] Canadian Bond Issues Abroad 1970–85*

	By Government of Canada	By Federal Government Enterprises	By Provincial Governments	By Municipal Governments	By Canadian Corporations	Total	Total as Percentage of GNP
	(millions of dollars)						
Average,							
1970–74	$ −55	$ −2	$ 774	$ 20	142	879	0.7%
1975	−53	7	2 992	459	700	4 105	2.5
1976	28	193	4 630	660	2 564	8 075	4.2
1977	111	467	2 798	277	1 383	5 036	2.4
1978	2 505	379	1 466	−62	943	5 231	2.3
1979	814	724	1 185	−251	544	3 016	1.1
1980	120	818	319	−97	1 355	2 515	0.8
1981	406	1 133	5 325	249	3 219	10 332	3.0
1982	1 321	1 851	5 665	309	2 769	11 915	3.3
1983	−365	643	3 577	20	565	4 440	1.1
1984	−176	450	2 498	520	870	4 162	1.0
1985	2 605	823	2 217	217	2 893	8 755	1.9

[1]Including retirements
(negative amount indicates retirements exceeded new issues)

SOURCE: Bank of Canada *Review*.

The foreign borrowing may also be linked to the large budget deficits of Canada's federal government. These deficits could have absorbed so much of Canadians' savings and pushed interest rates so high that provincial governments and corporations were crowded out of Canadian capital markets and forced to borrow abroad.

The combination of outflows of direct investment capital and inflows of borrowed capital is somewhat worrisome. Canada is, in effect, exporting productive, job-creating direct investment capital to other countries and replacing it with borrowed funds at high rates of interest. Furthermore, much of these borrowed funds is used by governments not for building productive assets in Canada, but rather for current spending on social services. Opponents of the current policy believe that Canada should redirect its government policies toward creating incentives for job-creating business investment, whether by Canadian or foreign firms.

The Balance of Payments and the Canadian dollar: an overview

Following late 1976, the Canadian dollar underwent a long period of decline against the US dollar, falling by about 30 percent from $1.03 US in 1976 to $.73 US in 1985. The decline in the Canadian dollar has both influenced and been influenced by the Balance of Payments. After late 1976, the decline was largely the result of current account deficits caused by increasingly heavy outflows of interest and dividends. These outflows were not offset by merchandise trade surpluses, because of Canada's high costs, or by direct investment, due to declining investor interest in Canada. As the Canadian dollar moved below $.85 US in 1980, Canadian products became more competitive with foreign goods and large merchandise trade surpluses developed. The trade surpluses more than offset the deficit on services, giving rise to current account surpluses after 1981.

Since there were also inflows of funds on the capital account, it seemed possible that the Canadian dollar had bottomed out at around $.73 US, and could be expected to recover to somewhat higher levels. As of late 1985, however, the recovery had not yet begun[4] — not due to the weakness of the Canadian dollar (which was strong against most other currencies), but rather due to the unusual strength of the US dollar. We will examine the reasons for the unusually high value of the US dollar in the next chapter.

DEFINITIONS OF NEW TERMS

Foreign Exchange Markets Markets, conducted through banks, in which currencies of different nations are bought and sold (exchanged for each other).

Exchange Rate The international price, or value, of a currency in foreign exchange markets.

Receipts International transactions in which a nation receives funds from other countries, causing the foreign countries to buy that nation's currency.

Payments International transactions in which a nation pays funds to other countries, causing that nation to sell its currency.

Balance of Payments A summary of a nation's receipts and payments for a given year.

Balance of Payments Deficit A situation in which a nation's payments have a tendency to exceed its receipts.

Balance of Payments Surplus A situation in which a nation's receipts have a tendency to exceed its payments.

Balance of Payments Equilibrium A situation in which a nation's receipts and payments are equal to each other.

---

[4]The delay could be explained by the "statistical discrepancy" at the bottom of Figure 18-12. In 1984, this discrepancy amounted to almost $6.4 billion — an unexplained outflow of funds that was large enough to more than wipe out the surpluses on current and capital accounts combined.

Floating Exchange Rate   A situation in which the international value of a currency is allowed to fluctuate freely with the supply of and demand for it.

Dirty Float   A situation in which a government influences the exchange rate by purchases and sales of currencies in foreign exchange markets.

Appreciation of a Currency   Increases in the international value of a currency.

Depreciation of a Currency   Decreases in the international value of a currency.

Foreign Exchange Speculation   Purchases and sales of currencies with the intention of earning profits on fluctuations in their values.

Direct (Foreign) Investment   Officially defined as "those investments in business enterprises which are sufficiently concentrated to constitute control of the concern," this term usually refers to investment by foreign firms in plant and equipment of their Canadian subsidiaries; it also includes provision of working capital for Canadian subsidiaries by foreign parent firms, and mergers in which the assets of Canadian firms are purchased by foreign firms.

CHAPTER SUMMARY

1. The international value of the Canadian dollar is determined by the supply of and demand for it in foreign exchange markets, with Canadian receipts from other nations generating a demand for Canadian dollars, and Canadian payments to other nations generating a supply of Canadian dollars.

2. The Balance of Payments summarizes, for a given year, Canada's international receipts and payments, classifying them into current and capital accounts.

3. Under a floating exchange rate, a Balance of Payments deficit will cause the exchange rate to fall, and a surplus will cause the exchange rate to rise. These adjustments will bring the Balance of Payments and the exchange rate automatically toward equilibrium.

4. Under a dirty float, the government influences the exchange rate so as to prevent excessively rapid fluctuations, by buying and selling currencies in foreign exchange markets.

5. In determining its exchange-rate policy, the government must choose a balance, or trade-off, between the goals of reducing unemployment (via reductions in the exchange rate) and combating inflation (via increases in the exchange rate).

6. In the 1950's and 1960's, Canada had current account deficits that were offset by inflows of foreign long-term capital, including substantial foreign direct investment in Canada.

7. After 1975, Canada's current account consisted of large deficits on services (mainly interest and dividends) and surpluses on trade in goods.

8. As the Canadian dollar declined after 1976, Canada's merchandise trade surpluses grew larger, and the current account balance changed from a deficit to a surplus.

9. After 1974, the inflow of direct investment into Canada turned to an outflow, and Canada borrowed large amounts of capital from foreign lenders.

QUESTIONS

1. What has been the trend in the Canadian exchange rate recently, and what are the reasons for this trend? (Sources of information for this topic include the Bank of Canada *Review* and the Toronto Dominion Bank's *Canada's Business Climate*.)

2. Has the Bank of Canada intervened recently in foreign exchange markets so as to influence Canada's exchange rate? If so, what were the purposes of such intervention?

3. If you were responsible for Canada's exchange-rate policy, would you favor action to increase or reduce the exchange rate at this time? Why?

4. Would you expect the international value of the Canadian dollar to increase or decrease over the next few years? Why?

5. Has the outflow of direct investment capital from Canada increased or decreased recently? What might explain this trend?

6. Has Canada's deficit on interest and dividends increased or decreased as a percentage of GNP? What might explain this trend?

7. Has Canada's merchandise trade surplus increased or decreased recently? Why?

8. If the Canadian government were to increase Canada's money supply much faster than the US money supply, how would this affect Canada's Balance of Payments and the Canadian exchange rate?

9. Classify each of the following transactions as either a Canadian receipt or payment on either current account or capital account:
(a) Canada exports wheat to Russia.
(b) Canadian tourists visit Florida.

(c) a Canadian corporation establishes a branch plant in South Carolina.

(d) an American investor buys shares in a Canadian oil exploration company.

(e) an American business ships its products on a Canadian Great Lakes freighter.

(f) the Canadian subsidiary of a US corporation pays dividends to its US parent company.

(g) American pension funds buy bonds issued by the Government of Ontario.

(h) a Canadian company contracts to use computer services supplied by a US firm.

(i) Canadian provincial governments pay interest to American holders of their bonds.

(j) US foreign exchange speculators transfer large amounts of money from US accounts into short-term Canadian dollar bank deposits.

CHAPTER 19

The international monetary system

For international trade and investment to flourish, it is essential that nations develop an acceptable and workable international monetary system. While some people advocate abandoning national currencies in favor of one world currency, this is not a practical or realistic proposal, as each nation insists on its right to control its own economic policies, a key part of which is its own money supply. Few if any nations would be willing to hand over such crucial economic policy decisions to an international agency.

It is essential to develop an international monetary system that facilitates the conversion of different nations' currencies into each other, such as the conversion of Canadian dollars into Japanese yen and other currencies. If a convenient and acceptable system can be established, it will encourage international trade and investment, to the economic benefit of all concerned. However, if a workable international monetary system were not developed, international trade and investment would be impaired, and everyone would suffer economically. One such system is the system of *floating exchange rates* which we examined in Chapter 18, under which the international values of currencies fluctuate with supply and demand, depending on the flows of trade and capital between nations. Another system, which we will consider in this chapter, is one of *pegged exchange rates*; under this system, governments hold the international values of their currencies at fixed levels.

Part A: The evolution of the international monetary system

The experience of the 1930's

During the 1930's, exchange rates became extremely unstable under the pressures of the Great Depression. Nations sought to gain exports and curb imports (and thus reduce unemployment) at each other's expense by deliberately reducing the value of their currencies. The game could be played by more than one, however, and the result was widespread *competitive devaluations* of currencies by governments, and international chaos due to the extreme instability of exchange rates. The effect of these misguided policies was to worsen the depression by further reducing international trade and investment.

The postwar system of pegged exchange rates

After the Second World War, the nations of the world were determined to avoid a recurrence of the experience of the 1930's. In 1945, they met to set up a system of pegged exchange rates, in which governments sought to prevent any significant exchange-rate fluctuations by undertaking to maintain exchange rates at fixed levels.

Under this system of pegged exchange rates, nations kept the international price of their currencies at fixed levels, through two approaches. First, and most basically, they undertook not to use any economic or trade policies that would destabilize international trade and investment, and thereby the exchange rates. Second, when exchange rates did tend to move away from their pegged levels, governments would stabilize them through purchases and sales of currencies in foreign exchange markets. For instance, if the British pound tended to lose value relative to the West German deutschemark, the British and West German governments would buy pounds and sell deutschemarks in foreign exchange markets so as to support the price of the pound relative to the deutschemark at the agreed-upon pegged level. As the West German government bought pounds, Germany's holdings of foreign currencies (its foreign exchange reserves) would increase, and as Britain sold deutschemarks in order to buy pounds, Britain's foreign exchange reserves would decline.

To oversee the system, an international agency known as the *International Monetary Fund* (IMF) was established. Its purposes were to provide a forum for the discussion of international financial problems, to promote stable exchange rates (the system of pegged exchange rates), and to help nations to keep the prices of their currencies at their pegged levels. To achieve this latter objective, the IMF would lend foreign exchange reserves (foreign currencies) to nations that had been forced to use up nearly all of their reserves in order to support their currency against downward pressure.

Gold and the US dollar in the postwar system

Due to the variety of currencies involved in international trade and uncertainties regarding their value, gold has historically played a central role in international finance, either as currency itself or as backing for paper currency, to establish the acceptability of paper currencies. Long after gold ceased to play any part in monetary systems *within* countries, it was still important in international financial dealings *between* countries — some nations would refuse to deal in anything but gold, or currencies that they could convert to gold on demand (that is, which were backed by gold). While placing gold in such a central position is not completely rational — after all, most countries, including Canada, use no gold in their domestic monetary systems — it does show the psychological importance of gold to people, and its association with value and money.

Because there was insufficient gold to finance the growing volume of world trade, nations also began to use paper currencies internationally. To make paper notes issued by one country acceptable in other countries, they were backed by precious metals. First the pound sterling, and later the US dollar, were the most acceptable and commonly used currencies internationally. Until 1968, foreigners could demand that the US government convert their US dollars to gold at the rate of $35 per ounce.

Because of this gold backing and the fact that the US economy was strong, the US dollar came to occupy a special place in the postwar international monetary system. First, the fact that the US dollar was widely acceptable internationally made it *the most widely used currency* in international trade. The US dollar became in large part the currency basis for world trade, with other nations often settling accounts between themselves in US dollars, because they were so acceptable and useful. The acceptability of the US dollar led to its second special role — that of *the main reserve currency*. As noted earlier, to maintain a system of pegged exchange rates, nations must hold reserves (consisting of gold and foreign currencies) with which to buy their own currency if its value tends to decline. During the postwar period, the US dollar came to be the most important reserve currency held by nations. Finally, the US dollar stood at the centre of the world system of pegged exchange rates — all other nations stated the value of their currencies *in terms of the US dollar* (and thus, indirectly, in terms of gold, since one ounce of gold was worth $35 US).

Because of its strength, the US dollar became the key currency in the international monetary system established after the Second World War. Pegged exchange rates were intended to eliminate the problems of

THE INTERNATIONAL MONETARY FUND

In 1945, the same year that the pegged exchange rate system
was established, 39 nations founded the International Monetary
Fund. The IMF had four basic objectives:

  (i) to provide a forum in which financial officials could consider and help resolve international monetary problems,
through consultation and cooperation,

 (ii) "to facilitate the expansion and balanced growth of international trade, and to contribute thereby to the promotion
and maintenance of high levels of employment and real income . . ." (from the IMF's Articles),

(iii) to help members attain sustainable balance of payments positions, and

(iv) to reduce restrictions on the movement of goods, services and
funds between nations.

    Originally, the IMF's main task was to preserve the system of
pegged exchange rates established in 1945. This was done
through annual consultations with member nations regarding
their balance of payments positions, policies and prospects, including reviews of their domestic monetary and fiscal policies.
The IMF would loan reserves to member nations that needed
them to maintain their exchange rates at their pegged level;

exchange-rate instability that plagued the 1930's by holding the values
of currencies relative to each other at agreed-upon fixed levels. However,
as we will see, the pegged system experienced problems of its own.

Strains on the pegged exchange rate system

It is not possible to peg the international values of all currencies indefinitely—some will tend to rise, due to Balance of Payments surpluses,
while others will tend to fall due to Balance of Payments deficits. If the
surpluses and deficits are short-term in nature and not too severe, governments can offset them; but if they are strong and persistent, it will
prove impossible to peg the currency values for long. To attempt to do
so would require buying or selling impracticably large volumes of currencies in foreign exchange markets.

Upward pressures on currencies were experienced by nations whose strong
international competitive positions put their currencies in high demand
on foreign exchange markets. For example, West Germany and Japan
gained vast export markets as they benefited from a combination of rising
industrial efficiency, relatively slow inflation and currency values that were

however, it became IMF policy that such loans be made on the condition that the recipient nations undertake economic policies to remedy their balance of payments deficits.

After the collapse of the pegged exchange rate system and the return of floating exchange rates in 1973, some critics argued that the IMF had failed, and others said that there was no further need for the Fund. However, as it had throughout its existence, the IMF adapted to the new circumstances. It amended its Articles to give floating exchange rates legal sanction, but also gave itself a mandate to "exercise firm surveillance over the exchange rate policies of its members". Thus, the IMF became a force for stability in the new and potentially unstable world of floating exchange rates. Furthermore, the IMF adapted to meet the needs of the developing countries, which have become the major users of the Fund's resources, by increasing its loan limits and extending its repayment periods. In 1982, the IMF gained recognition as having played a major role in averting a possible world financial crisis.

By 1985, the IMF's membership had grown to 148 nations from the original 39. Largely because of its ability to evolve with changing circumstances and needs over the years, it is regarded as one of the more influential and effective international organizations in the world.

pegged at quite low levels after the Second World War. As a result, the values of the yen and the deutschemark tended to rise. Since higher exchange rates would reduce their exports and increase unemployment, the governments of these nations strove to maintain their currency values at the old (low) pegged levels. However, to do so in the face of such high demand for the deutschemark and yen would require government sales of those currencies on a scale so large as to be impracticable: the governments involved would have to borrow or print deutschemarks and yen to an extent that would be damaging to their own economies. Despite the system of pegged exchange rates, the international price of strong currencies such as the deutschemark and the yen would eventually rise in relation to other currencies.

Downward pressures on currencies were felt by nations whose weak competitive positions caused their currencies to be in relatively low demand and high supply in foreign exchange markets. A good example is provided by Great Britain, which suffered from a combination of more rapid inflation than most other countries, lagging industrial efficiency and an overvalued currency that was pegged at an unrealistically high value. These factors combined to make Britain's goods uncompetitive in both domestic markets and export markets, causing large trade deficits that generated continual downward pressure on the price of the pound in foreign exchange markets. To maintain the pound at its pegged level, Britain was forced to buy large volumes of the pound, selling off its reserves of foreign currencies to do so. Eventually, Britain ran out of foreign currencies and was unable to continue to support the pound, which fell in value relative to other currencies.

Austerity programs

A common cause of downward pressures on a pegged currency was inflation. If a nation allowed its inflation rate to be higher than that of its competitors, its products would become less competitive in world markets, its currency would come under downward pressure and would then require support from its government.

Obviously, the appropriate approach to this problem would be to reduce the rate of inflation so as to make your nation's products more competitive internationally. Such anti-inflation policies would likely include tight money (scarce credit and high interest rates) and possibly curbs on government spending and tax increases. By depressing aggregate demand in the economy, these measures can slow down inflation, making your products more competitive and easing the downward pressure on your nation's currency.

However, combating inflation is not without economic and political costs, because a side effect of the depressed aggregate demand will be higher unemployment. When a government is forced to adopt anti-inflation policies because of deficits in its international payments, the anti-inflation policies are referred to as an *austerity program.*

Loans from the International Monetary Fund

Nations that experienced payments deficits that caused their foreign exchange reserves to become depleted could borrow additional reserves from the IMF. These foreign currencies could then be used by the borrowing nation to buy its own currency on foreign exchange markets, thus supporting its price and maintaining the system of pegged exchange rates.

This solution, however, was not altogether painless. The IMF would usually loan funds to a nation only on the condition that it take certain steps to correct its payments deficits, which usually meant an austerity program, with higher unemployment the inevitable result.

Devaluation of a currency

Despite austerity programs and assistance from the IMF, some nations, such as Great Britain, found themselves in a position where persistent and severe payments deficits were forcing their governments to continually buy their own currency, gradually exhausting their reserves of foreign currency and gold. What would happen to a nation that *ran out* of foreign currencies and gold?

A nation in such a situation could no longer buy its own currency. Since government purchases of its own currency are the only force supporting the price of the currency against downward pressures due to payments deficits, the price of the currency would undergo a *sudden decline*, as shown in Figure 19-1. The process of reducing the international price of a currency that had been pegged is known as devaluation of the currency. Devaluation is necessary when payments deficits have caused a decline in the exchange rate. Under a floating exchange rate, the adjustment occurs gradually, whereas under a pegged exchange rate, the adjustment takes place in one big step.

On the surface, devaluation of the currency seems to be a simple solution to the problem of payments deficits. The deficits are putting downward pressure on the price of your currency, so why not let it fall relative to others? With your currency costing less to foreigners, your exports should rise, and with other currencies more costly relative to yours, imports will cost more and should fall. Your receipts and payments could get back into balance, and your currency price would stabilize (although at a lower level).

FIGURE 19-1 *Devaluation of a Currency*

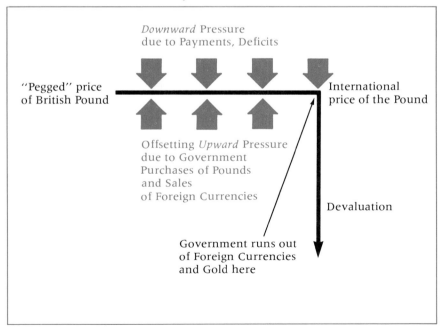

Unfortunately, however, there are problems with devaluing a currency, some of which are potentially quite severe. First and most serious, devaluation of your currency will have effects on your *trading partners*. With your currency cheaper compared to theirs, their people will tend to import more of your products. And with their currencies more costly compared to yours, they will be able to export less to you. As a result, you may solve your payments deficit by passing it on to them. And this reversal might cause them to devalue, too. The result would be that you would gain only very little, if anything, by devaluing your currency.

There are other problems, too. While devaluation makes your exports cheaper and more competitive, it makes your *imports more expensive*. Because your nation's currency is worth less, it costs your people more to buy foreign goods. The public will not be pleased when the price of a bottle of Scotch goes up. But the problem is not just political. If imports are a large part of your economy, their higher prices could cause the rate of inflation to rise, possibly triggering cost-push inflation as people seek to protect themselves against rising import prices through larger wage increases. If inflation does accelerate, your nation's goods will lose some of the competitive edge gained through devaluation of the currency.

Political considerations tend to make devaluation somewhat difficult, too. While the general public may not fully understand the reasons for devaluation, people know that it will make prices rise, and they often feel that devaluation indicates that something is wrong with the nation, or with the economic policies of its government. On an international level, there are also political pressures against devaluation, not only from trading partners who would be hurt by it, but also from the world community in general and the International Monetary Fund in particular. To them, the pegged system of exchange rates represents the only protection against the chaotic international monetary situation of the 1930's, and devaluations of currencies pose a threat to that pegged system.

Because of these problems, it came to be generally accepted that devaluation of a currency should only be undertaken as a last resort. For instance, if a nation suffered persistent and severe payments deficits because its currency was *overvalued* (pegged at a level that had become unrealistically high), it was considered reasonable to devalue that currency. As the USA, West Germany and Japan rose to dominance in world trade, it became totally unrealistic for Great Britain to try to maintain the pound at a pegged level more appropriate for an earlier era, when Britain was the chief economic, manufacturing and trading power in the world. The successive devaluations of the pound since 1945 were, therefore, accepted as a necessary and inevitable adjustment to changing economic realities. However, it was not considered appropriate or acceptable for a nation to devalue its currency simply to gain a competitive advantage in world trade, or because that nation's government had allowed excessive inflation to develop in its own economy. Devaluations for such purposes would only invite retaliation by other nations, which would threaten the entire system of pegged exchange rates.

As a result of the strains on the system of pegged exchange rates that have been described, since the Second World War there have been several major devaluations of currencies (including the British pound, French franc, Italian lira and Canadian dollar), in which the pegged value of a currency has undergone a sudden and often dramatic decline. Under a floating exchange-rate system, these adjustments tend to take place gradually, but under a pegged system the government will support the price of its currency and delay the adjustment as long as possible, so that when the decline in the value of the currency occurs, it happens all at once. Devaluations tend to be quite spectacular and important — one of the most dramatic and widely publicized of all economic events.

The Canadian dollar in the international monetary system

Unlike most currencies, the Canadian dollar was not part of the pegged system established after the Second World War. Due to Canada's high level of foreign trade and the high level of foreign investment in Canada, the Canadian dollar tends to be subject to strong and variable pressures (such as large increases or decreases in wheat exports or in foreign investment from time to time) that make it very difficult to establish and maintain a pegged level for it. The Canadian dollar floated in the 1950's at levels up to $1.05 US due to heavy foreign investment in Canada, and only after a sharp decline and loss of confidence in the Canadian dollar was it pegged at $.925 US in 1962. This level was maintained until 1970, when strong upward pressure made it impossible to hold it as pegged, and it was again allowed to float. The Canadian dollar, then, was at times part of the system of pegged exchange rates established after the Second World War, while at other times it was allowed to float apart from that system.

Summary: The international monetary system

After the Second World War, the nations of the world established a pegged exchange-rate system, in an attempt to avoid a recurrence of the instability of the 1930's. The system came under increasingly heavy strains as some currencies came under upward pressure and others became subject to downward pressure. Governments were able to maintain the pegged values of currencies against these pressures for some time, but not indefinitely, with the result that the system of pegged exchange rates has periodically seen major and sudden adjustments in currency values, such as the devaluations of the pound and the franc.

The biggest strain on the international monetary system was yet to come however, as the key currency in that system — the US dollar —

A COMPARISON OF FLOATING AND PEGGED EXCHANGE RATES

FLOATING EXCHANGE RATE

(a) Balance of Payments Deficit

Exchange rate moves downwards over a period of time causing receipts to rise and payments to fall, until the deficit is eliminated, and the exchange rate stabilizes at a new, lower level.

(b) Balance of Payments Surplus

Exchange rate moves upward over a period of time causing receipts to fall and payments to rise until the Balance of Payments surplus is eliminated and the exchange rate stabilizes at a new, higher level.

PEGGED EXCHANGE RATE

(a) Balance of Payments Surplus

Downward pressure on the exchange rate is resisted by the government's purchases of its own currency and sales of other currencies which can keep the exchange rate pegged unless or until the government runs out of foreign exchange reserves. The exchange rate will then move sharply to a new, lower level, or the currency will be devalued.

(b) Balance of Payments Surplus

Upward pressure on the exchange rate is resisted by the government's sales of its own currency and purchases of other currencies which can keep the exchange rate pegged unless or until the government decides or agrees that a higher exchange rate is appropriate. The exchange rate is then allowed to move sharply upward, or the currency is revalued.

came under intense downward pressure that would eventually shatter the system of pegged exchange rates.

Part B: The US dollar, gold and the international monetary system

As we have seen, the US dollar occupied a special place at the center of the international monetary system established in 1945. It was not only the key currency in the pegged exchange-rate system, with all other currency values expressed in terms of the US dollar, it was also the most acceptable and widely-used currency internationally, and the most widely-held reserve currency kept by governments. The key to the US dollar's position was that it was *backed by gold*—foreigners could convert their US dollars to gold on demand at $35 US to the ounce of gold. This fact established the international acceptability of the US dollar virtually throughout the world.

For several years, everything worked quite well—the US dollar was highly acceptable and widely used in world trade, and the USA had ample gold to back up its dollars held by foreigners. During the 1950's, the competitive position of the USA was very strong, largely due to the fact that Europe and Japan were not fully recovered industrially from the war. As a result, the USA was a major exporter, with large payments surpluses and a huge stock of gold reserves. As a result, the US dollar was very strong and highly acceptable; indeed, one concern during this period was that there were not enough US dollars in foreign hands to finance the growing volume of world trade. However, the situation was not to last.

US payments deficits in the 1960's

The situation reversed itself dramatically in the 1960's, as the USA had large and regular payments *deficits*. The result was a large outflow of US dollars into foreign hands, to the point where foreigners became concerned that the USA might not possess enough gold to back up its dollars. It is important to understand the reasons for this very significant development.

After the Second World War, merchandise trade was a strong positive factor in the US Balance of Payments, with exports exceeding imports. In the 1960's, however, the USA experienced *increasing foreign competition* from Japan and Western Europe (particularly West Germany), as these nations recovered economically from the war and advanced technologically, making their products increasingly competitive with US products. Foreign products such as automobiles (Volkswagen, Toyota, Datsun), electronic products (Sony, Hitachi, Yamaha) and even steel, made significant inroads into both domestic and foreign markets that had been dominated by US producers. Finally, in 1971, US imports exceeded exports, and one of the major strengths of the US Balance of Payments was lost. At about this time, US competitiveness in world markets was further undermined by *rapid rates of inflation* in the USA, largely due to the Vietnam War.

Related to the problem of foreign competition was the fact that the US dollar was *overvalued* (pegged at too high a value) by the 1960's. The high value of the US dollar was appropriate until the mid-1950's, because the USA faced little competition and its exports were very high. However, the rise of foreign competition by the 1960's made the price of the US dollar not only unrealistic, but a major handicap to the USA. The over-valued US dollar slowed down exports, and made foreign imports more attractive in US markets, thus aggravating the USA's payments deficits.

An important contributor to the US payments deficits was the fact that both the US government and US corporations were spending vast amounts of money abroad in the 1960's. Investment in other countries by US corporations and US military expenditures abroad (especially in Vietnam) gave rise to a heavy outflow of funds from the USA, generating larger payments deficits.

Problems due to the US deficits

The outflow of US dollars from the USA resulted in vast quantities of US dollars being held by foreign countries. This situation was not altogether bad — these US dollars helped finance world trade, as mentioned earlier, and many nations used them as foreign exchange reserves, to help maintain their pegged exchange rates. However, a problem arose in the 1960's, when the quantity of US dollars in foreign hands *far exceeded the total US gold stock*.

The danger this discrepancy posed was that foreigners *might lose confidence* in the strength and convertibility of the US dollar, and demand gold for their US dollars. Such a loss of confidence could cause a run on the US gold stock,[1] which would quickly be depleted as speculators, frightened by the lack of gold backing for the overly-plentiful US dollars they held, converted those dollars to gold on a vast scale. At times in the late 1960's and early 1970's, such speculative runs on the US gold stock did, in fact, occur, as foreigners converted their US dollars to gold on a large scale. This reduced the USA's gold stock even further, raising fears that the US dollar might lose its acceptability, disrupting international trade and investment flows and possibly even leading to a world-wide depression. Finally, it became necessary for the USA to take steps to deal with its Balance of Payments deficits and restore faith in the US dollar.

---

[1]There is an interesting similarity between the banks that we studied in Chapter 10 and the USA in the world economy. Both put out into circulation large amounts of paper currency on the basis of only a small amount of cash (gold) reserves. In both cases, the paper currency works well as long as people don't lose faith and try to convert it all to gold (cash). This is why the USA was sometimes called "banker to the world."

The USA's responses to the problem

The USA tried several approaches in the late 1960's and early 1970's (such as policies to curb inflation in the USA, policies to reduce investment abroad by US corporations and refusal to convert US dollars to gold for foreign speculators), but all of them failed to deal with the basic causes of the problem.

The fundamental cause of the deficits was a *basic shift in the world economy*, due to the industrial development of Western Europe (particularly West Germany) and Japan, and the resultant export success of those countries. The result was that the old system of pegged currency prices was no longer appropriate. The US dollar was overvalued, pegged at a high value that had been established when the USA was the dominant industrial nation in the world, and the leading competitor in world trade. By the 1970's, however, West Germany and Japan were competing successfully with many American goods in world trade. One reason for the trade success of the Germans and Japanese was that the deutschemark and yen were undervalued, or pegged at unrealistically low levels. This undervaluation gave them a substantial competitive advantage by making their products artificially low-priced in US markets. While such low values for the deutschemark and yen had been appropriate in 1945 when the pegged system was established, the industrial development of West Germany and Japan made these pegged values unrealistic relative to the US dollar.

Under the system of pegged exchange rates, adjustments in the international prices of currencies had not been permitted to take place. Consequently, for many years, the yen and the deutschemark remained undervalued, giving Japan and West Germany a competitive advantage in world trade, while the US dollar was at a competitive disadvantage because it was overvalued. The result, as we have seen, was that the USA experienced persistent and increasingly severe international payments deficits, accompanied by an outflow of US dollars into foreign hands and declining US gold holdings.

What could be done?

Since the US payments problems were fundamentally due to the overvaluation of the US dollar, or the undervaluation of other currencies (particularly the yen and the deutschemark), two possible solutions suggest themselves: either the US dollar should have been *devalued*, or the yen and deutschemark should have been *revalued* (their pegged values should move upward).

The USA was reluctant to devalue the US dollar. The dollar was the key currency in the international monetary system, and the maintenance of its value and acceptability was regarded as vital to the success of that system.[2] There were fears that a major devaluation of the US dollar could lead to devaluations by many other nations, shattering the system of pegged exchange rates and returning the world to the chaotic and destructive conditions of the 1930's, in which uncertainties regarding exchange rates would reduce international trade and possibly cause a worldwide depression. Consequently, due to the special role of the US dollar in the international monetary system, devaluation of the US dollar was seen only as a last resort.

Much more attractive to the USA would be the upward revaluation of other currencies, particularly the deutschemark and the yen. The complications and risks of devaluing the US dollar would be avoided by such a move. However, Japan and West Germany were very reluctant to agree to a revaluation, because by making their currencies more expensive relative to the US dollar, they would risk reducing their exports to the vast US market, and increasing unemployment in their own countries. Accordingly, Germany and Japan persisted in buying US dollars and selling their own currencies, in order to keep the price of the US dollar at its pegged (and high) level, against the wishes of the USA.

Finally, the USA *forced* other nations to revalue their currencies upward in 1971, by imposing a heavy import tax on foreign imports to the USA. (The USA would only withdraw the tax if other nations agreed to let the price of their currencies rise.) Consequently, the deutschemark rose by 31 percent against the US dollar, the yen rose 26 percent, the Swiss franc rose 23 percent and the British pound rose 6 percent. Also, the USA suspended the gold convertibility, or backing, of the US dollar, to prevent a further depletion of the nation's gold holdings and a possible loss of confidence in the dollar.

It was hoped that these increases in the prices of other currencies would correct the US payments deficits, but they did not do so. While the deficits were reduced, they did not disappear, and the outflow of US dollars continued. The USA was left with no alternative but to devalue its dollar against other currencies. In February 1973 the USA announced that the dollar would be devalued, officially by about 8½ percent. However, the significance of this event went far beyond a devaluation of 8½ percent.

---

[2] A devaluation of the US dollar would move its value downward, not only in terms of other currencies, but also in terms of *gold*. If the US dollar were devalued by 20 percent, it would be worth 20 percent less gold, or viewed differently, the devaluation of the US dollar would mean *an increase in the price of gold,* from, say, $35 US per ounce to $42 US per ounce. People who believed that a devaluation of the US dollar was inevitable had a strong incentive to convert their US dollars into gold so as to profit from the devaluation. Until 1968, foreign speculators could get gold from the US government at $35 per ounce; after 1968, however, the USA refused to convert dollars for foreign speculators, forcing speculators to buy gold in private markets, in which the price of gold was bid up to quite high levels. Such speculative selling of US dollars, of course, only made the problem worse.

The end of the pegged exchange rate system

When the US dollar was devalued, it was not repegged at a lower value; rather, it was permitted to float at lower levels. And, since the values of all other currencies were expressed in terms of a floating US dollar, their values were also floating. The system of pegged exchange rates had come to an end: not only was the US dollar no longer backed by gold, but exchange rates were no longer pegged to a US dollar of stable value.

In place of the pegged system there emerged a *dirty float*, in which nations' exchange rates floated, but under the guidance of their governments, which steered exchange rates upward or downward, depending on national circumstances or priorities. If the international value of a nation's currency tended to decline too rapidly, its government might buy its own currency on foreign exchange markets so as to prevent rapidly rising import prices from generating excessive inflation. On the other hand, if a nation's currency came under strong upward pressure, the government could sell its own currency in foreign exchange markets so as to prevent excessive increases in its exchange rate from jeopardizing the nation's international competitive position and employment.

The US decision to devalue and float the dollar generated strong criticism from other nations. Some feared that their competitive position in the vast US market would be endangered, while others feared that the abandonment of the pegged system of exchange rates would threaten world prosperity by a return to the conditions of the 1930's. However, the exchange-rate chaos of the 1930's did not reappear; in fact, most nations behaved quite responsibly in the management of their exchange rates, resisting the temptation to manipulate their exchange rates downwards to gain a competitive advantage. Fears were also expressed that a floating US dollar no longer backed by gold would lose acceptability internationally and that world trade would stagnate as a result. However, these fears did not materialize: despite its changed situation, the US dollar remained acceptable and held its place as the key currency in international trade and finance. The basic reason for this stability was probably simply that the world had *no ready substitute* for the US dollar — no other currency was both sufficiently strong and available on a large enough scale to play the role that the US dollar had played in the world.

The goal of the devaluation: a trade surplus to finance other activities

The USA hoped that the devaluation of its dollar would increase US exports and decrease imports sufficiently to give the USA a significant surplus on its merchandise trade with other nations. With the funds acquired from its merchandise trade surplus, the US could finance other activities throughout the world, such as *military and foreign aid spending* by the US government and *private investment spending* by US corporations in foreign nations.

There were two quite different views of this situation: some people felt that the USA needed a surplus on its trade transactions in order to fulfill its *responsibilities* (political, military and economic) throughout the world, while others argued that the USA wanted to sell more goods to other nations than it bought from them in order to maintain its own economy and to acquire the funds that it needed to finance its *excessive ambitions* (political, military and economic) throughout the world. In the view of some, then, the USA was trying to help (or even save) the world. In the view of others, it was trying to buy, control and police the world. In any case, it hoped to finance such international efforts through a surplus on its merchandise trade brought on by the devaluation of the US dollar in February 1973. At that same time, however, decisions were being made in the Middle East that would, within six months, shatter American hopes for a trade surplus and cause the greatest outflow ever of US dollars.

The OPEC oil-price increases: more deficits for the USA

In late 1973 and early 1974, the *Organization of Petroleum Exporting Countries* (OPEC), comprised mainly of Middle East oil-producing nations, finally succeeded in overcoming their mutual suspicion and mistrust sufficiently to unite on the question of oil prices. For years the industrialized nations had, through the multinational oil companies, bought crude oil at very low prices, obtained in part by playing off the oil-producing nations against each other. However, in late 1973 the OPEC nations agreed to present a unified front on oil prices, the result of which was a four-to-five-fold increase in oil prices over a period of a few months.

Because of its position as a large importer of OPEC oil, the USA's payments for imported oil soared, as did its merchandise trade deficit. A vast outflow of US dollars into foreign hands occurred, threatening the international value of the US dollar again. However, while the OPEC nations had agreed upon the oil-price increases, they had never reached ageement upon how much oil each should produce, and as a result, *overproduction* depressed oil prices: for about five years, the real price of OPEC oil (adjusted for inflation) actually fell, and the US payments deficits diminished. However, in 1979, OPEC managed to reduce the supply of oil, and prices shot upward, again generating massive US payments deficits and concerns about the prospects for the US dollar.

Notwithstanding these problems, the US dollar remained the key currency in world trade and retained its general acceptability, with even the OPEC oil producers preferring payment for their oil in US dollars.

As noted earlier, there is simply no ready substitute for the US dollar in international trade and finance.[3]

The recycling and investment of petro-dollars

In 1974, the year following the OPEC oil-price increases, the OPEC nations had a trade surplus on their oil sales of $62 billion; that is, $62 billion of funds — which became known as *petro-dollars* because of their source — flowed from the oil-importing nations to OPEC, in the largest transfer of wealth the world had ever seen. It was vitally important to the oil-consuming nations that these funds be recycled back into their economies, to avoid shortages of aggregate demand.

Generally, the recycling task took place quite smoothly. The OPEC nations bought substantial volumes of *consumer goods, capital goods and military equipment* from the industrialized nations, recycling large quantities of funds in the process. Further recycling occurred on a large scale through the *investment of Arab funds* in the industrialized nations. These transactions were handled by the banks of the industrialized nations, which accepted deposits from the OPEC nations and made on their behalf a variety of investments, mainly in safe, conservative securities such as government and corporate bonds and short-term securities. Also, the banks extended considerable *credit* to non-oil-producing underdeveloped nations, who were struggling under the burden of heavy payments for oil.

As time passed, the OPEC nations' investment practices became more sophisticated, as more petro-dollars were invested in shares of corporations and properties. By the end of 1980, Arab OPEC nations had over $340 billion of assets around the world. Arab investments in the USA included 4.9 percent of the equity of hundreds of America's top corporations (including many banks),[4] part of Eastern airlines, and a large percentage of the equity of oil companies such as Exxon, Texaco, Mobil and Getty. In Japan, Arab money has purchased substantial interests in the nation's high-technology industries such as Hitachi and Fujitsu, and in 1977 Libya purchased 10 percent of Fiat.

As the price of oil fell in the 1980's under the pressure of weakened demand and new sources of supply, the volume of petro-dollars fell, and concerns lessened regarding the Arabs' use of these funds. However, the

[3]During the 1970's, the US government pursued some extremely erratic monetary policies, expanding the US money supply extremely rapidly at some times and suddenly switching to tight money policies and extremely high interest rates at others. While such policies certainly shook the faith of other nations in American economic management, it is interesting to note that the US dollar still remained generally acceptable in the world.

[4]The 4.9-percent figure is significant. If it exceeds 5 percent, US law requires full public disclosure of the owners and the extent of their interest — a potentially explosive issue politically, which may be why the Arabs stopped at 4.9 percent.

petro-dollar outflow had contributed to yet another international financial problem—the banking crisis of 1982-84.

The banking crisis of 1982-84

In the early 1980's, the banking systems of the industrial nations underwent a serious financial crisis involving their loans to poorer nations. The origins of the problem lay in what are known as *Eurodollars*—US dollars on deposit in a bank outside the USA, usually in Europe. Because these US dollar deposits are outside the USA, the deposits—and loans based on them—are not subject to the US financial regulatory system, including US cash reserve requirements and other regulations intended to ensure prudent loan policies. Furthermore, because they are US dollar deposits, they are also not subject to similar regulations governing deposits and loans of banks in the nations in which they are deposited. Thus, the Eurodollar deposit pool presented banks with opportunities for the lending of US dollars in ways that were not regulated by monetary authorities in the USA or elsewhere.

In 1964, there were about 40 billion Eurodollars, but by 1980 the "Europool" had grown to $1 trillion, or twenty-five times that amount. This rapid growth was due to two major developments that led to massive outflows of US dollars from the USA: first, the *Vietnam War*, which was largely financed by the printing of money, then the *OPEC price increases*, which generated the outflow of petro-dollars, a large amount of which was deposited into European banks. Because these deposits were not subject to US regulations, they were often loaned in great volume to poor nations which were not particularly good credit risks, such as Mexico, Argentina, Poland and North Korea. These nations were anxious to borrow to finance ambitious development programs, willing to pay high interest rates and often had commodity exports as the basis for earning the foreign currency (usually US dollars) to repay their loans.

Nonetheless, these nations were often unable to meet payments on their loans in the late 1970's, so the banks renegotiated their loans, extending them further credit. Despite the fact that it seemed increasingly unlikely that many of the loans could ever be repaid, some banks continued to loan more money to them, to keep their outstanding loans from going bad. In some cases, banks even paid themselves the interest due on existing loans from their own advances for new loans to the debtor countries, reporting it as income, and adding it to the amount owed. Gradually, a fragile international financial structure was built on these Eurodollars.

By 1982, the situation had changed greatly. The growth of the Europool had stagnated as *tighter US monetary policies* and *oil-price declines* had stemmed the outflow of US dollars. The US monetary policies that made Eurodollars scarcer also made them more costly, as interest rates rose sharply. At the same time, the recession induced by these changes depressed international commodity prices, undercutting the ability of debt-ridden poorer nations to repay their vast loans.

The new developments left many banks in the industrial nations in a very exposed position, with large loans outstanding to borrowers whose inability to repay was increasingly evident, and loans totalling $400 billion appeared heading for default.[5] In August 1982, Mexico, with a foreign debt of $78 billion, announced that it was broke. Only a major bail-out plan organized by the International Monetary Fund, which included funds from 530 private banks, the IMF and the governments of several industrial nations, averted a crisis. By the end of 1984, 38 nations had required similar bail-outs, which included new loans to meet interest payments and longer repayment terms, to reduce yearly payments.

As these problems emerged, some banks failed, including the Continental Illinois (the seventh-largest US bank) and a British and a Danish bank. In each case, the government of the nation involved intervened through its central bank, to prevent the bank from collapsing and possibly starting a chain reaction of bank failures. In 1984, the US government gave Argentina $300 million to ward off default of that country's $47 billion in bank loans. That money went directly to the banks, to cover arrears on interest payments. Had they not been paid, the banks would have been forced to declare their loans *nonperforming*, exposing their financial weakness and possibly precipitating a financial crisis for many major banks. In defending this unusual use of taxpayers' money, the US secretary of the Treasury said that "We came up the edge of the abyss."

To ease these problems, the major governments involved, through their central banks, undertook the following steps:

(i) reduction of US interest rates, to head off a world recession and to ease the burden of interest payments on debtor nations.

(ii) movement of part of the poor nations' bank loans off the US dollar and into other currencies, to ease the interest-rate pressure on Eurodollars and make it easier for debtor nations to repay loans.

(iii) policies to keep the US dollar from rising further, as a rising US dollar would make it more difficult for debtor nations to repay loans denominated in US dollars.

Having rescued the banks from the consequences of their own loan policies, financial regulators have undertaken to monitor the banks' international activities more closely in the future, and thus, they hope, prevent a recurrence of the events of the 1974-84 period.

[5]The problems were not only to do with foreign loans. Banks had also made major domestic loans for energy-development projects which were based on the assumption that oil prices would continue to rise indefinitely. When oil prices fell after 1980, these projects became uneconomical.

Finally, the IMF has undertaken more strict regulation of borrowing nations, so as to discourage them from excessive borrowing. In order to receive IMF loan assistance, a country must agree to follow more conservative financial policies, including reductions in government spending and imports, tighter monetary policies and devaluation of its currency. While such requirements reduce the risk of poorer nations defaulting on their loans from industrial nations, they also undercut the economic development programs which debtor nations need so badly. These countries need US dollars for their development programs, and if their exports to the industrial nations are limited by trade barriers, their only alternative is to borrow the necessary funds, even if the terms and risks involved are unattractive.

The soaring US dollar

While the US dollar was weak relative to other currencies during much of the 1970's, it rose exceptionally and unexpectedly rapidly in the first half of the 1980's. From 1980 to 1985, the US dollar appreciated by about 60 percent against other currencies on a trade-weighted basis,[6] reaching record highs against the Canadian dollar, the French franc and the British pound, and almost reaching its record highs of the early 1970's against the Japanese yen and the West German deutschemark. By 1985, the strength of the US dollar had reached the point where it was a major matter of international concern.

The origins of the strength of the US dollar lie in the USA's robust economic recovery from the Great Recession of the early 1980's. The recovery was driven by two major forces: massive US federal government *budget deficits* (mainly due to a combination of tax cuts and heavy military spending) which approached $200 billion in 1985, and strong *capital investment spending*. While both of these factors boosted aggregate demand and the economic recovery, they generated very large borrowing requirements on the part of the US government and industry. At the same time, there was a shortage of capital in the US economy due to a *low personal savings rate* and a relatively tight *monetary policy* imposed to avoid the rekindling of inflation. The combination of a high demand for capital and a limited supply of funds generated *very high interest rates* in the USA, which attracted *large inflows of capital* from foreign nations—about $100 billion per year by 1984.

These heavy capital inflows from foreign lenders caused large volumes of foreign currencies to be converted into US dollars, boosting the demand for the US dollar considerably in foreign exchange markets. The result

[6]A method of calculating the average US exchange rate compared to the USA's trading partners, making allowance for the volume of trade the US does with each country.

was the exceptionally high US exchange rate referred to earlier, which would have widespread effects around the world.

On the positive side, the combination of the brisk US economic recovery and the strong US dollar generated very heavy demand for foreign goods and services in the US. This growing market gave some nations just what they had wanted—an export-led recovery from the Great Recession. In the words of the London *Economist*, "America has . . . pump-primed the world out of the 1980-82 recession" (September 22, 1984).

> From 1914 to 1982, the USA built up a net international creditor position of about $200 billion. Three years later, massive foreign borrowing had changed the USA's position into that of a net debtor for the first time in 71 years.

On the negative side, the high US interest rates pulled interest rates up around the world as competition for capital intensified.[7] The high interest rates are a particular problem for many debt-ridden poorer nations, but they did affect other countries as well. In Canada's case, the government was faced with the choice of raising Canadian interest rates in the midst of a weak economic recovery and sluggish business investment spending, or letting the Canadian dollar fall further against the US dollar, which would add to inflation. It chose a middle course, accepting some increase in interest rates together with some reduction in the Canadian exchange rate.

US protectionism

A more serious concern was the massive US *trade deficit*, which reached $120 billion in 1984. The trade deficit was the result of the strong US dollar, which boosted US purchases of imports, while dampening US exports. By 1984, US politicians were becoming increasingly concerned over the loss of American jobs due to the trade deficits, and were leaning toward enacting *protectionist legislation* to reduce imports into the USA. The threat of such legislation raised serious concerns in countries such

---

[7]High interest rates in the USA tended to spread to other countries because they attracted capital from other countries into US dollars. This outflow of capital from other countries to the USA caused heavy selling of their currencies, putting downward pressure on their exchange rates. This forced their governments to either increase their own interest rates to stem the capital outflow or allow their currencies to drop quite sharply against the US dollar. Most chose a middle course of action involving some exchange rate depreciation and some increases in their own interest rates.

as Canada and Japan, whose economies depend heavily on exports to the USA. By 1985, there was concern that the USA would take protectionist action against imports, and that other nations would retaliate, leading to a *trade war* such as the world had not seen since the Great Depression of the 1930's.

The G-5 agreement

On September 22, 1985, the Group of Five nations (G-5)[8] — the USA, Japan, West Germany, Great Britain and France — agreed to act together in foreign exchange market intervention to "bring the value of the US dollar down and the value of the other currencies up." While the agreement was vague regarding details, its main objective was a reduction in the US exchange rate that could reduce the US trade deficit and, it was hoped, head off protectionist measures before the US Congress.

JAPAN'S TRADE SURPLUS

The US protectionist sentiment was especially strong against Japan, which accounted for $37 billion of the USA's $120 billion trade deficit in 1984. Indeed, Japan's 1984 trade surplus of $44 billion on its trade with the world led to criticism from many nations, which wanted Japan to import more, voluntarily limit exports or invest more in production facilities in other nations. In 1985, Japan announced that it would lower its controversial barriers to imports over the next three years. However, there was considerable scepticism regarding the probable effects of such measures, as Japanese consumers are famous for their loyalty to domestically-made products.

The international monetary system in perspective

Figure 19-2 provides an overview of the developments in the international monetary system that are discussed in this chapter. As the overview shows, these developments can be broadly divided into three periods. First, there was the exchange-rate instability of the 1930's, which while partly a result of the Depression, also contributed to the severity of the Depression. In reaction to this, the pegged system was set up in 1945, to provide international monetary stability. Despite periodic devaluations of some

[8]Since then, Canada and Italy have been added to the group, expanding it to seven.

FIGURE 19-2 *The International Monetary System: An Overview*

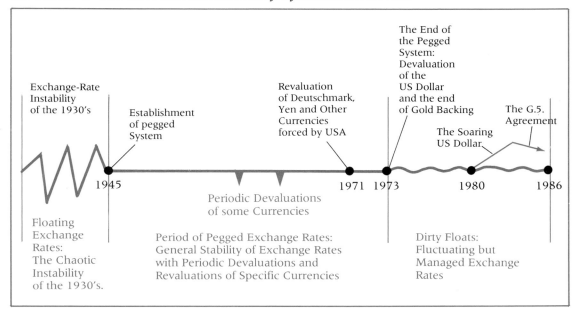

currencies, the pegged system endured until the weakness of its key currency, the US dollar, led first to the revaluation of various other currencies in 1971, then to the end of the pegged system in 1973, when the US dollar was devalued and floated and its gold backing removed. Since 1973, the international monetary system has been characterized by a dirty float, with exchange rates fluctuating, but under the influence of monetary authorities seeking to avoid excessive instability. During this period, the strength of the US dollar became a concern, and the US and other nations undertook to bring the US exchange rate down somewhat.

Following the announcement of the G-5 agreement, the US dollar moved somewhat lower relative to other major currencies. However, economists pointed out that the G-5 agreement dealt only with the symptoms of the problem—the high value of the US dollar. For the decline in the US dollar to be significant and sustainable, action would have to be taken regarding the causes of the problem—the huge US *federal budget deficits* that generated the capital inflows and kept the US dollar high.

According to economists, the US budget deficits were the key underlying factor in a potentially dangerous series of problems: high US interest rates, heavy capital inflows into the USA, the high value of the US dollar, the US trade deficits, the resultant protectionist sentiment in the USA and the associated risk of an international trade war. In the extreme, some feared, failure to reduce its budget deficits could lead the US government to print money to cover its deficits, touching off another wave of inflation such as occurred in the 1970's.

On the other hand, if the US budget deficit could be reduced, interest rates could fall and capital inflows to the USA could be curbed. The US dollar could also be allowed to fall, and the US balance of trade would right itself, heading off American protectionist sentiment. The world could look forward to a slower, but more sustainable pace of economic growth, with lower interest rates to encourage capital investment and less fear of a recurrence of severe inflation.

The future: should the world return to pegged exchange rates . . .

Some people view the floating exchange rate system that emerged after the devaluation of the US dollar in 1973 as unsatisfactory, because of the *instability* of floating exchange rates. Also, there is a temptation for governments to *manipulate* the price of their currency downward in order to try to secure a cost advantage for their exporters in world markets. Such action could result in retaliation by other nations, with a chaotic situation developing, as happened in the 1930's. Another argument against floating exchange rates is that they tend to be *inflationary*. Under a pegged exchange rate system, a nation that allows excessive inflation to develop in its economy suffers losses of exports and jobs, as its goods become overpriced and less competitive in world markets. Under a floating exchange rate system, however, that nation's exchange rate will decline, keeping its goods competitive and reducing the government's incentive to restrain inflation. In particular, the excessive increases in the US money supply after 1971 put the US dollar under downward pressure, causing the international values of other nations' currencies to rise, threatening their exports and jobs. To keep their exchange rates down, these other nations had to increase their own money supplies much as the USA had done; as a result, excessive and inflationary increases in the US money supply spread to many other countries, triggering the disastrous worldwide inflation of the 1970's.

Critics of the system of floating exchange rates would prefer the stability of a type of pegged system based on a new set of pegged currency prices, with the pegged exchange rates set at levels that reflect reasonably the present international economic situation, so that no currency is seriously overvalued or undervalued. Furthermore, they propose some arrangement that would permit exchange rates to change more readily as international economic circumstances change, rather than requiring currency prices to remain pegged at levels that have become unrealistic. Such unrealistic exchange rates cannot be maintained for long, and they place severe strains on the pegged system that, as in the case of the US dollar, can lead to the collapse of the entire system. While the system that they propose would be more flexible than the old pegged system, they argue that it could provide more stability than the floating system, to the advantage of everyone.

... Or continue with floating exchange rates?

Other people disagree. They argue that the real problem that led to the collapse of the pegged system in 1973 was the inflationary policies of the USA, which generated irresistible exchange-rate instability. A pegged system, they say, can only work in a period of relatively stable economic policies and conditions, which have not existed since the early 1970's. With such major international forces as the US Vietnam War inflation, the massive flows of OPEC petrodollars and the vast influx of foreign capital into the USA in the early 1980's, exchange-rate stability was simply impossible. If the nations of the world were to return to more stable monetary, fiscal and trade policies, exchange rates would be considerably more stable. Otherwise, no system of pegged rates could possibly be sustained.

The decline of gold

As noted earlier, key international currencies (most recently the US dollar) have traditionally been convertible into, or backed by, gold. After its gold reserves had been depleted by payments deficits and runs by speculators, the US government suspended the convertibility of the US dollar to gold. The US dollar was no longer backed by gold; its value and acceptability were based on faith.

However, speculators continued to buy gold in great quantities, as they expected that the USA would be forced by other nations to return to gold backing of its currency, and to devalue the US dollar. If the US dollar were devalued, gold would be worth many more US dollars per ounce — the holders of gold would become rich overnight. In anticipation of this event speculators bought great amounts of gold, bidding its price to very high levels.

While the devaluation of the US dollar did materialize (in February 1973), the anticipated return to gold backing did not. Instead, steps were taken to remove gold from its dominant role in the international monetary system, as the International Monetary Fund began selling off its holdings of gold at a series of auctions, with the proceeds to go to the benefit of underdeveloped nations.

Despite being phased out of its official role as backing for currencies, gold has continued to attract a great deal of attention from speculators who lack faith in paper money. Believing that governments have a natural tendency to overissue paper money, and seeking protection from the declining value of paper money due to inflation (not to mention profits from rising gold prices), these speculators have on various occasions (such as 1979-80) bought gold heavily, bidding its price up to very high levels. Generally, any event that could add to inflation or shake confidence in paper currencies, such as rumors of war, crop failures, or oil production cutbacks, generates heavier buying of gold and higher gold prices. It is important to note, however, that gold in these cases is being bought as a commodity that is predicted to hold its value better than paper money, not because it has any role as backing for currencies.

DEFINITIONS OF NEW TERMS

Pegged Exchange Rates   Exchange rates that are prevented by governments from moving from their fixed levels in relation to each other.

Foreign Exchange Reserves   Holdings of foreign currencies and gold maintained by governments for the purpose of stabilizing their exchange rates through purchases and sales of their currencies.

International Monetary Fund (IMF)   An international agency established to oversee and maintain the system of pegged exchange rates set up in 1945.

Austerity Program   An anti-inflation program imposed by a nation seeking to relieve payments deficits by reducing its rate of inflation so as to make its products more competitive internationally.

Devaluation   A reduction in the level of a pegged exchange rate.

Overvaluation   The pegging of an exchange rate at an unrealistically and unsustainably high level.

Undervaluation   The pegging of an exchange rate at an unrealistically and unsustainably low level.

Revaluation   An increase in the level of a pegged exchange rate.

OPEC   Organization of Petroleum Exporting Countries; established to control the supply and price of oil in world trade.

Petro-dollars   Funds (US dollars) earned by OPEC nations through petroleum exports.

Recycling   The process whereby petro-dollars are recirculated back into the economies of the oil-consuming nations, through purchases of goods and services and through investments by oil-producing countries.

Eurodollars   US dollars on deposit in banks outside the US regulatory system, usually in Europe.

CHAPTER SUMMARY

1. In 1945, to avoid a repetition of the exchange-rate chaos of the 1930's, the major nations of the world established a system of pegged exchange rates under the supervision of the International Monetary Fund.

2. The US dollar occupied the key role in this system: backed by gold, it was the most widely used and accepted currency internationally, the main reserve currency and the center of the system of pegged exchange rates.

3. Strains on the pegged system developed as the competitive positions of nations changed, placing upward pressure on some currencies (such as the deutschemark and the yen) and downward pressure on others (such as the British pound).

4. Nations used various measures to support the pegged system, including austerity programs and loans from the IMF.

5. As a last resort, the devaluation of chronically weak currencies was considered acceptable.

6. At times, the Canadian dollar was part of the system of pegged exchange rates, but at other times it was allowed to float.

7. After the 1950's, the USA experienced international payments deficits, largely due to increasing foreign competition, particularly from Japan and West Germany.

8. The result of the US deficits was a running down of the US gold reserves, and concerns about the international acceptability of the US dollar, which was no longer convertible into gold.

9. After a variety of measures to support the dollar, the USA was finally forced to devalue it in 1973.

10. Following its devaluation, the US dollar was not again pegged, so that the pegged system was in effect replaced by a dirty float.

11. The OPEC oil-price increases since 1973 caused the US payments deficits to continue despite the devaluation of the dollar; however, the US dollar remained acceptable internationally despite the deficits.

12. OPEC petrodollars contributed to the growth of the Eurodollar pool, which was the basis for massive bank loans to poorer nations that led to an international banking crisis in 1984.

13. In the first half of the 1980's, the US dollar was exceptionally strong, largely due to heavy inflows of foreign capital arising from large US government budget deficits and high US interest rates.

14. The strong US dollar contributed to very large US trade deficits. The deficits, in turn, led to protectionist sentiment in the USA that the G-5 nations tried to stem with a 1985 agreement to reduce the value of the US dollar.

15. Despite the fact that it is no longer used as a backing for currencies, gold is still bought (sometimes heavily) by speculators who lack faith in paper currencies.

QUESTIONS

1. Has Japan's trade surplus with the rest of the world decreased in recent years? If so, what has caused this? If not, are measures being proposed to reduce it?

2. Have there been any problems recently regarding the inability of poorer nations to repay their bank loans from the industrialized nations? If so, how have these been dealt with?

3. What have been the recent trends regarding:
  (a) the US federal budget deficit?
  (b) US interest rates?
  (c) inflows of foreign capital into the USA?
  (d) the US exchange rate?
  (e) the US trade balance?
  What are believed to be the basic causes of these trends, and how are they related?

4. Is the G-5 agreement now regarded as having proved successful? Why?

5. Have fears of increased US protectionism and possible retaliation by foreign nations proven correct? If so, what measures have been taken? If not, how has this been averted?

6. Has the price of gold changed significantly recently? Why?

7. Have exchange rates generally been relatively stable or not recently? Why?

8. If the USA printed money on a large scale to finance its budget deficits, what effect would this probably have on:
  (a) long-term interest rates?
  (b) the US exchange rate?
  (c) gold prices?
  (d) the Canadian economy?

CHAPTER 20

The Canadian Economy: A Time for Renewal?

As Canada's new government took office in the mid-1980's, it faced several major economic challenges. These included high unemployment, weak investment and productivity performance, and massive federal budget deficits, all of which were aggravated by high real interest rates and relatively weak confidence on the part of consumers and business. In this chapter we will consider each of these problems, and possible courses of action for dealing with them. First, however, we will review the background of recent Canadian economic developments, prior to the mid-1980's, so as to understand the situation better.

The Great Inflation of the 1970's

The 1970's brought the *Great Inflation*, which, as we saw in Chapter 12, originated with excessive money-supply growth. By the mid-1970's, the over-abundant money supply had generated inflation rates above 10 percent. The strong inflation psychology that developed after mid-decade helped to keep inflation severe and to make it particularly persistent.

Traditionally, inflation had been thought of as a disease of prosperity — an unpleasant side-effect of the high levels of aggregate demand that also bring low unemployment and rapid economic growth. The severe inflation of the 1970's, however, was accompanied by the unexpected and unwelcome phenomenon of economic stagnation: slow growth of output and productivity and rising unemployment, along with severe inflation, or *stagflation* as described in Chapter 15.

391

At the time, the combination of rapid inflation and high unemployment in the latter part of the 1970's seemed, in part, to be the result of temporary causes. For instance, despite the fast growth of employment, unemployment rose, as baby boomers and women sought work in unprecedented numbers. It is also possible that the rapid growth of employment contributed to the slow growth of productivity, as the economy absorbed many new workers, mostly into lower-productivity service-industry jobs and many into part-time jobs with low output per worker. Inflation was made worse by temporary factors, such as unusual increases in energy and food prices. Thus, some of the problems of stagflation were due to temporary causes that could be expected to pass.

However, economists grew concerned that there were also certain deeper, longer-term problems in the Canadian economy that had developed during this period—problems that would not resolve themselves, and would require changes in government policy to correct them. Weak capital investment, poor productivity performance, large federal budget deficits and a declining exchange rate combined with high and rising foreign indebtedness were some of the deeply rooted issues which demanded government attention.

(a) Weak capital investment

For the reasons outlined in Chapter 15, capital investment spending by business was depressed during the inflationary 1970's. As the decade wore on, investment was hurt further by weaker levels of demand, partly due to less expansionary monetary policies and partly due to the problems that high-cost Canadian products encountered competing with foreign products, both in Canada and abroad.

> From the perspective of economic growth, business investment in the 1970's has to be characterized as weak. . . . The strength of investment in the resource-based sectors masked weakness in other industries. . . . Investment in the 1970's never reached the high share of GNP attained in the previous decade. . . . We are inclined to attribute this weakness in investment to . . . the deterioration of the real return on capital, the confusion caused by inflation, and the increased uncertainty and risk.
>
> Economic Council of Canada,
> *Sixteenth Annual Review*, 1979

Fundamentally, the 1970's are regarded as a period in which a relatively small proportion of GNP was devoted to capital investment for the future, and a relatively high proportion to current consumption. While such a situation can carry living standards to *temporarily* high levels, it does not lay the groundwork for the growth of *long-term* prosperity.

(b) Poor productivity performance

As we have seen, productivity (real output per worker) is the key factor underlying a society's economic prosperity. In Chapter 5, we saw that Canada has suffered a productivity slowdown since 1974 that was more serious than in other nations. The productivity slowdown is a matter of serious concern, not only due to its implications for Canadians' *living standards*, but also due to its effects on the *international competitiveness* of Canadian industry, and on the *jobs* of many Canadians.

The causes of Canada's particularly pronounced productivity slowdown are complex and not fully understood (see Chapter 5). However, weak capital investment by business is generally believed to have been a major factor.

> . . . it is clear that the productivity slowdown is more than a cyclical deviation from a stable trend, and that changes in the level and quality of business investment are an important contributing factor. There is little doubt that the growth of Canada's productive potential has slowed down during the 1970's.
>
> Economic Council of Canada,
> *Sixteenth Annual Review*, 1979 (page 12).

(c) Federal budget deficits

After 1975, the federal government developed increasingly large budget deficits, for the reasons covered in Chapter 9. In part, these deficits were the result of the slackening of economic activity and higher unemployment in the second half of the decade, and were therefore to be expected.

However, part of the deficits was new, and of a different nature, in that it was *structural*, the result of a fundamental imbalance between the federal government's expenditures and its tax revenues. While there were several reasons for this imbalance, one major one was the *indexing* of transfer payments and the personal income tax. The result of indexing, as we saw in Chapter 9, is that inflation automatically forces government spending higher at the same time as it depresses tax revenues, creating ever-higher budget deficits. As the deficits grew, so did concerns that they would have an adverse effect on interest rates and business investment spending.

(d) The weak Canadian dollar and rising foreign debt

In Chapter 18, we saw how, during the inflationary 1970's, Canada developed large *current account deficits* on its international Balance of Payments. There were several reasons for these deficits, including high imports due to the lack of internationally competitive Canadian industries, and heavy outflows of funds to pay interest on Canada's large and mounting foreign debt. As a result of these current account deficits, the international value of the Canadian dollar declined considerably after late 1976. So, while Canada maintained quite a good employment-creation record during the inflationary 1970's, the Great Inflation left Canadians with an unhappy legacy of weak investment and productivity performance, large federal budget deficits, a weak exchange rate and a high, rapidly rising foreign debt. Underlying these problems, however, was the dominant economic problem of the decade: exceptionally severe inflation.

The Great Recession of 1981-82

By 1980, most countries had turned their economic policies toward the problem of combating the Great Inflation. An unfortunate side-effect was that the new tighter monetary policies began to push the world toward recession. In Canada, the adoption and impact of these policies were delayed somewhat, and demand surged quite strongly from mid-1980 to mid-1981. However, when the recession did strike Canada, after late 1981, it hit with exceptional severity. The unemployment rate was driven from 8 percent to 13 percent of the labor force within a year, and employment fell by 3 percent during 1982, as Figure 20-1 shows.

FIGURE 20-1 *Annual Percentage Change in Employment 1974-85*

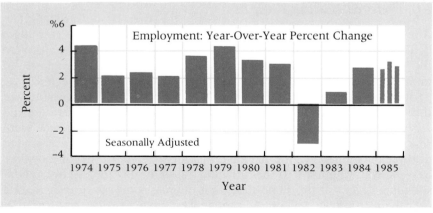

SOURCE   Toronto Dominion Bank, *Canada's Business Climate.*

While much of the recession was the result of depressed exports due to recession in other nations (especially the USA), domestic demand in Canada was even weaker than export markets. Consumer spending on new housing, autos and furniture declined. Business spending on plant and equipment also fell sharply, as interest rates peaked at more than 20 percent in mid-1981 and remained high well into 1982. The recession led to the demise of part of Canada's vulnerable manufacturing sector; plants closed in Ontario and Quebec, unable to cope with the combination of rising costs, heavy debt and high interest rates, along with low demand and foreign competition. As the recession deepened, government expenditures on unemployment insurance and welfare rose, while tax revenues were depressed, forcing the federal budget deficit up sharply into the $20 to $25 billion range in 1982-83.

FIGURE 20-2   *Inflation and Unemployment Rates 1980–85*

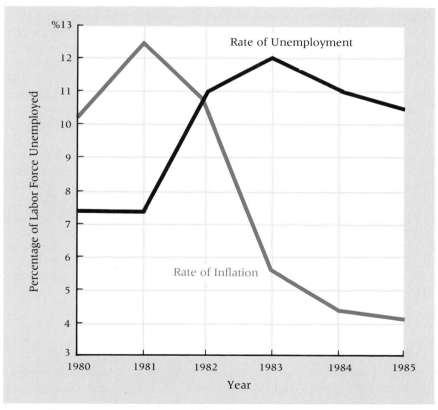

SOURCE   Statistics Canada, *Canadian Statistical Review.*

Figure 20-2 shows the impact of the recession on unemployment, which rose sharply in 1982, and the rate of inflation, which declined steeply in 1983, after a time lag. In particular, the pressure of wage increases on costs and prices eased greatly, as high unemployment moderated wage demands.

The recovery

After late 1982, the recovery from the recession was initiated by *increased spending* on consumer durables and housing, and by *increased exports* to the rapidly recovering US economy. In 1983-84, boosted by the low Canadian exchange rate as well as the strong US economy, exports were a major source of strength for the Canadian economy, and Canada's international current account deficits turned to surpluses due to large merchandise trade surpluses.

Canada's recovery, however, was *less robust* than the US recovery. Consumer and business spending were both restrained by a combination of past debt, uncertainty about the future and continuing high interest rates, and government spending growth was curbed by concern about already-high budget deficits. Consequently, Canada's recovery was relatively sluggish, with unemployment remaining in excess of 10 percent of the labor force through 1985 and forecast to stay in that range for several years. Partly because of the weakness of the recovery and the persistence of high unemployment, the federal budget deficit moved even higher, reaching almost $30 billion in 1984 and passing $35 billion in 1985.

Externally, the USA had been experiencing a strong economic boom, driven by massive federal government budget deficits and strong business investment spending. The borrowing requirements associated with such deficits and investment spending generated very high real interest rates in the USA, attracting large inflows of foreign capital. The resultant high demand for the US dollar in foreign exchange markets drove the US exchange rate to record-high levels, placing the Canadian dollar under downward pressure. Despite increases in Canadian interest rates to support the Canadian dollar, the Canadian exchange rate declined to the $.73 US range by mid-1985.

The situation as of the mid-1980's

And so, as we said, Canada's new government faced an economic situation without the severe inflation of the past, but with some familiar — and serious — concerns. We will consider each of these concerns in the following sections.

> Three problem areas that emerge from our analysis are the current poor performance of investment, the anticipated large federal deficits, and the persistent, high rates of unemployment. Even in the most optimistic case, all remain in a range that leaves much room for improvement. The main difficulty, however, is that initiatives that would reduce the deficit quickly are inconsistent with measures designed to reduce the rate of unemployment in Canada.
>
> Economic Council of Canada,
> *Twenty-First Annual Review,* 1984

(a) High unemployment

As we know, Canada's unemployment rate rose sharply during the recession, peaking at 13 percent of the labor force at the end of 1982. With the slow economic recovery, the unemployment rate remained uncomfortably high, at more than 10 percent for the labor force as a whole and over 16 percent for the 15-24 age group. It was forecast to remain in this range for most of the decade. While it could be argued that these figures were inflated by "voluntary unemployment" and that an unemployment rate below 8 percent could now be considered full employment, it could also be argued that the statistics missed a considerable number of discouraged workers who have given up looking for work because they believed no jobs were available. This latter group was estimated at 110 000 in 1983, which would add another percentage point to the official unemployment rate.

Ordinarily, an unemployment rate in excess of 10 percent would call for a large-scale counter-attack, through expansionary monetary and fiscal policies. However, there was little scope for the use of such policies in Canada. The *federal budget deficit* had become so vast that the federal government was not in a position to boost the economy with either spending increases or tax cuts. The Bank of Canada was equally reluctant to move to an easy money policy because this would imperil the hard-won gains against inflation and could send the Canadian dollar into a free fall against the strong US dollar.

Some Canadians favored a deliberate decrease in the Canadian *exchange rate*, because it would make Canadian products more competitive at home and abroad, and reduce unemployment. But a sharp reduction in the exchange rate was rejected by the Bank of Canada, on the grounds that it would prove largely self-defeating. In particular, the resultant increase in import prices would add to inflation, boosting wage demands and interest rates as inflationary fears were rekindled.

Notwithstanding its objections to a sharp reduction in the exchange rate, however, the Bank of Canada did allow the Canadian dollar to *depreciate* gradually from about $.85 US in 1980 to about $.73 US in 1985 — a decline of approximately 14 percent.[1] Gradually, and to a certain extent, employment in Canada was supported by a decline in the exchange rate. Canadians took a pay cut (in the form of a lower standard of living and higher import prices) in order to protect employment.

Nonetheless, Canada's unemployment rate remained uncomfortably high. With little stimulus available from fiscal, monetary or exchange-rate policies, there was little prospect for major government policy initiatives to reduce unemployment. Rather, the main hope for job creation was seen to be the *private sector*, with particular hopes for a revival of capital investment.

> Today, Canada's foremost requirements are business confidence and jobs. Without new policy initiatives and a major renewal of private investment, our projections . . . show little prospect of significantly lower unemployment rates for the medium term.
>
> Economic Council of Canada,
> *Twenty-First Annual Review: Steering the Course*, 1984

(b) Investment and productivity

In the aftermath of the Great Recession, real business investment spending was quite weak, as Figure 20-3 shows. Several factors contributed to the sluggishness of business investment spending. *Weak demand*, reflecting Canada's relatively slow recovery from the recession, was a significant factor. Figure 20-4 shows the percentage of Canadian industry's productive capacity that is utilized. After reaching the 90 percent range in 1979, the capacity utilization rate fell to 70 percent during the recession, and recovered to no better than 83 percent by 1985. With such a large amount of unused capacity, capital investment tends to be low.

The *heavy indebtedness of Canadian business* was another factor undermining capital investment. For a variety of reasons,[2] Canadian industry emerged from the recession carrying unusually heavy debt loads at quite high rates of interest. With the bankruptcies and near-bankruptcies of the early 1980's

---

[1]As noted in Chapter 18, this depreciation was not due to the weakness of the Canadian dollar, but rather to the unusual strength of the US dollar. While the Bank of Canada did raise interest rates to prevent a sharp decline in the exchange rate, it also accepted some decline in the Canadian dollar.

[2]The reasons for the high debt loads included a weak stock market, which made it difficult to raise capital through equity (share) issues; and a corporate tax system which favored borrowing because of the tax-deductibility of interest payments.

FIGURE 20-3 *Real Business Investment Spending 1974-85*

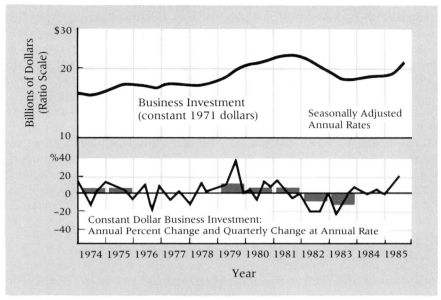

SOURCE   Toronto Dominion Bank, *Canada's Business Climate.*

FIGURE 20-4 *Industrial Capacity Utilization Rate 1974-85*

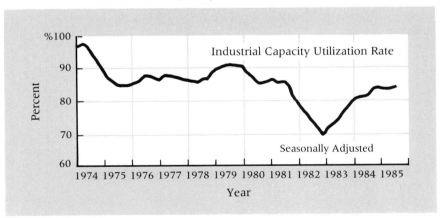

SOURCE   Toronto Dominion Bank, *Canada's Business Climate.*

(Massey-Ferguson, Chrysler, Maislin, Dome Petroleum, etc.) business leaders became sharply aware that their high debt made them vulnerable to both increases in interest rates and downturns in business. Interest payments must be met whether business is good or bad. In accountants' terms, Canadian industry was badly *undercapitalized*; its ratio of debt to shareholders' equity was dangerously high.

Businesses that are undercapitalized are not only vulnerable to severe financial difficulties, but also reluctant to spend on new capital investment. They tend instead to use available funds to reduce their debt and establish a sound ratio of debt to equity—a process known as *balance sheet restructuring*. According to the Economic Council of Canada, "Balance sheet restructuring is seen by many as one of the reasons for weak investment performance in Canada" (*Annual Review*, 1984).

Another problem underlying the slow recovery of investment in Canada was *weak business confidence*. Shaken by the instability of economic conditions and government policies in the past, and uncertain about the future, many businesses were reluctant to commit themselves to major capital projects. Of particular concern were the small size of the Canadian market and the federal budget deficit, which was seen by some as evidence of the government's inability to manage its finances. It is worth repeating here that while business investment spending remained weak in Canada, Canadian businesses invested substantially in other countries during this period. From 1982 to mid-1985, there was an outflow of nearly $10 billion in direct investment capital from Canada, mostly to the USA.

Finally, capital investment spending was depressed by *high interest rates*. While interest rates fell sharply after their peak in 1981, they nonetheless remained high in real terms; that is, adjusted for (or compared to) the rate of inflation. The important concept of real interest rates is explained in the next section.

In summary, business capital investment spending experienced a weak recovery after the recession, for a variety of reasons, including the weak confidence, low capacity utilization rates and heavy indebtedness of Canadian industry, as well as high real interest rates.

> We must build a climate which fosters investment—not only in machines and buildings, but in people. Investment is the key to job opportunity.
>
> Hon. Michael H. Wilson,
> *A New Direction for Canada: An Agenda for Economic Renewal*
> (Ottawa: Department of Finance, November 1984)

The weakness of investment spending was a serious concern for economists and government policy-makers. Stronger investment spending by business was badly needed by the Canadian economy for the benefits it would bring, not only to the demand side of the economy, but also to the supply side. On the demand side, stronger investment spending would boost aggregate demand, generating higher consumer spending, through the multiplier effect, and helping to reduce unemployment. On the supply side, investment would strengthen Canadian industry's productivity and international competitiveness, improving the prospects for both prosperity and employment for Canadians. On the other hand, continuing weak investment spending by business would contribute to a worsening of Canada's unemployment and productivity problems.

(c) High real interest rates

As noted in the previous section, high interest rates acted as a drag on the Canadian economy into the mid-1980's. Figure 20-5 shows how interest rates were driven up by the Great Inflation of the 1970's, then peaked at exceptionally high levels when policies were implemented to curb inflation in the early 1980's.[3] After mid-1982, interest rates declined considerably, as the graph indicates.

But this decline in nominal (or stated) interest rates is somewhat misleading, because if these nominal rates are adjusted for inflation, we find that the resulting real interest rates were actually rising to very high levels — a matter which requires some explanation.

There are two aspects to lending (or borrowing) money under conditions of inflation. First, there is the interest earned (or paid) on the loan; second, there is the reduction in the value of the capital loaned due to inflation.

FIGURE 20-5 *Interest Rates on Long-Term Corporate Bonds 1968–85*

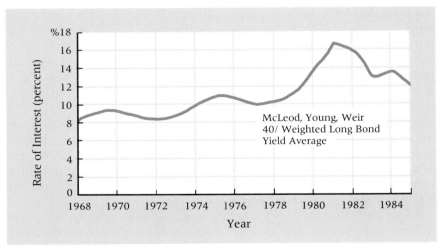

SOURCE   McLeod, Young, Weir.

[3]The interest rates shown are for long-term corporate bonds. These rates have been selected because corporate bonds are the type of borrowing most commonly used to finance business investment spending; however, other interest rates behaved similarly.

That is, the lender is repaid (or the borrower repays) in dollars whose value has been reduced by inflation. Depending on how these two factors balance out, either the lender or the borrower can wind up ahead (or behind) financially. Real interest rates, because they are adjusted for inflation, are useful in determining exactly who stands to gain in a transaction.

FIGURE 20-6 *Nominal and Real Interest Rates on a One-year Loan of $100*

	Example A *Nominal Interest Rate of 5%;* *Inflation Rate of 2%.*	Example B *Nominal Interest Rate of 9%;* *Inflation Rate of 11%.*
Interest Income	$5.00	$ 9.00
Loss of Value of Capital due to Inflation	–2.00	– 11.00
Real Return on $100 of Capital	+$3.00	–$2.00
Real Rate of Interest	+3.0%	–2.0%

Figure 20-6 contains two examples which illustrate the usefulness of real interest rates. In example A, the nominal rate of interest is 5 percent, and the rate of inflation is 2 percent. The lender of $100 receives $5 interest at the end of one year, plus $100, which has lost $2 of its purchasing power due to inflation, as repayment of the loan. Therefore, the lender is really ahead not by $5, but rather by $3, and receives a real interest rate of 3 percent on the $100. Conversely, the borrower has paid an interest rate of 5 percent but has repaid the loan in money worth 2 percent less, and so has really only paid 3 percent for the use of the $100.

In example B the nominal rate of interest has risen, to 9 percent. However, the rate of inflation is still higher, at 11 percent. Despite the fact that the *nominal* rate of interest is much higher, the *real* rate of interest is much lower; in fact, it is negative. Inflation has eroded the purchasing power of the $100 so badly, that the lender actually loses 2 percent on the transaction, and the borrower gains.

Figure 20-7 illustrates an important aspect of the economic situation in the mid-1980's: despite the fact that *nominal* interest rates declined considerably in 1982, *real* interest rates rose sharply. This underlying increase made borrowing considerably less attractive than it might seem from the decline in nominal interest rates, and contributed to the weakness in investment spending referred to earlier.[4]

[4]It also contributed to the weakness in consumer demand, by making saving more attractive.

FIGURE 20-7 *Nominal and Real Long-Term Interest Rates 1968-85*

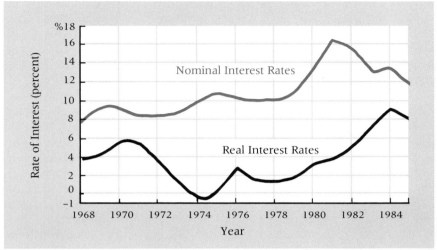

SOURCE   McLeod, Young, Weir Weighted Long Bond Yield Average.

These high real interest rates and their effects on the Canadian economy became a serious concern of policy-makers. In November 1984, the minister of finance stated that "The main uncertainty in Canada's economic outlook relates to interest rates and, more particularly, inflation-adjusted or 'real' interest rates. The level of real interest rates plays an important role in investment and other expenditure decisions. Measured in the conventional way, real interest rates have now reached near-record levels in both the United States and Canada. If real rates do not decline, a long period of lacklustre performance can be expected; if they increase further, a recession cannot be ruled out."[5]

It is worth examining why real interest rates were so high. The single most important factor was *high US interest rates,* which, as we saw in Chapter 18, pulled Canadian interest rates up. These high US interest rates were the result of an unusual combination of American economic policies — huge government budget deficits (which created a heavy demand for capital) and a fairly restrictive monetary policy (which limited the volume of funds available to meet this high demand for credit). While Canadian policies exhibited a similar distortion, this was not a problem that could be solved within Canada alone — Canadian interest rates could only come down if US rates did.

Another underlying factor behind these high real rates of interest was a *fear of renewed inflation* on the part of lenders. Savers and lenders had

[5]Hon. Michael H. Wilson, *A New Direction for Canada: An Agenda for Economic Renewal,* Department of Finance, November 1984.

been hurt by the unexpectedly severe inflation in the mid-1970's, which forced real interest rates to low levels (see Figure 20-7). They had grown wary of commiting funds to long-term loans, without attractive rates of interest to protect themselves against a return of severe inflation. One particular concern of investors was that the US government would fail to get its massive budget deficits under control and would resort to printing money to finance its expenditures. Investors remember that similar US policies had been a major factor in the severe world wide inflation of the 1970's, as we saw in Chapter 12. Similar concerns existed in Canada, where the federal deficit was almost twice the US deficit on a per capita basis, and was continuing to rise.

In the final analysis, the only way to reduce real interest rates would be for both the USA and Canada to maintain a low rate of inflation and assure savers and lenders that the future value of their capital would not be reduced. According to Gerald Bouey, Governor of the Bank of Canada, "Over time, our ability to achieve low interest rates in Canada will depend on maintaining a record of low domestic inflation. . . . the record shows that countries with the best inflation performance over time also have the lowest domestic interest rates."[6] To achieve such a reduction in interest rates would require action regarding the last of the problems to be discussed here, the federal budget deficit.

(d) Federal budget deficits

Another major problem facing Canada was the federal government's budget deficit, which by 1984-85 had grown to about $35 billion per year. While much of the deficit was cyclical in nature, reflecting the high unemployment of the period, there was also a large *structural* element to the deficit. That is, there was a fundamental imbalance between federal expenditures and tax revenues, such that even if economic conditions were excellent and unemployment at a minimum, the federal government would still have to borrow $10 to $15 billion per year (over $1000 per employed Canadian) to cover the excess of its spending over its tax revenues.

Furthermore, by the mid-1980's, the *interest payments* on the federal government's accumulated debt had grown, and it was feared that the deficit might acquire a momentum of its own, with more borrowing needed to meet interest payments on past borrowing. In 1985, interest payments absorbed approximately one-third of Ottawa's tax revenues, or nearly one-half of the government's new borrowing. Concerns were voiced that the vast interest payments on the government's debt would lead to a vicious circle of escalating interest payments, borrowing and debt.

There were further concerns that such large deficits could absorb excessive amounts of Canadians' savings and put upward pressure on interest rates. Canada's economic recovery could, consequently, be hampered by

[6]Bank of Canada, Annual Report of the Governor to the Minister of Finance, 1984.

> Projected federal deficits of $35-40 billion each year until the
> end of the decade would seriously harm Canada's growth pros-
> pects. By increasing the federal public debt faster than the econ-
> omy is growing, these large deficits would absorb an increasing
> share of Canadians' savings, reducing the amount available for
> the private investment needed for growth.
>
> Edward A. Carmichael,
> *Policy Review and Outlook, 1985: A Time for Decisions*
> C. D. Howe Institute, 1985.

depressed business investment spending and the crowding out of investment by government deficits as discussed in Chapter 9. According to
the Economic Council of Canada in 1984, "Canada has not suffered any
significant crowding-out of real economic activity from recent deficits,
but it could in the future if the relative size of federal deficits is not
reduced over the medium term."[7]

Despite the government's intention, the deficit rose substantially again
in 1984-85. One reason for the government's hesitation in dealing with
the deficit was *economic*; with unemployment high and the recovery weak,
the government was reluctant to reduce its spending or raise taxes. Another
reason was *political*; even with government spending nearly 40 percent
higher than its tax revenues, Canadians did not recognize the seriousness
of the government's financial situation and were therefore not willing
to make sacrifices to reduce the deficit. As a result, few observers expected
significant reductions in the deficits for several years, despite concerns
about their longer-term effects on the economy.

(e) External factors

Canada's economic situation was further complicated by changes in the
external environment. There was an apparent shift in the world market
for *natural resources*. In the past, Canada had maintained a relatively inefficient, tariff-protected manufacturing sector that had been carried by
a strong natural resource sector: Canada paid its way internationally
through strong exports of natural resources and resource products. It
was through the exporting of these resources that Canada earned the
foreign exchange (mainly US dollars) that made possible the heavy imports
vital to Canadians' high standard of living.

In the 1980's, however, the growth of demand in the high-income countries of the world was less toward the industrial products of the traditional
"smokestack industries" (that were major consumers of natural resources),
and more toward *services*, and the products of *high-tech and information
industries*. At the same time, competition in markets for natural resources

[7]Economic Council of Canada, *Twenty-First Annual Review*, 1984.

intensified as less developed nations entered the marketplace, anxious to sell their resources to pay their international debts and finance development programs. Canada, therefore, found that world markets were changing in ways that presented new challenges. Markets for resources — Canada's traditional strength — were not only slack but also more competitive, with prices and output generally depressed. In their place were rapidly growing markets for services and sophisticated manufactured goods. These markets offered great opportunities, but they were not markets in which Canadian firms (with some notable exceptions) had been particularly competitive. To succeed in these markets, Canadians would have to develop new skills, new approaches and new government policies.

> We must address the fact that natural resources will be less valuable in a low-inflation, knowledge-oriented world than they were during the inflationary 1970's. We will have to reduce costs and apply state-of-the-art technology throughout the economy. The outstanding question at the beginning of 1985 is whether Canada will ride the wave of change or be swamped by it.
>
> Edward A. Carmichael,
> *Policy Review and Outlook, 1985: A Time for Decisions,*
> C. D. Howe Institute, 1985

The policy problem

The new circumstances presented the government with a complex and difficult problem. Despite high unemployment, excess industrial capacity and sluggish investment spending, the government could not fall back upon the traditional policies of fiscal and monetary stimulation. The federal budget deficit was already considered too large to be increased further, and the Bank of Canada was reluctant to use easy money policies that could rekindle inflation. Consequently, the government was not in a position to use the "big levers" of monetary and fiscal policy to get the economy moving.

The circumstances of the mid-1980's also challenged Canada's past approach to economics and economic policy. For some time, Canadians had relied heavily upon exports of natural resources to support their standard of living. They had used part of their considerable wealth to support a manufacturing sector that had remained relatively inefficient by international standards, but was protected against foreign competition and did provide employment for a considerable number of Canadians. Government policies had been less concerned with incentives for the creation of wealth than with attempting to ensure an equitable distribution of wealth. Governments had undertaken to redistribute income through an extensive social welfare system. This system worked mainly through transfer payments, such as unemployment insurance, welfare, family allowances, pensions, subsidized health and hospital care, and subsidized education. There was also a wide variety of government programs created, to support groups, business firms and entire industries. Some observers described Canadian policy as reflecting a *resource wealth mentality*—the view that wealth is something that happens to society through the sale of resources, and that the main task of government is to ensure that this wealth is distributed fairly, through its taxation and transfer payments policies. Such an attitude, critics said, downplayed the importance of creating wealth, through incentives for enterprise, entrepreneurship, investment and productivity. In addition, since the mid-1970's Canada had adopted some policies of *economic nationalism,* such as the Foreign Investment Review Act and the National Energy Program, which discouraged foreign investment. Faced with weak capital investment in a sluggish economy and unable to use monetary and fiscal stimulation, it was necessary for the government to seek different approaches.

Policies for the future

The new government set itself three broad policy objectives: to contain inflation; to encourage business capital investment spending; and to encourage enterprise and entrepreneurship. We will consider each of these in turn.

(a) The containment of inflation

One of the most basic objectives of government policy was to keep inflation under control, to prevent a recurrence of the problems of the 1970's. By containing inflation, the government hoped to create a *more stable financial environment,* with *lower interest rates*[8] and a better economic climate for *capital investment.*

The main instrument for controlling inflation was monetary policy, through restraint in the growth of the money supply and high interest rates. But fiscal policy was *not* anti-inflationary, as the federal government had very large budget deficits rather than the surpluses ordinarily used to combat inflation. This discrepancy between monetary and fiscal policies led to a collision between heavy government borrowing requirements and relatively restricted credit availability that generated very high real interest rates in both the USA and Canada. Over the longer run, however, it was regarded as very important to reduce the budget deficits so as to achieve the lower interest rates made possible by slower inflation. By doing so, it was hoped that solid economic progress could be built on a base of productive business capital investment.

[8]As we have seen, Canadian policies alone could not ensure lower interest rates; the USA would have to take steps to reduce its interest rates as well.

Job opportunity and income growth for Canadians depend on a healthy level of business investment. Yet investment is faltering, at a time when the level of domestic savings is high. The past few years have witnessed large scale capital investment by Canadians in the United States; we cannot take for granted our attractiveness as a place to invest. Restoring investment growth, particularly among small and medium-sized business, is a critical component of the overall strategy for economic renewal.

Hon. Michael H. Wilson,
A New Direction for Canada: An Agenda for Economic Renewal,
Department of Finance, November 1984.

(b) Encouragement of investment spending

The single most fundamental objective of government policy was the encouragement of *capital investment spending* by business. This approach was explicitly supply side in orientation, and was intended to remedy the weakness in investment that had developed during the 1970's and persisted into the early 1980's. In basic terms, the objective was to reverse the trend of the previous decade, in which current consumption was stressed to the detriment of capital investment, and shift the allocation of economic resources toward investment.

Such an approach involves certain difficulties. Encouragement of business investment spending comes into conflict with at least two keynote elements of Canadian economic policy in the 1970's: *redistribution of income* and *economic nationalism.* A basic theme of government policy has been that it is desirable for government to redistribute income from those with higher incomes (including corporations) toward those with lower incomes. However, policies to encourage the saving-investment process appear to have the opposite effect, as they involve tax incentives (which some people say are unjustly preferential) for businesses and the higher-income Canadians who tend to save money. Nonetheless, in 1985 the Macdonald Commission recommended tax incentives for both saving and investment, on the grounds that these would promote the long-run prosperity of Canadians. However, because such policies benefit higher-income Canadians who have capital to invest, they tend to be politically unpopular, despite the longer-term economic benefits that they could generate for Canadians as a whole. Thus, government policies to encourage saving and investment necessarily involved some trade-offs against the goal of income redistribution, and the associated political risks.

Another theme of Canadian policy since the mid-1970's had been *economic nationalism,* as expressed mainly through the restrictions of foreign investment associated with the Foreign Investment Review Act and the National Energy Program. In an attempt to encourage investment, the

An example of the type of policy — and difficulties — involved in encouraging saving and investment is the government's $500 000 lifetime tax exemption on capital gains. By allowing tax-free capital gains on the sale of corporate shares, the policy was intended to encourage Canadians with savings to invest in stock. If they did, Canadian corporations would be able to raise more capital by selling shares, and reduce the heavy debt burden which was an obstacle to capital investment. Also, the capital raised by new stock issues could be used for new capital investment, for the benefit of Canadians generally over the longer run. However, it was also true that, at least in the short run, the main beneficiaries of the $500 000 capital gains tax exemption would be the wealthier Canadians with savings to invest, and political discussion of the policy tended to focus on this fact.

federal government substantially changed both of these laws. As with income redistribution, the pursuit of stronger investment involved certain trade-offs and, the government felt, the emphasis on economic nationalism had to be reduced.

The huge *budget deficits* of the federal government were also seen as posing a threat to the recovery of business investment spending. Not only were these deficits forcing interest rates upward, they were also undermining the business confidence necessary for strong capital investment. In the eyes of many business leaders, the massive size and continuing growth of the deficits called into doubt the financial management of the federal government and the future financial stability of the country. To reduce the deficit, however, the government would have to make difficult political decisions involving substantial reductions in government spending, or increases in taxes.

Another highly controversial issue was the question of *freer trade with the United States*. According to some economists, Canadian industry was too constrained by the small size of the Canadian market and needed guaranteed access to the US market in order to have an incentive to expand and invest in Canada. They pointed to the significant outflows of direct investment capital in recent years, as Canadian businesses increasingly tended to shift investment out of Canada in search of larger markets. This trend, these economists argued, would accelerate, unless a free-trade deal could be struck with the USA which would allow Canadian firms guaranteed access to the US market. In 1985, the Macdonald Commission made freer trade with the United States its keynote recommendation.

Others, however, saw freer trade with the USA as a serious threat to the tariff-protected manufacturing industries of central Canada, and opposed it. By the mid-1980's, political pressure from Ontario and Quebec against freer trade with the USA was mounting, making this yet another difficult policy decision for the federal government.

By mid-1985, there were some encouraging signs of recovery in business investment spending. However, investment remained well below its 1981 peak, and it remained to be seen whether the government would be successful in its attempts to revive business confidence and investment.

(c) *Encouragement of entrepreneurship and enterprise*

> In 1966, we could get away with running a closely protected domestic market for manufacturers, and still export our resources. We don't have as good a market for resources anymore, and even with protection, the developing world is starting to take our market away. If we want to maintain our standard of living, we're going to need a more competitive stance in manufacturing and services.
>
> Donald Macdonald,
> quoted in *The Financial Post*, September 14, 1985.

In the world that appeared to be emerging after the mid-1980's, Canada would no longer be able to rely on resource exports as its main source of continually rising wealth. Nor could it expect government policies to be aimed primarily at the redistribution of a national income that could be assumed to be rising indefinitely. As a result, the direction of government policy began a subtle but important shift away from *redistribution* of wealth and toward *creation* of wealth. New emphasis was placed upon enterprise and productivity, as Canadians began to realize the implications of their nation's poor productivity performance. Unless productivity could be improved, Canadians faced the prospect of falling farther behind in international competition, with stagnant living standards and lost jobs the result.

The Macdonald Commission recommended various policy changes to promote efficiency and enterprise. First, the commission recommended *tax reform*, to provide incentives for efficiency and growth, including incentives for saving and investment. Second, *less government regulation* of business was proposed. The commission noted that many government business regulations have the effect of restricting competition in the regulated industries, by controlling prices and production, and by restricting the entry of new competitors into the industry. According to the commission, many such regulations should be reduced or eliminated, so that competition could promote efficiency. Over the years, Canada had accumulated a great deal of government regulations. The range of these regulations was broad; it included major legislation, such as the Foreign

> We must ensure that government itself — through its taxation, expenditure and regulatory programs — does not impede the change and adjustment necessary to improve productivity and increase our international competitiveness. . . . we must encourage enterprise in this country. We must reduce the regulatory burden, not as an end in itself, but to release the creative energies of individuals and companies to experiment, to innovate and to produce better goods and services at lower prices.
>
> Hon. Michael H. Wilson,
> *A New Direction for Canada: An Agenda for Economic Renewal,*
> Department of Finance, November 1984.

Investment Review Act (FIRA) and the National Energy Program, as well as a multitude of lesser government regulations. It was estimated by the Economic Council of Canada in the late 1970's that there were 9000 pages of federal regulations, plus extensive provincial regulations (which in Ontario amounted to another 6000 pages).

Government policymakers also placed increased emphasis on encouraging the *small business sector* of the economy, which had provided a high proportion of the new jobs created in the recent past and was expected to play a larger role in the future. Unlike resource and heavy manufacturing industries, the emerging high-tech and service industries are not dominated by giant corporations; in fact, small size, innovation and flexibility are seen as advantages in these fields.

Another recommendation of the Macdonald Commission (the most controversial) was *freer trade with the United States.* The commission said that freer trade would promote efficiency in two ways: by exposing Canadian firms to foreign competition and by providing Canadian firms with access to the vast US market.

Short-term pain for long-term gain?

As with any economic policy changes, Canada's new policy directions involved certain trade-offs between costs and benefits. The unusual aspect of the new policy directions was that most of the benefits they offered were longer-term in nature while many of the costs — economic and political — would be felt in the short run.

While the encouragement of investment, enterprise and entrepreneurship could bring long-term gains in productivity, competitiveness, employment and prosperity, the shorter-term effects of policies to promote these were not as attractive. Policies to contain *inflation* necessarily involved slower growth and higher interest rates and unemployment than might otherwise have been possible, if only in the short run. Policies to encourage *saving and investment* involve tax incentives for higher-income Canadian investors that run counter to the objective of using the tax system to redistribute income from the rich to the poor, and attracting foreign capital could involve sacrificing some requirements that had been placed upon foreign investors. Reducing the *federal budget deficit* might please investors and promote business confidence and capital investment, but it would also require tax increases and restraints on government spending that would affect many Canadians directly. *Deregulation and freer trade* could promote efficiency, but they would also expose many Canadian firms to stronger competition than in the past. Even advocates of freer trade accepted that, in the short run, it would involve some difficult adjustments and dislocations for some businesses and their employees.

In the broad sense, the new direction of government policy was to shift the emphasis in the Canadian economy from security and consumption toward efficiency and investment, or from benefits that exist mainly in the present to longer-term gains. The success of such a policy initiative depends to a great extent on the willingness of the public to support it, which in turn depends partly on how quickly the promised economic benefits begin to appear.

Canada's strengths for the future

We must venture into untried ways that will demand open-mindedness, courage, innovation and determination. Can we not do better in the future? Our response to this question is a resounding 'Yes'!

Report of the Royal Commission on the Economic Union and Development Prospects for Canada, 1985

While Canada faces serious challenges economically in the future, there are also major opportunities. Canadian industries that could prosper in the future include energy, petrochemicals, natural resources and resource-related products (such as forest products, mining and pulp and paper), steel, transportation equipment, telecommunications and engineering and construction. These and other Canadian industries should benefit from the relatively low international value of the Canadian dollar in competing with foreign producers. The US market provides a particularly good opportunity because of its size, wealth and proximity.

However, it is important to remember that Canada's low exchange rate only provides Canadians with an opportunity. It is up to Canadians whether or not this opportunity will be seized. The competitive advantage made possible by the low Canadian dollar will only be realized if Canadians make their products competitive. To do so will require improvements in productivity, and keeping inflation in check. Only by achieving these objectives can Canadians gain the cost and price competitiveness (and the gains in output and employment) made possible by the low exchange rate. It remains to be seen whether Canadians will be able to achieve the great economic potential that they have always felt their nation possesses, and what price they will have to pay for its realization.

DEFINITIONS OF NEW TERMS

Balance Sheet Restructuring   The process whereby a corporation seeks to reduce excessive liabilities (debt) in relation to its assets, so as to build a sounder financial basis.

Real Interest Rate   The nominal rate of interest less the rate of inflation.

Resource-Wealth Mentality   The view that economic prosperity is the result of exporting natural resources rather than enterprise, competition, efficiency and investment.

Deregulation   Policies to reduce the extent of regulation of business by government, with the intention of promoting efficiency through increased competition.

CHAPTER SUMMARY

1. Canada emerged from the recession of the early 1980's with a much-reduced inflation rate, but with the following problems: high unemployment, weak capital investment, poor productivity performance, high real interest rates and massive federal budget deficits.

2. The situation was complicated by the fact that world markets for natural resources—Canada's traditional strength—were not only growing more slowly than in the past, but also were characterized by more intensive competition.

3. Due to concerns regarding the large federal budget deficits and the inflationary consequences of easy money policies, the government was not in a position to undertake large-scale stimulation of aggregate demand through fiscal and monetary policies.

4. The government set broad policy objectives that included:
   (a) the containment of inflation,
   (b) encouragement of capital investment spending by business, and
   (c) encouragement of enterprise and entrepreneurship.

5. Adoption of these goals, which stressed incentives for the creation of wealth, involved trade-offs against certain other policy goals, such as redistribution of income and economic nationalism. It also required serious consideration of other difficult policy choices such as the reduction of federal budget deficits, deregulation of business and freer trade with the USA.

6. It was hoped that these changes in government policy, combined with the low international value of the Canadian dollar, would revitalize Canadian industry and make Canada more internationally competitive and prosperous in the future.

QUESTIONS

1. Figure 20-7 shows that real interest rates fell to very low levels in the mid-1970's. Why might this have happened?

2. With unemployment in excess of 10 percent of the labor force, why would the Macdonald Commission recommend tax incentives to promote higher saving by Canadians?

3. Has the government succeeded in keeping inflation under control since 1985?

4. Has the unemployment rate increased or declined since 1985? Why?

5. In 1984, the minister of finance said, "Lack of business confidence is one of the most significant obstacles to investment and growth in Canada."
Has business confidence improved since then?
What is the recent trend in business investment spending?
What are the reasons for this, and what are its implications for the economy?

6. Has Canada's productivity performance improved recently? What are the reasons for this trend?

7. Has Canadian industry grown more or less competitive internationally over the past few years? What are the reasons for this trend?

8. In 1985, Edward Carmichael of the C.D. Howe Institute wrote, "Canadians still do not recognize the seriousness of the federal government's deteriorating fiscal situation." Have Canadians' attitudes toward the deficit changed since then? Why?

9. Has the government succeeded in reducing the size of the federal deficit? Why or why not?

10. Have nominal and real interest rates risen or fallen since 1985? Why? What are the implications of this trend for the economy?

11. Has the international value of the Canadian dollar increased or decreased since 1985? Why? What are the implications of this for the economy?

12. Has there been any move toward freer trade with the USA since the federal government expressed interest in such an arrangement in 1985?